"Read *Trials and Triumphs of Golf's Greatest Champions* as it delves into much more than the surface history of these famous golfers, detailing the obstacles and struggles with which they all had to deal."—Tom Watson, member of the World Golf Hall of Fame, winner of eight major championships

"*Trials and Triumphs* is the perfect affirmation of what makes golf the greatest game of all—overcoming odds and adversities to achieve greatness. As you will see, there is no other way!"—Jim Nantz, CBS Sports

"Here we have a unique instruction book on golf. It doesn't try to cure the slice; instead, it provides an array of inspirational stories about some of the game's heroes."—Dan Jenkins, *Golf Digest* columnist, author of *Semi-Tough* and *Dead Solid Perfect*

"Anyone who appreciates the cosmic connection between golf's seen and unseen worlds understands that success is inextricably linked to the player's ability—and determination—to overcome adversity in whatever form it comes. In this way, the game really is a lively microcosm of life, a human principle brilliantly reinforced in Lyle Slovick's outstanding new book."—James Dodson, author of USGA Book Award winners *Ben Hogan: An American Life* and *American Triumvirate: Sam Snead, Byron Nelson, Ben Hogan, and the Modern Age of Golf*

"Lyle Slovick points out many of the hardships my father faced in trying to fulfill his dream. All he wanted to do was to play the game of golf on an equal field."—Charles Sifford Jr., son of golfing great Charlie Sifford

"Lyle Slovick has a fine sense of the human condition and in this book brings it to an ever-fascinating subject—the will of an individual to overcome formidable roadblocks and succeed in a very difficult game. Well done!"—Al Barkow, former editor of *Golf Magazine*, author of USGA Book Award winner *Gettin' to the Dance Floor: An Oral History of American Golf*

"Why is golf one of our greatest games? Because it tests us—our patience, persistence, and perseverance—in ways we don't expect and often can't even imagine. In *Trials and Triumphs of Golf's Greatest Champions*, Lyle Slovick reminds us, through the soaring profiles of golf's most courageous fighters from Bobby Jones to Babe Didrikson Zaharias, that far more important than any golf lesson is the grit and greatness we find inside ourselves when we need it most."—Don Van Natta Jr., ESPN investigative reporter, Pulitzer Prize winner, and author of *New York Times* bestseller *First Off the Tee* and USGA Book Award winner *Wonder Girl: The Magnificent Sporting Life of Babe Didrikson Zaharias*

"Impressively researched, carefully documented, and clearly written, Lyle Slovick's *Trials and Triumphs* goes beyond tournament competition to examine the transcendent qualities of golf, offering a vivid, moving reminder of why the game matters so much to so many people. In an era when sports headlines draw our gaze downward to corruption, vice, or health risks, Slovick's book appeals to the better angels of our nature, sensitively and judiciously recounting the histories of such golf greats as Vardon, Jones, and Venturi, as well as those of lesser known heroes like Thomas McAuliffe. Poignant and uplifting, *Trials and Triumphs* is golf literature at its finest."—Stephen Lowe, professor of history and author of USGA Book Award winner *Sir Walter and Mr. Jones: Walter Hagen, Bobby Jones, and the Rise of American Golf*

"Every person in this book loved golf for golf's sake, the freedom and purity of the game, and was driven by it. It shows so much of the human spirit and an insight into the personalities of each person that one has not seen before."—Renee Powell, LPGA pioneer and member of the Royal and Ancient Golf Club of St Andrews

"Lyle Slovick's compassionate voice rings through the words of this book. The individuals featured demonstrate to the reader that even in the face of sickness, sadness, and cruelty there are the triumphant lessons of courage and perseverance. The connection may be about golf, but it is about life, too."—Susan Wasser, assistant director and curator, United States Golf Association Museum

"The title of this book is an understatement to the compelling stories of the great champions. Lyle Slovick has captured the incredible spirit and determination of those who strove 'with their last ounce of courage' to leave an impact on the game of golf forever. After reading *Trials and Triumphs*, you will never again lament an errant shot or a missed putt, rather be grateful that you have ever walked a fairway. Golf truly is analogous to the journey of life and if you ever doubted this statement, you will no longer at the conclusion of this masterpiece."—Jane Blalock, CEO of JBC Golf, Inc., winner of 27 LPGA titles

"In *Trials and Triumphs*, Lyle captures the same dedication to and love of golf that I've seen in so many of our nation's post-9/11 wounded and injured veterans. One comes away from the book with a reminder that the spirit of the game is truly timeless."—Jamie Winslow, co-founder/president, Salute Military Golf

"Sometimes, the more familiar a subject, the more you appreciate an author who synthesizes what you know in a new way, with unbridled enthusiasm, mature judgment, and a clear message. Lyle Slovick does just this in *Trials and Triumphs*—a meticulously researched, easy-to-read, truly inspiring tour de force of modern golf history."—Steven Schlossman, professor of history, coauthor of *Chasing Greatness: Johnny Miller, Arnold Palmer, and the Miracle at Oakmont*

"Human beings are far from perfect and it is these imperfections laid bare that somehow make the lives of those featured all the more poignant. For they overcame difficulties that most of us will never face; they triumphed over cruelties that fate can enforce and they show us that life is for learning . . . and we can all learn."—Angela Howe, director, British Golf Museum

"'The stories of these golfers, of their flaws as well as their virtues, offer lessons in perseverance, dignity, humility, faith, and of lives well lived.' Well said, and well written Mr. Slovick!"—David Joy, golf historian, author of *St Andrews & The Open Championship* and *The Scrapbook of Old Tom Morris*

"Ken Venturi was the very first person to 'go public' about his stuttering and has served as an inspiration for those who stutter for many years. *Trials and Triumphs* author Lyle Slovick does a brilliant job of highlighting why this remarkable man stands out as a beacon to so many."—Jane Fraser, president of the Stuttering Foundation

TRIALS AND TRIUMPHS OF GOLF'S GREATEST CHAMPIONS

A LEGACY OF HOPE

Lyle Slovick

Foreword by Bill Fields

ROWMAN & LITTLEFIELD
Lanham • Boulder • New York • London

Published by Rowman & Littlefield
A wholly owned subsidiary of The Rowman & Littlefield Publishing Group, Inc.
4501 Forbes Boulevard, Suite 200, Lanham, Maryland 20706
www.rowman.com

Unit A, Whitacre Mews, 26-34 Stannary Street, London SE11 4AB

British Library Cataloguing in Publication Information Available

Library of Congress Cataloging-in-Publication Data

Names: Slovick, Lyle, 1960- author.
Title: Trials and triumphs of golf's greatest champions : a legacy of hope / Lyle A. Slovick.
Description: Lanham : ROWMAN & LITTLEFIELD, [2016] | Includes bibliographical references
and index.
Identifiers: LCCN 2015036082| ISBN 9781442261181 (hardcover : alk. paper) | ISBN
9781442261198 (ebook)
Subjects: LCSH: Golfers—Biography. | Caddies—Biography. | Golfers—Conduct of life. | Cad-
dies—Conduct of life.
Classification: LCC GV964.A1 S56 2016 | DDC 796.3520922—dc23
LC record available at http://lccn.loc.gov/2015036082

∞™ The paper used in this publication meets the minimum requirements of
American National Standard for Information Sciences Permanence of Paper for
Printed Library Materials, ANSI/NISO Z39.48-1992.

Printed in the United States of America

For la luz de mis ojos, Isis Lari
my sisters Lynda and Dena
and
in memory of my parents Bud and Helen Slovick

CONTENTS

ACKNOWLEDGMENTS

Thanks must go first to my agent, Maryann Karinch, for offering to represent me and working tirelessly to find a publisher. At Rowman & Littlefield, my editors Christen Karniski and Andrew Yoder helped me get the manuscript into shape, and their patience and steadfast assistance has been much appreciated.

I must also convey my sincere gratitude to the numerous scholars who came before me, who did so much to shed light on my subjects, for without them this book would not have been possible. Among these men and women is Bill Fields, who has written eloquently for years on the game of golf and who graciously agreed to write the foreword for this book. Others include Audrey Howell, Sidney Matthew, Richard Miller, Catherine Lewis, Stephen Lowe, Ron Rapoport, Gene Gregston, Curt Sampson, James Dodson, Kris Tschetter, Martin Davis, Susan Cayleff, Rhonda Glenn, Don Van Natta, William Oscar Johnson and Nancy P. Williamson, Al Barkow, John Kennedy, Pete McDaniel, Calvin Sinnette, John Feinstein, and Herbert Warren Wind. I have been the beneficiary of the hard work they have done over the years.

Special thanks go to Karen Greisman and my sister Lynda Hanson for their tireless proofreading of the manuscript. Nancy Stulack at the USGA library provided me access to so many wonderful books, oral histories, papers, and clipping files, parts of which have found their way into this book. She is a treasure. Susan Wasser and Chris Keane at the USGA provided great help in locating photos for the book, as did Rachel Nordstrom at the University of St Andrews.

I was honored to have the late Ken Venturi graciously respond to a letter I sent him a few months before he passed away and appreciate his former colleague Jim Nantz for sharing a few memories of his friend with me. Tom Watson, my favorite golfer since I was fourteen, took time out of his busy schedule to review the chapter on Bruce Edwards. Thank you. I would like to acknowledge prolific golf writers Al Barkow and Art Spander for their kind encouragement, as well as St Andrews and Old Tom Morris historian David Joy.

To Bruce Clark, who taught me how to play the game, thank you for helping me realize a temper must be controlled in order to play well. To Dr. Arthur Martinson, who mentored me at Pacific Lutheran University, thank you for your faith in my skills as a historian. To my late mother and father, who instilled in me a good work ethic, I think you would approve of my efforts here. Finally, I wish to honor the memories of Harry Vardon, Bobby Jones, Ben Hogan, Babe Didrikson Zaharias, Charlie Sifford, Ken Venturi, and Bruce Edwards, whose lives provided me with compelling stories of trial and triumph.

FOREWORD

During an era when technology and statistics have ever more prevalent roles in golf, particularly at the elite level, the essence of an athlete, his spirit, can be clouded or minimized. That is unfortunate because, regardless of how weighted golf becomes with tools to dissect it like a laboratory frog, what really makes a player meaningful in the arc of this great game is still hard to measure. These intangibles can include the steel displayed on a Sunday afternoon when everyone is watching or the spunk required on a practice range or gym when no one is.

I've written about golfers most of my sports journalism career, famous ones and obscure ones, those born to the game and those who climbed their way to it one hard rung at a time. It might be easier for the former but not easy. Golf is hard, especially when unexpected or unusual obstacles are present.

Covering an important regional tournament this year, I was sitting on a hillside with the father of a player watching him make a mess of a par three. Seconds after the son made a five-footer for triple bogey, his dad said, "It's not how hard you get knocked down but how you get up." As if he heard those words, the golfer battled hard the rest of the afternoon. He eventually lost in a play-off but not for lack of effort.

Lyle Slovick's book, detailed and empathetic, is about golfers (and a well-known caddie) who got knocked down and got back up. Some are familiar tales to those of us with a substantial golf bookshelf, but Lyle brings a fresh viewpoint to them. They are important golf stories—human stories—and he tells them well.

We are sometimes too quick to talk of heroism or courage when chronicling games and the people who play them. A deft pitch off a tight lie to a tucked flagstick with a title on the line is a lot of things, but is it really brave?

The subjects profiled in this book were dealt truly tough hands— serious illnesses, debilitating injuries, mean-spirited societal attitudes. They did not wilt under the duress. Instead they listened to Henry David Thoreau, whom Lyle quotes: "However mean your life is, meet it and live it."

Bill Fields

PREFACE

In July 2015, I attended my third British Open at St Andrews, Scotland. I went specifically to see Tom Watson, my favorite golfer of all time, in his last hurrah at the Old Course, just as I had gone for Arnold Palmer's in 1995. But walking around the course, I was amazed by the number of people I saw with canes, on crutches, in wheelchairs, and in scooters watching the golf. Waiting for Watson to tee off in the first round, I stood next to a young man in his twenties who was missing a leg, craning his neck to see the action.

Another day, at the far end of the course—a long walk from the first hole—I saw another man in his thirties walking with a halting gait. It appeared as if he had muscular dystrophy or may have suffered a stroke, but there he was, following a group around slowly but surely. I thought upon seeing these people, "There but for the grace of God go I," and it only helped to reinforce the themes I touch upon in this book. Namely, that the human spirit is a mighty force that can help overcome the severest challenges life might throw our way.

We were all together, out there watching a game we love, treading over ground on which golf has been played for five hundred years. Amazing! Old Tom Morris was there in the 1860s, Harry Vardon in the early 1900s, Bobby Jones in the 1920s, long before the grandfathers of many of today's players were even born. It made me consider the transient nature of our lives, how we spend a little time on this earth, and when we leave, others will take our place.

Memories took me back to 1995 and following Tom Watson then. His caddy Bruce Edwards, whose story is one of those included in this book, was with him then but not this year. He's no longer with us, but his spirit lives on. He lived his life as he wished to live it, finding a profession that fulfilled him, and did something he loved. Each of us expresses our own gifts and talents in different ways, and for the people in this book, golf was their calling.

I was never a great golfer, the best I ever played was when I was a 12-handicapper in college. But I have loved the game and its history since I was 13 years old, and my calling has been to work in a world of old books and manuscripts found in libraries and archives. My historian's mind considers what has come before and how we all are part of a legacy passed down from previous generations. We can learn many lessons from people—famous and not so famous—who have faced difficult times and survived. We all face crises in our lives, and they are easier to deal with when we know we are not alone, when we realize others have struggled with the same or much worse and made it through the fires of trial. I believe the people found in these pages offer us many relevant and inspirational life lessons.

The idea for this book probably began almost 10 years ago, during my struggle to recover from back surgery. There were days when I could barely walk, let alone swing a golf club, and when I was finally well enough to return to the course, the results were not pretty. Immediately I was aware of a loss of distance—about 10 yards per club—due to the fact that my body couldn't turn as fast as it did before.

My swing, once a fluid motion from start to finish, was now an abbreviated and fairly ugly lunge. This was to be my "new normal," and although today I can still play the game, it will never be as it once was. This is disappointing, but in the greater scheme of things, a minor irritant compared to the challenges many people face. Yet it made me consider the great players of the game and how they might deal with a career-threatening illness or injury.

I recalled the great Old Tom Morris, who suffered many hardships in his 86 years. In his old age, with his wife and children all having passed on before him, he said that, without his God and his golf, he wouldn't be a living man. The game sustained him and gave him purpose, just as it would the lives of the people in this book.

I considered the trials of many well-known golfers in the history of the game and three years ago chose seven to write about. All shared in common strong characters that shaped the fiber of their beings and prepared them for the difficulties that befell them. Although their stories have been told before, I knew I could dig deep into some lesser-known sources to find information that would shed new light on their experiences. I trust that, as a result, the reader will learn something new about these compelling individuals. In an era when athletes have lost their luster as role models, the stories of these golfers, of their flaws as well as their virtues, offer lessons in perseverance, dignity, humility, faith, and of lives well lived.

Bedminster, New Jersey
August 16, 2015

THE GAME

"It All Comes Back to Character"

Out of suffering have emerged the strongest souls; the most massive characters are seared with scars.
—Khalil Gibran

Success is not final, failure is not fatal: it is the courage to continue that counts.
—Winston Churchill[1]

"Golf is the closest game to the game we call life. You get bad breaks from good shots; you get good breaks from bad shots—but you have to play the game where it lies."[2] So claimed O. B. Keeler, the famed golf writer who, from 1916 to 1930, traveled more than 120,000 miles covering the career of Bobby Jones. We do indeed play the game where it lies. Each day is different, even if the course remains the same, and the challenges are at once maddening and intoxicating. It doesn't matter if frost covers the ground in winter, if rain water fills the cups on the greens in the spring, or if wind blows sand in our eyes after a bunker shot in the summer. We just love to play.

Walter Simpson, in his 1892 book *The Art of Golf*, seems to understand the golfer's psyche. He writes that the game "has some drawbacks. It is possible, by too much of it, to destroy the mind."[3] His admonition notwithstanding, true golfers rarely get enough of it. We know that if we keep plugging along and keep trying, sometimes good things come to us when we least expect them, just as in life.

Golf is a game with incredible staying power, having been played for over five hundred years. Men and women, young and old, royalty and artisans, CEOs and taxi drivers, people with bad backs and creaky knees, amputees and the blind, all play it. A few even play from wheelchairs. What is it that draws people to golf and holds them in its grip until they are too old and feeble to play any longer? The reasons are many. The game engages both body and mind in a very particular way and, some might argue, the soul as well.

James Balfour, who began playing golf in Scotland in the 1840s, explains it this way in *Reminiscences of Golf on St Andrews Links*:

> It is a fine, open-air, athletic exercise, not violent, but bringing into play nearly all the muscles of the body. . . . It is a game of skill, needing mind and thought and judgment, as well as a cunning hand. It is also a social game, where one may go out with a friend or with three, and enjoy mutual intercourse. . . . It never palls or grows stale, as morning by morning the players appear at the teeing ground with as keen a relish as if they had never seen a club for a month.[4]

It is a game requiring not only physical skill but also the ability to control our emotions, as we try to beat our best scores each time out, as well as the scores of our friends who join us in the endeavor.

The game is different because the ball must wait for us. It isn't baseball or tennis where a ball comes toward us that we have to react to in a split second. The golf ball just lies there passively, sometimes seeming to taunt us. It's up to us to make it go. "There is no hurry," writes John Low in *Concerning Golf*, rather "we fix our own time, we give ourselves every chance of success." It is this deliberate quality of the game that "makes it so testing to the nerves; for the very slowness which gives us opportunity for calculation draws our nerves out to the highest tension."[5]

Golf certainly can make our stomachs churn and scramble our brains. Mark Twain famously describes it as "a good walk spoiled." In the short space of the 15 minutes or so it takes to play a hole, it's possible to experience a full gamut of emotions—you name it, and it can be felt in a million different combinations. Fear and trepidation of the opening tee shot, followed by joy and relief after a great drive nailed straight down the middle, then consternation at the fat second shot plunked into the water, and ending with sadness and disappointment as we walk off the green with a triple bogey. The challenges never end.

People are also drawn to golf because it takes them into the great outdoors, to open spaces away from the office. Theodore Arnold Haultain discusses the tactile lure of the course, each with its own personality and varied terrain, in his book *The Mystery of Golf*. Speaking of the delights of the game in 1910, he describes the varied elements that stimulate our senses:

> The great breeze that greets you on the hill, the whiffs of air—pungent, penetrating—that come through green things growing, the hot smell of pines at noon, the wet smell of fallen leaves in autumn, the damp and heavy air of the valley at eve, the lungs full of oxygen, the sense of freedom on a great expanse, the exhilaration, the vastness, the buoyancy, the exaltation.[6]

"We live in small spaces," writes Henry Leach in *The Happy Golfer*, "with many walls and low roofs."[7] Away from the city, and its cacophony of angry noises that strangle silence, the golf course provides us with a few hours of refuge. Steaming asphalt and concrete, honking horns, and the incessant buzz and clatter of people coming and going gives way to a quiet oasis of cool grass, green trees, chirping birds, and the smell of pine needles. "A golfer on the links is uplifted to a simpler, freer self," claims Leach.[8]

Michael Murphy, in his classic book *Golf in the Kingdom*, speaks of golf in terms of "walkin' fast across the countryside and feelin' the wind and watchin' the sun go down and seein' yer friends hit good shots and hittin' some yourself. It's love and it's feelin' the splendor o' this good world." To David Forgan, who crafted the "Golfer's Creed" in the late 19th century, golf offers "a sweeping away of mental cobwebs, genuine recreation of tired tissues. . . . It is a cure for care, an antidote to worry."[9]

As Balfour and Murphy assert, golf is also a social game, one we play with fathers, mothers, husbands, wives, sons, daughters, grandparents, aunts and uncles, friends in our Saturday foursome, and even with strangers who join us on the first tee. We may enjoy the park-like setting of the golf course, the competition, and the chitchat, but the most intriguing element of the game is trying to hit that little damn ball where we want it to go. "Without doubt," writes Haultain, "the ball must be impelled by muscular movement; how to coordinate that muscular movement—that is the physiological factor in the fascination of golf."[10]

When one considers the physics involved, this is a daunting task. We apply about 32 pounds of muscles to swing a golf club almost 4 feet long in an arc of 20 feet around our body, while shoulders and hips turn, arms move up and down, and 5 separate torques act upon the club.[11] All of this motion is focused on making solid contact with a ball 1.68 inches in diameter squarely in the center of a 2-inch-square club face on a path that will propel the ball with sufficient force to send it the correct distance to the target.

The ball is in contact with the face of the club for half a thousandth of a second (as the club travels about three-quarters of an inch), and the margins of error are incredibly slim. If the club face is open or closed just two or three degrees with a driver, the ball will fly 20 yards or more off line, depending on the speed of the swing.[12] Sometimes just hitting the ball at all is a challenge, and a proper club–ball contact that sends the ball straight to our intended target seems a minor miracle. All of these gyrations are produced with one objective: to put that ball in a four-and-a-quarter-inch hole placed in the ground hundreds of yards away. All the while we have to negotiate water hazards, bunkers, trees, and perhaps wind and rain—in addition to our own nerves and tempers.

Yet, in spite of these considerable challenges, on the occasions when things work—by design or divine intervention—and the ball is struck solidly on line, it provides a palpable physical thrill. As the old golf adage goes, "One good shot keeps you coming back." All the rest, the ones topped in the water or sliced into the woods, are shoved aside, as we choose to revel in our modest successes. "I did it once," we tell ourselves. "I can surely do it again, even better." Our minds and muscles drive us, and our memories plug into feelings of how we did it right yesterday, a week ago, or 10 years ago.

Pembroke Vaile, an intriguing and pensive man from the last century, wrote expressively on the "soul" of golf. Among its elusive elements, he claims, is "the sheer beauty of the flight of the ball," and the almost "sensuous delight which comes to the man who created that beauty, and knows how and why he did it."[13]

There is something intoxicating in the harmonically pure meeting of club and ball. Ben Hogan, one of the best to ever play the game, loved to practice and hit golf balls from sunup to sundown. He once said that the perfectly struck shot "goes from the ball, up the club's shaft, right to your heart."[14] This is the true essence of what has attracted people to the game for five centuries. For whether it's a hickory-shafted club from the 1800s or a modern, graphite-shafted, titanium driver, the player still has to execute the shot properly.

Golf is a game that has been called a microcosm of life, as every day offers a new set of challenges. To succeed you must work hard to develop your gifts, possess healthy doses of self-confidence and patience, and persevere when times get tough. Golf has been described as a "self-reliant, silent, sturdy," game, which "leans less on its fellows" and "loves best to overcome obstacles alone."[15]

Success or failure depends on one person, ourselves. There are no teammates to help us out when things go wrong, and unlike baseball, we have to play our foul balls. To excel at the highest levels, particular and rare talents are required. Not only physical skill but also a strong and resolved character is necessary to overcome the adversity that will undoubtedly come. As Charles Blair Macdonald, one of the founding fathers of American golf, put it in 1898: "No game brings out more unerringly the true character of a man or teaches him a better lesson in self-control."[16]

The people in this book all possessed confidence in their abilities and were dogged in their pursuit of excellence. But without natural talent, they would never have been heard from. Each of us is born into this world with certain gifts, which, if fully exercised, lead us to the life path we are meant to follow. There are different kinds of gifts and different kinds of work, but the same God works those gifts in all men and women.[17] So says the Bible. To express our gifts and build a fulfilling life around them is the highest expression of our true essence.

These champions—all of whom, with the exception of caddy Bruce Edwards, are members of the World Golf Hall of Fame—came from different times and had different backgrounds. None was a perfect human being. They all had their own particular faults and flaws but shared in common a gift for the game of golf. This is what defined them, just as our gifts define us. Horton Smith, winner of two Masters Tournaments, claims that "golfing genius strikes seldom. . . . It can be developed but before a man is a genius at golf, he must have within him a spark that is the gift of the Almighty."[18] Over a century ago, three-time British Open champion Bob Ferguson echoed the same sentiment as he claimed that nerve, enthusiasm, and practice are the three essentials to succeed in golf. But to be great, he asserted, requires the gift.

It is this unique and branded *gift* that set the truly great above all the rest. The men in this book—Harry Vardon, Bobby Jones, Ben Hogan, Charlie Sifford, Ken Venturi, and Bruce Edwards—and the woman— Babe Didrikson Zaharias—all had gifts they exercised freely and rigorously, never squandering them, even when circumstances might have forgiven them for fading away quietly.

They never quit, even when things looked bleak. Bobby Jones claims that golf "is the most rewarding of all games because it possesses a very definite value as a molder or developer of character."[19] It was character that guided these people's lives and girded them against persistent struggles in the face of adversity that threatened their very lives.

Harry Vardon was at the peak of his game when struck down with tuberculosis, but he resolved to play on, winning two more British Opens and acting as a mentor to promising new players; Bobby Jones was stricken with a rare and debilitating spinal disease that would confine him to a wheelchair when he was still a young man, but he kept building the Masters Tournament, writing about golf, and being an ambassador for the game; Ben Hogan nearly died in a car crash that permanently damaged his body and caused him chronic pain for the rest of his days, but he came back and won six more major championships and built a company bearing his name.

Babe Didrikson Zaharias was struck down by colon cancer but wouldn't quit. She became a spokesperson for the American Cancer Society and was an inspiration to fellow sufferers, especially after winning another U.S. Women's Open before the cancer returned; Charlie Sifford was the victim of incessant racism, which included harassment and death threats, but he never bowed and was a winner at the highest levels of the game, paving the way for the likes of Tiger Woods.

Ken Venturi lost his game after a car accident, and later to carpal tunnel syndrome, but would capture the U.S. Open in some of the most trying conditions the championship ever produced and later have a successful broadcasting career; Bruce Edwards was afflicted with ALS, or "Lou Gehrig's disease," but kept going and inspired people with his fight, carrying the bag for one final major victory with boss Tom Watson before succumbing to his illness. What kept them going? They all loved the game. It was what they did.

"However mean your life is, meet it and live it."[20] These words of Henry David Thoreau could describe the lives of all the people in this book, who faced tremendous physical and emotional trials in their lives, yet persevered and overcame. The strength and resilience of the human spirit—indeed, its stubborn persistence—was a common denominator in facing their struggles. Golf can be a vexing and cruel game and teaches us much about ourselves.

Golf has been described as "a contest, a duel, or a melee, calling for courage, skill, strategy and self-control. It is a test of temper, a trial of honor, a revealer of character." Jerome Travers, the great amateur of the early 20th century, believed the character of an individual is laid bare under "the microscope of golf influence. The good and bad qualities in our make-up are exposed to view under the spell which golf casts over man."[21] In the end, as with most of life, our success hinges on the character and spirit we possess.

How would our tempers be tested if we were struck down by a serious illness, a near-fatal accident, or some career-threatening injury from which we would never fully recover? How would our honor be preserved if we had people telling us we were washed-up, unwanted, and persona non grata on the golf course?

How would our character be revealed if Lou Gehrig's disease robbed us of the ability to walk and talk?

How would we face the fear? Would we give in to self-pity or persevere and keep going? Where would we find the strength to actually carry on with our careers with any measure of success?

The people in this book displayed their character vigorously by not giving up or giving in to the suffering that afflicted them. This is not a chronicle of the tournaments they won and lost but an examination of how they applied their gifts and pushed themselves to achieve success. Champion golfers have been identified as sharing certain qualities, among them tough-mindedness, confidence, self-sufficiency, and emotional stability: all of which provide players with the armor to press on when things look hopeless.[22] The very nature of the game prepares one for adversity and rewards a persevering spirit that doesn't accept surrender without a fight.

The stories of these champions not only bear witness to their courage and discipline but also to the love and support of family and friends who helped them. As Robert Tyre Jones, grandfather of Bobby Jones, claimed,

"No man ever accomplishes anything really worthwhile alone. There are always two additional forces at work—other people and Providence."[23] Their families and friends bolstered them, but the game itself offered them refuge and therapy for both body and mind when they were suffering.

In recent years, *Golf Digest* magazine has featured a series called Golf Saved My Life, which focuses on this therapeutic side of the game. Whether the men and women telling their stories have struggled with cancer, autism, bipolar disorder, or serious injuries brought on by war or accidents, they all reveal how the game has helped give renewed purpose to their lives.

This theme is nothing new. In 1965, *Golf Journal* ran the story of a James Ranni, 62 years old at the time, who had suffered a major stroke years earlier. The neurosurgeon who saved his life was a golfer and saw the game as a therapeutic measure to help patients overcome serious handicaps and regain health. As for Ranni, he claimed that when people spoke of "how close you can get to God on a golf course," he knew exactly what they meant. "I can't tell you how important it is to me to be an example of what golf can do in rehabilitating the disabled."[24]

The National Amputee Golf Association was formed in 1954 in response to World War II veterans who were returning home with missing limbs and who wanted to get back into the game. It has followed the motto, "It's not what you've lost, but what you have left that counts." Bert Shepard, who lost his right leg in World War II, spoke to *Golf World* in 1997. People claimed he had "the guts to go out and play golf and all that. What about some credit to the game of golf? I've seen guys who never got out of the house get fascinated with golf, and it changes their lives."[25]

The Salute Military Golf Association (SMGA) has positively impacted the lives of thousands of post-9/11 servicemen and servicewomen, as nearly 2,500 wounded warriors have been exposed to golf through the SMGA's programs. Many of them have spoken of the healing nature of the game, how it has helped them escape the dark days and given them a feeling of hope. Tim Lang, who lost a portion of his right leg in Iraq in 2006, is proof of that. "I would tell people who have physical handicaps who don't think they can play golf," he explained to *USA Today* in 2011, "that there are no limitations. To me, there are two types of people who have suffered a life-changing experience—ones who won't let anything stop them, and ones who will find any excuse to not do anything."[26]

This attitude of not letting anything stop you and doing the best with what you have left was certainly exemplified a hundred years ago by a man named Thomas McAuliffe. In spite of losing both arms in a horrible accident when he was nine years old, he learned to play golf. In 1915, the 22-year-old told his story to *Golf Monthly*. By gripping the club between his cheek and shoulder, and with a "combined swing and jerk of the body and shoulder," he was able to hit the ball 100 to 120 yards with a driver.

McAuliffe was certainly a positive thinker. "I never permit the thought of my accident to take possession of my mind," he declared, "nor do I think of anything being impossible for me to overcome. When the time comes, I just go ahead as best I may, and somehow, someway, I generally get there without any great difficulties."[27]

Somehow, someway, I generally get there without any great difficulties—this understatement of courageous determination and resolve is a common thread in the stories of Vardon, Jones, Hogan, Zaharias, Sifford, Venturi, and Edwards. The game was not only their livelihood but also a soothing therapy for them, as it has been for others not so famous.

Character is hard to measure, but it is evident in those who persevere, who believe they can and will overcome whatever hardships are placed in front of them. Golf is a test, Arnold Haultain claims, "not so much of the muscle, or even of the brain and nerves of a man," as it is a test of his or her innermost self . . .

> of his soul and spirit; of his whole character and disposition; of his temperament; of his habit of mind; of the entire content of his mental and moral nature . . . it is a physiological, psychological, and moral fight with yourself; it is a test of mastery over self.[28]

What is there to learn from the challenges these golfers faced and how they overcame them? Why should we care? Haultain once again offers insight: "In a picture, a sonata, a statue—the color, the sound, the form assuredly may interest us," but these "are but vehicles for the artist's thought and emotion." He continues:

> It is the artist's conception of life that is so interesting. So it is with sport. We like immensely to know exactly how a man boxes or fences or drives; *but underneath this, we like immensely to know how he*

fights the battle of life; for he will do the one as he does the other—that we feel [italics added]. So there is a great kinship between artist and sportsman. Each reveals himself in his work; and it is in this self-revelation that humanity takes an absorbing interest.[29]

For those who have the gift of golf, we wonder what it is that makes them special. This is especially true when they triumph over adversity that could just as well crush them. How do they deal with victory and defeat, both on and off the course?

The stories of the people I discuss here are connected, in more than a casual way, to each other by the game. Consider Harry Vardon, the greatest player of his era, who knew Old Tom Morris and played with Bobby Jones in the latter's first U.S. Open in 1920. He told reporters the young Jones would be one of the very best golfers ever seen, and he was right.

After Jones retired from competition, he played a 1934 exhibition in Houston attended by Babe Zaharias, an event she claimed "fired up" her own golf aspirations. That same year, Jones started the Masters Tournament, which Ben Hogan won twice. Jones used to say that if he had to choose one man to hit a shot to win a major championship, he would pick Hogan because of his "spiritual" assets.[30] Hogan, late in his career, saw a tenacity in Ken Venturi that he admired and took him under his wing. They became great friends, and Ken was a pallbearer at Hogan's funeral.

Venturi befriended Charlie Sifford in those days when racism dogged him. When the restaurant at the Pensacola Country Club wouldn't let Charlie eat there, Venturi spoke up, then took his own breakfast and joined Charlie in the locker room to eat. Bruce Edwards worked for Tom Watson, who was tutored by Byron Nelson, the same man who had helped Ken Venturi years earlier. The first tournament Edwards and Watson won together was the Byron Nelson Classic. Amazingly, the chain of golf history is often connected by one or two short links.

The talent of the seven people in this book, in concert with their character, defined lives that are remembered to this day. When golf icon Old Tom Morris died over a hundred years ago, his achievements as a golfer were well known and sure to endure. The greatest moral of his life, as stressed upon his passing, was that "no matter in what sphere, it is character that achieves the greatest victories." As Arnold Haultain writes plainly, "It all comes back to character; not intellect or acumen or ability . . . just character."[31]

In many ways, the legacy of how these champions dealt with the physical and emotional trials life handed them is more impressive than the records they set on the golf course. "We define and admire greatness," writes Mark Frost in his wonderful book *The Greatest Game Ever Played*, "not only by the magnitude of achievement but also for the degree of difficulty that person has to overcome."[32]

1

HARRY VARDON

"Never Despair"

Golf has no equal as a test of human strengths and failings. [1]
—Harry Vardon

He had the ideal soul for the game, a soul that took each break of the game as it came to him without a quiver or a complaint. [2]
—Jerome Travers on Vardon

In the months leading up to the 1903 Open Championship at Prestwick, Scotland, Harry Vardon had not been a well man. As he carefully packed the simple, rough-hewn wooden box that carried the tools of his trade, he was not looking forward to the long train ride to the west coast of Scotland. He felt listless, lacking energy, and was troubled by a persistent cough that wouldn't go away. Taking a breath, it felt as if someone had tied rope around his chest and pulled it tight. Sitting down, feeling much older than his 33 years, he stared at the box that had gone with him for over a decade. He felt more than punkish but would be damned if he was going to miss the most important tournament in the world, especially one he had won three times previously.

"I was a sick man then," he would write in his autobiography 30 years later. "The doctors said that I ought not to play." [3] However, in the end, despite periodic dizzy spells and that hacking cough, he made up his mind that he would go out and compete. His own brother, seeing Harry's ashen, gaunt face, tried to dissuade him from doing so. The decision was totally in keeping with the nature of the man, who was once described as a "gallant and great-hearted, if stubborn, soul." It may be argued that Harry's response was born of the strenuous upbringing he endured, combined with the professional work ethic deeply imbued in him. [4]

Prestwick was the site of the first British Open held in 1860, nine years after Old Tom Morris laid it out. It was a venue full of history, and the Open in 1903 was played June 9–10, 36 holes each day. As Harry stood on the first tee at 8:30 a.m. for that first round, he stared at the ball his caddy had teed for him on a mound of moist sand, hoping the sea air blowing off the Atlantic might refresh him. The weather was ideal, and he began the championship with an excellent first round of 73, but when he finished, he felt weak and had trouble catching his breath. [5] Concerned, he removed his Norfolk jacket and laid down on a bench in the professional's shop before teeing off again.

So ill he couldn't eat anything, he instead fortified himself with a bottle of Guinness, his hand shaking as he lifted the bottle to his lips. He lay on the hard, cool wood, sweat rolling off his forehead, his heart fluttering. Loosening his tie, he must have considered his options. In that long hour between tee times, he might have considered quitting. But he also may have remembered his lost childhood, when as a boy of 14 he was hired out by his father to work as a domestic servant. In reality, he became an indentured servant, toiling hard days for a stern master.

I've survived worse days than this. Alright now, let's get on with it. Calling upon some deep reserve of inner strength, Harry's weary body moved off that bench, and he plodded to the tee. The 77 he shot in the afternoon gave him a 4-shot lead. Harry didn't know what might happen the following day, but as he had done all his life, he would carry on as best he could and let the championship play out. After a meal and a hot bath, he turned in early. *Tomorrow will take care of itself.*

Considering his childhood and adolescence, it is a wonder that Harry Vardon became a champion of any kind. He actually played little golf as a boy. Yet, like Young Tom Morris before him and Bobby Jones after, Vardon was blessed with a genius for the game. He never took a single golfing lesson, and whatever style he possessed was "purely the result of watching others play and copying them when I thought they made a stroke on a particularly easy and satisfactory manner." [6] By the time he turned professional at the age of 20, Harry had played less golf than most ardent amateurs, yet he possessed a strident self-confidence to find success in the game.

Henry William Vardon entered the world May 9, 1870, in Grouville, on the isle of Jersey, a 46-square-mile piece of earth jutting out of the English Channel off the coast of Normandy, France.[7] His parents, Philip and Elizabeth, lived with their eight children in a simple, cramped cottage five hundred yards from the sea. Harry, as the family called him, was, in his own words, "a thin and rather delicate boy with not much physical strength."[8]

This, however, did not prevent him from enthusiastically joining his chums in playing cricket and football (soccer). He always loved outdoor activities. As a seven-year-old, he recalled gentlemen coming around to survey the grounds around his house. They were marking out places for tees and greens. "Then the story went out," Vardon said, "that they were making preparations to play a game called golf."[9] This signaled the beginning of the Royal Jersey Golf Club.

Harry Vardon, seen here on the first tee at St Andrews, circa 1905, with Old Tom Morris looking on (to the left with the white beard). Old Tom saw the best players from the 1840s until his death in 1908, and Vardon was at the top of the list. The *American Golfer* would note that Harry's swing was remarkable by virtue of its "utter ease and lack of physical effort. His hands, arms, body and legs appear to work as a well-oiled machine." *Courtesy USGA. All Rights Reserved.*

Like many boys of that and later eras who lived near a golf course, at age eight Harry began to caddy for players at the club, doing this twice a week or so for the next four years.

"We did not think much of it upon our first experience," he remembered, "but after we had carried for a few rounds we came to see that it contained more than we had imagined."[10] He got his first taste of the game, but "we had no links to play upon, no clubs, no balls, and no money. However, we surmounted all these difficulties." To begin with, the caddies laid out their own little course consisting of four holes, each about 50 yards long. "For boys of seven that seemed quite enough," he remembered. They made out teeing grounds, smoothed out the greens, and were soon ready for play.

In the absence of a real ball, they used a big white marble called a taw, which was about half the size of a real golf ball. For a club, after several experiments, they decided to cut a limb from an oak tree and trimmed it to resemble the heads of "the drivers we had seen used on the links." Many of their best matches took place under the moonlight, and they often made these 50-yard holes in three strokes, and "with our home-made clubs, our little white taws, our lack of knowledge, and our physical feebleness all taken into consideration, I say we have often done less credible things since."[11]

Harry caddied at the club and practiced his game when time allowed, which wasn't often. He never really had a childhood and from a tender age was always busying himself with work to help the family. He'd collect seaweed on the beach, which was sold for fertilizer and "for a sum that brought a nice few pounds a year into the family exchequer. I think that, whatever may have been my faults, I can claim to have been a boy who wasted little time."[12] He was a serious boy with adult responsibilities.

Theirs was a big family of six boys and two girls, and as Vardon remembered, "at the age of twelve I went out to work to do my bit in the maintenance of the home." Formal education had no appeal for him, and as he recalled, he was considered the dunce of his school. One day, as punishment, the teacher made him clean out a rabbit hutch. For some it might have been an unpleasant task, but for Vardon it was "a happy release. Anything in the nature of activity appealed to me far more than the acquiring of knowledge." He thus began a quasi-Dickensian existence, spending 60 hours a week working on a local farm and carrying clubs about twice a week at Royal Jersey. [13]

Work on the farm was cold, dirty, and extremely harsh work, which he did for almost two years. "At that time I had not the slightest thought of taking seriously to golf."[14] How could he? As a child laborer he had no time for leisure activities. He wasn't alone, as about 22 percent of boys in nearby England aged 10–14 were in the labor force at that time. [15]

Harry next entered the domestic service of Dr. Godfrey, working 14-hour days. "For four years I had virtually no golf at all. To be sure, I would go out occasionally with other boys on moonlight nights for a game, but I do not know that my spasmodic appearances on the links in these circumstances can be held to have constituted very serious practice."[16] His reflections on these difficult years were scant. At 17, he had the good fortune to leave the doctor's service and began work as a gardener on the estate of one Major Spofforth, who was the captain of Royal Jersey. It was a move that was to change his life forever.

Harry enjoyed working for the kind-hearted Spofforth. He was "keen on golf," according to Vardon, "and every now and again he took me to play." Vardon conceded at this time he was not "a diligent seeker of success on the links. I liked cricket and football, and went in a good deal of running, winning ten prizes as a sprinter." Apart from an occasional round with Major Spofforth, which inevitably made him feel nervous, Harry's golf was mostly limited to Christmas, Easter, and a few other holidays. Spofforth must have seen something in his young gardener, for one day, after one of their infrequent matches, the major said to him, "Henry, my boy, take my advice, and never give up golf. It may be very useful to you someday."[17]

Harry would never forget those words and would call upon them many times in the years after. As he awaited the final day's play at Prestwick in 1903, his thoughts might have carried him back to his beginnings, when he hadn't the wildest idea of becoming a champion. Now, years later, his golf had taken him all around the Continent and even to America. At times it was all a blur to him.

His tour of the United States in 1900—"the most interesting experience" of his career—had brought him a U.S. Open championship, he remembered that.[18] He also remembered the 20,000 thousand odd miles of monotonous travel, living out of hotel rooms, the heat and humidity of Florida and South Carolina, and playing shoddy golf courses with more dirt than grass. It was a grueling schedule that had him playing in different cities for weeks on end. He made it through that and had survived his time on the farm and with the doctor. *Surely I can make it through two more rounds of golf now, can't I?*

When Harry woke up on that final day of the 1903 Open, to his surprise—and relief—he felt a little better. He would shoot a miraculous 72 in the morning third round, the best of the entire championship. But between rounds it was the same as the day before; his strength was gone, his legs weak, the world unsteady under him. He returned to his bench to lie down. A coughing fit gripped him, and alarming amounts of blood covered his handkerchief as he pulled it from his mouth.[19] His brother Tom, who was also a contestant, begged him not to go out but to seek a doctor's attention. Harry, however, was more stubborn than he was afraid, and his eyes revealed a resolve that Tom understood.

The final round became an exercise in sheer survival. The crowd of six thousand cheered him on from start to finish, but Harry couldn't see them.[20] His chest was aching, and the taste of blood lingered in the back of his throat. More than once he felt so faint he feared it would be impossible to finish. "That I was able to last out until my final putt had been holed, only goes to show what it is possible to accomplish under adverse circumstances."[21]

He hung on and shot 78, but by the end, the only thing he could see was the brown turf his eyes strained to focus on as he trudged down the dusty fairways. He won by six shots over Tom and eight shots over Jack White. "It is strange," he once observed, "that sometimes when you are low-spirited and out of sorts you can hit the ball astonishingly well; golf seems to lift you out of yourself and cheer you."[22] Harry was beyond exhaustion, but instead of worrying about himself, he thought of his little brother. He would later say of that day, "Glad as I was of having equaled the record of the two Morrises, I could have wished, and did wish, that Tom had been the victor."[23]

Harry loved Tom, and trusted him implicitly. It was Tom who carried his bag in the play-off against J. H. Taylor in 1896 that had brought Harry his first Open. He had also been spurred on by Tom to become a professional. Tom was not only his support but also his competition. As Harry recalled years later, his first attempt to play golf in earnest was at the age of 20, when he entered the "competition for a vase given by the local working men's club."[24] Even though he played little golf up to then, he won easily and was encouraged.

Then, coincidentally, he learned that Tom, who had gone to England to try his own hand at professional golf, had won second prize in an open professional tournament at Musselburgh. "The award was £20," Harry remembered, which "seemed an enormous amount to me." His brother's success caused Harry "to think very seriously of the wonderful prospects which were possible as a golf professional." He figured that even as little as he played, he was as good as Tom. "If he could win that vast fortune," Harry concluded, "why shouldn't I?" Since Harry was making about £16 a year at the time as a gardener, he felt he had nothing to lose and everything to gain in seeing how good his golf game might be.[25]

Harry had come a long way from those days and by 1903 was recognized as the greatest golfer in the world. In the weeks that followed his amazing victory, Vardon felt no better. There were days when sheer force of will moved him from his bed to the golf course. Many a time Tom begged him to ease off his commitments and take time off to heal himself. Instead, Harry pressed on, doing three weeks of exhibition matches. Upon returning to his club, he suffered a severe lung hemorrhage, coughing up copious amounts of dark red blood. "It was now apparent," he reflected in his autobiography, "that I was in a real bad state of health," and he was ordered to seek treatment in a sanatorium.[26]

Harry underwent a thorough physical examination, after which the doctor delivered the bad news—he was suffering from tuberculosis. In the days before wonder drugs, Harry knew this could be a death sentence. He had no choice now but to follow his doctor's orders. In the late summer of 1903, he boarded a train at Liverpool Street Station in London for the trip to Mundesley, located in Norfolk, near the North Sea coast. It was England's foremost and most expensive facility and would be his home for the next six months.[27]

Tuberculosis has been present in humans for at least five thousand years. Many famous people have been stricken with it, including Anton Chekhov, Elizabeth Barrett Browning, Edgar Allan Poe, Vivian Leigh, Eleanor Roosevelt, Eugene O'Neill, George Orwell, and W. C. Fields. Without effective treatment, over 50 percent of sufferers will be dead within five years of its onset, their bodies wasting away to skeletal proportions (a physical decay that gave rise to the disease being referred to as "consumption" in earlier times). [28]

Tuberculosis is contracted primarily simply by the act of breathing; therefore, everybody is susceptible to the pulmonary form of the disease. Bacteria inhaled in water droplets settle in the periphery of the lung and grow very slowly until they form what looks like a cheesy boil. From this boil, the infection spreads and spills over into nearby small airways and forms more of these tiny boils. [29]

The second main way the disease is contracted is by drinking milk from an infected cow. The pathogen could have been in the milk Harry drank as a boy in Jersey, lying dormant for years. For the great majority of sufferers, we can compare the treatment of TB in those days with the methods for treating less curable forms of cancer today. Prayer became as important as medicine. Even 25 years after Vardon was first treated, 50,000 people a year died of TB in England and Wales (and 90,000 in the United States). In the United Kingdom it accounted for almost half the deaths in the population affecting men and women between 25 and 30 years of age. [30]

Whether Vardon contracted it from milk he drank or from the air he breathed on countless trains and coaches while traveling in England and in the United States, we don't know. It didn't change the fact that his life was now threatened. At Mundesley, Vardon was assigned a room with his own bathroom on the first floor. It was a large bright room with windows running the whole length of one wall. Attractive rugs covered the floors, and paintings adorned the walls. Confinement to bed was crucial, the rationale being that this would reduce the amount of oxygen required by body tissues, lessening the burden on the lungs. [31] Vardon slept 12 hours a day and passed time replaying rounds in his mind, wondering if he'd ever return to competitive golf.

For Vardon, nothing was pleasant about life in a sanatorium, for "the two things of which I was exceedingly fond were barred," namely golf and his pipe. Tobacco was prohibited. As he described those trying months: "My enforced rest cure was possibly more irksome than it otherwise would have been, owing to the fact that I had always experienced exceptionally good health," he would recall. "I had, too, all my life been extremely active. The thought that I would not be able, for goodness knows how long, to lead my usual active life was far from a pleasant one. However, we made the best of it." [32]

In the early 1900s, Germany introduced a new concept of treatment to the sanatorium movement. Patients, most of whom were between 20 and 35 years of age, were put on bed rest 24 hours a day for sometimes a full year or more, forcing sufferers to abandon careers.[33] Mundesley was operated along the same lines, with rest in a quiet environment, good food, and plenty of fresh air being the main components of treatment. In his first week, Harry was allowed to get out of bed for one hour in the afternoon, in the second week for two hours, and in the third week for four hours.[34] This left him plenty of time alone with his thoughts, perhaps to reflect on where his life had taken him.

He could remember how hard he had worked as a boy to help his family. He sacrificed much for them, but if it was truly appreciated, he didn't know. His father was a stern man, never enamored of Harry's ambition to become a professional. According to Vardon, his father, Phillip, didn't even see him play until he had won three championships. Curiously, his father had on numerous occasions watched Tom and always thought he had the potential to be a good golfer. But, as Harry explained, "he could not reconcile himself to the belief that a person who took such a dilettantish interest in the game as myself would ever excel at it."[35]

Even after Harry had won a large number of prizes, his father remained firm to his early convictions. He frequently remarked, "Harry may win the prizes, but it is Tom who plays the golf." This must have stung Harry, who was not simply better than Tom but one of the best players in the world. All Harry would say about his father's opinion of him years later was, "Happy and sacred his memory!"[36] Harry had been born into a hard life of the lower classes, forced to work to support his family, but he had a better plan for his life and believed he could achieve greater things.

Despite his father's misgivings, Harry Vardon believed in himself. In 1890 the 20-year-old Vardon left Jersey to take a job at Studley Royal Golf Club in Yorkshire, Ripon, England.[37] It was a tiny village in the middle of the country, and he served as greenskeeper and professional. The club was too quiet and offered little competition on the course to sharpen his game. "No true golfer is satisfied with a little of the game," Vardon remarked, "if there is no substantial reason why he should not have much of it." While there, an opponent in a match told him to "get away from here as quickly as you can, as you don't get half enough golf to bring you out." He took the advice "very much to heart."[38]

Vardon moved to Bury Golf Club, to the east and near Manchester a year later, again serving as keeper of the greens and professional combined, and did not play or teach until late afternoons.[39] The competition was better, and he grew by leaps and bounds. One blessing of the relative remoteness and "quietness" of his previous job in Ripon was that it offered him the opportunity to practice his game. As he put it, "Perhaps I was lucky in the fact that there were so few players in those days that the opportunity of a match rarely presented itself, and so there was nothing to do but practice."[40]

It was in that year "I learned most of my golf, including the overlapping grip, the low-flying back-spin shot with an iron club, and the other ideas that were useful in a later period." He had a gift, but he also worked it. "I practiced as assiduously as anybody in the land. Not one of my shots came to me as a gift pure and simple."[41] Later, men like Bobby Jones and Sam Snead were said to be "naturals" at the game, implying that they didn't have to work at the game. But nobody becomes good at something without assiduous practice, as Vardon attested to.

Vardon's practice regimen was to pay huge dividends by laying a sound foundation in all aspects of his shotmaking, and would serve him well the rest of his career. He had physical gifts that suited the game. Standing five feet, nine and a half inches tall, and weighing about 155 pounds, he had large, powerful hands and fingers that "looked like a bunch of sausages wrapped around a baton." With them—for Vardon's power emanated almost totally from his hands— "he performed feats of golf seldom seen before or since."[42]

Harry was a catalyst for great change in the way golfers swung a club. He revolutionized the way we hold the club, wedding the hands together in the finger instead of the spilt-grip method that held the club in the palms. He did not "invent" the popular "Vardon grip" but rather improved and popularized a grip British Amateur champion John Laidlay used in the late 1880s. "I believe in a firm grip," Vardon said. "The practice of holding the left fingers firmly and the right loosely, tends to wildness in direction. In my grip there is neither a left nor a right hand, for both are united by the overlapping (not an interlocking) of the little finger of the right down the shaft."[43]

As he became accustomed to his new grip, he began to have the satisfactory feeling that both hands were working as one. This feeling of unified hands working together is one all modern golfers strive to achieve. Most importantly, Vardon emphasized, was that the club head, hands, wrists, and arms all work together as one piece of machinery. [44]

Vardon also used shorter clubs than most golfers, feeling they gave him "better command." Harry developed his own style, one of an upright swing, which took the club on a more economical back-and-through motion. He claimed that he, his brother Tom, Ted Ray, and a few other Jersey golfers "all drifted involuntarily into the habit of taking the club to the top of the swing by the shortest route, whereas the popular way before was to sweep the club back flat at the start and make a very full flourish of the swing. Why we hit upon the other way we do not know." This flat, sweeping swing was much more a "hitting" motion than the "swinging" one Vardon popularized, but it was a shock "to the people who for years had worshipped the longer and flatter method known as the St Andrews swing." [45]

When Vardon first came to prominence in 1893 as a contender in the big events, those who watched him, including famed golf writer Bernard Darwin, thought his style ungainly, taking the club up abruptly and with considerable bend in his left elbow. "Whatever was actually the case," argues golf historian Herbert Warren Wind, "professional and popular understanding of the correct method to hit a golf ball was entirely different after Harry Vardon made his way to the top." Change always has its detractors, but Darwin himself came to admire Vardon's style, and asserted that "in his great years, no one had any real hope against him." [46]

His swing was so smooth, so rhythmical, that he came to be known as "the Stylist."

"The outstanding impression of watching Vardon play," notes the *American Golfer* in 1924, "is that of utter ease and lack of physical effort. His hands, arms, body and legs appear to work as a well-oiled machine." Henry Leach, a well-known British golf writer of the day, was convinced that of all the "men who have ever played golf, he is the supreme artist of the game." [47] Nobody else came close.

Besides golfing style, Vardon also had some interesting theories on proper clothing for golf. He believed that suspenders (or "braces" as they were called) kept his shoulders bound together and also recommended playing in a jacket, which had the same effect. He was also the first professional to play in knickerbockers—doing so because he disliked the cuffs of his trousers getting muddy on rainy days. Attired in his Norfolk jacket, "and with the flower in his buttonhole, he set a mode of gaiety and smartness to the rest, which younger men were not slow to follow."[48]

Harry Vardon was an artist, but he was no dandy, and his swing didn't lack power. Gene Sarazen remembered that "Vardon always played well within himself. He always kept 20 yards of his power in reserve and there were times, when he hit the ball flat out, he could add as much as 50 yards to a drive." Sportswriter Grantland Rice agreed with the notion that Harry played within himself. "Vardon's idea of driving is to hit a ball two hundred and twenty yards straight rather than two hundred and sixty yards off to the right or left."[49]

Considerable though they were, Vardon's physical talents formed only a part of his genius. Golf is a game requiring patience and keeping one's emotions in check. "At golf," he was fond of saying, "the ball soon puts you back in your place if you get annoyed with it."[50] His demeanor was perfectly suited to the rigors of competitive golf. Few players since have been able to analyze a course, holes to be treated with respect and those that might be attacked. He was probably the first practitioner of "course management," something Ben Hogan was revered for 50 years later. Harry Vardon "was the epitome of confidence. Imperturbable, taciturn, he seldom smiled on the course, but then he seldom scowled, either. He never threw a tantrum, never gave an alibi." Emotionally, he had "the equanimity of a plowhorse."[51]

These qualities of calm and self-control helped Harry during his stay at Mundesley. In that first month or two he was allowed out of his bed to venture outside for only a few minutes at a time. Out of breath after 50 paces, he would sit down on a bench and look out into the garden. The scent of roses wafted in his nostrils. Cheeks warmed by the sun buoyed his spirits. *By God, I'm still alive after all.* There was still beauty in the world. When the wind came up from the east, the smell of salt air reminded him of Jersey and faraway days when he felt his whole life was ahead of him.[52] Days when he thought it was possible to love and be loved.

While in the employ of his benefactor Major Spofforth, Vardon met a pretty young woman named Jessie Bryant. A quiet, shy girl, she was captivated by the dark, handsome young man with the penetrating eyes.

He hoped this was a woman whom he could share his dreams with and find a life together. The more they saw each other, the stronger their bond became, and both felt the pangs of separation when he left the island to take his first job in England in November of 1890. He returned home as frequently as he could to see her, often meeting on the links to walk and talk and dream of the future.

Before moving to his next job in Bury, he told Jessie that they would marry once he was established. She was thrilled at the proposal, although she did not relish leaving Jersey. The timeline for a wedding moved up when, a few weeks after returning from a trip to see her, she sent him a letter telling him she was pregnant with his child. As was the usual solution in those days, they married quickly, on November 15, 1891. Sadly, he would quickly realize that any interest Jessie took in his career during their courtship had been feigned. The truth was, she had no interest in his golf and never would.[53]

Harry returned to his job while she stayed with her parents, waiting for the baby to arrive. Clarence Henry Vardon was born June 25, 1892, but took sick soon afterward, the life ebbing from his tiny body with each passing day. He died August 5, 1892. After losing the baby, Jessie withdrew emotionally and physically. Harry was hurting too and was steadfast in trying to help her, but her Victorian response was reticence. Hoping to move on, he went back to doing his job, working and playing tournaments in England and Scotland while Jessie remained in Jersey for the next three years.[54]

In 1896, Harry took a job in Ganton, in North Yorkshire, about halfway between London and Edinburgh near the North Sea. The course was only five years old, and he saw possibilities to grow there. Most importantly, he convinced Jessie to go with him. Romance was renewed in the marriage, and by Christmas, she was pregnant again. Both had hopes of new happiness filling their lives. Expectations were high, but in the spring of 1896, Jessie sensed something wrong inside her. A doctor was called and confirmed the horrible news—she had suffered a miscarriage.[55]

This was a blow from which she never fully recovered. As with the death of baby Clarence, this tragic event drove the two apart again. Jessie, never fond of her husband's life of travel or comfortable with the higher social class he mixed with, stayed home and withdrew within herself.

Harry found his salvation in golf and did as he had before, going back to work.

The summer after the miscarriage, he won his first British Open with a score of 316. In 1893, a year after losing Clarence, Harry had played in his first Open at Prestwick. He finished 23rd, 22 shots behind winner Willie Auchterlonie. Next came a fifth-place finish in 1894 and a ninth-place finish in 1895. He was definitely a player on the rise.

It must be remembered that scores in golf are relative to the age that produces them. In Vardon's era of hickory-shafted clubs, a drive of 240 yards or more was a prodigious hit. Before the advent of the rubber-core ball in 1902, the old gutta-percha balls had less bounce and sounded like a billiard ball when hit. The irons were thin faced, light tools, attached to hickory that would twist violently during the swing, causing shots to go wildly off line. Add to that courses not groomed as they are today—greens were bumpy and fairways a mixture of dirt, clover, and weeds with a patch or two of smooth grass thrown in for variety.

At Muirfield in 1896, a few months after Jessie's miscarriage, Vardon tied for the Open lead with J. H. Taylor after 72 holes, then won the play-off. By 1896, the world had heard of the Vardons, but many thought that Tom was the stronger man. After all, Tom had finished 10th in 1891 and 12th in 1892 before Harry even got started, then 9th and 10th in 1895 and 1896. Taylor was not one of them. He told Horace Hutchinson, a two-time British Amateur champion, afterward that he realized "even then, even before the competition, what a terror this Harry Vardon was." He had good reason for thinking so, as two months before the Open Vardon thrashed Taylor eight and seven in a match at Ganton. "I played my game," Taylor insisted, "but who could stand against that? Vardon's not a man at all—he's a blooming steam engine."[56]

Vardon, along with Englishman Taylor and Scotsman James Braid, won among them 16 British Opens, and their dominance inspired the moniker, "The Great Triumvirate." They were that era's Hogan, Snead, and Nelson, or Nicklaus, Palmer, and Player. Hutchinson maintained it was "hardly to be questioned which of the three had the most perfect and beautiful style," adding that Vardon's "style was the perfection of power and ease."[57]

Vardon credited a putting cleek he found before the play-off with carrying him to victory. "I have never putted so well in my life," was the way he described it.[58] His brother Tom also played an important role.

Having finished 10th, Tom caddied for his brother in the play-off, offering him considerable moral support. For example, when Harry hit a shot out of bounds at the first hole in the second play-off round, Harry said Tom encouraged him, saying "Never mind Harry, you'll soon get those two back again." When he sunk the last putt and stood on the final green victorious, he was, by his own admission, "dazed, and unable to speak."[59] He had won the biggest championship in the world.

Yes, Harry, you'll get your game back, he might have thought to himself at Mundesley while playing bridge with his fellow patients, trying to keep his mind busy. *It's there for you still. Just carry on.*

Although Vardon would recall in his autobiography that he made the best of his forced rest, he must have suffered deep apprehension about ever being able to resume his career. In a letter to fellow pro W. C. Gaudin, he writes, "I am doing well here but cannot say if I will ever play golf again. If not, I shall never rest, as golf taken away from me would be as hard as giving up smoking!" He most surely realized the seriousness of his condition, adding, "If I get another hemorrhage, it may be all up for me."[60] Perhaps he would have felt more restful if he had a happy home life, but long gone were the days when he could turn to his wife for nurturing.

For years, Harry had spent long periods of time away from Jessie and was accustomed to the life of a bachelor who happened to be married. His strong mind and self-discipline kept him going forward. Jerome Travers, who was a great player and winner of the 1915 U.S. Open, said of Vardon: "His mental equipment was flawless. His disposition was even, unbroken, and placid—placid but not flabby. He had the ideal soul for the game, a soul that took each break of the game as it came to him without a quiver or a complaint."[61] It was within this cocoon that he existed, holding onto and reaffirming his mantra, "Never despair." He was alone and had learned at an early age the value of self-sacrifice and self-sufficiency.

As each week passed, the doctors allowed him more time on his feet, and he passed his time with card games on the porch and reading books in the library.[62] He must have missed his golf badly. Henry Leach recalled years later that during that time, Vardon "wrote to me piteously from there saying, 'They won't let me have my clubs!'" Harry put up a good front to the public, penning a letter in *Golf Illustrated* that autumn, telling readers he was staying there "for the winter, after which they tell me I will be a new man and able to take to the game I love so well."[63]

Harry befriended other patients, trying to give them hope as well. Memories of his childhood, playing under the moonlight with Tom and his fellow caddies must have bolstered him. After his breakthrough in 1896, Harry finished sixth in the Open in 1897, then won again in 1898 and 1899, and finished second from 1900 to 1902. It was in 1900 that Vardon made a tour of the United States and while there won the U.S. Open. He lost only 13 of the 88 exhibition matches he played on his tour, competing against the best ball of two and sometimes three other players. Given his estrangement with Jessie, the idea of a trip overseas had appealed to him very much. "I had played exceedingly good golf, the crowds had been large and enthusiastic, and the golf boom throughout the United States was already established."[64]

One reporter who interviewed Vardon during the tour shared with his readers that while "positive in his golf views, Vardon is not a great talker, nor is he at all of a boastful nature. He is as hard as nails in condition, very sinewy and as active as a sprinter in moving about."[65]

Now, three years later at Mundesley, Harry was the same man, quiet and polite and so unassuming that most of his fellow patients had no idea of his fame as a golfer. He was still "hard as nails," although his body had been assaulted by disease. He would come back, he believed, as he had so many times against his competitors on the golf course.

It was Andrew Kirkaldy, the great St Andrews professional, who christened Vardon "the Greyhound" because at the height of Harry's career other players were unable to catch him. Kirkaldy added that Vardon's dominating play could "break the heart of an iron horse."[66] That same spirit would now be harnessed to face the course before him, defeating his opponent—tuberculosis—and getting back home as soon as possible.

At the end of his fourth month, Harry was allowed to walk on the grounds and soon discovered the edges of the hospital golf course. The sight of it seemed to mock the fact that he was unable to hold a club in his hands, but the smell of the cut grass lifted his spirits. On Christmas Eve, 1903, Vardon and two others were allowed to go to the village for a short excursion and rode in Dr. Burton-Fanning's open-topped roadster—it was the first car ride for Harry. Christmas Day dinner was served in the dining room, with a tree in the corner, candles adorning the tables.[67]

Harry and his fellow patients may have felt like prisoners, but they could still try to find reasons to keep their hopes alive.

G. W. Beldam paid Vardon a visit at the beginning of 1904 and "found him in excellent spirits and greatly improved health. . . . The Open champion's condition is now so greatly improved that the doctors allow him to play a little, so that he is able to keep himself in some sort of practice."[68] Harry was getting impatient to return to his work, playing golf. At least he had another job to fall back on if his playing career was over, as in 1902 he had begun his association with the South Herts Golf Club in England, where he would serve as head professional until his death.

Perhaps, when he considered his release from Mundesley, he'd approach the game as he had when first starting out. Harry had not known what it is to be nervous, even in a championship round when his "fate depended on almost every stroke, and particularly on those at the last few holes. The feeling that was always uppermost in my mind is that I had everything to gain and nothing to lose." He played with confidence, simple as that, and "no stroke or game ever seemed to cause me any anxiety in those young days, and my rapid success may have been in large measure due to this indifference."[69]

Perhaps the best thing to do now was to play as if he had nothing to lose and everything to gain. After all, he was still alive, and that was everything. Once again, his demeanor would dictate his path. "Vardon has genius," Jerome Travers told people, "and with it, a rare combination, the capacity for infinite patience."[70] This trait of patience would be worth more than gold to Harry and bolster him in the years to come. His difficult past also prepared him for his trials. He was firmly convinced that the hard work he did as a boy was the best thing possible to prepare him for "the many adverse circumstances which must befall any young man when he starts out in the battle of life."[71] His experiences steeled his resolve, and his patience would guide him through difficult times.

During his fifth month in Mundesley, Harry borrowed a club and was allowed to putt on the hospital course. When he walked onto the green and took his stance, he looked down at his right hand and noticed a steady tremor running through it that he couldn't control. The tremor might subside for awhile but then "jump like a running salmon in his downswing."[72] He questioned Dr. Burton-Fanning about it, and the doctor asked Vardon if he had ever suffered an injury to his right hand. As Harry considered the question, it didn't take him long to recall an incident three years earlier. While playing soccer for the Ganton Club, which Vardon recalled as some of the most enjoyable days of his life, he suffered a broken bone near the outside of the wrist.[73]

The doctor explained that tuberculosis has the capacity to infect every internal organ, from liver to brain, from the finger tips to the delicate structures of our eyes, and that the tubercle bacilli had sought vulnerable tissue in his wrist and arm.[74] It didn't affect his full swings, only his putting. Though quite troubling, this was news Harry would have to accept as the "new normal" for his life going forward.

In February 1904, after five months in the sanatorium, Harry asked his doctors to be released, and they agreed he was well enough to go back home. He had made a solid recovery. After entering Mundesley weighing 140 pounds, a few months later he was up to 175.[75] Before leaving, Harry scored a hole-in-one on the facility's par-three fourth hole, which would turn out to be the only ace of his career.[76] The doctors told him a more moderate climate would better his chances of continued health. Harry stubbornly declared he would remain in England, responding defiantly that, even "if I have only a short time to live, it is going to be the most joyful period of my life."[77] He was determined to be the master of his life and not let his disease control him.

He returned home to find that his wife Jessie had moved into a separate room, ostensibly to ensure that his room would be kept clean and dust-free. They were never again to share a bedroom. After many years of an estranged marriage, Harry accepted Jessie's decision, as he did most unpleasant things in life, with quiet resignation. They had grown apart. Harry's fame had carried him into social circles unimaginable to him or Jessie a few years earlier. The rich and famous sought his company, which fed Harry's ego but which his wife wanted nothing to do with.[78]

Restless to do something after his confinement in Mundesley, he started work on his first book *The Complete Golfer*.[79] Published in 1905, it was met with critical and commercial success. Writing gave Vardon an opportunity to look back on his career and share his knowledge of the game with the masses. Years later, in retirement, he very much enjoyed teaching average golfers to play a better game. But for a man of 33, he faced a tenuous future.

By the summer of 1904, Harry was back on the circuit and went to the Open at Royal St. George's, where he finished fifth, six shots behind Jack

White. He missed a number of short putts in the third round, costing him a chance to win, and this would become a maddening pattern for the rest of his career. At the end of the summer, he suffered another small hemorrhage, and bed rest was ordered again for a brief period.

Vardon would never again be the golfer he was when he entered Mundesley. Before he went away for treatment, Harry was in a class by himself. "For a while he was," in the opinion of Horace Hutchinson, "two strokes in the round better than either Taylor or Braid, and, I believe, better than any other man that we have seen."[80] That changed when the tuberculosis felled him, for when Harry left Mundesley, he was plagued with the putting yips. Vardon himself said that there was little doubt that his illness had affected his game, "and indirectly this may have been the cause of my failing to add another championship to my list."[81]

The disease had affected the nerves in his right forearm, which puzzled a good many doctors and subjected Vardon "to indescribable mental torture."[82] It is fascinating to read Vardon's clinical analysis of his own problems. "As I stood addressing the ball, I would watch for my right hand to jump."[83] He added that it was only on putts close to the hole that he had any trouble, "so the affliction must have been born largely of imagination and environment."[84]

Obviously, he accepted the possibility that there was a mental component to his problem; at least it may have exacerbated his physical ailment. He explained that the instant he felt his right arm about to "jump," he'd make "a dash at the ball in a desperate effort to be in first with the shot, and what happened as a consequence of this haste may be readily imagined." He did note that "if no jump came on the first green, I knew I was safe for the round."[85]

Part of Vardon's putting problems can also be tied to the change from the gutta-percha to the Haskell rubber ball adopted almost universally in 1902 following Sandy Herd's win in the British Open. The new ball rebounded easily off the putter when struck, where the guttie had to be struck firmly to get it to the hole. With the rubber-core ball, a more coaxing stroke had to be employed. The jump in his arm, coupled with the fact that the ball also rebounded faster off the putter, made his life on the greens hell, as "those wretched two to three foot ones" tortured him for the rest of his career.[86] Adding to his agony was the feeling that the hole began to shrink away on shorter putts. With his mind in a panic, he would hit the ball as quickly as possible so that "with a little luck it may reach the hole before it goes away altogether and there is nothing to putt at."[87]

This torture has been well documented by many who witnessed it over the years. Henry Cotton, three-time British Open winner, stated that Vardon's "unbelievable jerking of the clubhead, in an effort to make contact with the ball from two feet or less from the hole, had to be seen to be believed."[88] Gene Sarazen, who first saw Vardon in the 1920 U.S. Open, maintained that he was "the most atrocious putter I have ever seen. He didn't three-putt, he *four*-putted." He remembered a time when Harry, faced with a four-foot putt, took a divot on the green three inches behind the ball.[89]

Archie Compston, who played on three Ryder Cup teams for Great Britain, and gained fame by beating Walter Hagen 18 and 17 in a 72-hole challenge match in 1928, recalled Vardon's trials on the greens: "You never knew when it would happen, and Vardon didn't know when either, but that nerve near his elbow would sometimes jump—you could see it jump—just as Vardon was about to strike the ball on his short putts. When it did, he would hit a three-foot putt a foot or more off line, to the right of the cup. I played with him once when he completely missed the ball when he was trying to hole a two-foot putt."[90]

To become so spastic on the greens was both frustrating and embarrassing for Harry, who defended himself in his autobiography, written four years before his death. To those who took it for granted that putting had always been a weak part of his game, he assured his readers: "This was far from the case. In the days of the guttie ball, and before my illness, my putting left little to be desired." In fact, J. H. Taylor said that in his prime, Vardon was one of the finest putters he had ever seen.[91]

Vardon soldiered on, as he always had. Golf was what he did, and he continued to win, despite his physical problems. The years passed. His marriage to Jessie offered little solace, as she never asked about his golf. One wonders what kind of relationship they really had, but unfortunately, we know more about his life on the golf course than off it during those pre-war years. The Open was still the crown jewel for golfers, and he continued to finish in the top 10 most years and won 13 lesser events between 1905 and 1910.

In 1911, at the age of 41, Harry caught lighting in a bottle, winning the Open at Royal St. George's. His total of 303 tied Frenchman Arnaud Massy, the 1907 champion, who he then beat in a play-off. This win

The tuberculosis that almost killed **Harry Vardon** affected a nerve in his right arm that made it "jump like a running salmon" in his downswing on short putts. This caused him, in his own words, "indescribable mental torture," and cost him many tournaments. He is shown here at **Siwanoy Country Club, Mount Vernon, New York** during his 1920 tour with **Ted Ray** of the U.S. *Courtesy USGA. All Rights Reserved.*

proved to Harry he could still win the big ones. That same year, his niece Mary came to live with the Vardons, and both would treat her as a daughter. The pleasant addition of his niece to the household was offset by the sadness of his brother Tom's immigrating to the United States to take a job there.

In 1913, Harry and Ted Ray, winner of the 1912 Open, made a tour of the United States, playing 40 matches and losing none. Before returning to Britain, they played in the U.S. Open at The Country Club in Brookline, Massachusetts, which will always be remembered for Francis Ouimet's historic victory over the two men from Jersey. Ouimet, an unknown 20-year-old amateur, scored one of the most improbable feats in the history of the game and changed the face of American golf forever, as his win spurred a great interest in the game in this country. Everybody loves an underdog, and Ouimet was certainly that. By his own admission, he believed fate had something to do with the outcome, as he publicly stated many times that Harry Vardon was the best golfer in the world and that he was lucky to win.

Vardon later claimed that he played his worst golf of that American tour the week of the U.S. Open. His putting was also not very good, but he took the defeat graciously. "We have no excuses to make," he said, "for we were defeated by high class golf." Ted Ray commented, "I have no hesitation in saying that he played better golf the whole four days than any of us." Golf writer Bernard Darwin, who kept Ouimet's scorecard and who would write so poignantly about that day, said simply: "Finest thing I ever saw."[92]

As journalist Henry Leach said of Vardon, "He wins modestly, and he takes a beating well. He is never ungenerous, and I have never known him to make a disparaging remark upon the play of any man who has ever beaten him."[93] This is exactly the way he acted at Brookline. The next day, he and Ray were on the road, playing another match, and when the year ended, Vardon had won three tournaments.

1914 was a year that changed the world. Archduke Ferdinand was assassinated in Sarajevo on June 28, and World War I began a month later. In between, Harry Vardon would win his sixth and final Open championship. The venue was Prestwick, where he had won twice before, including his heroic 1903 victory. Vardon shot rounds of 73, 77, 78, 78 for a 306 total, which won by three shots over J. H. Taylor. He did it with only nine clubs in his bag.[94]

As it was since the day he left Mundesley a decade earlier, his putting was suspect. Even though the "jump" would leave him entirely for a month or two, early in the final round, "the wretched thing suddenly reasserted itself. I felt the 'jump' with a thrill of apprehension that is far from being a pleasant memory."[95]

Playing with Taylor, he didn't want him to know anything about it, since his opponent was "well aware as I that if the distress became serious, I could miss putts down to six inches." Vardon recalled how odd it was to be walking down the fairways trying to keep his secret, making sure that not "the smallest inkling of this development must be allowed to reach Taylor's ears, lest it should stimulate him to believe, as almost certainly it would have done, that he had me as good as beaten. Perhaps it was just this diversion from the thought of the possibilities of the jump itself, that enabled me partially to overcome it and to struggle home first. As a test of nerve, that last day's play at Prestwick was far and away the most trying I can remember."[96]

Harry was able to persevere one last time, and won three other times that year. To win again at the place that gave him his most meaningful victory must have given him a deep satisfaction, especially knowing he wasn't the player he once was. He remarked: "I can hardly believe that I have won when I am not within four strokes a round as good a player as I used to be."[97]

With the coming of the Great War, golf in Britain was shut down almost completely for five years. Although Harry won three small tournaments and several War Relief exhibition matches between 1915 and 1920, he could not turn back the years. When the war ended, he was 48 years old. He would finish eighth in the Open in 1922, but that was as close as he'd ever get to holding the Claret Jug again.[98] The war robbed him of five years, and although he was already an old war horse, who knows if he might have been able to add another title—perhaps doing something like Jack Nicklaus, who won the Masters at age 46, or Julius Boros, who won the PGA at 48. We will never know.

Harry's last hurrah came in 1920, at the U.S. Open at Inverness, in Toledo, Ohio. He and Ted Ray had decided to make another tour of the United States, which saw them win 60 of 84 matches.[99] As in 1913, they tried their hand at the U.S. National Open. A Donald Ross–designed course, Inverness opened in 1903 but was hosting its first national championship. A total of 265 players tried to qualify, with 70 making the final field. Finding some old magic, the 50-year-old Vardon shot rounds of 74-73-71 to lead after three rounds with a 218 total. Pursuing were Leo Diegel and Jock Hutchinson at 219, Ted Ray at 220, and Bobby Jones and Jim Barnes at 222. "To find myself leading the field," recalled Vardon a dozen years later, "and playing almost as well as I ever did in my life was something in the nature of a remarkable feat."[100]

Harry started the last round well, but missed a three-foot putt for a birdie four at the long ninth to be under par. He had played an excellent front nine in 36 strokes, but that miss was a portent of things to come. He started home 4-3, picking up a stroke at the 359-yard 11th. At this point he was five strokes ahead of the field. Surely he could hang on.

As Harry was playing the 10th and 11th holes, a great black cloud began climbing up from the horizon behind the clubhouse, but the air remained calm. Then, on the 522-yard uphill 12th, "a strong, whipping wind came leaping from under the black cloud; a sudden half-gale, straight in his face, as he teed the ball and looked down the long, narrow fairway."[101] So recalled sportswriter O. B. Keeler, who was there covering Bobby Jones's first U.S. Open.

He continued:

> Harry struck his drive straight down the alley into the wind; and then two more shots—not a yard off line, and still a half-pitch shot short of the upland green. Four shots to get on, and all of them well struck. That 6 there spelled disaster. He was well on the green of the short thirteenth, pitching craftily in a sweeping cross-wind—and he took three putts. Two strokes in two holes. Now the old boy was turning for the fourteenth, with his back to the wind; he could use it there; the fourteenth was a good, big two-shotter. And the wind died, swiftly as it rose. And it blew no more. The great black cloud slid off toward the west and vanished. There was no rain. But old Harry was done.[102]

Since that day at Mundesley when he saw the tremor in his right arm while stroking a putt, Vardon knew he was powerless to stop it. He had been able to overcome it at Prestwick in 1914, but this day it controlled him. On the 13th, where his two-foot putt for par hit the "back of the cup and jumped out, he would have gone six feet over if the tin hadn't intervened."[103] He followed this with three-putt bogeys on the 14th, 15th, and 16th.

Incredibly, Vardon could still win with pars on the last two holes, but when he hit his second shot on the 17th into the water and took a six, it was over. He got his four at the last hole—his first par in a run of seven holes—and was tied for the lead at that point with Jack Burke after coming home in 42 for a final round 78.[104] Ted Ray, playing behind him, came in with a 75 to grab the title at 295, a single stroke over Vardon, Diegel, Hutchinson, and Burke.

Grantland Rice, another iconic sportswriter, writes that the crowd had "forgotten the dividing line of nationality between British and American in the deeper human sympathy for a great veteran, the greatest master of the game, struggling against the inevitable—those two unbeatable monarchs of destiny—Time and Fate."[105] One reads this, and it could have been Tom Watson in the 2009 Open at Turnberry that Rice was writing about. It is amazing how history repeats itself. People remember the 1920 U.S. Open as the one Vardon lost, not the one that Ray won at the age of 43 (making him the oldest champion until Ray Floyd broke that record in 1986). They remember 1920 for Vardon, just as people will remember 2009 for Tom Watson and not the victor, Stewart Cink.

Harry explained his play at the 17th, where he tried to carry the creek 200 yards away and reach the green, as one of desperation. After wasting so many shots with his bad putting, he had to take a chance. "I knew my only chance to get home was to put my body into the swing, something I never like to do." When the shot hit the little brook on the fly, he realized, "that my bid for the championship had failed. Even as tired as I was, I can't see yet how I broke so badly. Why, I am sure I could go out now and do better by kicking the ball around those last few holes with my boot. I cannot understand it. On the other hand, I can't understand how I was so close, only one stroke out, after missing all those short, simple putts that any other man could have holed with ease."[106]

"It seemed he was set," recalled O. B. Keeler. "He was playing as smoothly and confidently as ever; if the weight of his fifty years was pressing, he did not show it. I shall always believe that it was fate, and fate alone, that broke the winning spell."[107] As the Bible tells us, "time and chance happeneth to them all." It was Ted Ray's time and not Harry's, just as it had been Francis Ouimet's in 1913. It was also a very sad reminder that tuberculosis had robbed him of something he could never get back—his putting touch.

The sting of this defeat was not erased by Harry's victory in two other small tournaments, but something else occurred that year that changed his life, for good and bad. During a trip to Hoylake for a tournament, while staying at the Royal Hotel, Vardon met Matilda "Tilly" Howell, an employee there. Before the war, Tilly and her sister Constance had embarked on a stage career. They formed a song and dance act and toured music halls and theaters auditioning for shows and doing charitable events. To make ends meet, they also took jobs in hotels, which brought Tilly to Hoylake, leaving her home in Liverpool to work at the hotel.

When Harry met her she was 28 years old and on her own, as her sister had moved back home to be with her boyfriend. Tilly's life since the war had not been a happy one. She saw her fiancé off to war from Liverpool Station on a cold November day in 1915, only to lose him in the trenches two years later. Like many other women who lost men in the war, she picked herself off the ground and kept going, and her life was routine when she met Harry Vardon. Then, one day she saw him as he walked through the hotel, dressed nattily and cutting an attractive figure, and she felt alive again. Recognizing him, she asked for his autograph, which he happily provided. He was flattered. Signing his name, he took in the figure of the slim, attractive, dark-haired young woman who carried herself so gracefully and liked what he saw.

Vardon's playing career was at an end, and when his niece Mary moved out of his house to get married, he realized his life was changing yet again, and he didn't want to waste the rest of it. He found Tilly's world of theaters and music halls fascinating and was smitten with her.

When he returned to the same hotel a year later, their paths crossed once again. They were two people emotionally lonely and in need of something—or someone—to fill their needs. Vardon was an older man, 22 years her senior, charming, worldly, and well mannered. He treated her with gentle kindness, which endeared him to her.

For Vardon, Tilly was like a breath of fresh air in his weary life. After so many years of living with a wife who was emotionally distant and who took no interest in his golfing life, Tilly enjoyed hearing about his exploits on the golf course and off. She was able to brush aside the invisible screen he had unknowingly built to protect his innermost thoughts. The spark she gave him could not have come at a better time. With the dark days of the war years over and his career on the decline, they both hoped the 1920s would herald a brighter outlook on life.

Harry found himself falling in love with Tilly. He would share her euphoria at passing an audition, as well as her disappointment at being turned down. He enjoyed her youthful spirit, enjoyed being with her, but also knew he would not walk away from his marriage to Jessie. Like many men then and now, he chose a different alternative. He would travel as often as he could to be closer to Tilly, always being discreet in his comings and goings. He had someone who was happy to share with him the joys and frustrations of his life, and he selfishly did not want to give that up. Eventually, he suggested she move to London to be closer to him, since he was living in Totteridge, a little village in North London. Jessie, whether she did or didn't know of his double life we cannot be sure, but she never questioned his movements.

In 1925 Tilly became pregnant, creating a bit of a crisis for the well-ordered world Vardon had created. His heart may have belonged to Tilly, but he still felt a loyalty to his wife and could not leave her. He thought she had been victimized by the circumstances of her life and felt responsible for her well-being. This was in keeping with his lifelong devotion to her and his own sense of self-sacrifice. He had been sacrificing for his family since those youthful days when he gathered seaweed on the beach.

Tilly would return to Liverpool to have the baby, born January 26, 1926, whom she named Peter. He was a "healthy child, born with a sunny disposition, and when Vardon saw him he burst into tears, overcome with emotion and the unfairness of fate."[108] In the end, Tilly accepted her sister Connie's offer to raise the boy with her husband Walter, as they had no children of their own. The world was a different place then, and publically claiming the baby and leaving his wife to make a home with Tilly would have done irreparable harm to Harry's reputation. He could not live being ostracized from the golfing world and in the end never left his wife.

We can only imagine how difficult these years were for Harry, and Tilly, as there is no record as to their feelings on the matter. It was only through a 1991 biography of Vardon that we learned of his affair with Matilda Howell and of the child they had together. Harry continued to play in the Open until 1929 and finished 17th the year Tilly became pregnant. Afterward, he made the cut only once, in 1928, when he finished 47th.

In 1927, the Open was played over the Old Course at St Andrews, never one of Harry's favorite venues. Bobby Jones won it with a record score of 285. "What a dramatic little episode that must have been on the third green at St Andrews," recorded the *Literary Digest*, "when Bobby Jones, with his retinue of 5,000 hero worshippers, met old Harry Vardon, who was playing the homeward nine. The correspondent draws a graphic picture of Vardon, conspicuous for his loneliness, swallowed up by the milling mob which swarmed in Jones's wake. What thoughts must have burned through Vardon's brain as he stood . . . above his ball, arms outstretched to fend off the rabble which threatened to trample him."[109]

Perhaps Harry recalled the day at Prestwick in 1914, when the thundering herd cheered him to his sixth Open championship. Vardon knew his time had passed, and when he looked at Jones, he realized here "was one so young and yet who had the game at his finger tips," innately knowing that "he would be one of the very best golfers ever seen."[110] This precocious Jones boy was the vanguard of change, notes the article: "The old order changeth, yielding place to new. Sport can be mercilessly cruel. There is pathos in the picture of Vardon struggling to save his ball as the man-pack surges around the latest Caesar. Few in that thrill-drugged crowd noticed Harry Vardon. Fewer still recognized him if they saw him. Some day even Bobby Jones will know that stilly quiet, the silence that roars with the echoes of vanished ghosts."[111]

Harry realized his life was more than half over, but his son offered a second chance to have a family, albeit a secret one. For Peter's third birthday, Vardon presented him with a toy Rolls Royce car, big enough to sit in and pedal. He later fashioned a golf club for him, sadly aware that in different circumstances he would have been able to openly teach and nurture the child.[112]

But it was not to be. Vardon would visit as often as he could until the boy was old enough to wonder who the "nice man who brings presents" was. Tilly thought it best that Harry not have any contact with the child after that point, which must have been heartbreaking for Vardon. He continued to send Tilly money to care for the boy. It was not until Peter reached adulthood and after his father had died that his mother told him the true story—when he finally found out why his Uncle Walter kept a scrapbook on Vardon and seemed so determined to tell Peter that Harry was the greatest golfer in the world.[113]

"I was frustrated," said the late Peter Howell in a 2000 interview. "I thought my mum should have told me while he was still alive, but she couldn't face up to it. In those days, it was hush-hush. I would have liked to have known him." Instead, his mother spent most of her life trying to hide the fact in the days when children born out of wedlock were looked down upon. "I would like to have thought that I could have talked to him as a young man without letting the cat out of the bag if someone had given me the chance. But it was an awkward situation. My father had a wife, of course, and he loved her as well."[114]

Harry stayed with Jessie and spent the rest of his days playing golf and teaching, trying to fill a void left in his life by the absence of Tilly and Peter. One can only imagine how difficult it was for him to grow old and see his golf skills fade and also be deprived of a family life that would have helped sustain him, especially when his old friends and rivals like J. H. Taylor and James Braid had children. Vardon had a son he wanted to love, a son who wanted to know him, but the conventions of the time prevented both from being part of each other's lives.

As Vardon faded from the championship stage and as his health declined, he found a comfort in imparting his acquired knowledge to players of all levels on the lesson tee. "He bore the deprivation with philosophy and sweet temper," Bernard Darwin writes, "enjoying teaching when he could not play and always anxious to watch the younger players."[115] When Henry Cotton won his first Open in 1934 at Royal St. George's, Harry had followed him around the course. Too ill the last day to get out to watch, Cotton recalled that when he took up to Harry's bedroom "the old cup he had so gloriously won on six occasions, tears came into his eyes, and he could not say a word, nor could I, for I was crying too! Harry was always most encouraging to me."[116]

Vardon penned an autobiography in 1933, in which he shared much about his life (but obviously not everything) and his notions of the game. He spoke of the evolution of the game and was concerned with equipment changes—putting him in good company with the likes of Arnold Palmer and Jack Nicklaus in today's age. Harry felt that much of the skill of the game was left behind in the wake of improved clubs and balls, and he regretted very much the passing of the guttie ball. "In the days of the solid ball it was necessary for the drives to be properly struck if anything approaching a good round was to be recorded."[117] With the rubber-core Haskell ball, however, even a miss-hit shot would go a decent distance, and as a result, the penalty of a poor shot had been measurably lessened.

Harry was also a realist, acknowledging that the average golfer did not wish for any restrictions on the distance the ball could travel. Their views were to be respected, he maintained, for golf is a game for the multitude, not for the champion, he believed.[118] But he did believe that the game had been made too easy owing to the improvement in the clubs and the balls used in modern times.[119] To combat that, he felt the hole should have been narrowed by a quarter of an inch, giving a higher premium on accuracy, since lesser players would have fewer chances to make up strokes on the greens.[120]

As a parting shot to those who might have thought the old guard could not play a good game, he said it "must be remembered, however, that lower scores do not necessarily mean a higher standard of skill."[121] He wanted people to remember that, long after they were gone, he and his peers could play a fair game.

Vardon believed that to succeed in golf a player must be "to a certain extent highly strung, like a racehorse, always on his toes. Once the first ball is hit the nervousness goes." Without this edge of intensity, he believed it was impossible to "achieve the highest honors in golf." Beyond this, there also must be "the will to win, along with true sportsmanship."[122] Harry Vardon had a burning will to win and pursued his career with unflinching dedication and professionalism. He was Kiplingesque in his approach to life and the game. He met triumph and disaster and treated both the same. He forced his heart and nerve and sinew to serve him long after they were gone and held on when there was nothing in him except the will to hold on.

The tuberculosis that felled him in 1903 continued to dog him for the rest of his life. Being a lifelong smoker didn't help his case, and lung cancer would ultimately take him on March 20, 1937. In memorializing him after his death, Bernard Darwin told his readers that Vardon had "remained what he always was, a modest, reserved, kindly creature, who said little and that little not about himself."[123] A private man who kept his secrets well, he would be dead 50 years before the existence of his son Peter was revealed to the world.

Toward the end, as friends visited Harry, they noticed the same attitude he had always shown, one of acceptance and resolve. J. H. Taylor noted that "Harry never lost his cheery optimism. . . . He was at all times most anxious with his help and advice. He was the kindliest of souls, and to know him was to love him."[124] When he passed away, those who knew him tried to tell the world what Harry Vardon meant to the world of golf. Darwin claimed Vardon "did what only a very great player can do—he raised the general conception of what was possible in his game and forced his nearest rivals to attain a higher standard by attempting that which they would have otherwise deemed impossible."[125] *Golf Illustrated* opined that Harry Vardon "was a golfing genius, something that occurs only occasionally in the history of the sport, or in the history of a sport, or in the history of art, letters or music. This is the way of genius, something at which we lesser mortals can only gaze in profound and hallowed wonderment."[126]

As for Harry, he would forever remember his greatest moment in golf. "I unhesitatingly say that whatever good achievements I have accomplished, my victory in the Open Championship in 1903, under the existing circumstances," was the "finest achievement which I have ever accomplished."[127] To us mere mortals who have never known what it is like to be inside the gallery ropes, we see what he achieved and indeed share a "hallowed wonderment" of it all.

2

BOBBY JONES

"We Have to Play the Ball as It Lies"

The main idea in golf, as in life, I suppose, is to learn to accept what cannot be altered, and to keep doing one's own and resolute best whether the prospect be bleak or rosy. [1]
—Bob Jones

Of all the fellows who ever played golf Jones is the most ruthless, ravenous destroyer . . . [2]
—Tommy Armour

Bobby Jones finished his lunch in the clubhouse of the Royal and Ancient Golf Club of St Andrews, and was looking forward to a casual round with friends around the Old Course. Turning his gaze out the large bay windows to the first tee, he was surprised to see it packed with people, with a swarm of others fanned down the edge of the fairway. "Are they having a tournament?" he murmured to himself, wondering if it might delay his tee time.

Six years after capturing the British Amateur title here in 1930, and on his way to the Olympic Games in Berlin, he and his party had stopped over in Scotland for a little golf. After playing Gleneagles 50 miles to the west, his thoughts had turned to St Andrews. Being so close to the course he considered the most fascinating in the world, and one which held such enduring memories for him, he just had to make the short trip to the Auld Grey Town.

People saw the name "R. T. Jones, Jr." on the sign-up sheet by the starters hut that morning and spread the word. Shopkeepers on South and Market Streets went from one to another, saying, "Bobby Jones is coming."[3] Signs were placed in windows announcing the news, and the town effectively shut down. As Jones passed outside the clubhouse doors into the bright sunshine of a lovely summer day, he was astounded to see two thousand townsfolk there to greet him, a number that would double by the time he finished. There was no tournament; they were all there waiting for him. "He should be king of Scotland," said one man to sportswriter Grantland Rice, who was in Jones's party. "This is where he belongs."[4]

A feeling of panic struck Bobby. His game had lost considerable luster, and the prospect of performing in front of so many people was more than a bit unsettling. Willie Auchterlonie, winner of the 1893 British Open and resident professional, played with him after the rest of the foursome dropped out. "Whatever the cause, and very much to my astonishment," Jones recalled years later, "I played as well that afternoon as I ever played in my life, at least for ten holes."[5] Perhaps it was the familiar smell of the air coming off the North Sea, or the comforting spirits of Old and Young Tom Morris that permeate the place, but that day he found a magical elixir.

Years later, Jones would remember the holiday atmosphere in the crowd that day, which spurred him on. Warm memories and good feelings carried him to an outward nine of 32, including a birdie on the par-three eighth. There, after a punched four iron left him eight feet from the hole, he handed the club back to his young caddy, who said under his breath, "My, but you're a wonder sir." Bobby could only smile and pat him on the shoulder. "I have ever been thankful that for at least part of what was to be my last golfing at St Andrews I was permitted to play so well." Nobody seemed to care about the 40 coming home, and as Jones said, "the thirty-two out was good enough for me." After finishing with a birdie on the final hole, he spent 30 or 40 minutes signing autographs for the crowd, many of them women and children. It was a fitting end to what had been, according to him, one of the great days of his life.[6]

Bob Jones would return to the city 22 years later, as captain of the U.S. team for the inaugural World Team Amateur Championship. But he wasn't the same man. The once strong hero was now a cripple, confined mostly to a motorized cart that took him around the course. A degenerative neurological disease, which afflicted him in 1948, was slowly taking his life from him, but as he had done since the day he was born, he kept fighting the odds and left the rest to fate.

Bobby's parents, Robert and Clara, could have never imagined him becoming a champion of any kind when he was born. They had welcomed another son into the world before Bobby, a boy they named William. This poor child had the misfortune to be stricken with a mysterious intestinal disorder shortly after birth, one that doctors could not successfully treat. William did not thrive but instead grew weaker and weaker, dying when he was but three months old. [7]

Clara, a frail woman physically who stood five feet tall and weighed 90 pounds, blamed her child's death on the fact that she and her husband were living in Canton, Georgia, a small town without benefit of high-quality medical facilities. The death of William devastated her, so much

Bobby Jones played the Old Course at St Andrews for the last time in 1936, and the town virtually shut down to watch him play. After finishing with a birdie on the final hole, he spent thirty or forty minutes signing autographs for the crowd, many of them women and children. It was a fitting end to what had been, according to him, one of the great days of his life. *Image courtesy of the University of St Andrews Library, GMC-1-57.7.*

so that in the future she could not bring herself to use his name, referring to him only as "the baby that died."[8] Soon she was pregnant again, and when she insisted on moving to Atlanta, her husband agreed.

Their second son, born March 17, 1902, was named Robert Tyre, whom they called "Rob." He was a small baby, five pounds at birth, and also a sickly child, afflicted by the same digestive problems that had taken the younger brother he never knew. In his first few years, "he lived rather from day to day. One doctor after another, to the number of six, told Bob's parents it would be a miracle if they raised him."[9]

Clara and Robert fretted over their son, who for the first five years of his life was unable to eat solid foods. "Beaten eggs and milk and all sorts of peptonoids made up his diet," recalled his father. "That was Bobby's first battle, the battle for life," claimed friend and sportswriter O. B. Keeler. Things changed, Jones recalled, in the summer of 1907, when "we moved out of the city to board with Mrs. Frank Meador in a big house about a mashie pitch from what was then the second fairway of the East Lake golf course of the Atlanta Athletic Club, five miles from town."[10]

Tiny Bobby, who at age five weighed only 40 pounds, took to the outdoors, joining other boys in games of baseball. This activity boosted his health, asserted Keeler, "and it may be that some hardy inherent fighting quality in the frail little chap asserted itself, for in a very short time, he was eating anything he could bite."[11] When his parents took up golf, they allowed him to tag along, on the condition that he keep up. A fellow boarder, Fulton Colville, provided Bobby with his first club, a cut down cleek (similar to a present day two iron). Later, he would add a brassie (two wood), given to him by his mother, and a mashie (five iron), from his father, to his arsenal.

As Jones recalled, he didn't take to golf at first, preferring baseball instead. When the summer ended, the family moved back to the city. They would return the following year, and when they did, a new professional was on the job, Stewart Maiden. Jones maintained that Maiden's arrival to East Lake in 1908 "was the very luckiest thing that ever happened to me in golf. His speech was so full of burrs that for some time after he arrived I thought he was speaking a foreign language, as I stood looking up into his face."[12]

The young boy was fascinated by watching Maiden play the game. "When I followed Stewart, I didn't even carry one club. I just watched him. I liked golf pretty well, he was the best player at the club, and I liked watching him perform." Bobby mimicked Maiden's swing and, after following him four or five holes, would return to the house, a new place his parents had rented just off the 13th green of the old course. There he would "get a cap full of old balls and my mashie and putter and pitch them all on and putt them out, over and over again. It was pretty good practice, I suppose."[13] He was so successful at copying the movements of the pro that as he grew into young adulthood people would see him swing from afar and confuse him with Maiden.

The game came to dominate Jones's days and strengthened his puny body. In his later years he reflected, "I doubt that without this playing I should have lived to see a full maturity."[14] His father, who friends began to call "Big Bob" to differentiate himself from his son, "Little Bob," was proud of his accomplishments and encouraged him at every turn. Big Bob, a successful lawyer, had been a good athlete in his youth but was thwarted from playing major-league baseball by his domineering father, Robert Tyre Jones, a wealthy and very religious man who believed playing games was a waste of time.[15]

This tension led the son to rebel against the father who overshadowed him—as Big Bob drank, swore, and told dirty jokes—all attributes his own son adopted in adulthood. As Big Bob explained it, "Rob was our only child. He was a good son—no man ever had a better. Golf was the game he loved, and it became the ambition of his mother and myself to see him progress in it, and to help him all we could."[16]

It was quickly apparent that Bobby had a gift for the game. He also had the wonderful fortune of having two friends at East Lake who gave him adequate competition—Perry Adair and Alexa Stirling. Perry was two years older and Alexa five years older than Jones, and both pushed him to fulfill his potential. Alexa would go on to win three consecutive U.S. Women's Amateur titles, the last in 1920. "A liking for golf grew on me," Jones remembered. "When I was nine years old I won the junior championship of the Atlanta Athletic Club, playing against a boy of sixteen. I won a cup. I was amazed at myself, and awfully pleased. I think I've liked golf ever since."[17]

When he was 11, Jones witnessed an exhibition match at East Lake featuring the great Harry Vardon and Ted Ray. Jones was impressed with Vardon's consistency, as he shot 72-72 for two rounds. It put in Little Bob's mind the idea that he'd gladly "take 4s anywhere, at anytime."

Years later, after winning his first U.S. Amateur in 1924, he'd conclude, "If you keep on shooting par at them, they'll crack sooner or later."[18]

At 12, Bobby shot a 70 at East Lake, and at 13 lowered it to 68. His name was becoming known nationally.[19] On the invitation of friend Perry Adair's father, George, Jones accompanied Perry north to Pennsylvania to compete in his first U.S. Amateur at Merion. His 1916 debut was auspicious. As Bobby put it, "I was in my first national tournament, scared stiff at the end of the first qualifying round when I found myself leading the field," after a wonderful 74. "I struck a proper average by leading the field at the other end, in the afternoon round," when he shot a horrible 89. He won his first two matches before eventual runner-up, Robert Gardner, sent him home.[20]

Grantland Rice, who over the course of his fabled career wrote 67 million words devoted to the world of sports, told his readers after seeing the pudgy 5-foot 4-inch 165-pound Bobby perform that he would win more than one championship: "For he has shown at fourteen the two ingredients of success—the ability to play well, and the courage to go into the battle with unbroken determination and to fight every step of the journey. And efficiency plus determination is about the hardest combination to check that any game or any existence has ever known."[21]

Jones was clearly a young man with promise, "the most remarkable kid prodigy we have ever seen," according to Rice.[22] But he was still more boy than man, as evidenced by the quick temper he displayed. Bobby had "the face of an angel and the temper of a timber wolf," and with each missed shot, his "sunny smile" could turn "suddenly into a black storm."[23]

This vicious temper was a character flaw Bobby would struggle with for years. It almost did him in and generated considerable criticism. As Alexa Stirling recalled, by the time Jones was eight, he was obviously destined to become a remarkable player. "He was a handsome boy, with a gentle, wry way of smiling." Even then, adults watched his game with envy. "However, he had one flaw—his temper. Let him make a poor shot and he'd turn livid with rage, throw his club after the ball, or break it over his knee, or kick at the ground and let out a stream of very adult oaths."[24] Off the course his manners were impeccable, but on it, he was a terror.

Even so, his game was good enough to capture the Southern Amateur in 1917. When World War I broke out, Jones and Stirling played in numerous exhibition matches sponsored by the Red Cross. She never forgot one moment. On the eighth hole at Brae Burn in Boston in 1918, "he missed an easy shot. I saw the blood climb his neck and flood his face. Then he picked up his ball, took a full pitcher's windup and threw the ball into the woods. A gasp of surprise and shock went through the large crowd watching us." Later, when she chastised him, Jones shot back, "I don't give a damn what anybody thinks of me."[25] He told her he only got mad at himself. Suddenly, she saw him as a 15-year-old boy driven by the demand for perfection.

When he fell short of his expectations, disappointment turned to rage. "Worst of all, he knew that these temper outbursts released a psychological poison within him that upset his game." Jones would remember that day as well. "I read the pity in Alexa's soft brown eyes and finally settled down, but not before I had made a complete fool of myself."[26]

Jones's fiery temper was not easily squelched. Jerome Travers, 1915 U.S. Open champion, recalled a 1919 exhibition he played with Jones in Canada. "On the first green Bobby missed a small putt and became so enraged that he hurled his club far over the heads of the crowd into a cluster of trees and stubble bordering the course."[27]

People gave Jones a lot of slack due to his age, and as a young star with plenty of charisma, he was an acceptable "bad boy." Stars get preferential treatment, and, if not condoned, their poor comportment is more easily excused than that of the run-of-the-mill player. Not everyone gave Jones a pass, however. After the Brae Burn incident, a newspaper warned that his outbursts would have to be contained "if this player expects to rank with the best in the country. Although Jones is only a boy, his display of temper when things went wrong did not appeal to the gallery."[28]

As Alexa Stirling knew, perfectionism drove Jones. His mentor Stewart Maiden claimed he was "certainly born with the soul of a perfectionist looking only for perfection."[29] Charlie Yates, a legend of Georgia golf and a friend of Jones, remembered Jones once getting upset with a shot that landed close to the hole. Yates asked why he was mad. "I wanted to make it come in left to right and it went in right to left."[30]

Bernard Darwin, who covered the game from the days of Harry Vardon to Jack Nicklaus, noted that "Bobby did hate missing a shot. Perhaps that's why he missed so few. . . . He set himself an impossibly high standard; he thought it an act of incredible folly if not a positive crime to make a stroke that was not exactly as it ought to be made and as he knew he could make it."[31] Even so, neither Harry Vardon before him, nor Ben Hogan after him—both perfectionists in their own right—ever threw clubs or swore on the golf course. Jones's struggle with his temper would continue, and his emergence as a champion would be inexorably tied to overcoming it.

Jones was a young man with a temper, but he also possessed a curious, precocious mind. He graduated high school at the age of 16 and then went on to Georgia Tech, graduating at 20. He was well liked by professors and fellow students. Georgia Tech Dean Emeritus George C. Griffin said of him: "He was a real gentleman in every respect, modest, unassuming, never mentioning his golf game. . . . He also had a great sense of humor."[32]

Classmate K. Walter Coxe remembered Jones as a "friendly, healthy, fun-loving, smart, modest and hard working man on campus."[33] His interests were eclectic, as he enjoyed listening to opera and reading the classics. His granddaughter Merry Black remembered him reading "the dictionary as most would read a book," adding that he had "a command of the English language that few possess."[34]

While in school, however, classwork was not his highest priority. At Georgia Tech, he enjoyed his friends and socializing and was a member of several societies, including the ANAK Society, which honors upperclassmen who demonstrate both exemplary leadership and a true love for the school. Gentleman Cs were prevalent on Jones's transcript at Georgia Tech. Except for college algebra (95) and plane analytic geometry (96), in four years Jones didn't excel in any subject, with his average for all courses being 74.5.[35]

Golf, of course, took up a good deal of his time, and in 1919, Bobby finished second in the U.S. Amateur, Canadian Open, and Southern Open. Although only 17 years old, he was impatient to win a major tournament. Jones, like everyone, was shaped by the people around him. Next to his father, Oscar Bane (O. B.) Keeler played as important a role as anybody in developing Bob Jones the man. He met Keeler—"Pop" to his friends (Jones also called him "Keela")—at the 1916 Georgia State Championship. Together, they would travel some 120,000 miles over the next 14 years, and Keeler would witness each of Jones's 13 major championships. It is hard to think of Jones without Keeler, who served as his publicist, friend, and, perhaps most importantly, sports psychologist.

They were, on the face of it, strange bedfellows. Keeler, 20 years his senior, was not college educated but was a voracious reader with a photographic memory. In December 1908, just when Bobby was starting in the game, Keeler, depressed with his life as a lowly office worker, contemplated drowning himself in the Chattahoochee River. At the last minute he thought better of it. His ambition had been to work for a newspaper, and in a last-ditch effort, Keeler offered to work without a salary for the *Atlanta Georgian*. He convinced the editor to give him a chance and within two weeks was on the payroll at $18 per week.

After a year, he left the *Georgian* for a three-year stint at the *Kansas City Star*, where he worked alongside a young Ernest Hemingway, covering murders, fires, and, whenever possible, sports. He soon became an avid, if indifferent, golfer. Just over six feet tall with broad shoulders, he looked like a man who could knock the cover off a golf ball, but he never came close.

O. B. returned to the *Georgian* in 1913 and in 1920 joined the *Atlanta Journal*, where one of his responsibilities was covering Bobby Jones's tournament exploits. Keeler had a calming influence on young Bobby. Above all, Jones noted, Keeler was "an acutely sensitive, instinctively gallant, and wholly unselfish friend whose loyalty and devotion could never once be questioned." Bobby's mother, Clara, appreciated Keeler's influence, telling him when they got on trains for tournaments, "O. B., you look after Robert now."[36]

In 1920, Jones competed in his first U.S. Open, playing with the great Harry Vardon, who lost the championship by one shot. Jones came very close to winning himself, but a final round 77 did him in. Bob finished tied for eighth but later claimed it "was as fine a thing as ever happened to me. If I had won that first Open, I might have got the idea that it was an easy thing to do!"[37]

Vardon, the lion of the previous generation, and Jones, the heir apparent to the crown, both took something from their meeting. "Vardon's face was the most patient I had ever seen," Jones remembered. "It seemed rather the face of some quiet, placid minister, . . . thoughtful and reflective," adding that never "a flicker of resentment crossed Harry's face" after hitting a bad shot. As for Vardon, he recounted in his 1933 autobiography that he saw enough of Jones's game "to convince me that the high praise which had been bestowed upon him was soon to materialize. . . . I thought this young amateur had a big future before him."[38]

Technically, Jones's swing was smooth and powerful and served as a bridge between the old and the modern techniques. At 5 feet, 8 inches, 170 pounds, he had an ideal golfer's body. Bernard Darwin described Jones's swing as being graceful, with "nothing hurried or slapdash about it." It had a "certain drowsy beauty which gave it a feeling of slowness."[39] The feeling of slowness was due to trying to time the swing properly—"wait" on the shot as the old-timers would say—so that the hickory shaft would not bend inordinately, thus sending the ball off line.[40]

Jones was not a great putter in his early years and worked diligently to improve it. When he did, with the help of the great Walter Travis, his combination of excellent tee to green and short game put him head and shoulders above the competition.[41] Still, he needed a breakthrough and had the feeling that, no matter what he did, something always seemed to happen to keep him from winning on the national stage.

At the 1921 U.S. Amateur in St. Louis, Jones asked Keeler if he'd ever win a big event. Keeler responded, "Bobby, if you ever get it through your head that whenever you step out on the first tee of any competition, you are the best golfer in it, then you'll win this championship and a lot of others."[42] But Jones continued to be held back by fits of rage on the course. Earlier that year, in the British Amateur, he had been "petulant and irritable; in short had lost his temper and his nerve. . . . He kicked at an inoffensive gorse bush which had the audacity to catch a pulled drive, and generally this glorious boy golfer was a mass of nerves."[43]

Then, during the British Open at St Andrews, he quit during the third round, picking up on the 11th hole in a fit of pique and walking in. A less publicized incident occurred in the earlier rounds, when he missed a three-foot putt on the 16th hole and tossed the putter to the ground as he began to leave the green. Jock Hutchinson, the eventual winner who played with him that day, reprimanded him on the spot. The *Dundee Courier* commented that, "Master 'Bobbie Jones' is a boy, and a rather ordinary boy, after all."[44]

The final straw came at the U.S. Amateur a couple of months later. Jones threw a club after skulling a pitch over the green during a tight second-round match. The club bounced along the ground and struck a woman on the leg. Newspaper reporter Kerr Petrie, who would later refer to Jones as a "mechanical man," reminded readers that Bob was a lad of promise, "but then, everyone knows what they say about promises."[45]

The United States Golf Association finally put its foot down. President George Walker sent the impetuous Jones a letter, stating in clear terms that he would never play in a USGA event again unless he could control his childish temper.[46]

For years, tacit approval had glossed over his behavior. PGA and U.S. Open champion Jim Barnes had told Grantland Rice: "Never mind his club-throwing. It simply means Bobby is never satisfied with any pretty good shot. It has to be perfect, or it is no good at all. That's the way any great artist must feel." George Duncan and Chick Evans also defended these as actions of an "artist," who "strikes for perfection or destruction," but the act had worn thin.[47]

After being so impressed by Harry Vardon's stoic attitude on the course in 1920, Jones went to the Amateur that year and was a "veritable icebox" in the first round. But by the third match, his "fundamental golfing fault showed up" as his "face became flushed with anger" when shots flew array. Even after the reprimand from the USGA, Jones claimed, "I was a year or two more, getting my turbulent disposition in hand. It wasn't an easy matter."[48] But it was a turning point.

Sportswriter Al Laney met Jones in 1919 and believed there was more behind Bobby's anger than adolescent angst. There were demons being fought. He related a story from the spring of 1920, when he was traveling with Jones and some friends to a tournament in Chattanooga, Tennessee. On a country road in Georgia, the car got stuck in the mud, and Jones became incensed.

Laney recalled Jones's rage and was afraid for him, "for I had seen him flushed and shaking in a rage of sudden anger, then drained white a moment later in sudden fear at the nearness of evil. In a sense I shared his deep inner struggle to overcome what, with his intellect, he knew to be ignoble. He knew well he was poisoning himself with anger, that he must find the inner strength to rise above it."

Alcohol may have played a part as Jones admitted he drank a lot in those days, a reaction to so many weighty expectations being placed upon him. Jones later told Laney he had feared this battle inside himself was "the critical match I thought I was losing."[49]

Later that year, Laney ran into Jones after Bob had played Francis Ouimet in a U.S. Amateur match. "I could see at once that he had changed," Laney recalled. "Francis helped me," Jones told him. Laney began to see the reverence Jones had for Ouimet, who was nine years older, as a friend and a mentor. Ouimet was the hero Jones had followed in the newspapers during his historic victory over Vardon and Ray in the 1913 U.S. Open, and from that moment on, Jones idolized him. Ouimet may have helped his friend, but Jones admitted that to "the finish of my golfing days, I encountered golfing emotions which could not be endured with the club still in my hands."[50]

Fortunately for Bob Jones, he had an active and varied life that helped him focus on things other than golf. In September 1922, he entered Harvard University (mostly to please his parents) to complete a second bachelor's degree in English literature. Jones was a "pass man" at Harvard, the term for a C student, and did enough to get by, just as he had at Georgia Tech.[51] While a student there, his breakthrough finally came on the golf course and opened the flood gates to success.

After finishing tied-fifth in the 1921 U.S. Open and tied-second in 1922, Jones came to Inwood Country Club on Long Island, New York, in 1923 with high expectations. The pressure, however, wore heavily on him. "The whole heft of responsibility seems to have hit me," he recalled three years later, "the idea of being a great golfer (as people kept saying) who couldn't win."[52] He was near the top of the leader board throughout the championship and took the lead in the last round, only to finish bogey, bogey, double bogey. On the last hole, he pulled his second shot way to the left of the green and then had to wait to hit his third shot, which he flubbed into a bunker.

Even with this collapse, it still appeared he would win. "I don't want to win the title this way," he told Keeler. "I know what they're saying. They think I'm a quitter because I had the championship in my pocket and chucked it away. And they're right. I fell down shamefully when all I had to do was chip over that little trap."[53] Keeler tried to pump him up, saying he played like a champion. Jones had none of it. "I didn't finish like a champion. I finished like a yellow dog."[54]

Bobby Cruickshank, still on the course, had a chance to tie. A Scotsman who had fought in the Great War and survived being taken prisoner by the Germans, he knew all about pressure. This was just golf. The last hole was a 425-yard par 4, a stout test in those days, with a second shot requiring a carry over a water hazard that guarded the front of the green. Cruickshank had birdied the 18 in the morning round, so he knew it could be done. A good tee shot found the middle of the fairway, but he was still a long way from the green. He took a one iron and hit a career shot, the ball flying on a line right at the hole and coming to rest six feet from it. He then stroked the putt right into the heart of the cup to force a play-off.

Jones was rendered inconsolable by his tortured finish. Four strokes up with two to play, he finished 5, 6 to Cruickshank's 4, 3, a stunning turn of events that opened the door for Cruickshank. What thoughts must have gone through the mind of Bobby Jones that night as he pondered a play-off? Golf historian Herbert Warren Wind, in his classic work *The Story of American Golf*, claims the double bogey Jones took on the final hole epitomized his years of failed attempts to win a major championship. As Wind describes it, "There was always something wrong. At one time it had been inexperience. He had outgrown it. Later it had been a wicked temper. He had conquered it. Sometimes it had been just plain bad luck."[55]

For Jones, the play-off offered a chance for redemption. He described Cruickshank's birdie at the 72nd as "one of the greatest holes ever played in golf. It was far and away the greatest for me. It gave me a chance to get square with myself." Jones contended that had Cruickshank parred or bogeyed the last hole, "I'd never have felt I had won that championship."[56]

The play-off was a back-and-forth affair, as neither player gained a clear advantage. All even coming to the 18th, Jones recalled, "The strain had killed us off; anyway it had killed me." When Cruickshank hit a poor half-topped drive, forcing him to lay-up his second shot, the advantage seemed to be with Jones. His drive was pushed to the right and was lying on some sandy turf, not a great position but not bad.

"I did think of playing safe," Jones admitted later. "But it seems I didn't do it. I guess I just banged away at it."[57] Bang away he did, catching the ball perfectly flush with a long iron and sending the ball like a laser toward the flag 190 yards away, where it settled 6 feet from the hole. It was a heroic shot. Stewart Maiden, standing behind Bobby's caddy Luke Ross, was so excited he smashed his straw hat over the top of Luke's head.[58]

When Cruickshank put his third in a bunker, it was all over. Years later, Jones claimed, "I have absolutely no memory of hitting that ball," saying all he remembered was the sight of the white ball rising into the foreboding grey sky. Maiden claimed he had never seen Bob hit a shot more promptly or decisively. Jones savored the victory. "The first conscious thought I had," he remembered, was "'I don't care what happens now.' I had won a championship." The next day the *New York Times* asserted that Jones's victory had restored the faith of his "most enthusiastic admirers," who had doubted his "ability to shake off the jinx that seemed to be pursuing him."[59]

Cruickshank, reflecting on his defeat 50 years later, was philosophical, saying he and others had their chances against Jones. "That's the way the Lord makes it, really. I have no regrets. . . . I think things work out for the best and if you win you win. And if you don't, you don't. It's fate's work, you see." Without Inwood, Jones sometimes felt he would have gone on to the end of his career "in the shadows."[60]

Victory, however, took a toll on his nervous system, just as defeat had. Grantland Rice saw Jones after that final round and described a man older than his 21 years, with "deep circles under his eyes, a weary sag to his body, and the look of one who had been mortally hurt."[61] If Jones believed in fate as Cruickshank did, he also must have accepted that suffering was part of it. Bobby Jones once remarked that desire was the most important quality in order to become great but added, "Remember the good Lord is the boss."[62] His grandfather would have agreed. Robert Tyre Jones stressed duty to family, discipline, hard work, and an absolute moral code based upon the Bible. He also believed that "no man ever accomplishes anything really worthwhile alone. There are always two additional forces at work—other people and Providence."[63]

For Bobby Jones, perhaps people and Providence were married together. He counted Stewart Maiden coming to East Lake when he was a boy the greatest bit of luck he had, his father encouraged his talent and allowed him to compete against the best players in the world, and he had the good fortune to have O. B. Keeler with him to cheerlead and portray him in glowing terms. All played unmistakably important roles in his life, especially his father, who was his best friend. Jones maintained that if it "hadn't been for Dad, I don't think I would have persisted in trying to win any championship matches. He said all along that I could win, and that encouraged me."[64]

Stewart Maiden spoke in later years of the special qualities Jones displayed even as a boy, including his powers of concentration and willingness "to practice and play all alone, hour after hour, while other kids were playing other games. He was never lonesome with a golf club in his hands. He must have been born with a deep love for the game." Maiden also saw in him the God-given talent to swing a golf club "at a time when beginners are awkward looking. Even then he had an uncanny knack of timing. He had the feel of what his hands were doing with the club head."[65] Although Jones did not take formal lessons from Maiden, he spoke of the many hours they spent together, "most of them profane," coaching him when he "was in a slump with one club or another." He believed Maiden's success was due to an observant eye that "went always to a point of basic disturbance."[66]

O. B. Keeler served a number of roles in service to Jones. First and foremost was as his chronicler. Ralph Trost of the *Brooklyn Eagle* contends: "Keeler made Jones. He WAS Jones. He told us what Jones said, what he hoped, his aims. He told us what he had done—and much about what he was going to do, and did. Far more than Bob Jones can ever realize, many of us got to know Bobby through O. B."[67] This is indeed true, as much of what was written in the magazines and newspapers of the time had Keeler's name in the byline. Men like him and Grantland Rice were always sure to portray Bob in the best light.

Jones was astute enough to know that to become famous it wasn't enough to do the job. "There must be someone to spread the news," he said and acknowledged that whatever measure of fame he enjoyed was "due in large part to Keeler and his gifted typewriter."[68] But the connection was as personal as professional. They traveled together, shared trains and hotel rooms together, ate and drank together, commiserated and celebrated together. Keeler was a surrogate brother and friend and a very real calming influence.

For example, in the first qualifying round of the 1927 U.S. Amateur, Jones shot a 75 and was afraid he might not qualify. Worried, he turned to Keeler, saying he planned to go out in the afternoon and try to win the medal and then asked his friend to walk a few holes until he calmed down. "I wanted just the satisfaction," Jones explained, "of having an understanding soul with me to get over that feeling of aloneness which comes when your confidence is gone. It worked like a charm. I let O. B. go after the fifth hole, finished the round in sixty-seven for a course record and the medal, and went on to win the championship."[69]

Keeler was also a great public-relations man and did his job well, creating certain myths about Jones that persist to this day because they have rarely been challenged. He made it appear as if Bobby came from a very modest family with little money (an impression Jones himself fueled), when in truth his father was a man of standing in the community, a successful lawyer who represented many of his father Robert Tyre's business interests, as well as other companies, including Coca-Cola.[70]

Another myth was that Jones played less formal golf than any other first-rank golfer.[71] Jones played as much golf as a dentist, it was said, which would be true if that dentist practiced for hours on end as a youth and then played in numerous exhibitions for the Red Cross during the war, as well as exhibition matches (two to four a month) from January through March to begin many of his golfing seasons. Opponents in exhibitions and early-year tournaments included Hall of Famers Gene Sarazen, Leo Diegel, Jim Barnes, U.S. Open champion Johnny Farrell, and British Open champion Arnaud Massy. The competition was more than just casual and helped sharpen his game. Jones's grandson Bob Jones IV has said, "There are so many myths about him. People think of my grandfather as The Natural, as if it all came so easily to him, that he didn't have to work at it. The truth is, he studied golf obsessively."[72]

In the winters of 1925 and 1926, he played almost every day with Tommy Armour in Florida, where Armour had taken his first job as a professional.[73] Curt Sampson, one of the few authors to challenge the Jones myths, claimed that although Jones did devote serious time to play and practice in preparation for a competitive season, he did curtail long practice sessions during tournaments "for the same reason he didn't practice tying his shoes. He'd gotten it, and four rounds a week, nine months a year was plenty for him to keep it."[74] This was similar to Byron Nelson not practicing much when he was in his prime in the 1940s—he felt it would be counterproductive. Luke Ross, who caddied for Jones in many tournaments from 1920 to 1926, said that Jones "seldom practiced for more than an hour, except on the putting green."[75]

One aspect of Jones's philosophy of golf, and by extension, life, that has been accurately portrayed is the notion of fate. In his early years, Jones believed he had runs of bad luck that could not be explained. In 1919 it was the loud shouting of a marshal through a megaphone that upset him on the 12th hole at Oakmont against Davey Herron in the finals of the U.S. Amateur. The next year it was a bee buzzing above his ball in a match with Francis Ouimet that upset him and threw him off his game.[76] It seemed like something always happened to make him the victim, be it some odd incident or an opponent going "wild" on him with a streak of incredible scoring.

In the 1920 Amateur, Jones saw Chick Evans make an improbable par on the last hole of an early match to force extra holes. He won the match, then went on to win the title by demolishing his opponents 7 and 6, 10 and 8, and 7 and 6, the last being Francis Ouimet in the finals. Keeler believed it was "right there that Bobby began to feel that there really might be a destiny that shapes the ends of golf." Jones writes in his 1927 book *Down the Fairway* that "very lately I have come to a sort of Presbyterian attitude toward tournament golf; I can't get away from the idea of predestination." William Woodward echoes this theme in a 1930 article. Jones was "an ardent fatalist," he writes. "'It is written in the book,' is one of his favorite expressions, meaning that no matter what one does, the result will come out in its predestined way."[77]

Jones contended that the championships he won "seemed sort of inevitable. I hadn't much to do with them. But the championships I lost, . . . what a lot of fighting in those, fighting against myself."[78] That internal struggle involved a battle of temper and nerves that shattered him by the time a championship had concluded. Jones was a high-strung individual, and what made him such a great player—his competitive nature—amplified his nerves and threatened to rip him apart.

The year after winning his first major championship, Jones married Mary Rice Malone, the sister of two of his friends at Tech, on June 17, 1924.[79] Ten months later, their first child, Clara, arrived. As 1925 dawned, the added responsibility of a family moved Bob to seek a way of making a living. Mary had grown up in a wealthy family, and her upbringing gave her a feeling of entitlement. While she enjoyed her husband's fame, she hated sharing him with the world. Privately, she could act tempestuously when in a jealous mood and, therefore, was not the easiest woman to live with.[80]

She counted as her happiest day the day Bobby retired. But in 1925, her husband needed a job. The Florida real-estate boom was at its zenith, and his friend Perry Adair was involved in the market there through his father's real-estate company. Jones spent much of February and March working as a salesman, along with keeping his game in shape playing almost daily with Tommy Armour.[81]

His adoring public didn't care that he worried about his responsibilities. They just wanted their hero to play golf. Play he did, but the competitive strain was enormous, what he called "that stretching and stretching and stretching inside your head."[82] Golf is a game played at such a slow pace; there is no opportunity to "work off steam in physical activity," as he put it. He felt uncomfortable with leads, feeling it was easier for him to play from behind, when he could be positive and aggressive. "The one thing I could not cope with on the golf course was the fear of looking ridiculous—not only to other people but to myself—by throwing away a big lead."[83]

During a tournament, Jones was like a man on a high wire. Throughout the early morning of every competition he found himself "continually on the verge of active nausea."[84] He had trouble eating and for most of his career would limit himself to a lunch of toast and tea, routinely losing 10–15 pounds in every tournament he played. "It can't be the physical strain," he would maintain. "I could play 36 holes of golf every day in the week and weigh the same at the end. It's the major championship golf that wears you out." He lost 20 pounds the week of the 1919 U.S. Amateur and 12 pounds during the three days of the 1925 U.S. Open. "Perhaps these physical symptoms," he concluded, "help to explain the furious toll exacted from the spirit, under the stress of tournament competition."[85]

Jones wished he could approach the game differently, but he knew only one way, total concentration and dedication. "Oh, no. Bob didn't like to lose," remembered Charlie Yates, "whether you were playing for a dollar."[86] Tommy Armour, who played golf with Jones perhaps more than any other great professional, said of him: "Of all the fellows who ever played golf Jones is the most ruthless, ravenous destroyer," explaining that he went after all opponents "with the idea of winning by 10 and 8, or by 40 strokes."[87]

When Jones met his friend Watts Gunn (also a member at East Lake) in the final of the 1925 U.S. Amateur, Watts jokingly asked if he'd get his usual two shots a side, as Jones would accede in casual matches at home. Bob looked him in the eye and replied, "I'm going to give you hell, you little s.o.b." He did, winning eight and seven.[88]

Francis Ouimet once said of playing against Jones: "It is just as though you got your hand caught in a buzz saw. . . . If the young man were human, he would make a mistake once in a while, but he never makes any mistakes. He manages to do everything better than anybody else." Ouimet told golf writer Herbert Warren Wind, "You have no idea how good Bobby was!"[89] Armour acknowledged that Jones was high strung but in control: "Those are the fellows who are nervous but have it under control.

Famed golf writer Bernard Darwin described Bobby Jones' swing as being graceful, with "nothing hurried or slapdash about it." It had a "certain drowsy beauty which gave it a feeling of slowness." With a powerful swing and wonderful putting touch, friend Tommy Armour called Jones, seen here in the late 1920s, "the most ruthless, ravenous destroyer," on the golf course, explaining that he went after all opponents with the idea of beating them by the widest margins possible. *Courtesy USGA. All Rights Reserved.*

They're the toughest to beat."[90] In reality, Jones may have been able to reign in his temper, but the fires still leapt within him.

Chick Evans, who had the ability to play to the gallery and joke with them, recalled Bobby telling him once, "If you miss a shot you can laugh it off. It is all a big outing to you, but I just can't seem to get into a joking mood on a golf course, and I can hardly keep from getting piping mad when I make a bad shot." Behind the façade of invincibility, Jones feared failure. "There are times, when I feel that I know less about what I'm doing on a golf course than anyone else in the world. I really mean it."[91] He had put in years of practice to the game and went out and played by instinct, trying to hang on while his nerves jumped inside him.

Jones, as one of the icons of the so-called Golden Age of Sports—Babe Ruth, Jack Dempsey, Red Grange, Bill Tilden, and fellow golfer Walter Hagen, among others—was head and shoulders above his competition, and being an amateur playing against professionals in many events, he was even more admired for his accomplishments. The public also appreciated his modesty and integrity, as twice, in 1925 and 1926, he called penalties on himself during the U.S. Open.

In the first instance, the ball moved while addressing the ball in heavy rough on the 11th hole during the opening round. USGA officials saw no movement, but he was adamant. When applauded for his honesty, Jones said famously, "You might as well praise a man for not robbing a bank!" The penalty led to a tie, and a loss in the play-off to Willie MacFarlane. In the second round of the 1926 event, the ball moved as he addressed a putt on the 15th green. This nearly affected the final outcome, as he was able to win by a single stroke. These events did wonders for his reputation of unwavering integrity and helped repair the damage done earlier by his ill temper.[92]

By 1926, Jones had won a U.S. Open and two U.S. Amateurs but had other things on his mind, most pressing among them how to provide for his family. A year earlier, he had lamented to a newspaper reporter, "I am twenty-three years old and I'm a failure. Do you realize that I cannot do anything well, except play golf?" He not only felt a need to find his own way and break away from his father's shadow but also admitted he could be a bit lazy at times. "It seems I love almost any pursuit except work," he tells readers of his book *Down the Fairway*. "I even like going to school, which I am doing again, right now."[93]

After spending two years with Adair Realty, Jones decided that sales were not for him. In a business that required an aggressive personality, Jones's rather shy approach to things outside of golf did not lend itself to the task.[94] He wanted to do something but had trouble figuring out what it was. He was adamant about not turning professional, which was quite understandable in an era when there was no money in tournament golf.

Jones earned his degree at Harvard in the spring of 1924 and, with another baby on the way, decided to enter Emory Law School in September 1926, seemingly prepared to follow his father's career path. That same year, the idea of winning the national championships of both the U.S. and Great Britain also entered his thinking. He once said: "No one knows what will happen in golf until it happens. All you can do is work and suffer and wait for fate."[95] He would continue to work toward his high goals and suffer.

When he lost to an unknown player by the name of Andrew Jamieson in the British Amateur in the spring of 1926, fate dashed his plans that year and also portended a troubled future. He woke up the morning of his match with Jamieson with what he called a "crick" in his neck. "I felt, and am sure heard," he recalled, "the muscle up the left side of my neck give a loud, rasping creak like a rusty hinge." Barely able to lift his arms above his head, he decided at the very last moment to play, lost four and three, and told those around him not to reveal the fact of his injury to the press. No excuses were to be made. Wanting to show the country he "really could play golf at times," he remained for the British Open, and his neck improved.[96]

His game regained its sharp edge, and he captured his first British Open at Royal Lytham and St Annes in England that June. His victory came down to a spectacular 175-yard iron to the green from a sandy lie on the penultimate hole. He realized just how fortunate he had been, saying, "You know, an eighth of an inch too deep, and the shot expires in front of your eyes." At the presentation ceremony, J. H. Taylor, who played in the age of Old Tom Morris, spoke briefly and emotionally, telling the crowd that the "greatest golfing prize has been won by the greatest golfer."[97]

Jones returned to the States and the next month won the U.S. Open at Scioto Country Club (later Jack Nicklaus's home course) in another tight finish. The last day, he woke up feeling quite ill and found a doctor early that morning who prescribed some medicine to quell the nausea, which caused Bob to lose his breakfast. Entering the final round three shots back, he was able to rally and birdie the last hole to gain the lead in difficult, windy conditions. His knees were shaking on his second shot to the green, a rocket of a four iron to the par five, and they nearly buckled as he walked after it.[98]

He went back to his hotel room and waited for Joe Turnesa, his closest competitor, to finish. As his mother packed his things, the tension that had built within him suddenly let loose. As he would describe it, "I blew up completely for the first time in my life. Anyway, I never did sit down and cry before."[99] Clara told her son it would be a good idea if he didn't play any championships for a while. When Turnesa was unable to catch him, Jones was again champion, but the fight left him so completely drained that he asked USGA officials not to call on him to make a speech at the ceremony.

Bobby believed that last round was touched by fate, saying later, "If anybody had told me, as I stood on the seventh tee, that I must finish with two 3's and ten 4's to win, I'd have laughed at him—if I'd had the strength. Two under 4's in that wind, and the last dozen holes of an open championship! Don't tell me it isn't destiny." Jones called it destiny, while others just saw it as a manifestation of his incredible talent. "He had the ability to produce his best under duress," recalled Tommy Armour in 1960, "like Arnold Palmer, which of course is the mark of a champion. . . . He never gave up." [100]

Adding to the pressures of competition itself, Jones had to live up to the role of "world beater" every time he walked onto the course. He was always *the* man to beat, and he knew it, and the notion added to the pressure he felt to succeed. As Grantland Rice wrote in 1925, "Jones was merciless in criticism of himself" and "made no attempt to cover up any fault." [101]

Thus, at the end of a tough day on the course, he would, in the words of friend Charles Price, "soak himself in a hot bath to calm the nerves nobody thought he had, sip a little bourbon and then . . . go out and exchange inanities with the back slappers, autograph hounds, favor seekers, story tellers, party crashers, name droppers, social opportunists, self-promoters, kissin' cousins, drunks, and the other assorted pests." Being the center of attention wore on Jones. "I do not have anything against the human race as a tribe," he once claimed, "but I prefer them in small doses." [102]

The idea of being a role model didn't set well with him either. "Of course it's nice to have people say nice things about you, but honestly, when New York papers make me out such a glowing example of moral discipline, I don't know what to make of it." [103] He wasn't simon-pure as most sportswriters claimed, and he knew it. He was just trying to win golf championships.

Paul Gallico, a sportswriter who admired Jones greatly, also addresses some of his foibles. He writes of Jones playing at East Lake with his father and friends before the 1930 U.S. Amateur. "They called each other 'son-of-a-bitch,' and called the ball the same or worse. . . . Jones threw clubs and broke them and sometimes threw the pieces in the lake. Liquor was involved." Away from the spotlight, Jones let loose a few of his demons, even though two years earlier he denied having a fierce temper. "Have I ever been such a bunch of fireworks?" he asked a reporter. Gallico's observations seem to suggest that Jones could indeed be like a "bunch of fireworks," but he concludes truthfully that his hero behaved "very much like a human being."[104]

Perhaps the most pivotal year in Jones's career, 1927 began with him winning the Southern Open in March by eight shots against a strong field. At the U.S. Open at Oakmont, he finished 11th, his worst performance ever in that event. It proved a fateful result as it spurred him to enter the British Open at the last moment. Previously, he had stated he would not play, citing first the "pressure of business."[105] He not only played but also would produce the best score ever in the event, a 285 total that broke the championship record by 6 shots. Jones felt both pleased and vindicated. "I am happy, supremely happy . . . because I have won at a place where golf was played nearly five centuries ago."[106]

Harold Hilton, the great old English champion, said Jones's returning to St Andrews to defend his title "was a sporting thing to do, and our people, who already loved him, now simply adore him. He has won British hearts as well as British championships." Bernard Darwin added, "Not even when Francis Ouimet beat Vardon and Ray was there such a riot of joy."[107] As 15,000 spectators rushed to touch their hero after he putted out on the final hole, a spectator standing by the green muttered, "The man canna be human."[108]

Jones told the press, "I would rather have done what I did than any-thing else I ever accomplished in golf or am ever likely to." He acknowl-edged that on his first trip over in 1921 he had behaved "rather badly" and added, "I may well confess that I could never quite get the sting of that incident out of my memory, and in some ways it appeared to me that by coming back to the same old course and assaying a defense of the title, I might retrieve that boyish error of six years ago." Jones had further en-deared the British people by saying at the awards ceremony that he wanted "this wonderful old club" to do him the favor of accepting custo-dy of the cup for the coming year, instead of him taking it home.[109]

Later that summer, Bob won the U.S. Amateur in a contentious final match against Chick Evans and in 1928 would defend that title after losing the U.S. Open in a play-off to Johnny Farrell. In December 1927, Jones took the Georgia bar exam and, to his delight, passed. He dropped out of Emory Law School and took a job in his father's law firm.[110] Bob had taken his studies at Emory seriously, and in his first year, finished second in his class of 25. H. M. Quillan, one of his professors, said Jones had "one of the finest legal minds of any student" he had ever known.[111]

O. B. Keeler contended that Jones's legendary year of 1930 would have never happened if not for the putt Jones made on the final hole of the 1929 U.S. Open. Squandering a large lead coming down the stretch, he needed a par four on the last to tie Al Espinosa. After pulling his second shot, he left his pitch short. The hole remained 12 feet away, downhill with a foot of break from left to right, on a green as fast as ice. It had to go down for a tie.

In Keeler's words, "If he missed, it would be the first time he had scored as high as 80 in the Open Championship. He would have blown a lead of six strokes, and one more, in the last six holes." Al Watrous, who played with Jones that day, said the putt was so perfectly stroked that if the hole had been a four-and-a-quarter-inch circle on the green, the ball would have stopped in the middle of it.[112] "If he hadn't sunk that putt," Keeler later reflected, "there wouldn't have been any Grand Slam in 1930. . . . I think it might have broken him up."[113]

Jones remembered that it "was nice to sink that one. I sure needed it. It was awfully rough going. But, you know, after every year of play, whether I won or lost, I would always look back and think, 'Why should I punish myself like this over a golf tournament?'"[114] Jones thus considered 1930 his last chance to go after all four national championships in a year. Fate seemed to be on his side as the year began, as he warmed up with wins against strong professional fields in the Southern and Southeastern Opens, the latter a 13-stroke victory over Horton Smith. Bobby Cruickshank told Keeler: "Bobby is just too good. He's going to Britain, and he's going to win the British Amateur and the British Open, and then he's coming back here and win the National Open and the National Amateur. They'll never stop him this year."[115]

Jones acknowledged almost 30 years later that, in fact, "I did make my plans for that golfing year with precisely this end in view, and so prepared myself more carefully than I had ever done before."[116] It began in St Andrews with the British Amateur in May. The turning point may have come when Jones needed a putt of around 12 feet in his semifinal match against George Voight on the 17th to keep the match all square. "I could see the line as plainly as if it had been marked on the green," Jones remembered. "I knew before I swung the putter that I would surely hole the putt."[117]

Two holes down with five to play, he won the match at the last. He beat Roger Wethered in the final seven and six and won the title he craved most. In his victory speech he said, "I have never worked harder, or suffered more, than in trying to get it." He told Keeler his "little expedition" was a success, no matter what happened the rest of the way.[118]

For Keeler, the result reaffirmed his idea that "golf tournaments are a matter of destiny," as he recounted the many crises Bobby faced in eight matches. Yet every time, "he stood up to the shot with something I can define only as inevitability and performed what was needed with all the certainty of a natural phenomenon." Others may have thought it was supernatural, as one man in the gallery was overheard saying: "They ought to burn him at the stake. He's a witch."[119]

Next, Jones went to Hoylake on the west coast of England for the British Open. In control during the final round, he was staggered by a seven on the eighth hole after being just short of the par 5 in two. "It was the most inexcusable hole I ever played. An old man with a croquet mallet could have got down in two."[120] After settling down and making a birdie on the par-five 16th after a brilliant bunker shot with a concave wedge given to him by Horton Smith, he followed it with a good putt for par on the 17th and won by two shots over Leo Diegel and Macdonald Smith.

The strain was mounting, and Keeler saw it on the countenance of Jones. "When are you going to quit?" Keeler asked his friend. "Pretty soon, I think—and hope," answered Bob. "There's no game worth these last three days." He told reporters, after pouring himself a stiff drink, "I have never had such a terrible time in my life."[121]

The show moved back across the ocean to Minneapolis for the U.S. Open at Interlachen. Played in withering heat, Jones claimed, "I don't believe I ever hit my shots better in any tournaments." Fate again played its part as he was lucky to have a miss-hit second shot skip over the water hazard guarding the ninth hole in the second round. What could easily have been a bogey or worse was turned into a birdie. As Keeler put it, "If your name is up, the ball will walk on water for you."[122]

Leading in the final round coming to the 17th hole, a 262-yard par 3, Jones hit his tee shot into the swamp to the right of the green. He claimed the wind had fooled him, and a double bogey was the result. Many people have claimed he received a controversial ruling, since the ball was not found, but the USGA official on the spot saw the ball travel inside the margin of the water hazard, and the local rule allowed Jones to drop in the fairway 50 yards short of the green. Case closed. [123]

The margin of victory increased to two shots over Mac Smith when he holed a 40-foot birdie putt at the last. Bernard Darwin wrote that the time had come for Jones to call a halt to his self-torture. "Golf had always taken a prodigious toll and now I thought it had taken too great a one. The time to go, even at twenty-eight, was fast approaching."[124] Eddie Williams, who finished tied for 35th, told of going to the locker room in the first round to escape the stifling heat and use the facilities. "Who was there but Jones himself being quite ill. After that I did not feel so bad since a player of his caliber couldn't hold his breakfast any better than little old me."[125] Grandfather Robert Tyre Jones claimed the arms of the Lord had been around the neck of his boy to come out victorious, while all Bobby could muster was an understated "I am mighty glad to have won this tournament."[126]

Jones had a respite of sorts after Interlachen, as the U.S. Amateur, the last of his events, would take place in September, at the same course his career began, Merion. During that time, he tried to relax a bit with his father and friends at East Lake. When he arrived in Ardmore, Pennsylvania, the golfing world was waiting and watching. Could he do it? The frenzy was so terrific that the *Philadelphia Evening Bulletin* alone had 16 reporters and photographers covering Jones, including one to follow him off the course. More than two million words would be written about Jones and the other participants during the six days of the event. The USGA, concerned about security, had 50 Marines assigned to follow Jones and keep order. [127]

What most people didn't know was that Jones was under the care of two doctors. The previous week he had played an exhibition at East Lake and was stricken with severe abdominal pains. At first feared to be appendicitis, he was diagnosed with a severe nervous disorder and given medicine to last him through the competition. [128] On the course, Jones plowed through his opponents, winning no match by less than five and four before closing out Gene Homans eight and seven in the finals. The world wouldn't find out for a couple of months, but Bobby Jones was done. "I felt the wonderful feeling of release from tension," he explained, that "I had wanted so badly for so long a time. I wasn't quite certain what had happened or what I had done. I only knew that I had completed a period of strenuous effort, and that at this point, nothing more remained to be done."[129]

Jones made the decision to retire after winning the U.S. Open, and his feelings were reinforced after Merion, when he realized golf had ceased to be fun anymore. "Hell, I had more fun then playing against my Dad and the members of East Lake."[130] When he began his career nothing much "was expected of me and I had a lot of fun battling with the boys," but around 1925 "golf became a serious business. I was expected to win or finish well up. It got worse and worse and the pressure got heavier and heavier." After 1930, he decided he had had enough.[131]

Bobby Jones announced his retirement on November 17, four days after signing a contract with Warner Brothers to make a series of instructional films. This, along with his agreement to design golf clubs for Spalding in 1931 and his investments in Coca-Cola bottling plants in the United States and South America, helped secure his financial future.[132] This suited Jones's lifestyle, as he was not the kind of man willing to toil long hours in his father's law office. Sportswriter Paul Gallico writes, in the late 1920s, that the law was Jones's "mental hair shirt. . . . He admits frankly that he doesn't like to work . . . [and] admits a great longing for financial independence from the routine of desk slavery." Jones now had the freedom to pursue his true passions.[133]

Among Jones's greatest legacies is the Augusta National Golf Club, where the Masters Tournament has been played since 1934. Architect Alister MacKenzie acknowledged that Jones had rendered him "assistance of incalculable value" in designing the course and hoped "for accomplishments of such unique character that the holes will be looked upon as classics in themselves."[134] Jones was coaxed out of retirement to play in his tournament, but the magic was gone, and he knew it standing on the fifth tee of the first round.

The nervousness that used to leave him within a hole or two hadn't abated, and when the whirring of a motion-picture camera disturbed him, he stepped away. He pushed his ensuing drive into the trees, and in that moment, he "realized that this return to competition was not going to be much fun. I realized, too, that I simply had not the desire nor the willingness to take the punishment necessary to compete in that kind of company."

As he said in 1966, it wasn't so much the "question of playing in a golf tournament every week, it's a question of mental conditioning." His putting touch had also left him, which he admitted was a very "intricate and delicate" thing, and he wasn't the same golfer as before. Jones finished 13th, his best showing in the 12 Masters he played through 1948. He may have continued longer, but fate had other plans. [135]

Tommy Barnes, who Jones mentored as a young man, recalled the last round of golf Jones played on August 15, 1948. Bobby was not hitting the ball as far as he normally did that day at East Lake, and on the next-to-last hole, he duck-hooked his tee shot and made a double bogey. A par at the last gave him a 72. When a member of the foursome inquired about his health, Jones replied that he had been "having some numbness" in his limbs. [136] His problems started earlier that year, when for six weeks he experienced double vision of distant objects. By May, he was having difficulty using his right hand and was stubbing his right foot while walking. When he swung a golf club, a burning sensation seared down the left side of his body. [137]

After numerous exams and tests, an operation was performed October 30 at Emory University Hospital, a seven-hour procedure on the fourth, fifth, and sixth cervical vertebrae in his neck to remove a bone growth doctors felt was affecting a nerve. Although newspapers reported that "a complete recovery is hoped for and expected," the surgery was not a success. [138] By the following year, Jones said his spine had been twisted out of shape, and that the pressure on the nerve was affecting his legs. The problem became apparent when he would sit down to the table to have a couple drinks and then not be able to get up. "My head would be clear and I'd be cold sober, but I couldn't work my legs." [139]

On May 18, 1950, a second operation was performed. This one took place at Boston's Lahey Clinic and lasted five hours but was no more successful than the first. Jones even went so far as to have several bad teeth removed after being told they might be poisoning his system. [140] Nothing helped. Thus began a steady physical decline, as his legs became weaker and walking impossible without canes and braces.

Alexa Stirling, Jones's childhood friend, recalled seeing him in 1950 on a visit to Atlanta, shocked at what greeted her. "On the retina of my memory was impressed the picture of a handsome young man in knickers, swinging a golf club with tremendous power and grace. In tragic contrast there stood before me a man slumped on two canes, a brace on his right leg, his face gray." Jones quickly put her at ease and would "be damned if he was going to have any soupy sympathy. About this point he was profanely specific."[141] Even though he was in constant pain, he went to his law office every day and to the East Lake golf club frequently.

When Stirling asked Jones if he had made the adjustment to this new life, he bristled. "Adjustment? If adjustment means acceptance, I'd say no. I still can't accept this thing. I fight it every day. When it first happened to me I was pretty bitter, and there were times when I didn't want to go on living, so I had to face the problem of how I was going to live. I decided I'd just do the very best I could."[142]

He continued to try to improve and didn't wallow in self-pity. Before leaving Atlanta on that visit, Stirling went with Bob to a rehabilitation center where he was taking some physiotherapy. He got out of the car and began "his torturous trip to the building entrance, dragging his legs one after the other." When he made it to the door, he turned and gave her a "fleeting smile of triumph—the same expression he always wore when he made a good recovery from the rough, or blasted up to the pin from a sand trap."[143]

In 1956, a final diagnosis of Jones's condition was made by H. Houston Merritt, a world-renowned neurologist who specialized in diseases of the spinal cord. He was a "powerhouse," according to Dr. T. Glenn Pait, former chairman of the history section of the American Association of Neurological Surgeons, and his word was gospel. Jones had syringomyelia (*sir-ring-go-my-eel-iah*), a degenerative disease in which cysts form within the spinal cord, expanding and elongating like fingers over time, restricting and eventually terminating the function of the sensory and motor nerves. This leads to progressive weakness and muscular atrophy in the back, shoulders, arms, and legs; an inability to feel extremes of hot and cold (especially in the hands); and dull, chronic pain. Today, an estimated 40,000 people in the United States suffer from the disease.[144]

Dr. Pait, whose opinions are presented in Ron Rapoport's book *The Immortal Bobby*, gained access to Jones's records and believed that he suffered from a spine problem, not a spinal-cord problem. Pait didn't believe an exact diagnosis was possible from X-rays and dyes used in the years before magnetic resonance imaging (MRI) technology. The possibility of a misdiagnosis aside, Pait nevertheless concluded there was no reason to believe Jones's surgeries were botched but produced results consistent with the limitations of surgical techniques in the early years of treating spinal-disc disease.[145]

There had been warning signs, Dr. Pait believed. The "crick" Jones had felt in his neck during the 1926 British Amateur that produced a rasping sound was probably bone on bone irritation. Jones also described a "click on the lower part of the left side of the back of my neck," when he got out of bed before the Southern Open in March 1930. He felt the effects for a few days but soon recovered. These ailments were ignored, and unlike today, Jones didn't have access to on-site physical therapy, MRI, or other modern medical exams. A preexisting condition may have been aggravated by the twisting motion of the golf swing, but we will never really know. Whatever the cause, as a medical book of that era describes the disease, "Most neurologists and neurological surgeons have found all forms of treatment very disappointing."[146]

Jones could have benefited from physical therapy, and the 30 cigarettes, 2–6 drinks, and 4 cups of coffee he consumed daily didn't help. Smoking and drinking cause a vascular compromise, and with his condition, he needed all the blood he could get going to his spinal cord. Bobby's breathing, oxygenation, and endurance were all compromised. But he was also living in a time when many people, including doctors, believed smoking relaxed you.[147]

As the years progressed, Jones's body continued to atrophy, leaving him confined to a wheelchair by the 1960s. Writer Pat Ward-Thomas visited him in 1961. By then Jones could still walk with two canes and leg braces, but it took him 10 minutes to go 50 yards. "It seemed as if his body had become too fragile to support the splendid head, which never lost its noble outlines, but the mind remained wonderfully sharp, the humor lively and the manner unfailingly gentle." Alistair Cooke remembered meeting Jones and looking at his once strong hands, "twisted like the branches of a cypress, gamely clutching a tumbler or one of his perpetual cigarettes in a holder. His face was more ravaged than I expected, from the long-endured pain I imagine."[148]

By 1968, the last year he would attend the Masters, Bobby Jones's health had slipped from "the terrible to the abysmal," in the words of friend Charles Price. His eyes "were bloodshot from years of excruciatingly sleepless nights." He was put into and taken out of bed by a male nurse, "who was the size of a linebacker," according to Price. "'He handles me like a flapjack,' Bob said by way of complimenting the man when he introduced us." His body was full of codeine to deaden the daily pain, his feet and ankles swollen to four times their normal size and purple from lack of circulation.[149]

That year Jones wrote a telling letter to Dr. Houston Merritt, the specialist who had diagnosed his condition in 1956. "I hope you appreciate that I am saying this with all the good humor of which I am capable, but I am getting pretty fed up with this 'relatively good prognosis.' My life, day and night, is about as nearly miserable as one can imagine. . . . I have wasted away to a bare skeleton and keep going only with the aid of three or four devoted people." Two days later, Jones wrote his personal physician Dr. Ralph Murphy. "I have a very real horror of spending my final years lying paralyzed or in twisted agony," he confided. "Any other way out, no matter how quickly it comes, would be better. I am sure you will agree."[150]

No longer able to act as host at the Masters, Frank Christian, the tournament's official photographer, noted that Jones's "facial muscles and hands were horribly crippled. He could barely lift his cigarette holder to his mouth, and he was unable to control his saliva."[151] Clifford Roberts, the other driving force behind the Masters, was concerned that Jones would be seen on television like that and eased him out of the presentation ceremony. Some think Roberts was protecting his friend's dignity, while others thought he was being boorishly controlling.[152]

Jones's decline was difficult for all to witness. Former champion Doug Ford recalled, "It just broke your heart to see how much he was going downhill each year," but despite this, Jones "was still smiling and greeting everybody and being the perfect gentleman. . . . He was in a lot of pain, but you would never know it." Granddaughter Merry Black remembered that, as the disease progressed, "you could see the pain in his face and you could hear a muffled groan, but I never heard a selfish complaint."[153]

In his last years, it was hard to imagine Bob Jones as the "ravenous destroyer" his old friend Tommy Armour once described. He continued to write about the game and cement his legacy with each passing year through his Masters Tournament. Perhaps it was because he was a believer in fate that he coped as well as he did. The results in life, as well as in golf, were all "written in the book," according to him. He once told sportswriter and friend Al Laney early in his illness, "I know I can only get worse. But you are not to keep thinking of it. You know, in golf we play the ball as it lies. Now, we will not speak of this again, ever."[154]

Bob Jones died December 18, 1971. In 1972, St Andrews honored his memory by naming the 10th hole on the Old Course "Bobby Jones." It provided the opportunity to reminisce about his impact on the game and recall the last time he visited the town in 1958. The occasion was the inaugural World Team Amateur Championship, in which he served as captain of the U.S. team. While there, in a ceremony at the University's Younger Hall on October 9, he was given the Freedom of the City award, which in effect granted him genuine citizenship. He became only the second American to receive it—the first was Benjamin Franklin. "Within the few seconds it took me to make my way to the lectern," he would recall, "I found out how a man's life, or a great part of it, can flash through his mind in an instant."[155]

Jones spoke for about ten minutes, of his youthful indiscretion in withdrawing in 1921— the most "inglorious failure" of his golfing life as he once described it—of his victories in 1927 and 1930, and of his last round there in 1936. He told his friends in the audience, "You people have sensitivity and an ability to extend cordiality in ingenious ways." He added, "I could take out of my life everything except my experiences at St Andrews and I'd still have a rich full life."[156]

After his remarks, he left the stage and got into the electric golf cart he used to get around the course as captain. Herbert Warren Wind remembered that, as he exited, "the whole hall spontaneously burst into the old Scottish song "Will Ye No' Come Back Again?" So honestly heartfelt was this reunion for Bobby Jones and the people of St Andrews (and for everyone) that it was 10 minutes before many who attended were able to speak again with a tranquil voice." Jones would call it "the finest thing that ever happened to me."[157]

In retirement, Jones devoted much of his time to Augusta National, and Frank Christian, who grew up around the club as the son of its official photographer, remembered Jones. "He would always ask how my father was, how I was doing in school, and how was my golf game progressing? Was I practicing?" When Jones talked with him, he gave his full attention to the young man and seemed genuinely interested in the answers. "Jones was that way with everyone, and I think that is one of the reasons people loved him. He was never boastful, nor did I ever hear him say anything about himself or his own golf game. I think his reputation as a gentleman, for his courtesy and sportsmanship, were genuine and came from within the man."[158]

Jones's accomplishments on the golf course were incredible, but how he lived life when stricken with his illness is even more impressive. He kept his sense of humor, kept fighting, and kept his friends around him, not to reminisce about old times but to enjoy new ones. The game helped prepare him for later life because it had stripped his soul bare and provided him with the armor to face the difficult physical trials he would endure for the last 23 years of his life. He had battled his mercurial temper as a young man and succeeded in concealing it for most of his life. When stricken with syringomyelia, he concealed equally as well his suffering, as best he could. He didn't ask the world to feel sorry for him, but rather, to paraphrase his own words, he "played the ball as it lay."

As Jones maintained, the "main idea in golf, as in life, I suppose, is to learn to accept what cannot be altered, and to keep doing one's own and resolute best whether the prospect be bleak or rosy." More than 40 years after his death, his presence remains prominent in the world of golf. The late English journalist Henry Longhurst said of Jones that night at Younger Hall in 1958, "If he came back in a hundred years' time, he would still not be forgotten."[159]

3

BEN HOGAN

"The Human Body Is a Great Machine"

Quite simply, it is the story of the spirit within the man—the spirit that springs from faith. [1]
—John Ames, USGA President

It seems to me that every time somebody said I couldn't do something, I just got more determined. Not to disprove them, but to prove to myself I could do it. [2]
—Ben Hogan

Ben Hogan loved to practice, but on this warm Texas day his body was working through the recovery process following surgery to remove troublesome calcium deposits from his collar bones. Before going under the knife, it looked as if the top half of a golf ball was sitting under his shirt, nasty residuals of the car accident that nearly killed him two decades earlier. The condition was painful and had impeded his shoulder movement. [3] Although retired from competition and now an old man, he still loved the game and enjoyed hitting golf balls out to his caddy Jody Vasquez.

Hogan took a fairway wood, testing his progress. "Then, as he swung forward at the ball," recalled Vasquez, "all I saw was a blast of turf exploding into the air. The ball jumped forward about 50 yards in front of him. He must have hit inches behind it. . . . Mr. Hogan stood looking down at the ground for what seemed like an eternity." Hogan leaned on his club, shoulders slumped, head bowed. After a few seconds, he walked over to his cart and sat down.

"This icon of a man looked suddenly mortal," according to Vasquez. "He was tired, physically and mentally," and "must have simply been asking himself, 'Why am I doing this?'" Finally, he got up off the cart seat and continued hitting shots.[4] There was no quit in this man. He accepted this difficult day as he had each tough day since he was nine years old and kept pushing forward.

Sportswriter Charles Price once described Ben Hogan as "a myth everybody knows, and a man nobody knows."[5] William Benjamin Hogan was born August 13, 1912, the third and youngest child of Chester and Clara Hogan. The family lived in Dublin, Texas, until 1921, when Hogan's father, a blacksmith, was beset with bouts of depression. Early that year, he ceased going to church and at times never left the house to go to work at his blacksmithing shop, which, in an age when automobiles were becoming ubiquitous, was making his trade obsolete.

Clara sought treatment for him at a sanatorium in Fort Worth, 70 miles to the northeast, and moved the family there. Chester underwent calming mineral baths and mild electrotherapy treatments and five months later declared himself cured. He returned to Dublin to open his shop again, telling friends he would bring his family back with him. But he was not a well man. He was drinking and displaying manic-depressive tendencies, in good spirits one day and down the next. He came back to Fort Worth in February and tried to convince Clara to move back to their old home. Clara objected, telling him she thought it best for the children, Royal, Princess, and Bennie, to remain in school until the end of the term. Arguments followed throughout the night.[6]

Despondent, 37-year-old Chester Hogan grabbed his .38-caliber revolver on Valentine's Day 1922, put it to his chest, and pulled the trigger. He was rushed to the hospital but died 12 hours later. A newspaper reported that "his six-year-old son, who was playing on the floor," was present in the room with him. In that moment, Bennie Hogan's life changed forever. "Ben's father was his idol," explained Hogan's wife, Valerie, years later. "I was told that at his father's funeral, they were not able to get Ben to go into the church, that he couldn't bear to see the casket."[7]

The little boy had to grow up in a hurry. Chester's death left the family in difficult straits financially. While Clara took in sewing, Ben sold newspapers at Fort Worth's Union Station. "I was skinny and small and I wasn't getting much sleep," he'd remember, "between selling papers and trying to go to school. I don't think it did me any good." When he was 12, he also began caddying, walking seven miles each way to the Glen Garden Golf Club. His mission in life from that point on, he would say years later, was to not be a burden to his mother. "I sold newspapers until I found out caddies got 65 cents for 18 holes. That was a lot more than I was getting staying up to 11:30 and 12:30 every night selling newspapers."[8]

When Ben reported for caddy duty, he "was given the works," according to friend and former Masters champion Jimmy Demaret. Hogan was shoved forward in front of the biggest kid and told to fight him. His opponent soon wished someone else had been picked for the task, notes a *Sport* magazine article in 1953. "The skinny kid tore into him with the sharp fury of a wildcat in battle." As Hogan remembered it, "They threw me in against one of those fellows and I got the better of him."[9]

His initiation wasn't over, as next he was stuffed into an old barrel and rolled down a hill behind the clubhouse. After traveling 30 or 40 yards and dropping 20 feet, he emerged a bit battered but more determined than ever to show his peers he would not be intimidated. He was also determined to do a good job. Some Saturdays he would sleep in a bunker, using newspapers as a blanket, to be first in line for a bag on Sunday morning. According to Demaret, when Ben spoke of those early days, he'd only say, "They were real rough," and let it go at that.[10]

The game appealed to Hogan from the start. In high school he had tried to play football but was too small, and baseball just didn't catch his fancy. "Why golf did I do not know, but I just loved it."[11] He played and practiced as much as he could. "The grocery where my mother used to send me on errands," Hogan told *Look* magazine in 1941, "was a half a mile away and I used to hit a ball all the way there and back. At home I wore our lawn bare hitting golf balls off it." When Walter Hagen came to town in 1927 to play the PGA championship in Dallas, an impressionable Hogan took notice. Hagen arrived in a purple car and raiment fit for a king. "I made up my mind," Ben would remember, "that if golf could make it possible for a fellow to live like that, then I would have a fling at it myself."[12]

But Hogan was no instant prodigy as was Bobby Jones. What Jones was born with, Hogan had to acquire, and he also had to overcome the objections of his mother, Clara, who was not happy with all the time he spent on the game. She told him in those early years that he'd never get anywhere fooling around on a golf course. "It's time you went to work," she'd say. To which Ben replied, "I'm going to work harder than anybody you ever knew," adding that someday he was "gonna be the greatest golfer in the world." He would work hard, and when self-doubt crept into his mind, he used anger to drive away the fear.[13]

The same year he saw Walter Hagen, he also met a man who would become a mentor and act as a surrogate father. Marvin Leonard was a successful businessman whose doctor told him he needed more exercise in his life. In golf, Marvin found an ideal game. He would rise early to play nine holes, then go home and eat a big breakfast before heading off to work "feeling like a new man." When he found young Ben in the caddy yard, there was something about the kid he liked. He told Ben he was a rank beginner, but that didn't matter to Hogan. He thought he could help his player and told Leonard as much. In Marvin Leonard, Hogan would find a decent, widely respected man and the transformative role model he needed.[14]

Leonard, 17 years older than Ben, would serve as a surrogate father or older brother, just as O. B. Keeler had done for Bobby Jones. The friendship and support was welcomed by Hogan, who felt the pressure of living up to his mother's expectations. He was always hearing, "Why don't you do it like your brother?" Ben's older brother Royal had become Clara's rock after Chester died, working hard to help the family. Ben's golf, on the other hand, was "nothing," according to his mother. "And nothing divided by nothing is nothing." This, ironically, would become one of Ben's pet sayings. Hogan's wife, Valerie, always contended that he "had the misfortune to be the youngest of the family."[15]

For Ben, golf became the driving force in his life, notwithstanding his mother's disapproval. At Glen Garden, he also found a boy his age who was not only his greatest competition but also would become one of the greatest players in the history of the game—Byron Nelson. Friends, but never close ones, they would find distinctly different paths to greatness. Byron began a pattern of superiority in the early years when he beat Ben in the caddies' tournament at Glen Garden in 1927. When Nelson was given junior membership at the club instead of Hogan, it left Ben embittered.[16] He would be spurred by Byron's early success, and a rivalry was born, in part perhaps rooted in Ben's jealousy of Byron's easygoing personality that made him very easy to like.

Ben would caddy until he was 16, then went to work in the golf shop at Glen Garden. On weekends, he'd polish clubs until 3 a.m. "Boy, I'd look at those clubs and they were the most beautiful things, Nichols and Stewarts, all made in Scotland. I got my own set of mongrel clubs out of a dime store barrel for a dollar a piece."[17] Hogan kept working on his game and turned professional at the tender age of 17. His first tournament, the Texas Open in February 1930, began a 10-year struggle to find his place in the world of golf.

As Ben told *Sports Illustrated* 25 years later, "I didn't think I was good enough to win anything as a professional, but I figured if I played enough I might make some money. . . . They thought I was nothing divided by nothing. Although I practiced day and night, I was so small a lot of people didn't have faith in me."[18] Apparently, he didn't have much faith in himself either in the beginning, withdrawing from his first two events. In his first attempt, he shot 78-75 and withdrew, then did the same thing after opening the next one with 77-76. "I found out the first day I shouldn't even be there," he would remember and decided, if he couldn't handle the pressure and play any better than that, he "had no right to be out there at all." From the beginning, he was an unforgiving perfectionist, a trait that would define his life.[19]

He returned to Fort Worth and tried to improve his game, doing it on his own. His method was to watch the best players and try to emulate them by practicing as much as daylight would allow.[20] Aniela Goldthwaite, a prominent amateur golfer and member of the Curtis Cup team in 1934, met Hogan when he was caddying as a young man. She saw promise in him and gave him a dozen brand new golf balls and a new pitching wedge. A month or so went by, and Hogan went to see her and asked politely is she might be able to give him more balls. Had he lost them all, she asked? He gave her the box with all the balls inside, with covers so worn that the dimples were almost smooth. There were no cuts or creases; Hogan had simply worn them out.[21]

As he kept wearing the dimples off his practice balls, he found various jobs to put money in his pocket. He was a mechanic, he worked in a bank and a hotel, and he even worked as a croupier at the Blackstone Hotel before trying the circuit again in 1932. "I don't know why Ben denies having been a croupier," said Jimmy Demaret. "He was a hungry kid. It was an honest game. Hell, there was nothing to be ashamed of." Hall of Famer Paul Runyan recalled card games in the clubhouse with Hogan and marveled at how he dealt cards "so fast they just spilled out of his hands."[22]

After going bust on the tour again during a brief stint in 1932, Ben returned home and rented the golf shop at Oakhurst Country Club. "No friend ever showed up," he told writer Herbert Warren Wind two decades later. Said Wind: "I've never heard a man so bitter."[23] At Oakhurst, Hogan practiced four hours a day and hustled gamblers in his spare time. Hogan would bet that he could hit drives to his friend Buell Matthews from 220 to 240 yards and have Matthews catch them barehanded. This ploy hooked a lot of suckers, who would usually give up after Matthews shagged maybe 7 of 10 without breathing hard.[24]

Even after another failed try to play the tour in 1934, including a missed cut in his first U.S. Open, Hogan was not deterred. He was stubborn, practiced all the time, didn't seek help, and rarely hung out with other players in the bar at the end of the day. Aside from golf, he was also spending considerable time with Valerie Fox, a pretty young woman he had met when he was 14. She was attending Texas Christian University, majoring in journalism, when they started seeing more of each other.[25]

She would recall the early struggles before they were married. "When he got home one year, he talked about the day he hit bottom." He was playing well, with Horton Smith in his group. If he made a putt on the last hole, he would have made a nice sum of money. But as his ball approached the cup, the caddy couldn't get the flagstick out of the hole in time. She didn't know if the ball hit the stick or what, but he finished out of the money.[26]

Valerie remembered Ben describing that day. "I went over and sat on a bench and just felt like I didn't want to live," he told her. "But then Horton Smith came over and sat next to me. Horton told me, 'Ben, I know you think the world is against you because that was a bad break, but you must get over this and go on. You've got a wonderful future.'"[27] Even if he was only trying to be gracious at the time, Smith turned out to be a prophet. Part of that bright future began when Ben and Valerie married on April 14, 1935. They both found in each other something they needed. She believed in him and pushed him when his resolve flagged. Ben's mother claimed: "Valerie is the only one who can honestly say, 'I told you so.' The rest of us hoped Ben would make it, but Valerie was always sure he would."[28]

Of the relationship, Valerie's niece Valerie Harriman believed they filled a void in each other's lives. "She needed his strength of character and he needed someone to wholeheartedly believe in him through thick and thin. He provided her with a life she could never have found on her own, and she rewarded him with unwavering devotion and loyalty."[29] When Hogan ventured out on tour again in 1936, she went with him. When he ran out of money after missing the cut again in the U.S. Open, Marvin Leonard, who over the years had built a small business empire with his brother, never forgot his young friend and helped Hogan out financially. In January 1936, Leonard also opened Colonial Country Club in Fort Worth, which would host the U.S. Open in 1941 and remains one of the most famous courses in America, thanks in large part to Hogan's later association with it as winner of five Colonial National Invitation tournaments. But success was only a dream when Ben Hogan ran out of money again in 1937.

"I tried to quit this game thousands of times, because I didn't feel I was taking care of my wife in the manner I should have." They were staying in cheap hotels and driving broken-down cars. But Valerie wouldn't let him quit. "She kept saying, 'You can't give up now. You're so close. I just know it.'. . . So in a lot of ways, in those days, my wife was my sports psychologist."[30]

When he complained to her that he wasn't making enough putts to win, she suggested matter-of-factly that he should just hit the ball closer to the hole.[31] Jimmy Demaret claimed that Ben hit the ball as well in the 1930s as he did in the late 1940s, but he couldn't buy a putt. As Demaret put it, "I thought that he would never get the touch. Most good putters are born that way, not made. But Ben made himself into a great putter. To me, that will always be one of the most amazing parts of his success."[32]

Hogan kept pushing himself to make it on the tour, perhaps motivated by the fact that his old caddy mate Byron Nelson had won the Masters in 1937. But it was not an easy life. Bob Harlow, founder of

Golf World and early manager of tour events, once said that the tour was an "education in survival of the fittest. . . . If you found a way to make it one week, well, you graduated to another week. . . . Pro golf was like university education, a higher institution of hard knocks."[33] By 1938, Hogan had an advanced degree in hard knocks, and the turning point of his whole life would come early that year. By the time he and Valerie reached Oakland, they had $86.00 left out of the $1,400 bankroll they started with. He had promised her that if he could not make it this time—if they ran out of money—he'd give it up and find a job in Fort Worth.

They were staying in the Lemington Hotel, which gave the pros the best rate in the city, and he parked his car in a lot across the street. As he told the story, he was playing fairly well and on the last day had a chance to make some much-needed money: "I had a fairly early starting time and left the hotel after breakfast and went across the street and my car was jacked up. And my two rear wheels are sitting on rocks." Sam Snead and some other pros saw what happened. "He was as close to tears as that tough little guy can get," recalled Snead.[34]

Hogan later told Jimmy Demaret that at that moment he didn't have a bit of hope left, but Valerie bucked him up. "Don't be silly" she told him. "Things will be okay. We'll just ride out to the club with somebody else. Don't get upset about it."[35] He got a ride to the course, but it is interesting that in a 1983 interview he could not remember who took him there—his old friend and rival Byron Nelson. "So I played. I won $385.00. It was the biggest check I'd ever seen in my life. And I'm quite sure it will be the biggest check I'll ever see."[36]

This was his defining moment and a turning point. Later that year, Hogan teamed with Vic Ghezzi to win his first event, the Hershey Four-Ball Invitation. Ghezzi said in an interview 15 years later: "Maybe I was imagining things, but his face seemed to turn gray from the almost violent effort he put into every shot. I knew from that day on nobody, but nobody, was going to stop Hogan."[37] By the end of the year, Ben finished 15th on the money list.

Before he got to Hershey, Hogan had earned the admiration of that year's Masters champion, Henry Picard, who hadn't even seen him play. Hogan's reputation as a hard worker made Picard curious. When Ben arrived for the tournament, Picard sought him out for a practice round. "And on the third tee," Picard recalled in a 1990 interview, "I watched that swing and I said, 'You can beat the world.' That's what I saw."[38]

Picard was also a kind man who offered Hogan financial support if he needed it. He recalled seeing Ben and Valerie arguing in a Chicago hotel. Their finances were low, and they were a long way from home, and Picard sensed their predicament. "Well, I don't have all the money in the world," he told Hogan. "But I've got enough to support you. . . . And that's the way it's going to be. And of course he never did call me for money."[39] Hogan never forgot that gesture. "Picard gave me a terrific boost. Even if you're digging as hard as you can, you like to have somebody on your side." In 1948, he would write in his book *Power Golf,* that "knowing that help was there if I needed it helped me forget about my troubles."[40]

In the next couple of years, Hogan would seek out Picard for practice rounds and pick his brain. In early 1940, he asked Picard why he wasn't winning. "What are you worrying about, a duck hook? We can change that in five minutes." He weakened Hogan's left-hand grip, and Hogan liked the results. Hogan practiced at Pinehurst for 12 days in preparation for the North and South Open, a major event in those days. They played together, and Picard was amazed by the display of golf. "I've never seen such power in my life from a man that size." Hogan was hitting it 25–30 yards past long-hitting Craig Wood. Hogan broke through, winning three tournaments in a row by an accumulated 34 under par, remarkable scoring in those days.[41] He ended up the leading money winner with $10,655.

Hogan won four tournaments in 1940 and five in 1941 but was still fighting the hook off the tee. "I hate a hook," he would tell *Sports Illustrated* in 1955. "It nauseates me. I could vomit when I see one. It's like a rattlesnake in your pocket."[42] That rattlesnake had its origins in the caddy yard at Glen Garden, when the caddies would have driving contests to determine who would shag the balls they hit. Hogan, being small, employed a strong grip and long backswing to maximize his distance, but it was an action that created a tendency he fought until the late 1940s.

In the 1942 Miami Biltmore Four-Ball, the hook rose up with a vengeance as he lost in the first round with partner Lawson Little. He sought out Picard, who weakened his left-hand grip again. Harry Cooper also noticed that Ben was re-gripping the club at the top of the swing, and told him so.[43] The struggle with the hook would continue, but when World War II came, many players, including Hogan, enlisted, and he lost two years of his career to the war.

Before entering the army, he was quoted as saying, "I know a lot of people don't like me. They say I'm selfish and hard, that I think only of golf. Maybe I do. But there's a reason. I know what it means to be hungry. I sold papers around the railroad station in Fort Worth when I was twelve. I never intend to be hungry again." Forty years later, when asked what drove him so hard to succeed, he responded: "Three things. One, I didn't want to be a burden to my mother. Two, I needed to put food on the table. Three, I needed a place to sleep."[44]

Hogan would never forget the "hunger" he spoke of and could never escape the tragic consequences of his childhood. His behavior in adulthood was not difficult to understand. Counselors who work with suicide survivors point out that a child without an adequate support system lacks a strong capacity for intimacy and trust. This leads to detachment and bitterness, and the child often becomes a loner. Many become workaholics as adults.[45]

Hogan's dedication to the game was his obsession and left little room for friendly banter on the golf course. "He let it be known early that he was all golf and no fooling around," Paul Runyan remembered. "Some of the fellas began to even fear getting near Hogan—that icy look he would give you that said, 'That's far enough, friend.'"[46] Hogan would explain his approach when he started out this way: "I was so broke I couldn't afford to talk to other people, because I was afraid of losing my focus. So I stayed to myself on the golf course."[47]

Hogan's refusal to let up, no matter what the score, was never better demonstrated than the 1941 Inverness Four-Ball. He and partner Jimmy Demaret were five up, when Demaret suggested they coast to a win. "We're five up now," protested Hogan, "but what's wrong with winning by eight or ten?" His perfectionism was legendary. "You got the feeling," noted Sam Snead, "that he hated—I mean, hated—the mistakes he made."[48] This is the answer to why he kept trying to build a swing he could rely on.

Even though he won six times in 1942 and—after the forced break caused by the war—5 in 1945, he was still troubled by the hook that crept into his game. Where most people would be content to win and accept an imperfect swing, Hogan could not. "I was in Chicago, as I recall it," he told Ken Venturi in 1983, "and I was hooking so badly that I couldn't get a 4-wood off the ground, and I had to use iron clubs all the time. I came home and I said to myself, 'you can't play this way.'"[49]

In the famous 1955 *Life* magazine article that describes the "secret" to his success, he relates how he found his flash of genius in 1946: "I left the tour and went home to Fort Worth about as desperate as a man could be. I sat and thought for three or four days. I didn't pick up a golf club, although I wanted to in the worst way. One night while laying awake in bed I began thinking about a technique for hitting a golf ball that was so old it was almost new."[50] What he came upon was the concept of pronation—that is, rolling the hands gradually to the right on the backswing, which opened the face of the club. He weakened his grip a bit and cupped his left wrist about five degrees at the top of the backswing, which he called the "real meat" of his "secret." This allowed him to keep it bowed outward coming into the ball, and swing as hard as he wanted without the clubface closing and causing a hook. "It worked. It worked all day long. And the next day. And the next day, too."[51]

Hogan was resilient enough to try new things and had the strongest of minds and spirits when dealing with adversity. After losing the 1946 Masters by three-putting from 15 feet on the last hole, he didn't curl up and disappear, but came back to win three of the next four events. That June, after failing to get into a play-off at the U.S. Open—again on the final hole—he came back the next week to win the Inverness Four-Ball with Jimmy Demaret.[52] Then, at the end of the summer, he won his first major championship, the PGA, in Portland, Oregon. He beat Ed Oliver in the final, but it was his thrashing of friend Demaret in the semifinal match that drew the attention of reporters. Lawton Carver writes that Hogan was the most "ruthless, most cold-blooded and least compassionate" of competitors. "He doesn't merely want to beat you. He wants to trample you underfoot."[53]

Even after winning 21 tournaments since breaking through in 1938, Hogan claimed he "never felt genuinely confident" about his game until 1946. "But my self-doubting never stopped," he admitted. "Regardless of how well I was going, I was still concerned about the next day and the next." The cold, merciless automaton of a man admitted he was human— he had doubts in his own abilities. He did realize he had to stop trying to

Ben Hogan circa 1940, was just developing into the golfer we remember. Henry Picard, member of the World Golf Hall of Fame, met Hogan in 1938 and curious about his talent, sought him out for a practice round. "And on the third tee, I watched that swing and I said, 'You can beat the world.' That's what I saw." *Courtesy USGA. All Rights Reserved.*

do everything perfectly, as it became apparent that "the ambitious over-thoughtfullness was neither possible nor advisable, or even necessary."[54]

Another seven victories in 1947 brought him into 1948 playing the best golf of his life. In June he won his first U.S. Open at Riviera with a record score of 276 that stood for almost 20 years before Jack Nicklaus beat it in 1967. Hogan became the best and stayed that way through incessant practice. "It seemed like it took me a month to three months to get back those three days where I was when I took a rest," he would tell Ken Venturi in 1983. "I had to practice and play all the time. I told you before, my swing wasn't the best in the world and I knew it wasn't and I thought, well, the only way I can win is to outwork these fellows. So, they might work two hours a day and I might work eight."[55]

Bobby Jones once said Hogan was the hardest worker he'd ever seen. Gene Sarazen said it exhausted him just to watch Ben practice but feared he left his finest strokes on the practice grounds. "They used to laugh at me for practicing," Hogan was fond of saying.[56] He was a pioneer of long practice sessions. Until the dawn of steel-shafted clubs in the 1930s, players generally practiced only enough to acquire the feel of a club or a swing, not to hone their skills. The game was played on the course, not the practice ground, and the hickory-shafted clubs of that era couldn't stand up to the beating of repeated blows practice demanded.

But was Hogan's incessant practice a symptom of something else? For someone like him, who suffered the loss of his father through suicide, repeated activities or rituals, according to experts, are "soothing devices used to fill an emotional emptiness caused by under parenting or impaired receptivity to parenting." His mother never encouraged his golf and was always telling him to get a real job and to be more like his older brother, Royal. In golf, he found an escape and a comfort. "Repetition brings familiarity, and familiarity is the opposite of the unknown." Hogan's behavior, however, was not pointless. As biographer Curt Sampson wrote, "He was single minded in turning his negative past into a future filled with glory."[57]

Hogan didn't have much use in later life for biographers' trying to analyze his life, saying derisively of Sampson that he was nothing but a "broken-down old golf pro passing himself off as a writer."[58] Hogan did things his way, obsessively but with purpose. He used to putt on the carpet in hotel rooms to a quarter, feeling when he got to the course the hole would look as big as a bucket. "Once, when he strode through the lobby of a hotel carrying a putter and wearing a scowl," wrote Arch Murray in 1941, "he was asked the reason for his poor humor. 'I just three-putted two carpets upstairs,' he snapped. But next day he shot a record 62."[59]

Gene Sarazen called Ben Hogan the most merciless player of all the modern golfers. "His temperament may derive from the rough, anguishing years of his childhood or the hostility he encountered as a young and over-determined circuit chaser," Sarazen noted. Whatever the reason, Hogan was the kind of man that could be aptly described as "perpetually hungry."[60]

But Hogan's drive to be the best had consequences in his personal life. He and Valerie had no children. After Ben's death in 1997, Valerie explained, "It didn't happen. We always felt if it happened, fine. But Ben didn't think the tour was any place for a mother and child. So he'd have stayed home with me and done something else. Our happiness was more important to him than his career."[61] Ben wanted his wife with him as he traveled the tour. Sam Snead's wife told Valerie, after a short break when she stayed at home while he played, "I'm glad you're back. I think he's the most lonesome man I've ever seen on the road."[62]

Valerie said at the end of her life, "We didn't miss children like some people did because we had so much to give each other in our marriage."[63] Yet in 1955, in an interview with Margarette Curtis of *Golf Digest* during the week of the U.S. Open, the wife of another player had commented to her that she had only one child. To which 44-year-old Valerie replied softly, "One is better than none."[64] We can never know for sure what was in their hearts and minds concerning the subject, but Hogan's career did not make room for children. The game was his life, and at the end of 1948, he was at the top of the golfing world. That would all change in one violent moment on a Texas highway early the next year.

Hogan had started the New Year by winning the Bing Crosby National Pro-Am and the Long Beach Open and had finished second to Jimmy Demaret when he and Valerie were driving home for a break. It was February 2, 1949. A Greyhound bus, behind schedule and trying to make up time, was barreling down a foggy road 30 miles from Van Horn, Texas. As Hogan rounded a corner, the headlights of the bus were staring straight at them. "Honey, I think he's going to hit us," said Valerie in disbelief.[65] As 19,250 pounds of bus bore down on Hogan's 3,900-pound Cadillac, Ben flung his body across Valerie, saving him from being impaled by the steering wheel. "It was the end. We had no chance," Valerie would recall.[66] The force of the crash thrust the steering column into the driver's seat, hitting his shoulder and breaking his collarbone, and slamming the engine into his left leg and stomach. His head banged into Valerie as he lost consciousness briefly. "I thought he'd die on my shoulder," she'd say.[67]

Valerie, who miraculously suffered only cuts and bruises in the horrific collision, pulled her husband from the wreckage. Ben lay on the ground with a fractured pelvis, a broken collarbone, rib, and ankle. In addition, he suffered a deep gash near his left eye, a bladder injury, and massive contusions on his left leg.[68] No one called an ambulance immediately, and with his golf clubs scattered around him, Hogan, conscious but suffering shock and in great pain, waited an hour and a half before an ambulance finally arrived. It was four more hours before he was carried into the Hotel Dieu Hospital in El Paso, 150 miles west of the accident scene. Hogan was delirious, at one point motioning with both hands to keep an imaginary gallery back.[69]

A team of doctors worked on him, and his brother, Royal, came from Fort Worth to be with him and Valerie. "I'm lucky to be alive," he told a reporter at the hospital.[70] His injuries were treated, and he began to recover. He was scheduled to be released on February 16 when things took a turn for the worse, as an embolism passed from the pulmonary artery into his right lung. "It was as if someone had struck a knife into my chest," Hogan would remember, "and was grinding and twisting it, deeper and deeper."[71] Dr. J. Leighton Green told Valerie that the next one could be fatal, fearing that a clot might form in his left leg and "move up and obstruct the artery completely. It is damn bad. He is seriously ill, no question about it. I think it will be touch and go to save him."[72]

On March 2, a second blood clot was discovered in his leg. So serious was the condition that the AP transmitted a 16-paragraph obituary to member papers and radio stations. A decision was made to operate and tie off the vena cava, the large vein that carries deoxygenated blood from the lower half of the body into the right atrium of the heart. It was not a common operation at the time, and Dr. Alton Ochsner of New Orleans, an expert in the field, was recommended for the job.[73]

After Valerie made a call to General David Hutchinson, commanding officer of El Paso's Biggs Field, who had visited Ben several days earlier, a B-29 on a training flight was ordered to New Orleans to get Ochsner and bring him to the Hotel Dieu Hospital. The question of Hogan's survival was in the balance, and Valerie wanted him to make the decision. After the doctors explained the procedure and risk involved, Hogan asked if he would be able to use his legs and play golf again.[74] They told him he would, and he consented.

The operation lasted two hours, and the vena cava was tied off so no blood clots could go to his heart or lungs, allowing for smaller veins to reroute the flow of blood. Hogan awoke to find a heavy cast encasing him from hips to armpits. The circulation of blood to his legs would be forever impaired, but his life had been saved. He was still not out of the woods, as his appetite disappeared and his weight dropped.[75] But he hung on, and the doctors were heartened when he said he was hungry again.

The cast was removed a week later, and on March 14, Hogan was rolled out to the grounds to see some sunshine. "He has shown me more willpower through this terrible spell than he ever did on a golf course," declared Valerie. "Ben realizes how many friends he has everywhere. People have been wonderful." But not many gave him a chance to resume his career, including his doctors. Golf writer Herb Graffis visited him and remembered, "I left the hospital sick at heart, stomach, and head, but hoping for a miracle."[76]

Ben was a good patient and followed directions precisely. His doctors and nurses liked him and admired his self-discipline and determination. On April 1, he left the hospital and went home to Fort Worth. The doctors told him it would be at least five months before the swelling in his legs disappeared and he could only build his strength by walking. He started by doing laps in the front room of his house. On April 30, he went to New Orleans for a checkup with Dr. Ochsner. "They say I'm going to be alright," he said after, but tournament golf was a different story.[77] In May, Hogan sent in his entry for the U.S. Open, a symbolic act that told people he'd be back, maybe not that year but certainly the next. "Listen, a lot of people have had bad injuries," he said. "They came back and so will I."[78]

In September, Bill Rives wrote in *Sport* magazine that Hogan had been a fighter his whole life and couldn't be counted out, noting his "wild, almost irrational, resolution." Ben said he was more determined than ever, knowing where he had come from. In his younger days, he said, many times it "seemed that I couldn't possibly make the grade. But I hung on."[79] He intended to do the same now. As he had told golf writer Charlie Bartlett before leaving the hospital, "You work for perfection all your life, and then something like this happens. My nervous system has been all shot by this, and I don't see how I can readjust it to competitive golf. But you can bet I'll be back there swinging."[80]

The support of the public through his trials was a true source of inspiration. People from all over the country wrote to him and Valerie, offering prayers and encouragement. "I never realized just how swell the American public can be," he confessed.[81] By summer, he had improved enough to go to Britain as captain of the Ryder Cup team. While there, he met with golf writers Leonard Crawley and Henry Longhurst, telling them he would win again. "Longhurst and I looked at one another," recalled Crawley, "and when Hogan left us we said in the same breath: 'How pathetic.'"[82]

By November, he began hitting balls at Colonial. A caddy there recalled Hogan's first attempts. "He would putt awhile, then chip some. But when he started to swing a wood, it was pathetic. I couldn't believe I was watching Ben Hogan."[83] His legs were weak, and his broken collarbone still bothered him, but he pressed on. He played his first full round on December 10, riding a golf cart, and did so the next day, shooting a 71 and 72. A week later, he walked a full 18 holes, but was so spent he went home to bed.[84] Back on the practice tee the next day, he kept at it and a few days later filed his entry for the Los Angeles Open, to be played in January.

What followed was both the beginning of an improbable comeback and, in another sense, the end of his formidable career. His legs would never again allow him to play but a handful of tournaments a year, and he would never swing the club consistently as well as he had before. He lost the L.A. Open in a play-off to Sam Snead and would tie for fourth at the Masters. Then came the U.S. Open at Merion, site of Bobby Jones's last victory in his 1930 Grand Slam year.

The accident forced Hogan to endure a three-and-a-half-hour pre-round ritual. First, he soaked in a tub of Epson salts for an hour. In the second hour, he took his aspirin and rubbed liniment into his shoulders and wrapped his legs from ankles to crotch in elastic bandages, which were meant to minimize swelling. He would arrive at the course an hour and 20 minutes before his tee time, change his shoes and maybe have a glass of ginger ale, which he believed made his hands feel thin, before warming up on the range and putting green.[85] But he didn't like the attention the press gave him at times. "You fellows have been good to me. Real nice. But I'm damn tired of being called an invalid. I wish you wouldn't write it anymore."[86]

The 1950 U.S. Open has become a thing of legend, as have many events surrounding Hogan. In third place after three rounds, he was fighting for the lead in the last round when he arrived on the 12th tee, and his legs locked up after hitting his drive. Harry Radix, a golf official and acquaintance, was there, and Hogan remembered the moment years later. "I told him, 'Let me hang on to you for a little bit.' I started moving my foot real slow. I told Harry, 'My God, I don't think I can finish.' My legs had turned to stone."[87]

After struggling to his third bogey in six holes at the 17th, Hogan's two-stroke lead was gone. He was forced to make a par four on the 458-yard last to force a play-off with Lloyd Mangrum and George Fazio. Everyone remembers the iconic Hy Peskin photo of Hogan hitting his one-iron second shot to the green, but few recall the four-foot putt he made to secure the par. Hogan, exhausted and hurting, remembered it this way: "I thought 'The devil with it.' I didn't rush, understand, but I put my putter behind the ball and hit it. It went right into the middle of the cup. I could care less. I was so discouraged at losing those three shots. I had it won easy."[88] As he would tell friend Kris Tschetter many years later, it was "one of the greatest two-putts of my life to get into a play-off the next day. Folks today don't want to hear the truth. . . . They'd rather think I hit it to a foot to win."[89]

Robert "Skee" Riegel, who tied for 12th, said that after Hogan finished he "looked completely beaten, as bad as I've ever seen a man look after a tournament. I wouldn't have bet you a buck he was capable of playing any more golf that week." Ben had to soak for hours in a hot bath that night to fend off the awful leg cramps that felled him on the 12th, but knew he'd play on, win or lose.[90]

He was on the first tee the next day and prevailed, shooting a 69 to beat Mangrum by 4 and Fazio by 6. Hogan would claim that his win at Merion gave him his greatest satisfaction in golf. As his opponent Lloyd Mangrum said before the play-off, "If you're supposed to win, you win. If you're not, you don't."[91] He was right. Mangrum had won the Open in 1946 when it was his time, but Hogan's victory in 1950 was a truly storybook ending. Sportswriter Red Smith wrote that this "was a spiritual victory, an absolute triumph of will," while John Ames, president of the USGA, claimed it was "the story of the spirit within the man—the spirit that springs from faith."[92]

For Hogan, it was just who he was. Longtime friend Gene Smyers put it this way: "This may sound odd but Ben was proud of the hard things he'd endured." He genuinely believed that the difficult times he had survived—from losing his father to having to fight his way into the caddy yard—prepared him for being the best he could be in life. "That's why he never showed a ripple of fear or intimidation to the world at large—and certainly not another golfer. If he did, he knew he wouldn't make it, might not survive."[93]

Ben Hogan as a young man created an alter ego—Hennie Bogan as he'd refer to himself in the third person—the boy who wanted to be more like his rival Nelson perhaps, likeable, soft-spoken, as opposed to the aloof persona of Ben Hogan. But his life created a different path. As he said, "I don't think I could have done what I've done if I hadn't had the tough days to begin with."[94] The accident was another setback in a life full of setbacks, and he used his strength of will to not give up his career when his body threatened to fail him.

As he explained years later, "Golf isn't a game you play with pain. It's not like football or other games where you can sit on a bench while your substitute takes over. I didn't like to talk about my legs because it's no good when you feel that people feel sorry for you."[95]

Two-time U.S. Open champion Cary Middlecoff in 1950 called Hogan "a walking miracle," but it wasn't a big enough miracle to make Hogan's body whole again.[96] After the accident, he played only a half dozen or so tournaments a year. CBS radio broadcaster and friend John Derr remembered Hogan's reluctance to play unless he was totally prepared. "But that preparation was a physical ordeal," in the years after the accident. "It just all wore on him, and it kind of wore him out."[97]

Hogan successfully defended his U.S. Open at Oakland Hills in 1951 after winning his first Masters that April. After three rounds, he trailed Bobby Locke and Jimmy Demaret by two shots but in the final round shot the best round of the entire championship, a 67, to win. "Under the circumstances, it was the greatest round I ever played," he would say. "I didn't think I could do it. My friends said last night that I might win with a pair of 69s. It seemed too much on this course. It is the hardest course I have ever played."[98]

That same year, a movie was released that told his life story. *Follow the Sun* was a somewhat melodramatic treatment (typical of the 1950s) that attempted to show Hogan's more human side. "There's absolutely no question that accident and the stories that came out about it completely changed the image most people had of Ben Hogan," said Tommy Bolt. "Up till then he'd been seen as a cold and unsympathetic character who didn't give a damn about anybody but himself." Yet Bolt claimed he and a select few that Hogan trusted soon saw a very different man. Ben helped some of the younger players, giving them advice, even offering to lend money if things got tough, though he never wanted any of that known. "I guess he feared people would mistake such kindness as weakness," concluded Bolt. "But that car accident changed everything—even Ben himself."[99]

Another thing became apparent after the accident. As Jimmy Demaret wrote in his book, *My Partner, Ben Hogan*: "Ben has a deep respect for the one Being who is a lot bigger than all of us combined. 'I couldn't have done a thing—I wouldn't even be alive—except for the help of God.' Ben is following religion closely these days. Not in any stuffy manner, but in the coherent, deep faith of a person who knows what the Lord did for him."[100] In Rev. Granville Walker of the University Christian Church, Hogan found a spellbinding speaker who appealed to his newfound spirituality. While Valerie only went to church for Christmas

Ben Hogan standing next to the wreckage of the car he was driving when it was hit by a bus in 1949. He came close to dying, but vowed to come back. When he won the Masters, U.S. Open, and British Open in 1953, he believed his accomplishments would "give courage to those people who are sick or injured and broken in body as I once was." *Courtesy USGA. All Rights Reserved.*

and other special occasions, Ben became a regular attendee for the rest of his life.[101]

In 1953, Hogan achieved the greatest success in golf since Bobby Jones in 1930, a year that would stand alone in professional golf until Tiger Woods supplanted it in 2000. Ben won the Masters with a then-record score of 274, asserting he played as well as he could. "I'm talking about four rounds of hitting good shots."[102] Putting was a different part of the game to him. In June, he won his fourth U.S. Open at Oakmont. Johnny Bulla played behind Hogan in the third round and marveled at how he could save shots when in trouble. "I thought the guy was shooting 80 in the morning," remembered Bulla, "but he made some great saves. Like Tiger and Nicklaus, he didn't throw away any shots."[103]

The USGA was conscious of pace of play in the Open and tried to push the players along. Hogan was not a fast player, and others complained about the double standard. Hall of Famer Denny Shute played one round in three hours seventeen minutes (unheard of these days). "I want to see them rush Hogan the way they did us," he said at the time. Clayton Heafner added, "I want to see what they do with Ben Hogan this afternoon. We played in three and a half hours. . . . It took Hogan four and a half hours yesterday."[104] Hogan may have earned more respect from fans after his accident, but his fellow-competitors still found him irascible at times.

If it hadn't been for Valerie, Hogan might not have entered the British Open that year. After the Masters, legends Walter Hagen and Tommy Armour, along with Bobby Cruickshank, called and told him his career wouldn't be complete unless he went to Scotland to compete in the oldest championship in the world. Ben told Valerie after the Masters that he thought he'd enter the British Open if he won the U.S. Open. He would recall that "all she said was, 'I should think you'd want to play in the British Open if you didn't win the U.S. Open.'"[105] He sent in his application.

After winning at Oakmont, the pressure kept building on him and multiplied when he arrived in Carnoustie. "I kept asking myself, 'What am I doing over here?' You know, a great many people built up in their minds a mythical Hogan who could win whenever he wanted to win. Well, life does not work that way." He felt if he didn't win the "people over there would have thought, 'Well, American players aren't so good as they're supposed to be, especially under British conditions.'"[106]

Hogan might not have even played once he got there had not the National Cash Register Company provided him use of a guest house when he discovered his original hotel didn't have a private bath, an absolute necessity for soaking his injured legs before and after play. The company even provided a driver for him. The guest house staff took good care of the Hogans, and the fans appreciated his stoic talents on the course, referring to him as the "Wee Ice Man."

Outward appearances notwithstanding, Hogan was touched by the response of the Scottish people, who were steeped in the history of the game and appreciated his golf. "Their warmth warmed him," claimed Valerie.[107] He won by four shots over a quartet of players including five-time champion Peter Thomson, despite a case of the flu that overtook him after the second round. He woke up with a temperature of 103 on the last day. John Derr knew of this, but Hogan wouldn't let him go on the air with the information and took a shot of penicillin to help get him through the final two rounds.[108]

Bernard Darwin said of the victory: "I'm happy to have lived long enough to see Ben Hogan play golf." As he told Derr, "I distinctly got the feeling he could have done whatever was required of him in order to win. He could have shot 65 if he had needed it." Gene Sarazen asserted that Hogan "is the greatest player of all time. No ifs, ands, or butts about it, boys. Got it? Good. Print it."[109]

When Ben returned to the guest house to pack his things and prepare to return home, the staff gathered and asked that he open his golf bag. He discovered a number of personal trinkets and good luck charms in the lower pockets of the bag—amulet stones, personal notes, an ancient British coin, a treasured family locket. The woman who managed the lodge said they were put there for good luck. Valerie confided to her sister Sarah later that Ben was so touched he couldn't even speak. "I've never seen him so deeply moved by anything. He couldn't believe they would do something like that and he had tears in his eyes saying good-bye to them all."[110]

When he and Valerie arrived in New York on the return home, he was given a parade down Broadway. Hogan told the crowd "Right now I feel like crying." He added, "I have a tough skin but a soft spot in my heart and things like this find that soft spot. This tops anything I've ever received."[111] Later that year, reflecting on what he had done, he said, "It had been a long, tiring road to that lead, and every step of the way reaffirmed my belief that no one does anything unless the Lord's with him. I think it was fate, and supposed to be, that I won this tournament." He also contended he won the three majors of 1953 for a reason. "I hope that purpose," he confided, "is to give courage to those people who are sick or injured and broken in body as I once was."[112]

Even the greatest players face an end to their careers. Hogan would never win another major and only one more tournament after 1953. He had some close calls, the best chance coming in a play-off loss to Jack Fleck in 1955. It was a shocking defeat for Hogan. As he remembered it, "As the Open moved along and there seemed to be a good chance for victory, I began to feel stronger. At the final hole, I believed I had won by at least five strokes."[113]

But Fleck, an unassuming man who practiced yoga but who had also been tested on Utah Beach during D-Day, birdied the last hole to tie. Hogan hated play-offs, feeling they were somewhat of a letdown. "You can't help feeling somewhat empty," he would tell *Sports Illustrated* later that year. "At least I can't." Fleck didn't have a letdown in the play-off and won by three shots with a 69.[114]

It was for Hogan the end of his tournament career as he saw it. He would play in select tournaments for the next 15 years but would be content to concentrate on his business interests. He had begun the Ben Hogan Company in 1953, and the first run of clubs came to stores in the summer of 1954—in a cruel twist of fate Jack Fleck would play Hogan clubs.[115] With his demand for excellence, people knew they were buying quality. Valerie maintained it made the company stronger because "people knew they could trust Ben to put out a golf club that was up to his standards, which everyone knew were very high." As Hogan said of his company, "I know I've picked a tough business, but it's competition again. I love competition."[116]

Hogan loved tournament golf but did not like to put his game on public display when he couldn't perform to his standards. The accident robbed him of his legs, and his nerves robbed him of his putting touch. "The accident had left my legs somewhat impaired," he acknowledged, "but there was no reason to make a fuss over it. Many thousands of people had far worse handicaps and continued without special notice or praise."[117] He could deal with his legs much better than he could with the injury to his eye that the accident produced. His left eye would refuse to focus on his target, and as the years went by, he lost almost all sight in it.

Considering how important depth perception is to a golfer in hitting the ball and judging distances, it was a severe handicap, yet one he never shared with the press. [118]

He still hit quality shots from tee to green, but once there, trouble started. "It was a nerves situation, and it was embarrassing for me out there in front of people."[119] Friend John Derr remembered Hogan telling him the one thing that signified a great golfer was control. "First off, you must control yourself, your mind," Hogan said. "Then you control your muscles, you control your club. And if you control your club, you can control your ball. That's all golf is: control."[120] But by the mid-1950s, Hogan had lost control on the greens.

At the U.S. Open at Oak Hill in 1956, he needed pars on the last two holes to tie Cary Middlecoff but missed a 30-inch putt on the 71st hole. John Derr was in the gallery. "I had my watch on him. He stood over the ball for at least sixty-six seconds, an eternity, and finally made a terrible little stab at the ball. You could see he was in pure agony." He missed a play-off by a shot. Hogan remembered it well. "I got to where I couldn't get the putter back. I could get it through if I could get it back, but I couldn't get it back! I would just stand there and shake, and it wouldn't move. And people would say, 'Oh, for crissake, hit it!' I was saying to myself, 'For crissake, hit it!'"[121]

Even though he claimed he was retiring from tournament golf, he really didn't, even though his putting continued to be abysmal at times. At the 1960 Masters, he would say, "Every time I stand over the ball I feel like the hole is filled with my corpuscles"—as if his blood and cells were draining out of him. [122] But two months later, he held together well enough to almost win a fifth Open at Cherry Hills.

Tied for the lead on the 71st hole, his third shot on the par five was hit a bit heavy and carried just over the water hazard but then slowly rolled back in. He was able to play out to 15 feet but missed the putt. With that bogey, the wind went out of his sails. A tee shot into another hazard on the last hole led to a seven, when two pars would have put him in a play-off with Arnold Palmer. In an interview with Ken Venturi in 1983, Hogan admitted the disappointment of that moment had never left him. "I find myself waking up at night thinking about that shot, right today. Well, that's been twenty-three years ago and there isn't a month that goes by that doesn't cut my guts out."[123]

Jack Nicklaus, who was paired with Hogan that final day, recalled that Ben "handled himself really well, right down to the end, and he was still the same person, the same gentleman at the end as he was at the beginning. I admired him for that in him, and I enjoyed that."[124] Nicklaus had first become aware of Hogan when he first took up golf as a 10-year-old. His teacher Jack Grout had toured with Hogan, and that experience influenced his approach with Jack. "He had a lot of influence on my left-to-right ball flight," claimed Nicklaus. "Grout and I worked hard against the hook, and Hogan had a lot to do with it."[125]

Hogan played his last tour event in 1971. A year earlier he had played with Lee Trevino at Houston in 1970, where he finished ninth—along with Trevino. "We were paired in the final round and he began the day four shots out of the lead," said Trevino, "and birdied four of the first seven holes. His ball always went straight to the flag. . . . This man must have been unbelievable when he was out there all the time."[126]

In retirement, Hogan devoted himself to his company and continued to play and practice for his own enjoyment. He would go to Shady Oaks, built by his good friend Marvin Leonard and opened in 1958, every day for lunch. "You hear stories about me beating my brains out practicing, but the truth is, I was enjoying myself. I couldn't wait to get up in the morning so I could hit balls. I'd be at the practice tee at the crack of dawn, hit balls for a few hours, then take a break and get right back to it. And I still thoroughly enjoy it. When I'm hitting the ball where I want, hard and crisply—when anyone is—it's a joy that very few people experience."[127]

He would share that enjoyment in the last decade of his life with a junior member of Shady Oaks. Kris Tschetter was a freshman at Texas Christian University when she met Hogan. An outgoing person, she was not intimidated by his aura and one day said hello to the 73-year-old icon. Later, he saw her practicing and took to her, telling her to keep working at it. Thus began a friendship that would last until his death 12 years later, one that was more like a father and daughter than teacher and pupil.

Hogan would practice with Tschetter, hitting a few balls and then going out and picking them up himself. She was surprised that he still loved to practice because she could tell he was in pain. "Sometimes he would wince when he swung," she'd remember, "and sometimes I'd see him catch himself when his knees would almost buckle. He would never talk about it, even if I asked."[128] Hogan's personal physician, Dr. Jim Murphy, would say that all Hogan would use for the pain was Tylenol.

"He was just pretty tough, I can tell you that. I can't remember him complaining much about pain. But I knew he was in a lot of pain."[129]

Contrary to the cold man most portrayed him as, she found a man with a sense of humor and a kind heart. "Mr. Hogan was naturally shy and with his fame came cautiousness, so meeting new people made him a bit uneasy." But to those who gained his confidence, he was a warm and loyal friend. Tommy Bolt contended, "You have to give Ben a chance, that's all he wants. He's the friendliest guy in the world, but most of these guys either don't want to believe it or they're scared to approach him."[130]

Kris Tschetter wasn't afraid to get to know him. They would practice together, lunch together, talk about her boyfriends and family. He took her under his wing, as he had done Ken Venturi in the late 1950s. When she made it to the LPGA Tour, he encouraged her and even came out to watch her when she had a chance to win the U.S. Women's Open when it was held at Colonial in 1991.

When she asked him once why he didn't let more people see the lighter side of him, he explained that when he was playing, the only way he could succeed was to focus on what he was doing and it carried over to the rest of his life. He believed galleries paid their money to see good golf, not "an affable clown or a floor show," as he said in 1955. "But my outwardly cold, reserved manner did not make me the gallery favorite on the circuit."[131]

His accident changed things, as he received thousands of letters from fans wishing him a speedy recovery. "They gave me a life with an entirely new meaning. I knew that I had never taken a good look at them before. From that day on, I promised myself that if I were ever fortunate enough to walk on a golf course once more, I would never become so determined that I would again neglect all human values."[132] He was still tough as nails and not universally loved, but others did see the human values he spoke of.

Mickey Van Gerbig, former Florida state amateur champion, recalled Hogan coming to a player's barbeque at the 1973 Trans-Mississippi Amateur. "He sat there for two hours answering questions. And he was funny, too. He told Ben [Crenshaw] and me we needed haircuts. He was very private, but that didn't mean he looked at everybody like they were jerks."[133]

Hogan's life was golf, and after his playing days, he put his time and energy into his company. In 1960, he sold the company to American

Machine and Foundry (AMF), but he stayed on and went to the office every day. AMF sold it in 1984 to private investor Irwin Jacobs, who in turn sold it four years later to Cosmo World, a Japanese firm. In 1992, Cosmo sold it to Bill Goodwin, who moved the plant to Virginia.

This was a crushing blow to Hogan. On the day before the plant in Fort Worth closed in June 1993, he turned the lights out and put his hand on the wall, letting it linger a long time, as if saying goodbye to a loved one he'd never see again. "Don't ever grow old," he repeatedly told his secretary Sharon Rea, who was there to witness it. The new owners legally prevented him from starting a new company under his own name, which was the final straw, claimed Rea. "That just finally broke his heart and spirit."[134]

John Mahaffey, a fellow Texan and 1978 PGA champion, remembered an occasion when Hogan gave a glimpse of his emotional side. "I was at a testimonial dinner—there were probably twenty-five pros there—when he broke down and cried because he was losing his company. . . . It was pitiful to see him break down in tears."[135]

Kris Tschetter had her own experiences with a side of Hogan most never saw. One day they were discussing a friend of hers who was having some problems, and she mentioned that the friend had a tough childhood. "'Tough time?' Hogan said quietly. 'I'll tell you about a tough time. Imagine a little boy walking into a room as. . .' His voice trailed off, but he stuck out his index finger like a gun and made an unmistakable gesture of a man shooting himself." Tschetter said tears welled up in his eyes, and the shattered look on his face was one she would never forget. Until then, she hadn't known about his father's suicide. "Mr. Hogan, what do you mean?" she asked. He waved his hands and said, "Never mind." Not knowing what to say, she simply gave him a hug. "Never mind," he said again, and the subject would never be broached again.[136]

That Tschetter did not know the circumstances of Hogan's father's death was not surprising. Valerie didn't even learn about it until they were married, when his mother told a writer.[137] Hogan had adored his father, according to Valerie, and the suicide affected his childhood and indeed his later adult life. Hogan's chauffer Elizabeth Hudson shared many conversations with him in his later years. "He said he spent his whole life wondering why his daddy did that," she'd recall, "because he loved his father very much. . . . You could tell that he'd spent his whole life tryin' to figure that out, why his father did that. It bothered him terribly, not knowing."[138]

His father's death made him less trusting of people and made him somewhat dour and serious, not hard to understand. Yet he was not an unfriendly person according to those who knew him best. "He always had liked people," said Jimmy Demaret in 1954, "but his temperament never permitted him to step out and grab a man by the hand to say hello. He seemed to feel he was forcing himself on people, and the only reason they would talk to him was because of his success as a professional golfer."[139]

After the accident, Demaret said that changed, but Hogan would remain wary of people for the rest of his life. Ken Venturi contended that if "you didn't like him, you never met him," adding that what "people fail to appreciate about Ben is that he is a very shy and a very humble man. Those simple qualities have so often been misinterpreted."[140]

Shyness was a quality Kris Tschetter noticed in Hogan as well, but she and others also saw his kindness. Niece Valerie Harriman remembered Hogan as a warm and friendly man. "Children have a natural instinct about these things," she said of her childhood. "It was clear that this man . . . really loved children." Another niece, Jacqueline Hogan Towery (brother Royal's daughter), said Ben loved her "as much as an uncle could love a niece. When we were at dinner he would reach over, hold and pat my hand, and tell me how much he loved me. We really had a great relationship."[141]

The people at Shady Oaks also saw the caring side of Hogan. Charles Hudson, a waiter at the club, recalled driving Hogan to get fitted for a suit. "When he was through, he told the tailor to fit me for a suit, too." Rosalva Rodriguez, a bartender there in the early 1980s, told of the time her sister Rosalinda was shot in a mugging. Hogan "raised money from the members—about $9,000 or $10,000 in a month's time." Rodriguez added that he took an interest in their lives. "He took time to talk to us. He'd talk to us about our families, if we were married, had children, you know."[142]

Some people only remember Ben Hogan as the cold and calculating man who surgically dissected golf courses. He had a good sense of humor, but John Derr claimed Hogan never wanted the public to see that side of him.[143] Valerie Harriman remembered Hogan attending a debutant ball with her. "There was Uncle Ben, the famous Iceman, dancing with some other debs on top of a ballroom table," all laughing, and "having the time of their lives."[144] George Archer played with Hogan for the first time during the last round of the 1967 Masters. Hogan, who had shot a 66 in the third round and was close to the lead, surprised Archer with his behavior by talking to him as they walked down the first fairway. "He was very cordial that day. We talked quite a few times while sitting on benches that day. The whole time I'm thinking. 'Is this the Ben Hogan I've read and heard about?'"[145]

The man Kris Tschetter knew was polite and humble. "Mr. Hogan wanted to be remembered for being a gentleman," she'd say.[146] She considered herself fortunate to practice and play with him and wondered what he must have been like in his prime. She asked him if he ever hit the ball as well after the accident. "Not even close," was his immediate response. When once reminiscing about the late 1940s with friend Bill Flynn, he seemed almost bemused by that period. "He'd say, 'Bill, it was a hell of a thing: It wouldn't matter what shot I tried, I hardly ever missed one.'"[147]

The accident changed all that. Hogan once told Carol Mann, World Golf Hall of Famer, that from the day of the accident he never knew a day without pain. He changed his swing to accommodate his "new" legs and carried on. "Ben never again felt really good physically on the golf course," claimed Ken Venturi. "Something was different. He overcame it with his mind and his guts and his talent, but he knew he had lost something."[148] Valerie said at the end of her life: "Ben was cheated out of years of golf by the accident. We always looked at it as how fortunate he was to play again, that God let him live. But, as he got older, there was a sense of loss. There was sadness. He would have loved to have played forever."[149]

He couldn't play forever, but because of his friendship with Kris Tschetter, we are able to know about his last round of golf, nine holes on the back side of Shady Oaks played August 28, 1986, with Kris and two of her college teammates. He shot a 36 that day from the back tees with 2 birdies and 15 putts and joked with Kris that he'd play more if he could always putt that well.[150] Although he'd hit balls at times for another five years, this was the last time he played, as health issues would soon overwhelm him.

The following year, he almost died after his appendix burst. He spent nearly seven weeks in the hospital and lost 30 pounds. That same year, he agreed to an interview with *Golf Digest* magazine, and in a wide-ranging back and forth with Nick Seitz, he was asked if he had ever gone through a long slump in his prime. "This sounds stupid," he answered, "but I thought I was always in a slump."[151] Hogan was never fully secure in his own abilities and had to constantly work to maintain what he had.

Ben confessed to *Sports Illustrated* in 1955: "I have never achieved what I thought was success. Golf to me is a business, a livelihood in doing the thing that I like to do. I don't like the glamour. I just like the game."[152] It was difficult to get old and not be able to compete for tournaments and play the game as he had. Shady Oaks pro Mike Wright recalled Hogan in his final years, remembering how on days when he didn't practice he would go to the bag room and "just hold his clubs, just feel them." The last time Wright recalled him hitting balls was around 1991. One day, out of the blue, the 78-year-old Hogan came to the golf shop and asked for his driver. He had three balls in his hand, and he went out to the back tee on the 10th, a 380-yard par 4. He hit the balls—with a wooden driver with a very stiff steel shaft—and they all landed 260–265 yards out within about 30 feet of each other. He went out to pick up the balls and gave the club back to Wright. It was his goodbye to the game.[153]

In 1995, Hogan had surgery for colon cancer, from which he never fully recovered. As bad as this was, an even worse condition was afflicting him. Around 1992, Kris Tschetter noticed that his memory was slipping. He'd be sitting at his table in the clubhouse and say "Looks like the rain's going to blow in late this afternoon." Then 15 minutes later, he'd repeat himself.[154] Hogan's symptoms were masked by his regimented routine, but Valerie knew something was wrong. When he drove around Fort Worth for four hours but hadn't remembered where he went, Valerie took his car keys from him.

Dr. Murphy used to check in with him after his colon surgery. "I went by every week or two weeks—almost every week the last two years. We'd shoot the bull, but you know he had Alzheimer's, and he couldn't remember anything." Attorney Dee Kelly recalled one of the last times he updated the Hogans' wills. "Ben could impressively remember in detail everything he'd ever done on a golf course or an oil well deal he'd made forty years ago, but he couldn't remember what he said to me five minutes before."[155]

Valerie spoke cautiously of her husband's condition, telling reporters he'd talk about hitting balls, then forget. "Naturally there are times when he's a little depressed because he cannot do what he once did," she said.

"When you stop to think, most everything has been taken from him. It's a marvel to me that he smiles and still sees the humor in things." Dr. Murphy wanted Ben to see more people, but Valerie didn't want them to see her husband in this condition. She became more protective and was jealous of anyone who got close to him, telling him he couldn't be all things to all people.[156]

"He simply didn't understand what was happening to him," said chauffeur Elizabeth Hudson. He would ask her why nobody came to visit him, and it tore at her heart. "Mrs. Hogan would say he wasn't up to having visitors. It was always the same. Every day they came, seems like, and every day she said no. And he got a little bit sadder each time." Valerie's sister Sarah had once warned Elizabeth, "'Everything has to be her way. Valerie's always been that way.' And, I found that to be pretty true."[157]

The dedication Valerie showed for her husband their entire lives together now became a curse at times, as she felt she knew what was best for him. Hogan had said in 1953 that she was "a wonderful wife, partner, companion, trainer and adviser who deserves more credit than I can possibly give her for any success I've had."[158] Since they were teenagers, each had been dependent on the other. "He gave her the strength she needed to face people," Hogan's great-niece Charissa Christopher said, "and she gave him the unqualified belief in him that helped Uncle Ben become the Ben Hogan people now read about." She added, "He was shy and very sweet. As he got older, this sweeter side of him came out. Unfortunately, Aunt Valerie went exactly the opposite way." She may not have meant to do it, but she knew no other way.[159]

Dr. Murphy claimed that, "in a sense Valerie was pretty paranoid, and she was very protective of Ben." She constantly blamed Murphy for his medical treatment of her husband and didn't allow Ben to have radiation or chemotherapy treatments after the cancer surgery that may have prolonged his life. With his onset of Alzheimer's, she was even more protective.[160]

Valerie didn't want him to smoke or leave the house, but when she'd go out to attend to Hogan's business, Elizabeth Hudson would let Ben sit in his car and smoke his cigarettes. "She never knew anything about it, but it made him extremely happy." He would talk to her about his life and how he missed going to church. "One more thing he missed," Hudson lamented. Hogan's secretary Sharon Rea, when reflecting on Valerie's treatment of her husband, conceded, "Whatever else is true, she gave her life to that man, and he returned her love for all that loyalty."[161]

Unlike some Alzheimer's patients who may demonstrate angry outbursts, Kris Tschetter saw an "added sweetness" in Hogan. "He was much quicker to smile and seemed much softer around people."[162] When Hogan's brother Royal died at the end of 1996, it was a further blow, and his health continued to decline. Even through all of this, when Kris Tschetter saw him in the hospital just months before he died, he told her the story of Henry Picard offering to loan him money in the lean years. All those years later, and through the devastating fog of Alzheimer's disease, he never forgot the kind act of a fellow professional who had believed in him and told him he had a swing that could beat the world.[163]

When Ben Hogan died July 25, 1997, the golfing world lost another icon. At his funeral, Dr. Charles Sanders, associate minister of the University Christian Church, read from the book of Romans: "'Suffering produces endurance and endurance produces character and character produces hope.' I think Ben Hogan's life underlined the truth of that passage."[164]

When asked what it was that drew him to Hogan, Henry Picard once said, "I was never quite sure what that was but I liked Ben. He kept to himself but he had an air of dignity that appealed to me. He wasn't afraid to work."[165] Johnny Miller, like Hogan and Picard, a member of the World Golf Hall of Fame, claimed that there never has "been a golfer who influenced the swing more than Ben Hogan. In fact, if you named the next three guys they wouldn't be as influential as Ben Hogan. I studied his book as if it were true scripture."[166]

Dave Marr, 1965 PGA champion and longtime television broadcaster, said of Hogan's passing, "We lost the unicorn. Did he really exist? Valerie laughed when I said that, but it's true." The enigmatic unicorn, Ben Hogan himself, once said, "I have always thought of golf as the best of all games—the most interesting, the most demanding, the most rewarding. I cannot begin to express the satisfaction I have always felt in being part of a game with such a wonderful flavor and spirit."[167]

Hogan's own spirit lives on in the game. The Ben Hogan Award—given to an individual who overcomes serious injury or illness to actively be involved in golf—was created in his honor in 1954. One of its recipients is Dennis Walters, a famous golf trick-shot artist who tours the country with his entertaining show. When Walters was paralyzed in a tragic accident in 1974, he received a letter from Ben Hogan. In part it read: "We know the human body is a great machine and can absorb many shocks. Even though it may seem slow, recovery is possible provided one has faith, hope, will and determination."[168]

This sentiment inspired Walters, as it had Hogan. Doctors had told Ben that he would never walk again, but he knew they were wrong. "If you want it bad enough, you can do it," he believed. "You can do anything you set your mind to."[169] These words are fitting testimony to the spirit Ben Hogan demonstrated his whole life in overcoming considerable physical and emotional shocks to become the man who still captures our imaginations today.

4

BABE DIDRIKSON ZAHARIAS

"Spiritual Muscle"

I feel as though I have been a prisoner in this thing. I've been like that gal who fought to get the women the vote, you know, the one who started the battle for women's suffrage.[1]
—Babe Didrikson Zaharias

Discouragement was not within her psychological makeup, and she possessed courage which would not admit the thought of failure.[2]
—Louis Didrikson

Babe Zaharias approached the green slowly, the spikes on her shoes dragging across the fairways of the Tam O'Shanter Country Club outside Chicago. It was the third round of the All-American tournament, and she was only at the fifth hole, but both her legs and swing were a little shaky. After three-putting from four feet and cringing over opening rounds of 82-85, her resolve was weakening. She walked to the next tee, sat down, and buried her face in her hands. Tears of pain and frustration rolled down her weathered cheeks, as her husband, George, and playing partner Betty Dodd tried to comfort her. Betty put a hand on Babe's shoulder, hesitated, and knelt down next to her, telling her quietly there would be no shame in withdrawing. "I don't pick up the ball!" Babe pushed back. "I'm not a quitter."[3]

The feisty response was typical. Two good shots on the next hole put Zaharias on the green, where another three-putt followed. Feeling she was letting down thousands of cancer patients who were looking to her for inspiration, Babe would remember this as the "blackest of moments." She whispered a prayer to God, asking for the strength to continue.[4] She got up and kept going, shot an inspired 34 on the back nine and the next day finished the tournament in 15th place. This was a remarkable accomplishment for a woman who only 14 weeks earlier had undergone drastic surgery for cancer of the rectum, surgery that had left her with a colostomy bag hanging from her waist.

Time magazine commented that "with doctors marveling at her recuperative powers (the Babe calls it 'spiritual muscle'), she was back on the golf course," trying to win tournaments. Babe contended, "I'm just going to keep walking around the course and see if I can get in shape for the world."[5] She was born to compete, and cancer was just another obstacle in a life that had been full of challenges. The great Bryon Nelson once observed, "In Texas we call someone like Babe Zaharias 'a piece of work,' but as brash as she could be at times, she sure did have the talent to back it up."[6] Babe was a woman the public loved, but her private friends were few, and beneath her bravado was a stinging insecurity she never quite overcame. She was driven to win at everything she did.

Mildred Ella Didriksen was born June 26, 1911, in Port Arthur, Texas. Her parents, Ole and Hannah, had welcomed six other children before she arrived. The family moved to Beaumont when she was four years old, and it was there, on hardscrabble sand lots and dusty basketball courts, that she became one of the most famous female athletes in history. Mildred, given the nickname Babe by her mother, grew up in an era that was generally unsympathetic to women. As a female athlete, she was looked upon by many as a freak. She was insulted, ignored, and laughed at, treatment that would make her tough and even bullying at times—character traits she maintained throughout her life.[7]

From the start, Babe was rambunctious and obstinate. Her father, a carpenter, built a crib for her that she was forever trying to escape. Ole once remarked to his wife that he didn't think he could build a crib that would hold her.[8] As a child, she liked being with people and doing things more than attending school and reading books (unless it was a rule book to some game). She loved running wherever she went and playing games with the boys in the neighborhood.

Raymond Alford, a neighbor who was himself a good athlete and someone she admired, recalled their childhood. "All of us from the South

End were poor. Not on welfare, but darn poor." He remembered that when kids gathered on the sandlot Saturday mornings, Babe would always be there. Even though she was the only girl, she was also one of the first to be picked for various baseball or football teams.[9] She loved being the center of attention. Her older brother, Louis said that, from an early age, she wanted to be "where the people were. She would cross the street to join a group and participate in the conversation. More often, she would dominate it."[10]

Beaumont's South End was a dead-end place to live, neither particularly pretty or comfortable, and it shaped both Babe's stubborn temperament and physical talent. Equally influential was her father Ole. Although no athlete himself, he believed in keeping his children active. "Get plenty of exercise and keep your bowels clear," was his advice to them. He did his part by building a backyard gym, telling people, "I'll build good bodies for them." Babe would contend in later life that her father "was more responsible than anyone for making me a great athlete."[11]

As a young girl, Babe knew exactly what she wanted to do when she grew up: the greatest athlete that ever lived. Her brother Louis recalled, "If she ever heard about something involving use of the hands or legs, she wouldn't rest until she had given it a whirl."[12] As she grew and came to appreciate her natural athletic abilities, she saw sports as a way of escaping her dreary life in Beaumont. Until that day came, she was intent on finding work to help the family.

At 12 she got her first afterschool job at a fig packing plant and the following year found one sewing potato gunnysacks for a penny a bag. Come payday, she would keep a nickel or dime for herself and give the rest to her mother. "I want you to buy little things for yourself," she would tell her mother, whom she adored. Instead, Hannah told her daughter to buy something for herself. Babe bought a harmonica after earning money cutting a neighbor's yard, which she would play often and with considerable notoriety to the end of her life.[13]

It was in high school that she changed the spelling of her last name from Didriksen to Didrikson. She'd explain that she didn't want people to think she was a Swede, as if there was something wrong with that.[14] Babe Zaharias fit the description of a tomboy, happiest when sweating and grunting and playing any kind of sport—and even better when competing against boys. By the time she reached Beaumont High School, people knew about this tall, thin girl with the flat chest, muscular legs, and thin-lipped smile. She was a friendly, rowdy soul who enjoyed practical jokes and was also blessed with raw talent and skill in widely diverse sports. [15]

Babe's gift for sports was resented by her female classmates, which didn't bother Babe, since she had no use for "girly" things. "She should have been a boy," contended Sigrid Hill, a classmate. "She was tough." Ruth Scurlock, wife of one of Babe's media allies, noted that her "very excellence at sports made her unacceptable to other girls. She was an alien in her own land, believe me." Belligerence was an intrinsic part of her personality as a youngster trying to prove how tough she was and would turn to violence often when crossed. [16]

Insecure about her looks and social background, athletics were a way of gaining respect. Betsy Rawls, who was Phi Beta Kappa and competed against Babe, saw it this way: "Well, Babe grew up being a fairly unattractive female I think. . . . And I think she just felt like nothing, except sports . . . made her feel like a worthwhile person and that was a sure way of proving herself." Raymond Alford, a friend, claimed that sports were an equalizing agent, and he believed that's what "carried Babe through and made her work so hard." [17]

In the classroom, Babe was not an outstanding student but wasn't as poor as some have portrayed her to be. She got mostly Bs and Cs, along with a few As in physical-education courses. Her life was in the arena, where she was driven to succeed. As she once said, all her life she "always had the urge to do things better than anybody else." [18] Her yearbook photos revealed a serious figure wearing a grim expression under her Dutch boy haircut. Even then, she was all business.

While a member of the high-school basketball team, she met Bill "Tiny" Scurlock of the *Beaumont Journal*, who became a great booster and her early biographer. He described her as "flamboyant, down-to-earth, apparently gruff at times, perhaps, but considerate, humorous, friendly, warm-hearted and generous." [19] For the next several years, he would help build the myth of Babe Didrikson, although she was often the driver of her own publicity campaign. It was Babe's performance on the basketball court that brought the greatest attention and had the best possibility of turning her ability into a paid career as an athlete.

In the days before the existence of college athletic programs for women, the Amateur Athletic Union (AAU) provided a structure for women's teams playing each other on a national scale. The AAU, founded in 1888 to establish standards and uniformity in amateur sports, worked closely with the Olympic movement in its early years to prepare athletes for the Olympic games. The AAU also conducted basketball tournaments; the National Men's Championship began in 1897, the first Women's National Championship in 1926. Companies formed teams as a way of giving employees a chance to play organized ball and to also put the company profile before the public. Scouts would scour the land looking for good players, and Babe Didrikson became a highly-sought-after talent as she dominated her high-school competition.

Colonel Melvorne Jackson McCombs, manager of the athletic program at Employers Casualty Company in Dallas, took notice of Babe. After convincing her parents to allow her to leave home, he signed her to play for his team immediately upon the completion of her senior year at Beaumont High. Babe's sister Lillie remembered the discussions that took place. When Ole made up his mind, he told Babe, "Goddammit! You go!" Although Hannah hated to see Babe move away from home, she sided with her husband. After all, they had come from Norway in order to give their kids everything America had to offer, and this was an opportunity not to be passed up.[20] If Ole had said no, Babe most likely would have gone anyway, since when she wanted something she usually got it.

Babe left for Dallas (275 miles from Beaumont) to play basketball for the ECC Golden Cyclones the day after her last high-school game. She would work as a typist for the company—she once won a typing contest in high school averaging 86 words a minute—and was paid a salary of $75 a month, $900 per annum.[21] This was a good salary for the times, when the average household took in less than $2,000 a year. The games were popular entertainment for the people and drew one thousand to four thousand fans per game.[22]

Babe's team was not only good, but also they could destroy opponents—they beat one team 62–9 and another 82–5 (Babe scored 36 points in the latter).[23] The relationship Babe had begun with Tiny Scurlock took full flight when she arrived in Dallas, as she wrote often, asking him to publicize her exploits. Realizing her value as a commodity, she wanted to exploit it.

Coach McCombs had seen athletes come and go for 28 years but had never coached one, man or woman, who matched her natural ability. But she was also immature and petty. She was a ball hog and showboat and played for herself first and her team second. "She was out for Babe, honey—just Babe," recalled teammate Reagan Glenn years later. Glenn remembered Didrikson's physical strength and claimed she was born to run and to jump, adding that she got all the publicity and was "out for fame."[24]

After a couple of years—which included a national championship in 1931—Babe was feeling underappreciated, underpaid, and afraid her talents were going to waste. In January 1932, she wrote to Tiny Scurlock, admitting she was deliberately playing poorly and missing shots on purpose, "'cause I don't want to play with them for nothing."[25] She complained about her pay, telling Scurlock that $90 a month was too little to live on. In fact, it was almost as much as a schoolteacher was making in 1932 and double that of steel workers.

In the depths of the Great Depression, with 24 percent of the people in the United States unemployed, the 21-year-old Didrikson was whining about being underpaid.[26] Her self-absorbed thinking was evident, as she told Scurlock she had to make her athletic ability pay off economically. "I'm tired of working and giving them all this advertisement for nothing." Despite her temporary "strike," Babe returned to her normal good play soon thereafter and made the All-American team for the third-straight year.[27]

In the spring, McCombs, knowing the depth of Didrikson's talents, resurrected ECC's track-and-field team to showcase her talents. As Babe told it, "The colonel decided to have a track team, and I was it." She wrote Tiny Scurlock, saying that right after the track season she was going to train for the 1932 Olympics with fervor and "show everyone I have ants in my pants."[28] She would make good on that promise.

McCombs entered Babe in the AAU's Women's National meet, which served as the trials for the Olympic Games to be held that summer in Los Angeles. Over the course of two and a half hours, she won five of the eight events she entered for 30 total points and beat the next-best team (with 22 athletes) by 8 points.[29] Sportswriter Paul Gallico notes, "I cannot think of any male athlete, with the possible exception of Jim Thorpe, who has come even close to spread-eagling a track meet all by himself in this manner." She was almost superhuman, people thought, and being a woman made her even more "different."[30]

Didrikson often "wore a half grin that was equal parts friendly and cocky, conveying a mix of mirth and contempt," writes biographer Don Van Natta. She was a masculine-looking young woman, with a prominent nose and jaw and had a unisex haircut that made her appear even manli-

Babe Didrikson Zaharias, circa 1950. From an early age, she loved to compete and win at whatever she did, first in high school and later in the Olympics. When she turned to golf, fellow player Betty Hicks summarized Babe's aggressive demeanor on the course, in the heat of battle, this way: "Babe Zaharias was openly, hostilely, aggressively, bitterly, laughingly, jokingly, viciously and even sometimes lovingly competitive." *Courtesy USGA. All Rights Reserved.*

er.[31] Her five-foot five-inch frame was 130 pounds of sinewy muscle. She reveled in her physical prowess, and her confidence knew no bounds. After winning the AAU national meet, she said to herself, "I guess I'll take the Olympics too."[32]

Her cockiness rubbed a lot of people the wrong way, especially her fellow competitors, but to her it was just the truth. As she told the *Saturday Evening Post* years later, "But I *am* a natural. I've always been real flexible and I don't tighten up in the clutch."[33] Al Besselink, who teamed with Babe to win a team tournament in 1952, backed up this assessment. "She had the [nerve] of a Trojan. The more pressure you put on her the better she played."[34]

The same *Post* article maintained that "Babe accepted the early popular concept of herself as a tomboy and muscle moll with a grimly set jaw. Her temperament and the body Nature had given her made her a 'loner.'"[35] Her public image would evolve over time, but this was an accurate portrayal of who she was in 1932. Didrikson went to the Olympics and won the gold medal in the javelin and 80-meter hurdles and the silver in the high jump. What's more remarkable is how the other women on the American team came to detest her.[36]

Before she even arrived in Los Angeles, bad blood was stirred. When the train carrying the team stopped in Albuquerque, Babe found a bicycle next to the Western Union office and rode it around the platform. Evelyne Hall, whom Babe beat in a controversial finish in the 80-meter hurdle, remembered Didrikson yelling to the people gathered there, "'Ever heard of Babe Didrikson? You will!' She was exactly like Muhammad Ali even then. Such a braggart."[37]

Kathleen Speer Peace, who played with Babe on the AAU teams, believed that her cockiness was a defense. "I think she exaggerated her roughness," claimed Peace, "because there wasn't time, in the world she had chosen, to slow down. Most likely, she never thought she could smooth it off, and instead elevated it to a sort of red badge, born of subconscious anger."[38]

Regarding her competition, Didrikson told the press she didn't wish to demean her teammates' abilities but explained she had an advantage over them since she grew up "competing against wiry, tough boys and that gave me experience that most of the girl runners today never had."[39] After she beat Hall in the hurdles, many members of the team hoped she would be beaten in the high jump. Jean Shirley was Didrikson's rival in that event. "She constantly wanted to be on center stage," recalled Shirley years later. "I have often wondered *why* she was so obnoxious." Hall recalled, "We were very high-strung and we put a lot of pressure on Jean to beat this obnoxious girl."[40] They were pleased when Babe finished second after the judges determined she went over the bar head first (which was illegal at the time) after she had tied Shirley at a height of 5 feet 5¼ inches.

Mary Carew, a 400-meter relay runner, admitted that everything Babe "bragged about she could do. . . . She wasn't liked by the other girls because nobody likes a bragger, but she didn't care, evidently." In a 1991 interview, Peggy Kirk Bell seemed to agree with the last part of Carew's observation, saying, "I don't think Babe really cared what you said about her as long as you spelled her name right. She would say that frequently."[41]

Babe put her teammates off, not only by her brashness but also because she was masculine. "We weren't used to having any girls that were her type," said Evelyne Hall. "Most of the girls were ladylike."[42] Babe may not have cared what people thought of her, but the notion that she was less than a lady would haunt her in the years to come. The Olympics thrust her upon the national stage, and the press helped build Babe's pedestal. She became a working-class heroine; she talked like them and shared their backgrounds.

Grantland Rice, the legendary sportswriter, saw Didrikson's performance in the Olympics and was introduced to her. He asked if she'd like to join him and fellow sportswriters Paul Gallico, Westbrook Pegler, and Braven Dyer for a round of golf. A game was arranged at Brentwood Country Club, and the legend was retold for many years that, having never swung a golf club before, she shot in the low 80s that day. The truth was, she had played the game in high school and went around that day in about 95 strokes.

Bea Lytle, Didrikson's high-school physical-education teacher, introduced her to golf when she was a freshman and recalled in 1975 that Babe's first attempts to hit a golf ball were not totally successful. "She could outdrive me after a while," said Lytle, "but it took quite a few rounds." Also, while Babe was working for Employers Casualty, she mentioned to Tiny Scurlock in a 1931 letter that the president of the company was giving her free golf lessons at Dallas Country Club.[43]

Didrikson made it sound as if golf was completely foreign to her, which helped craft the legend to her liking. She did show promise, however. Olin Dutra, the club pro at Brentwood who would win the 1934 U.S. Open, gave her a few tips before teeing off and remembered she "had great timing, the kind of timing you can't teach." Rice believed that if Babe took up the game seriously, "she would be a world beater in a short time."[44] Babe must have agreed, for soon after, she told a reporter in her home town that golf was what she was going to tackle next. She said she had no time for a vacation and had to practice her golf. "You see, I'm planning on winning the women's championship."[45]

Less than a novice, she was audacious enough to believe she could be the U.S. Women's Amateur champion, but she still needed a job to make a living. Anything was considered, as long as there was money in it for her, her parents, and family. For awhile after the Olympics, she did a vaudeville show. When the AAU banned her temporarily after her words appeared in an advertisement for Dodge automobiles, without her knowledge or consent, she decided to give golf her full attention. Fortunately, she had a fallback position at Employers Casualty if things didn't work out (they raised her pay to $300 a month after the Olympics), and indeed she would go on and off its payroll a number of times. [46]

After saving $1,800, she headed to California in the spring of 1933 in search of a pro to help her with her game. She told a reporter that it was her intention to win the U.S. Women's Amateur championship within three years. [47] In Los Angeles, she found Stan Kertes, a young pro who was the teacher of many Hollywood celebrities, including Bing Crosby and Bob Hope. "Babe was like Arnold Palmer, she bulled the ball around," Kertes recalled years later. He recognized her talent and agreed to teach her for free. "I worked with her in Los Angeles and Chicago, mostly on style. I tried to give her a picture swing." [48]

A routine day began at 9 a.m. and lasted until late in the night. "Babe used to hit a thousand, fifteen hundred balls every day," said Kertes. "We'd work until eleven o'clock at night. . . . For eight months she hit ball after ball until her hands began to bleed." [49] Babe needed the practice. As she told a reporter in 1933, "Most things come natural to me, and golf was the first that ever gave me much trouble." Her brother Louis would maintain that Kertes "put her through the mill. Probably he was a greater influence on her golf, than was anybody else." [50]

Babe returned to her job at Employers Casualty in the fall, and when her father took ill and needed an operation at the end of the year, she needed to do something to make more money. When Iowa promoter Ray Doan offered her $1,000 a month to be part of a barnstorming basketball team, she eagerly accepted. One of three women on the team—Babe Didrikson's All-Americans—she played 91 games from the Midwest to New England. When that tour ended in the spring of 1934, she then joined another of Doan's teams, a men's baseball team called the House of David. She was a pitcher and went from coast to coast with the team as it played two hundred games to the end of the year. As the only girl on the team, she helped draw big crowds, justifying her $1,500-a-month salary. [51]

Babe's exploits mixing with male athletes drew attention to her less-than-feminine ways. Paul Gallico, who had played with Babe in that famous round after the Olympics, became one of her detractors. In an article for *Vanity Fair* in October 1932, he described her as a "muscle moll" and "girl-boy" and more than a dozen times used the word "boy" to describe her. Gallico also said she was the vanguard of a breed of women "who made possible deliciously frank and biological discussions in the newspapers as to whether this or that woman athlete should be addressed as Miss, Mrs., Mr., or It."[52]

Gallico added that because she was not pretty she couldn't "compete with the other girls in the very ancient and honored sport of mantrapping." Westbrook Pegler, who played with Didrikson, Gallico, and Grantland Rice after the 1932 Olympics, said that "Babe probably did not know it but she was a beautiful woman—from the mouth down. I certainly do not mean to be unkind in saying this," he added, but he was unkind.[53] Sentiments like these stung Babe, especially when writers said she didn't have much interest in men. She dug in, becoming more arrogant and self-centered than before. She also began to act more mannish and seemed to glory in a coarse demeanor.

If she could not be feminine and pretty, then she would be as absolutely unfeminine and unattractive as possible, just to spite her critics. One Sunday feature in a Dallas newspaper made note of her "almost wholly masculine" features and "husky voice." When the reporter tried to ask her if she wore brassieres and other feminine lingerie, she was indignant. "The answer is no. What do you think I am, a sissy?" To her, "sissy" was synonymous with a lady "loser."[54]

Being thrust into the national spotlight was a heavy burden for an unsophisticated, uneducated young woman to carry, and Babe had difficulty coping. Arthur Daley of the *New York Times*, after meeting Babe in 1933 and discussing her future plans, left the interview feeling sorry for her. She came off as brittle, self-hating, and spoiled, hardly a good role model. Almost overnight, Babe became a symbol of the negative effects competitive sport could have on women. In her home state of Texas, signs were posted in women's gyms: "Don't be a muscle moll."[55]

Dr. Belle Mead Holm, a former dean of the Women's Physical Education Department at Lamar University, spoke in 1975 of how Babe had been a pioneer and how she overcame the "viciousness" and "cannibalism" displayed by women who despised her. "There had to be fierceness in her," said Holm, "a killer instinct of some kind. Babe simply had to have a warlike spirit."[56] Didrikson broke through barriers of prejudice regarding female athletes on a number of levels. Only 10 years before Babe won her gold medals, the Metropolitan AAU in New York City still barred women from running events over one-half mile because they were considered too strenuous (the reason given was that longer distances would put their reproductive health at risk).

Years later, Babe would acknowledge the strain of being a trailblazer. "I feel as though I have been a prisoner in this thing," she told *Sport* magazine in 1948. "I've been like that gal who fought to get the women the vote, you know, the one who started the battle for women's suffrage."[57] Ruth Scurlock was convinced that Babe also suffered from the added responsibility of providing assistance to her family. Babe knew there had to be money, not only for her but also her family. "They always had their hands out to her," said Scurlock, which was a source of constant strain.[58]

The years 1933 and 1934 were difficult ones for Babe. As she explained in her autobiography, these years "were a mixed-up time for me. My name had meant a lot right after the Olympic Games, but it had sort of been going down since then. I hadn't been smart enough to get into anything that would really keep me up there." When she saw her idol Bobby Jones play a rain-shortened exhibition in Houston the summer after the House of David tour ended, he "sort of fired up" her own "golf ambitions."[59]

Those ambitions had been put on hold when she toured with her basketball and baseball teams, even though she tried to hit golf balls whenever she could during off days. Now she went back to practicing full-on. Didrikson claimed that during the "first four years I played golf there wasn't one day in which I didn't hit at least a thousand" golf balls.[60] Gene Sarazen said of Babe's practice regimens in the mid-1930s, "I only know of one golfer who practiced more than Babe and that was Ben Hogan." While she was practicing her game during these "mixed-up" years, the press was slowly forgetting her. Two years after the Olympics, the *New York Evening Post*, in an article about headliners of the past, stated: "At an age when most people are wondering when the first break is going to come, Mildred Didrikson is one of our most illustrious has-beens."[61]

For a woman of Didrikson's ability and determination, who also loved being in the limelight, this was another challenge to be taken up. She would prove them wrong and turn the world of women's golf on its head. In November 1934, she felt it was time to test her game at the Fort Worth Women's Invitation. After shooting a 77 to earn medalist honors by five shots, she saw her name in the headlines. As Babe said, "It was like 1932 all over again. Even though she lost in match play the next day, she set her sights on the next year's Texas Women's Amateur. In her words, she "settled into as tough a siege as I've ever gone through for any sports event in my life."[62]

All her life she had been competing—and competing to win. From January to April of 1935, she put in 12–16 hours a day on her game. She would practice three hours before work at Employers Casualty, work on her putting on the carpet of her boss's office at lunchtime, then at 3:30 leave for the golf course for lessons and play. After dinner, she would read the golf rules book. By the time the tournament came around, anything less than victory would be unacceptable.[63] She didn't care what detractors thought of her, she just wanted to win.

If Stan Kertes helped shape Babe's golf game, a woman named Bertha Bowen would help transform her into a lady. Bertha and her husband, R. L., were prominent within Texas golf circles. She met Babe at the Fort Worth tournament, and when Babe came to play in the Texas Women's Amateur, Bertha invited her and Helen Dettweiler to stay at their house. They ended up staying three weeks. "That's how our friendship started," recalled Bowen almost 50 years later.[64]

At the time she and Didrikson met, it "wasn't ladylike to be muscular," recalled Bowen. "Of course, that's where her courage came in. I never understood how she had the strength to overlook the snubs and slights and the downright venom of a lot of women."[65] Babe accomplished her goal, winning the tournament by beating Peggy Chandler two up in the final.

It was Chandler who said before the competition began, "We really don't need any truck driver's daughters in this tournament," a clear swipe at Babe's working-class background.[66] Golf was not as democratic then as it is now, and its history in this country has been "interwoven with money, privilege, exclusivity, and social class." Bertha Bowen said that Chandler was a "fine person and a fine golfer. But Babe just didn't fit; she just didn't."[67]

Paul Gallico marveled at her win, but couldn't help taking a jab at her, hypothesizing that "maybe it was Mrs. Chandler's neat and feminine clothing that made Didrikson mad. The Texas Babe seems to be working out a lifelong vendetta on sissy girls."[68] There were many who were less than thrilled with Babe's win, given her class background and history of playing sports for pay. Peggy Chandler appealed to Joe Dey, the executive director of the United States Golf Association, asking that Babe not be allowed to "get away with this."

Dey, college educated and soon to marry into a wealthy family, may have shared the same class prejudices that Chandler had. One day after her win, the USGA declared that Babe was a professional because she had taken money for playing other sports. In that era, being a professional in one sport made you a pro in all.[69]

Didrikson could ask for reinstatement five years after her last professional appearance and then had to wait another three years to regain amateur status. Bertha Bowen believed the rich wanted to protect the game for high society. "I was just furious at those people who had been so cutting to her. The fact that she was poor and had no clothes did not mean she had to be ruled a professional." In fairness to the USGA, a precedent had been set years earlier, in 1927, when Mary K. Browne was suspended for playing tennis for money.[70]

Babe took the suspension with unexpected grace and kept working. Bertha and R. L. Bowen became like second parents to her, treating her like a daughter. Reports chronicled that Bertha took Babe to "Neiman-Marcus for seven hundred dollars' worth of new clothes, advised her on a more feminine hairdo, and applied subtle makeup." Bowen maintained that "Babe was eager to be proper."[71]

After the USGA's ban, Gene Sarazen, who had won the Masters that April, offered Didrikson $150 per appearance to tour with him. For two months, they did some 18 exhibitions in the Midwest and East Coast. "People wanted to come out and see this freak from Texas who could play golf," Sarazen would candidly recall.[72] "She was strong as an ox" and had all the physical tools to play well, he asserted, adding that she was "very intense and wanted to learn." It was a great training ground for her, as she would play with him and then go out and practice. As Didrikson remembered it, she knew she wasn't a finished golfer then, but if "I was going to be the best, I wanted to learn from the best."[73]

She loved to play to the galleries, and Sarazen said it came naturally to her, as it would later for another great Texan golfer, Lee Trevino. But Sarazen claimed Babe "was too much show business to ever develop a really sweet swing," the kind Kertes wanted to give her. Instead, she just wanted to "wallop the ball because that pleased the public."[74] This may be true, as Didrikson never had a classic style.

She hit a low, powerful shot that could bore into the wind but often failed to shift her weight to her left side properly on the follow-through. It was a "fire and fall back" method. She did love the crowd and admitted that, sometimes, "when I connect with one clean and pretty and it goes streaking down the fairway making a white line in the air like a piece of string, I turn to the gallery and say 'How'm I doin?'" She pulled them into her game, and they loved becoming part of the action.[75]

For a while Babe considered playing tennis and went into serious training for tournament competition. However, when she was told that her history of playing professional sports would make her a professional in tennis as well, she decided to stick with golf and played wherever she could. She was also fortunate to have signed a contract with sporting-goods company P. Goldsmith Sons after her USGA ban. It paid her $2,500 a year, easing her financial worries while she spent most of her time in California, working on her game.[76]

The press was also taking notice of her physical transformation under the influence of Bertha Bowen. Henry McLemore of the United Press writes of Babe in 1937: "Her hair is worn in a soft brown, curly cluster about her face. Her figure is that of a Parisian model." Paul Gallico, seeing Babe after her exhibition tour with Sarazen in 1935, claimed that he hardly recognized her, writing, "The tomboy had suddenly grown up."[77]

Although Bertha Bowen had helped her friend become more feminine in appearance, Babe still had to deal with misogynist sentiments. Muscular women were offensive and unfeminine, according to some journalists. Masculine traits also led some to wonder about her sexual orientation. "Her physique, her trousers and plain shirts, her short-cropped hair," writes biographer Susan Cayleff, "and her sheer competence in the male realm of competitive sports presented an intimidating image" to a society that saw these traits as a threat to the ideal image of femininity and put into question her sexual orientation.[78]

Didrikson said of this time that she was called a "tomboy" but noted that others were as well. Hall of Famer Patty Berg, for example, as a young girl played football with neighborhood boys in Minneapolis, including Bud Wilkinson, who would go on to coach at the University of

Oklahoma. Yet nobody inferred that she was a lesbian because of this behavior.

Babe's brother Louis recalled a conversation she once had with "an unscrupulous fellow" who pushed her into the topic of her sex life. "She responded by telling him that she wondered what would be turned up, in a check of his own personal life? That stopped the creature's wagging tongue." Babe's switch to golf helped quiet things, as it was seen as a gentile sport played by ladies, not "muscle molls." Didrikson would later tell her good friend Peggy Kirk Bell that she was glad she'd gotten into golf because it had quieted "that talk." But it was not until she married George Zaharias that such talk ended. [79]

Babe met George at the 1938 Los Angeles Open, when she was 27 and he was 29. He was a celebrity in his own right, a famous wrestler who had honed his role as a villain. "The fans hate me, but pay money to see me wrestle, probably in the hope that I'll get my neck broken."[80] They were both media hounds and hustlers and found each other instantly appealing. They soon became inseparable and married December 23, 1938.

His "manliness" reaffirmed her femininity, which helped her in the eyes of the press, and he also was wealthy enough to support her in her pursuit of her golf career. There were trade-offs, however. She gained companionship but lost control, as George ruled supreme and was over-bearing at times. [81] By the time World War II came along, George had quit wrestling and become her full time manager, and she was playing in exhibitions with Ben Hogan and Byron Nelson.

Babe was able to play in a handful of tournaments a year, and won the Women's Western Open and Women's Texas Open in 1940. She was reinstated as amateur by the USGA at the beginning of 1943. After winning two more Western Opens and another Texas Open in 1944 and 1945, she went on a tear in 1946–1947, winning 14 straight. [82] The crowning achievement in this streak was her victory in the British Ladies Amateur, won despite a chipped bone in her thumb. First played in 1893, Didrikson became the first American to win it. One disconsolate Scot, impressed by Babe's power, said, "It seems a shame to send our girls out against a game like that." Another was heard to say that he had seen Walter Hagen, Bobby Jones, and Gene Sarazen, and none of them could "hit the ball better than this girl can." The British press loved her outgoing manner with the galleries, as well as her competitive fire, and called her "Tough Babe."[83]

On August 14, 1947, Didrikson, at the height of her popularity, turned pro and hired Fred Corcoran as her manager. Corcoran, who also represented Sam Snead, Stan Musial, and Ted Williams, acknowledged that they "were great guys, but when it came to getting headlines, Babe had them all beat. She had a fantastic feel for publicity."[84] As Babe told the *Saturday Evening Post* a month later, "I haven't really learned to play golf yet," explaining that she needed to work on her accuracy and consistency.

The article also notes how she had changed since her Olympic days, both in terms of physicality and personality.[85] Readers were informed that her figure, which in the early 1930s was described as "slat-thin and flat-chested" and "born halfway between masculine flats and the rubbery curves of femininity," had developed into a shapely 38-27-37 on her 5-foot 7-inch, 140-pound frame.[86] Her manner of dress was also not as "Spartan as it once was. Perfume, lipstick and fingernail polish lie on her dressing table. Style and class hang in her closets. . . . Such frills and fripperies are a far cry from the cotton union suits she once wore, and the make-up she defiantly *didn't* wear."[87]

Jack Sher, writing for *Sport* magazine, concluded that Babe had earned a new legion of fans, who "just want to look at the Babe. There is a strangeness and mystery about her. She will always have that quality."[88] When she played an exhibition in Atlanta in 1948, teaming with Patty Berg against Louise Suggs and Dorothy Porter, six thousand people came out to watch. Bobby Jones, a Georgia native, acted as referee for the match and commented that he had never seen anything like it.

Fans were in awe of her and amazed at the way she hit the ball. "I was the first woman to play the game the way men play it," Babe claimed. "I mean to hit the ball instead of swinging at it. Now all the women do it that way. I used to outdrive the other girls from twenty to forty yards, but I'm not far ahead of them anymore."[89] The crowd also loved her personality, which was brash and confident. For her part, she loved playing to her fans, and her brother Louis maintained his sister had "a degree of ham in her. Most of all, she wanted to make people laugh, and could do it."[90] But she didn't work for free.

Babe loved money and publicity, and the two were always intertwined, for both her and George. "Ah can remember them hamburger days in Beaumont," she would say in her folksy manner. "Ah want nothin' but filets now."[91] She recognized the power of her personality, and when talk came of forming a professional tour for women, she knew she would be the main attraction. Other golfers like Patty Berg and Betty Hicks had won tournaments on a national stage, but Babe had the fire-power in her game and personality to attract spectators.

The Ladies Professional Golfers Association had its beginnings in 1949 through the efforts of Fred Corcoran, who had been the tournament director for the PGA, and L. B. Icely, president of Wilson Sporting Goods. With nine tournaments and $15,000 in prize money, it was a very modest beginning—by 2016, the number of tournaments had increased to 34 with $63 million in purses. When the LPGA formally incorporated in 1950, it had 11 charter members, with Patty Berg serving as president from 1949 to 1952 and Babe from 1953 to 1955.[92]

From the beginning, it was her show. Fred Corcoran insisted that Babe made the women's tour a success, making it clear that "she was the color, the gate attraction." She was also a headache for her fellow players, much as she had been for her Olympic teammates 20 years earlier. Her insis-tence on personal press coverage, undeniably egocentric, was powerful.[93]

She loved publicity, said Betsy Rawls, a 55-time winner on the LPGA tour. "She was one that would get upset if there were not a press confer-ence to go to or interviews to give. She really liked being in the public eye." And she loved entertaining the fans. Betty Hicks, who served as the LPGA's publicity and tournament director in the early 1950s, said of Babe, "Oh, how she gave them a show!" As Zaharias would tell the crowd, "Watch close boys, 'cause you're watchin' the best."[94]

Those early years were difficult. "We couldn't skip one tournament," Hicks said. "If one or two people dropped out of a 30-player field, it could be disaster. The competition was still there, and Babe could be extremely difficult at times. There wasn't a great deal of love lost among the top players, no matter what the TV documentaries claim. It was com-petitive, and yet at times, the camaraderie was quite excellent."[95]

Camaraderie wasn't so good when Babe would arrive in the locker room and, as Walter Hagen had done to the men 25 years earlier, ask her fellow-competitors, "Ya gonna stick around and see who'll finish second this week?" Peggy Kirk Bell recalled the time Zaharias called a meeting of the players, telling them matter-of-factly that she was the star and they were all the supporting cast. "I get the money and if it weren't for me, half of our tournaments wouldn't even be."[96]

Every important player was there, according to Bell, including Patty Berg and fellow Hall of Famer Louise Suggs. Babe added, "Do you want to go back home and be secretaries or work in a store or teach school? Go ahead. If you want to be out here playing golf, you'll do it my way."[97] Bell understood the reality of the message but believed it could have been delivered more diplomatically. But Babe didn't have a filter and said what was on her mind, consequences be damned. She also thought she would win everything, no matter what it took.

Betty Hicks summarized Babe's aggressive demeanor on the course, in the heat of battle, this way: "Babe Zaharias was openly, hostilely, aggressively, bitterly, laughingly, jokingly, viciously and even sometimes lovingly competitive."[98] Louise Suggs, who won 61 times on the LPGA tour, contended that "Babe had to win and didn't give a damn how." Betsy Rawls said of Babe, "It was almost as if she hated everyone that she was competing with. She had such a need to beat people." Zaharias did hate to lose. "She would get angry at everybody around her," recalled Rawls. "Oh, she would sulk. She would even resort to intimidation on the golf course sometimes."[99]

She would also take advantage of her position as *the* star of the LPGA by often choosing her own tee times and playing partners, or by trying to influence the local committees in setting up the golf courses. Babe would go to the tournament director and ask that tees be moved back on certain holes because she believed a longer course gave her an advantage. Rawls contended "she would even go so far as to threaten not to play in the tournament if they didn't do things the way she wanted."[100] Peggy Kirk Bell explained that in those early days they would start the tournament in the middle of the men's tees and by the last day would be on the back of the men's tees. "And pin placements were tough," added Rawls. "But nobody ever thought of complaining."[101]

Betsy Rawls maintained that sponsors often treated them in a high-handed manner because they were women and also because the sponsors knew the players needed them more than they needed the players. There was still little money in the professional game at that time, with the exception of Babe. In addition to doing exhibitions at $500 per (she did 656 during a three-year period in the early 1950s), she routinely asked for appearance money (usually $1,000), even though the LPGA had a rule against it. "That didn't apply to her though," claimed Louise Suggs, at least not "as far as she was concerned." Betty Hicks believed that appearance fees "were her ego trips. Her self-concept carried a price tag."[102]

Babe and George were constantly looking for ways to make a dollar. In 1947, before the tour was formed, Babe suggested to Betty Hicks that they start a faux "feud." If they did so, she told Hicks, "then we can play exhibitions and make a lotta money." Babe shared her husband's sense of the dramatic, and he, the former wrestler, was in complete agreement. When the LPGA came along, he affirmed that "women's golf is just like wrestling. It's a racket, and you've got to run it the same way." That attitude, Betty Hicks asserted, "detracted from the dignity of our activity."[103]

George and Babe were always looking for deals or trying to get something for free, and Babe did get a lot given to her, according to Betsy Rawls. Bertha Bowen's husband, R. L., contended that George, through his business connections around the country, could get anything at wholesale or for free based on his name. Actions such as these created considerable friction with Babe's fellow players, but they were reticent to speak up, especially in the early years when her agent Fred Corcoran also served as the tournament director.[104]

The public saw none of that—they just enjoyed seeing Babe perform. Patty Berg, a founding member of the LPGA and one of the greatest ambassadors the world of golf ever had, always supported Babe. "You know people loved the Babe and they clung to her for her wit and humor and enthusiasm and really for her love of life." Peggy Kirk Bell believed the "USGA loved her. They pulled for her to win. She brought in the crowds. She was their star." No one would argue that women's golf grew because of Babe Didrikson Zaharias.[105]

She also transformed the woman's game. "She came along with that great power game and it led to lower scores and more excitement," said Berg. "Babe would swing high and hard. And she brought all that humor and showmanship to the game. She humanized it. . . . Her tremendous enthusiasm for golf and life was contagious—even the galleries felt good when Babe was around."[106] Suggs acknowledged that Zaharias was "very charismatic" but also called her a bully because "she was going to have it no matter what, no matter who, what or whatnot. And that's where she and I got into it because I kept calling her on it. Nobody had the guts to call her."[107]

When Suggs would call Zaharias out, Babe wouldn't pay attention to it. "In fact," said Suggs, "I had people tell me, 'You better be quiet Suggs, you'll get kicked out of the tournament.' I always got the worst end of it, frankly, because there was nobody there to back me up."[108] The most publicized incident was probably the drop Babe took in a tournament in 1951 that Suggs felt was improper. She refused to sign Babe's card in protest, but a tournament official finally did. Suggs never forgot this instance of preferential treatment.[109]

It is ironic that Zaharias stated in her autobiography that you have to "play by the rules of golf, just as you have to live by the rules of life. There's no other way." Although Betsy Rawls asserted she didn't think Babe cheated, "she did bend the rules. Above all, she wanted to win and she would sacrifice other things to win."[110]

Adding to the ill feelings among her fellow players was the fact that no matter what Zaharias's competitors did, the headlines usually emphasized her performance. For example, from 1950 to 1955, Babe won 29 tournaments, and Louise Suggs won 25, but the headlines usually read something like "Babe loses" rather than "Suggs wins." Betsy Rawls claimed, "She would use every device she knew to win a golf tournament. And that's what she lived for. That was her life. . . . Her self-worth was based on winning, on beating people at something—if not golf, anything."[111]

Babe was so serious about winning that when she worked on the 1952 movie *Pat and Mike* with Katherine Hepburn, the last scene had to be rewritten so that Babe won the match. Art imitated life. That intensity and singleness of purpose was something she had demonstrated since she was a young girl. Raymond Alford, her childhood chum, remembered, "She had a temper. She wanted to excel. She wanted to show you up." And she didn't care if she irritated people.

Journalist Lawrence Lader contended she demonstrated "a cold indifference to what people think or say about her." Babe's brother Louis reaffirmed this sentiment, saying his sister "never agonized over who was pulling for her and who wasn't."[112] Both she and George could be overbearing, but he became the least loved of the two within LPGA circles.

George also became an increasing strain on her, as he controlled the money even though she earned it. "Everything I do I do for George," Babe had told the *Saturday Evening Post* in 1947. "He's the only thing I've got on my mind. I'd give up golf if he couldn't be with me." This, however, was the public façade. As Babe's friend Betty Dodd remembered it, "After a while George got to be a burden on her. Here she was trying to climb up socially and he was dragging her down."[113]

All her life, Babe had tried to escape her past as an athletic freak from poor beginnings and felt golf, with its elite caste, might allow her a new life. She didn't like to talk about the Olympics, those days before she was a "lady," and actually hid her medals in a coffee can. Bertha Bowen believed she used her bravado as a defense. "It's hard to break into society when they don't want you," she said. "And if you have once been poor, you never really feel that being rich is quite, well, quite natural."[114]

George faced many of the same social judgments. He had become rich through his wrestling but was still a rough-talking, uncouth man. When they married, he was 250 pounds of mostly muscle, but as he got older, he quit taking care of himself and put on weight, ballooning to 400 pounds at one time. Babe used to joke, "I married a Greek god and now he's just a goddamn Greek." But it wasn't funny; it was an embarrassment for her. By 1950, the marriage had been troubled for many years.

George drank too much and ate gluttonous amounts of food. Marilynn Smith, like Betsy Rawls and Louise Suggs, a member of the World Golf Hall of Fame, hosted a dinner at her home during the 1950 U.S. Women's Open and invited the Zahariases. George took two chairs to the table. "He didn't exactly swallow up two," Smith recalled. "He just sort of overran one."[115]

Louis Didrikson spoke of his sister's rocky marriage, with separations that became more frequent in the early 1950s. "Mildred was welcome everywhere, but George wasn't. He started drinking a lot. I personally thought he was overbearing and unjust with Babe." Sometimes she would bear bruises from their clashes. "But she stood by him."[116] George felt overshadowed by his famous wife, and that grated on him. "We started getting at each other's throat much of the time," he once admitted. "We both had tempers." R. L. Bowen remembered that when George felt Babe was "full of herself," he would yell, "Goddammit, Babe, I was a celebrity in my own right—and don't you forget it!"[117]

Not being able to have children also saddened Babe greatly. In 1932, she had told reporters, "At least I know I like children, and expect to have some of them." During the war, Babe had at least one miscarriage, which left her fairly depressed. She once told friend Peggy Kirk Bell, "I'd give up every trophy I ever won if I could have a baby."[118] The couple tried to adopt once but were told they traveled too much to be acceptable candidates. As Babe's marriage was becoming a place of discomfort instead of joy, she turned to her friends and family for support.

Bertha Bowen introduced her to a young golfer from San Antonio named Betty Dodd in 1951, when Betty was 19 and Babe was 40. Babe asked Dodd's father to permit his daughter to move in with Babe and George in their home in Tampa and work on her golf game. "I would have walked underground to China for Babe in those days," recalled Dodd in the 1970s, appreciative that she had been Babe's protégé. It was a friendship that lasted until Babe's death.[119]

Babe saw in Dodd a younger version of herself: untamed, boyish, and talented. Dodd claimed that Babe was lonely, that she needed someone to talk with and travel with. She "wanted a playmate and a friend. And she didn't have anybody else." Bertha Bowen saw Dodd as an agent that exacerbated the sore points in the Zaharias marriage. "She was just the oil of the misery," she contended, adding, a "close girlfriend can cause trouble between a couple, not meaning to."[120]

Some have hypothesized whether it might have been a lesbian relationship. Her close friends thought not. "Gay? Babe wasn't gay," said an adamant Peggy Kirk Bell. "We had a lot of trouble keeping her away from the men!" When asked by a reporter in the mid-1940s to describe the most thrilling experience of her life, Babe responded, "The first night I slept with George."[121]

Louis Didriksen claimed his sister, as a teenager, had a "wholesome interest in boys" and that she liked them "as much as did any girl, but she never sought association with them on any continuing scale. She didn't have time for them." He added that perhaps she was a bit "on the rough side for most boys." Whatever the substance of the relationship with Dodd, it created tension among the three, as Babe became more dependent on her. By 1953, Babe and George were sleeping in separate beds.[122]

Babe kept pushing to continue building her professional career and kept a hectic schedule. Her brother Louis remembered she was always on the go, unable to turn down requests for her time. "We kept telling her and her husband, too, that she was overdoing it, and that no human could hold up under that much stress and strain."[123] After winning nine times in 1951, her total fell to five in 1952, due in part to being sidelined with an operation for a femoral hernia. She recovered but had no energy, "no gas" as she put it. Since 1948, she had been having recurrent pain and swelling in her left side. She acknowledged that she should have seen a doctor but was always "too busy" and always found excuses to put it off. [124]

Between 1952 and the winter of 1953, she disregarded serious symptoms of a problem, symptoms that would have sent anyone else scurrying to their doctor. She had noticed blood in her stool a few months earlier. "Aw, Babe," George would say, trying to reassure her and probably himself, "it's just them hemorrhoids." She skipped most of winter tour in 1953 and finally saw her family doctor, Dr. W. E. Tatum, in April. He told her she needed more tests and sent her to a proctologist in Fort Worth, where she and George stayed with the Bowens. [125]

Bertha Bowen recalled the day they returned from the doctor's office. "Babe threw her purse down on the chair and flopped down on that bed. 'Well B. B., I've got it, and it's the worst kind, grade three,' she said." [126] Cancer of the rectum. Bowen knew Babe didn't like going to doctors. "She was rough in spots, but she was modest too, and she didn't like to have physical examinations. She waited too long; that was her big trouble." Since her childhood, Babe had enjoyed a cohesiveness and confidence between body and mind that few ever know. The onset of cancer, a dreaded disease Americans didn't talk about openly then, was devastating. [127]

In Babe's words, the cancer "hit me like a thunderbolt" and claimed the tears she shed were the first her husband George had ever seen. "I kept saying to myself, 'God, why did I have to have this? Why does anybody have to have it?' But my idea has always been that whatever God intended for me in this life, I'd go along with." [128] Trying to put on a brave front and perhaps convince herself, she had said a day after the diagnosis, "I am definitely not out of sports. I feel confident that with God's help, I will be back soon to play and win." Her humor was still evident when she told Tiny Scurlock before going into surgery on April 17 that she was tired of being in the sports pages. "Put me on page one," she said. [129]

The three-hour surgery was performed by Dr. Robert Moore of Galveston at the Hotel Dieu Hospital in Beaumont. The operation went well, but the malignancy had spread to surrounding lymph nodes, signaling doom. [130] George went into hysterics and walked out of the hospital when told the news. Even with the difficulties in their marriage, he still loved his wife. "I think his whole life was Babe," said Peggy Kirk Bell. [131] Betty Dodd asked Dr. Moore how long Babe had to live. He couldn't answer that but did not think she could survive. Betty and George followed Dr. Moore's advice and didn't tell Babe the cancer remained despite the surgery, a common practice then. [132]

The operation rerouted her intestinal tract to allow solid waste to pass through an incision in the left side of the abdomen, called a stoma, through which digested material would collect into a bag. In the 1950s, the bag was held in place by a nylon belt wrapped around the abdomen, with the incision protected by absorbent paper. Irrigating the colostomy was done every other day. Emptying and cleaning the bag was a painful routine, but a chore Betty agreed to assist Babe in doing as a team. One morning after her bath, Babe had an accident. "You never knew when something is going to happen," said Dodd, and from then on, "she wouldn't let anyone take care of her but me." [133]

Dr. Tatum, who assisted with the operation, announced afterward, "I don't know yet if surgery will cure her, but I will say that she never again will play golf of championship caliber." This in itself was enough to fuel Babe's competitive fire. There was no quit in her. As her brother Louis said of her: "Discouragement was not within her psychological makeup, and she possessed courage which would not admit the thought of failure." [134]

While trying to recover from the major physical and psychological trauma she had suffered, Babe received some unexpected inspiration from her nurse, Sister Mary Daniels. She told Babe there were sicker patients than her in the hospital, and knowing Babe's love for her harmonica, asked her to play for others. Babe did so, with Betty Dodd sometimes joining on the guitar. [135]

While working to get her strength back, Babe believed that "when you get sick, God is the one you go to. He gives you the spiritual muscle that you need." She visited a nun in the hospital, Sister Tarsisis, who had an ulcerated colon and was down to 65 pounds after refusing surgery. She needed a colostomy, and Babe tried to comfort her, telling her the operation wasn't so bad. "Maybe the good Lord sent you to me," the sister told her. "If you have that much faith and courage, I must have it, too." [136] She ended up having the surgery. Though Babe admitted she wasn't a "real church-going Christian," she said the prayers she had learned as a child and promised "if He made me well, I'd do everything in my power when I got out to help the fight against cancer." [137]

There were those who saw a new attitude in Babe after her surgery. Fellow pro Beverly Hanson wrote in *Golf Digest*: "During her amateur golf career and much of her pro life the Babe gave many the impression she thought the sun revolved around her, but in recent months she has not only acknowledged the existence of others but is now working for them."[138]

As she recovered, Babe devoted herself full force to this new opponent, forming the Babe Didrikson Zaharias Cancer Fund and doing public-service announcements. She said she wanted to "help crush cancer into the earth" and "shout from the housetops a warning against the disease."[139] She even went on *The Ed Sullivan Show*, where Mr. Sullivan wanted to show the nation that she had "licked" cancer. The colostomy was a big physical change but one she believed "the body can adjust to it." She wanted to get back to as normal a life as possible.[140]

Babe was in the hospital for 43 days, and only 14 weeks after surgery, she returned to play in George May's All-American Championship at Tam O'Shanter Country Club outside Chicago. Her game was rusty. After starting with 82-85, in the third round she turned in 44 and then, after wondering if she could go on, resolved not to quit and came home in 34. She knew she could still perform, and this was the beginning of her comeback. She ended up finishing in 15th place, and the next week, her hopes were buoyed when she finished 3rd in the World Championship tournament.[141]

Bertha Bowen spoke of Babe's comeback, saying she had many low moments and that it "was just pure spirit that got her through."[142] Zaharias not only had to overcome her physical problems but also her mental command of her body. "You go out there thinking you're going to hit it hard," she told reporters, "and then you feel like you're going to pull everything loose and you ease up on a shot." It was not an easy task playing in front of three thousand people with a colostomy bag. "What grit. *All* grit," said fellow pro Betty Jameson.[143]

Babe won 2 of the 24 tournaments she competed in, finishing sixth on the 1953 money list. She won the Ben Hogan Award in 1954, given to the player who has stayed active in golf despite a physical handicap or serious illness. In September, she opened up to Bill Rives in an insightful interview for *Sport* magazine. Regarding her cancer, her first reaction was to wonder if God had something against her. "I just didn't feel that I deserved it. I'd always tried to help people. I never did a wrong thing in my life. I couldn't understand why this had to happen to me."[144]

She then turned philosophical. "Maybe He wants me to set an example. If He is willing, I'll beat this thing."[145] Babe told readers she had always wanted to win and was determined to win her battle with cancer too and urged them to go to their doctors for regular checkups. She explained that she was still alive because her doctor found the cancer when it was still localized, which was a lie.

She had ignored signs for months before going to a doctor and wasn't even aware at the time of the interview that the cancer had spread to her lymph nodes. "I think of all the people who have cancer," she said, "and I think of those who live in fear of it." She wanted to be an inspiration to them by continuing to play, concluding, "I think of how wonderful it would be if I could return to the top."[146]

Babe started 1954 strong, winning her first tournament since the operation that February, the Serbin Open, beating Patty Berg. She called it "the biggest thrill of my life. I didn't think I would ever win another one."[147] The crowning achievement of the five-win season came in the U.S. Women's Open at Salem Country Club in July, where she rolled to a 12-shot victory. The last day—36 holes—she played with 19-year-old Mickey Wright, who would later win a record 82 LPGA tournaments.

Babe showed fans she hadn't lost her ability to do provocative things, as she stopped in the middle of the fairway in the final round to remove her slip, which she said was bothering her on the warm day. This drew laughs from the crowd and embarrassed her playing partner, but that wasn't the only thing Wright recalled about that day. "I do remember her as a showman," she'd say. "I thought she had the strongest-looking legs and arms I'd ever seen on a woman."[148]

Zaharias called her doctors after finishing, thanking them for all their encouragement. "You did it yourself, Babe," Dr. Moore told her. "It was your faith . . . that and your courage."[149] In an emotional speech at the trophy presentation, she told the crowd that, when she was lying in her hospital bed a year earlier, "there were reports going out that I'd never play championship or tournament golf again. I said, 'Please. God, let me play again.' He answered my prayer, and I want to thank God for letting me win again."[150]

She told reporters that for the first time since the operation, she felt like her "old" self. "My prayers have been answered. I wanted to show

Babe Didrikson Zaharias came back from cancer to win the 1954 U.S. Women's Open at Salem Country Club in Peabody, Massachusetts, by 12 shots. "My prayers have been answered," she said afterwards. "I wanted to show thousands of cancer sufferers that the operation I had, a colostomy, will enable me to return to normal life." *Courtesy USGA. All Rights Reserved.*

thousands of cancer sufferers that the operation I had, a colostomy, will enable me to return to normal life. I've received some 15,000 inquiries from those who have undergone the operation. This is my answer to them." She added, "I'll go on golfing for another twenty years."[151]

Babe spoke of her and George drawing closer to God. "We feel we know Him. For He was there when we called for Him," adding that "we see Him all round us, taking many forms." In the hospital she had seen Him in the doctors and the nurses who helped her. "We see Him in the many people who showed such real concern over whether I'd be able to play golf again."[152] Babe wanted to show people that there was hope in the face of cancer and would visit hospital patients.

One article described how she would sit down and give them words of encouragement from her own experience. The hope, however, ebbed when the cancer reappeared in 1955. Louis Didrikson said of that time,

"The twilight was beginning to dim, and we could do nothing to stop it."[153] Babe and George moved into a new home that March, and soon thereafter she hurt her back while trying to dig her car out of the sand on a beach on the Texas coast.

She kept playing, and won two tournaments that year, but knew something was wrong. In June, she had an operation for a herniated fourth lumbar disc, but the pain continued. In July, it was discovered the cancer had spread, and on August 5, the doctors told her she had a "small cancer lesion" at the base of the rectum and the sacrum, the wedge shaped bone at the base of the spine. In an eerie twist of fate, Babe's tape-recorded autobiography ended on the same day.[154]

She kept fighting, as she always did. In a letter to the Bowens October 9, 1955, she writes, "I don't think it will be too long before I can play again as I am feeling so good and strong. Oh for the day!" At the end of the month, Peggy Kirk Bell visited her in Tampa, and they played golf. Her strength sapped, Babe was unable to send her tee shots her customary 20–30 yards past Bell's and joked, "How do you break 100 only driving this far?"[155]

Babe tried to convince herself she was improving, again writing Bowen that she thought "it's just getting better by the day." It wasn't. By early December, she had to return to the John Sealy Hospital in Galveston. She was able to spend Christmas with the Bowens and on December 26 asked to go to a golf course. "I took her over to Colonial," said Bertha, "where you could drive up to the second green. She got out of the car in her pajamas and robe. She could barely walk. She just went over and knelt down and put her palm flat on the green," telling Bertha she just wanted to see a golf course one more time.[156] Friend Peggy Kirk Bell remembered Babe's sense of waning strength and invulnerability. One day she was lying in bed and put her leg up, showing Bell how her calf muscles had atrophied. "This is what made me great and it's gone."[157]

Zaharias left the hospital in January 1956 but had to return in March and remained there until her death. In February, she gave Joan Flynn Dreyspool of *Sports Illustrated* an interview, telling her, "The thing I don't understand is I've taken such good care of my body all my life. You go through it and you fight and you fight and you hope and you pray, then something worse hits you like this last one, cancer of the sacrum."[158] There would be no comeback this time.

Betty Dodd claimed her friend's "will to live was so great that she just wasted away to nothing; it was a very slow death."[159] Babe's brother Louis remembered her not conceding, until the end, "that she was dying, but she did know it. Her courage had stood firmly. That was the Babe way, but I'll admit that she had begun to cry a lot. She couldn't master this new obstacle, and it wouldn't go away. Her pain, except when she was heavily sedated, was excruciating."[160]

The pain became so great that doctors performed a chordotomy in July, severing the spinal nerves and paralyzing her from the waist down. George didn't visit much, and most of the care-giving fell to Betty.[161] On August 6, Dr. Robert Moore performed another operation to remove an obstruction from the lower bowel. Dodd saw her 11 days before she died. Babe had wasted away, and they talked about how victims of the Nazi concentration camps had been down to 80 pounds and came back. "She was flat on her back and she had tubes everywhere," Dodd recalled sadly. Babe asked her to shave her legs, but they were so thin, she worried she might cut her friend in the process. Even though emaciated, Dodd remembered that "she still had muscles. The nurses told me she should've died six months before she did."[162]

It wasn't until September 23 that the hospital admitted publicly that the end was near. On September 27, the nurses and doctor couldn't find a vein to put in a feeding tube. They told Babe she'd be dead in 15 minutes if they couldn't find one. "Then leave it out," she whispered. She told George: "I'll be going now Honey, thank you for everything."[163] George was crushed. He told the press that the end was "real nice and peaceful, as peaceful as a baby. She just floated away. It's been a long battle and the Babe fought it the way she knows how to fight, giving ground reluctantly all the way, an inch at a time. She's had enough agony, sadness, and pain." He reminded people that when she prayed, "she asked Him to ease the pain of everyone, not just her own."[164]

Babe's friends believed she had been kept alive needlessly at the end. A nurse told Peggy Kirk Bell that if it had been anyone else, they wouldn't have taken such extraordinary measures. But she was famous and a symbol of hope. "They kept her alive with needles," recalled an angry Bell years later. "It was stupid. She weighed 62 pounds when she died and she didn't know what end was up, they had her drugged so."[165]

Bertha Bowen agreed. "At the end her teeth were protruding and her face was so thin. She could barely whisper. I guess she never gave up.

She kept her golf clubs in the room right to the end." It was Babe's wish to be cremated. "I didn't want my beautiful body, now eaten up with cancer, to be buried in that condition," she had told her sister-in-law Corrie Didrikson.[166]

Zaharias was such an iconic figure that President Eisenhower made a statement upon her passing. "She was a woman who, in her athletic career, certainly won the admiration of every person in the United States, all sports people over the world. And in her gallant fight against cancer, she put up one of the kind of fights that inspired us all." Bobby Jones said she "took her final illness just as she played her games—giving her best."[167] Babe's manager Fred Corcoran remembered her as a "grand showman. She had a flair for the dramatic and a raw, earthy sense of humor. She loved life and loved people. She loved the color and glory of the passing parade and wore her role of champion as naturally as Walter Hagen did."[168]

Babe Zaharias was a woman many thought crude and brash, obsessed with winning at any cost. But like Ben Hogan, she had a softer side that not everybody saw. She loved practical jokes and would have fun with people by disguising her voice on the phone, putting on outlandish German accents, or pretending to be a little girl. Peggy Kirk Bell asserted, "Life was never dull with Babe. She was just a great big overgrown kid who loved living. She loved every minute, more than anyone I've ever known." Bell recalled the time they teamed to win a four-ball tournament in 1945 and she roomed with Babe. "Just when I was dropping off to sleep she grabbed my foot," Bell said. "I screeched and leaped a mile and she just laughed and laughed."[169]

Betty Hicks spoke of how Babe "would edge as close to illegality as she could to win a nickel in a golf match" but then would give "struggling golf professional Alice Bauer $100 for her baby's layette, without any of the fanfare Babe demanded for her other acts of charity."[170] Betsy Rawls, who was critical of her intimidating ways, in the end conceded, "But I loved Babe. She was good to play with, fun to be around. She was very witty and kept the gallery laughing all the time. Wisecracks all the way around. Very uninhibited. She was a little crude, and some things she said shocked me a little because I was just the opposite, but the gallery loved her. There will never be another like her."[171]

Sportswriter Paul Gallico believed Babe was "probably the most talented athlete, male or female, ever developed in our country. In all my years at the sports desk I never encountered any man who could play as many different games as well as Babe." He also stressed that not enough had "been said about the patience and strength of character expressed in her willingness to practice endlessly" and her incessant hard work to perform at her maximum level.[172]

Ben Hogan, a man who appreciated hard work, stated that she "dominated women's golf because she had strength, willpower, and desire to win. . . . I think the best way to describe Babe is that she turned out to be a diamond. As we all know, a diamond is a piece of coal that's been hard pressed for many years."[173]

Babe had been hard pressed her entire life and never bowed to a challenge. She "competed with life," contended Betty Dodd, an apt description that might well have served as her epitaph.[174]

5

CHARLIE SIFFORD

"What Kept Me Going? I Don't Know . . ."

Golf is a little too intimate a game for many white people's tastes; they'd prefer their black sports heroes to maintain a respectable distance.[1]
—Charlie Sifford

The word "nigger," you see, sums up for us who are colored all the bitter years of insult and struggle in America.[2]
—Langston Hughes

Charlie Sifford remembered, with a mixture of anger and sadness, a tournament he played in 1989. It was the pro-am round of the Showdown Classic, in Park City, Utah. He was making routine small talk with one of the members of his group, a prominent local businessman. On the 16th tee, this heretofore nondescript man asked Charlie where he made his home. Houston, Texas, came the answer. The man then said something Charlie couldn't believe. "Why I have a nigger maid who's from Texas too. And so is my nigger cook."[3]

The man broke into laughter after saying he wished he could take his cook with him when he died. The veins in Charlie's neck pulsated wildly upon hearing this, but he had learned many years earlier that nothing would be accomplished by taking a swing at every redneck he encountered. That vulgar word possessed the same strangling power it had when he was a child. As far back as 1837, Hosea Easton, an abolitionist minster of mixed race, wrote that the shameful term was "employed to impose contempt upon [blacks] as an inferior race. . . . It flows from the fountain of purpose to injure."[4]

But this was Utah in 1989, not Mississippi in 1837. To hear someone casually talking about "niggers" as if he was a character out of *Gone with the Wind* was too much for Charlie to bear. Blood boiling, he finished the round and left the course as fast as he could, livid at having to endure such behavior. He used to say that if he was a violent man he wouldn't have lasted three months on the golf tour because as far back as he could remember there were people who tried to disrupt him on the golf course. Would it ever end?[5]

How would you feel, he once asked, if the best years of your life were spent waiting on the sidelines when you knew "you had a God-given talent for something, but weren't allowed to do it because of the color of your skin." Wouldn't it have an effect on your whole life?[6]

Charlie Sifford was a black man playing a white man's game. That was true when he began his professional career in 1948 and is sadly still true today. That he persisted for decades to pursue his chosen career in spite of the racism that dogged him is a testament to his heart and soul. He not only carried the weight of his own struggles but also of those who saw him as a standard bearer, a soldier in the long struggle for civil rights. His burdens were multiplied a hundredfold by those who he pulled along with him.

That he survived makes him a special man. That he succeeded and won makes him an incredibly strong and talented man. The men who came after him, including the multiethnic Tiger Woods, realize the debt of gratitude Charlie, and other black pioneers, are owed. As Sifford said in 2003: "It's a good thing what Tiger is doing, but most kids don't know nothing better than Tiger Woods. . . . They should know where the game started from, they should know their history."[7]

Kids aren't the only ones in need of a history lesson. Race has been a problem in the United States since the first slaves arrived on its shores in 1619, and it still defines us. In 1944, when the world was at war to defeat tyranny, and four years before Charlie Sifford embarked on his professional golf career, Gunnar Myrdal wrote *An American Dilemma: The Negro Problem and Modern Democracy.* Its main thesis was that the "Negro problem is a problem in the heart of the American," a problem of "distinctly negative connotations" that suggests "something difficult to settle and equally difficult to leave alone."[8]

This racial problem, which Myrdal outlines exhaustively in his massive 1,500-page book, is in conflict with the "American Creed," as he called it. People may think, talk, and act as if under the influence of high national and Christian precepts, but at the same time, they are affected by personal and local interests and long-held prejudices, which are "defended in terms of tradition, expediency and utility."

It is the struggle between our ideals—as Lincoln put it, "the better angels of our nature"—and the reality of hatred, violence, and de jure and de facto segregation that have defined our actions as a nation. Even though conditions have improved since that book was written, African Americans at all levels of society were (and to a certain degree, still are) affected by this "problem," including those who wanted to play golf, both recreationally and professionally.[9]

Tiger Woods has acknowledged that golf has afforded him "a stage for free expression. That freedom, however, was a gift paid for by many determined people who endured all kinds of indignities just to be able to play the game."[10] This lineage goes back to the late 1800s, when golf took hold in the United States. There may have been a number of African Americans in those faraway days who had the ability to play a great game of golf, but they never had the opportunity to try.

It is informative to consider parallel developments in history. In 1896, a 16-year-old black man named John Shippen, who many consider this country's first homebred professional, tied for sixth place in the U.S. Open.[11] That same year, the Supreme Court upheld the constitutionality of state laws requiring racial segregation in public facilities in the case of *Plessy vs. Ferguson*. Thus began the doctrine of "separate but equal." The plaintiff argued that enforced separation of the two races stamped the "colored race with a badge of inferiority," summarized Justice Henry Brown. "If this be so, it is not by reason of anything found in the act, but solely because the colored race chooses to put that construction upon it."[12]

The court was no friend of the black race. *Plessy* thus legitimized segregation practices begun earlier in the South and provided an impetus for the passage of further laws aimed at keeping blacks and whites segregated. Legislative achievements won during the Reconstruction Era were erased through means of this "separate but equal" doctrine, which was the law of the land until 1954, when the court overturned this decision in *Brown vs. Board of Education.*

The very year Mr. Shippen came close to winning the national championship of this country, the laws codified that members of his race could and would be treated separately from white citizens. Golf would parallel society in its treatment of African Americans. The country Charles Luther Sifford was born into on June 2, 1922, was a much different place from today. The Dyer Anti-Lynching Bill passed the House of Representatives that same year, but was blocked in the Senate by Democratic senators from the South. While politicians were debating in Washington, 51 African Americans were lynched in the United States in 1922 and 6 whites.[13] Separate—but definitely not equal—treatment was the reality that Charlie grew up with.

Charlie Sifford was raised in Charlotte, North Carolina, with his three sisters and two brothers, in a simple, but comfortable house. Theirs was a strict Baptist home in which mother Eliza was "the boss." She was quite religious and stressed the importance of education to her children. Their father, Roscoe, who went by "Shug," was a strong, quiet man with a good sense of humor, according to Charlie.[14] Both parents worked hard to provide for their family.

By the age of 10, Sifford discovered golf, which had much more appeal to him than school did, to the disappointment of his mother. The family lived down the street from the Carolina Country Club, and he got a job caddying there, a job that allowed him to contribute to the family's finances. Charlie recalled with pride that, by the time he was 13, he was bringing home almost as "much in tips from the rich, white members of the club" as his father from his job in a fertilizer plant carting 100-pound bales of manure. He got 50 cents a bag and a dime tip each round.[15]

In his youth, racial tension and segregation were virtually absent in his neighborhood, which was a mix of working-class whites and blacks. Their next-door neighbors were white, and the kids played with each other often at one another's homes. Charlie believed everybody was equal, and when he discovered in his teens that "not everybody thought that way, it made it that much harder to understand, let alone accept."[16] He knew about "white" and "colored" restrooms and water fountains, but that was not part of his daily life. It wasn't until later in life that he would encounter the incessant racism and segregation entrenched in Southern culture.[17]

Charlie enjoyed caddying and found many of the members friendly and helpful to him. "I was in love with the golf course," he'd recall, and something about it appealed to him from the start. He also enjoyed being able to make some money and helping his men get around the course as best they could. Caddies were allowed to play on Mondays, and he was shooting par golf by the time he was 15 or 16 years old.[18] This was an amazing feat considering the caddies all shared clubs, although they could never seem to find a decent putter.

Self-taught, he took no formal lessons but picked up the game by watching others. He believed this was why he developed such an unorthodox swing. Jim Murray, late columnist for the *Los Angeles Times* and supporter of Charlie, would say years later, "His swing is nothing to get drunk over. He looks like a guy who has just fouled off a low outside 0-and-2 pitch. But when Charlie gets around the green and smells money, he's like a surgeon."[19]

No matter how unorthodox his technique, Sifford felt he had found something he could do well, "and I was stubborn enough even then to stick to it until I got it right." He used to tell people that he started playing because he realized one day that he could hit the ball just as easily as he could hand the club to somebody else. Sifford realized he didn't have as much natural ability as other players but did possess a fierce determination to succeed. Talent wasn't enough, he believed, unless it was coupled with dedication.[20]

Sifford had the good fortune to caddy for Clayton Heafner, who frequented the club and would go on to win four times on the PGA Tour. Eight years older than Charlie, they would also play money matches on occasion, which sharpened the 16-year-old's game. Charlie learned a great deal about the game from Heafner—the way he sized up each hole, the way he could fade or draw the ball depending on conditions and the nature of the hole, and the way he could save strokes around the green with his short game.

Just as he was coming into his own, Sifford was told he couldn't play at the course anymore. Shocked, he couldn't understand why he was being denied access to the course. What did they think he was going to do, "tear up the greens? Hit our women over the head with a 3-iron? Take a leak on the 15th green?" It would not be the last time he was denied access to a golf course, and it felt like a slap in the face to him.[21]

This was a turning point in young Charlie's life. The owner and professional at the club, Sutton Alexander, met with Charlie's parents and told them he believed their son had a future in the game if he were allowed to leave Charlotte and move to Philadelphia, where an uncle lived. Charlie's mother and father talked it over and agreed that, if their son got a job to support himself once he got there, he could go. [22]

Sifford was set on moving to Philadelphia but wasn't sure of the timing, since winter was coming. But in February 1939, something happened that hastened his departure. The owner of the general store, a huge man close to three hundred pounds named Jim Green, was friendly with Charlie's parents when he was sober, but when he went on a drinking binge, he became ugly quickly.

On this particular day, when Charlie saw the drunk Green stagger up to him, he sensed there might be trouble. Green called him "nigger," and Charlie told him his father wouldn't like that. Green said the word again and a flash of anger ignited inside young Sifford. He told Green if he called him that once more, he'd hit him over the head with a Coke bottle. Green did, and Charlie, true to his word, knocked the big man out cold.

Charlie ran home and told his folks what had happened. They knew Green's reputation, but he was white and their son was black. They sent Charlie to live with his aunt Betsy across town until things cooled off, but when Charlie returned to caddy a couple weeks later, the police arrested him. [23] His father and Alexander bailed him out, and the next day put him on a bus north.

Gathering together some clothes and a few dollars he had saved, he passed by the golf course on the way to the station. Looking out over the green fairways, Charlie wondered if he'd ever play golf again. His father's words must have rung in 17-year-old Sifford's ears, words he would remember. "When I was a kid, my dad told me, 'Be a man.' That didn't sound like very specific advice, but when I got caught telling a lie, he'd say, 'A man doesn't lie.' When I'd slough off on my chores, he said, 'A man works hard.' Though he didn't say as much, being a real man means obeying your conscience and being honest with yourself."[24]

As that bus chugged along the country roads of North Carolina, up through Virginia and Maryland on its way to Philadelphia, Charlie was being honest with himself by pursuing his dream. "I prayed to God that he would see fit to let me continue playing, and I promised if He would, I would do everything in my power to stick with the game."[25]

Charles Sifford in 1984 playing the Senior (now Champions) Tour, with his familiar cigar. He began smoking at the age of 12 and the cigars helped him relax as a black man playing a white man's game. While discussing the impact of Tiger Woods on the game in 2003, Sifford said it was good what Tiger was doing, "but most kids don't know nothing better than Tiger Woods. . . . They should know where the game started from, they should know their history." *Courtesy USGA. All Rights Reserved.*

By this time, Sifford had reached his adult size of 5 feet 7 inches and 185 pounds, solid through the chest and legs. Making good on his promise to his parents, he got a job as a shipping clerk at the Nabisco factory and worked there for three and a half years. He played no golf until one morning, after emerging from an all-night poker game, he ran into a man rushing to catch the street car with a bag of clubs on his shoulder. Wondering where he was going, Charlie jumped on board and followed him to Cobbs Creek, where he found blacks and whites playing side by side.

The course, built in 1916, played to around 6,200 yards and was the home of many very good African American golfers. It became Charlie's second home. Had he not jumped on that streetcar, it is possible the world may have never heard of Charlie Sifford. At Cobbs Creek, he found a proving ground for his own game, since one of the best black players in the United States frequented the place—the long-hitting, cross-handed-playing Howard Wheeler.

Charlie had bravado, and after getting the rust off his game, he felt he was ready to challenge Wheeler, who had just won the first of five Negro National Open championships. This was a tournament conducted by the United Golfers Association, which was created to give African Americans a place to play, since white golf circles excluded them as contestants. Sifford approached Wheeler one day and announced: "I'm Charlie Sifford, and I'm gonna whip your ass on that golf course." They played, and Wheeler took $10 from him, teaching Charlie an important lesson. Up to that point, Sifford admitted he hadn't been truly dedicated to the game, nor had he realized the deficiencies in his game. Howard Wheeler, he asserted, changed that in one morning, and he got to work, buying a new set of clubs and practicing hard for two weeks before asking for a rematch.[26]

This time, Charlie was victorious and called it one of the most satisfying wins of his career. After that, he and Wheeler teamed up and beat all-comers at Cobbs Creek. Charlie credited Wheeler with teaching him the subtleties of the game. One thing that set Sifford apart from the other good golfers he competed against was his desire to persist and push to become the best. He believed Howard did not have the personality to get into big-time pro golf but was content to be the local favorite and take on anyone who wanted to challenge him for a few bucks.

World War II put a stop to Charlie's golf for the duration as he served in Okinawa. Following the war, he quit his job and played in his first National Negro Open. As he writes in his autobiography, he had traveled a lot of miles in his career, but that car ride from Philadelphia to Pittsburgh would prove the most significant trip he ever made.[27]

The United States Colored Golfers Association, later renamed the United Golfers Association, was formed in 1925 as a response to the reality that very few courses were open to blacks. "The object of the national organization," stated the press release announcing its formation, was to "gather all colored golfers and golf associations into one body." UGA tournaments helped the whole African American community when they came to town, as hotels, restaurants, barber shops, and other businesses benefited from the influx of revenue during a tournament. Sports figures such as Sugar Ray Robinson, Joe Louis, Jackie Robinson, and Jim Brown made appearances at UGA events, and Cab Callaway, Count Basie, and Duke Ellington played at balls held at them. [28]

Charlie met some big names in the game at that 1946 UGA National Open, including Ted Rhodes, Bill Spiller, and Joe Louis. The latter, Charlie claimed, was the most "big-hearted man" he'd ever met in his life. Ted Rhodes served as Louis's personal coach and, according to Charlie was the best black golfer he ever saw, as good as any of the best white players of his era, including Sam Snead and Ben Hogan.

Rhodes introduced Sifford to bandleader Billy Eckstine, who ended up hiring Charlie to work for him as his personal golf pro and valet, a relationship that lasted 10 years. He was paid $150 a week, plus all expenses on the road. "Not only did this keep me from starving," recalled Charlie, "I had a great time." It afforded him the opportunity to travel the country and meet many fascinating people, including the best jazz musicians and black athletes in the land. [29]

The world was changing for Charlie and would take another turn when he met a pretty girl name Rose Crumbley one night at a dance. After a brief courtship, they were married in 1947, and later would welcome two sons into the family. This turned out to be a strong union, even though Charlie was away from home for extended periods touring with Eckstine and playing in golf tournaments. Sifford's son Charles Jr. said in 2014, "My mother was the main one who really kept him going. She encouraged him and knew how to calm him down when he got mad." [30]

When Sifford turned pro in 1948 and wanted to try his hand at the big-time tour, he was fortunate enough to meet with Jackie Robinson, who broke the color barrier in baseball the year before. Robinson asked Charlie if he was a quitter. "I told him no. He said, 'If you're not a quitter you're probably going to experience some things that will make you want to quit.'" He advised Charlie to control his temper and take care of his business. "I promised him I would. But if it hadn't been for the good Lord, a lot of days I would have taken one of those golf clubs and started swinging." Years later, reflecting on his journey, Sifford said he had wanted to prove to the world that "a black man could play golf as good as a white man, so I knew I was going to take everything they threw at me and accept it." [31]

Charlie wasn't alone in his struggles. In those days, PGA rules stipulated that players finishing among the top 60 one week were exempt from qualifying for the next tournament. In the 1948 Los Angeles Open, Ted Rhodes and another black golfer, Bill Spiller, did just that and headed north to play in the Richmond Open, outside Oakland. But upon arriving, they, and another black player named Madison Gunter, were denied entry, prompting the *New York Times* to editorialize: "The Professional Golfers Association refusal to accept the entry of two Negro golf professionals . . . is neither sportsmanlike nor American."[32]

Golf World magazine asserted that "Negro golf has grown to the point where something is going to have to be done about it." With assistance of Jonathan Rowell, an African American Oakland attorney, the three promptly filed a $315,000 lawsuit against the PGA and Richmond County Club, claiming they had been deprived of "their constitutional right to earn a living at their chosen profession."[33]

In September 1948, just before the suit went to court, the PGA pledged that it would no longer prevent blacks from playing in its tournaments. They still couldn't be members of the PGA, however, due to a clause that stipulated members had to be of the "Caucasian race." The three players dropped the suit without getting a dime in settlement money. Then the PGA quickly changed its tournament policy—an "open" became an "invitational" event, meaning that the tournament committee had the power to invite only those golfers it wanted to participate.[34]

According to Al Barkow, who has written extensively on the history of the PGA Tour, the lawsuit at Richmond "was a turning point." It drew attention not only to the discrimination blacks faced in golf but also to the basic truth that they actually played professional golf. "The word got out," Barkow claimed, "and it got into the system; people started thinking about it."

It would be years before things really changed, and those years were wasted on Charlie. As *Sport* magazine proclaimed after the Richmond case: "The colored pros have very little chance to make any legitimate money out of the game. They can't play in the endless string of big-money PGA tournaments."[35] Charlie would play wherever he could, but he kept fighting for the right to play wherever he wanted.

By the early 1950s, with financial backing and the time to devote to his game, Charlie began finding success. His first professional win was the 1951 Southern Open on the United Golfers Association tour, beating old partner Howard Wheeler with rounds of 66-62-68-69. The following year, he won his first of five UGA National Opens, beating Ted Rhodes, making him the top player on the circuit. He would go on to win, but he craved the big time. In looking back, Sifford figured it was probably in the late 1940s when a question started crossing his mind, one that came to him constantly, like a persistent itch deep inside him that he could never scratch. Why, he'd ask himself, in this free country of ours, was he being denied the right to try to prove himself against the best players, black and white?

He may have been finding more success on the golf course, but the trouble was finding a place to play. In those days, a handful of African Americans waded into PGA-sponsored events. As Sifford recalled, at the Los Angeles Open, the Tam O'Shanter, and the Canadian Open, black players were accepted as equals. He singled out players like Jimmy Demaret, Ed "Porky" Oliver, and Bob Rosburg as going out of their way to make the black participants feel comfortable. But the sponsors who ran the tournaments, and the PGA by extension, were not as willing to welcome black players into their fields. One man who would make a difference was not a professional golfer. As Charlie recalled, the only person who "could make a dent in the system was the one black athlete whom everyone respected—Joe Louis."[36]

Heavyweight champion of the world from 1937 to 1949, Louis ruled the boxing world and was a source of pride and inspiration to African Americans. In retirement, he loved to play golf and became the patron saint to black golfers. He was a mid- to high-70s shooter and loved to gamble on the course. In January 1952, he declared his intention to play in the San Diego Open, which had never been open to blacks. He, Bill Spiller, and Eural Clark drove from L.A. to San Diego and petitioned the PGA to allow them to enter the tournament. Joe made sure to keep the media informed of what was going on, and the story began to appear in newspapers all over the country.

Louis announced: "I want the people to know what the PGA is. We've got another Hitler to get by. Horton Smith believes in the white race—Hitler believed in the super race."[37] Smith was the president of the PGA, former two-time Masters champion, and would later be elected to the World Golf Hall of Fame. The head of an organization of three thousand members and with less than two months on the job, he met with Louis to try to smooth things out.

Because Louis was an amateur, he would be allowed to play as a sponsor invitee, but the others would not. Smith believed he was only following the rules as they existed at the time. Louis played, but said he would continue his fight to "eliminate racial prejudice from golf, the last sport in which it now exists."[38]

Smith did appoint a committee to confer playing rights on black golfers, and the next week in Phoenix, six would play. At the end of January, the PGA voted on a new rule—blacks could play if they were given one of ten sponsor exemptions or if they were invited to be one of ten golfers who could compete for open spots in a qualifying round. In addition, a committee of five black players would be formed to maintain an "approved list" of golfers who were qualified to play in events.[39] As it was, a black professional would be lucky to play in 10 tournaments a year but hardly enough to make a living.

Following the San Diego Open, Louis asked for invitations for seven blacks, including himself and Charlie, to enter the tournament in Phoenix, and they were allowed to attempt to qualify. But hotels and restaurants turned them away, they weren't allowed in the locker room, and all were sent out first in two groups. Sifford was never to forget that qualifying round. On the first hole, he walked up to pull the flagstick from the hole, and something was wrong. He glanced down at the cup. "I had the flagstick half raised, but I shoved it back into the cup." Someone had filled it with human excrement, "and from the looks and smell of it, it hadn't been too long before we got there that the cup had been filled."[40]

Shocked and angry, he played badly and failed to qualify, but three others did. After such an introduction to PGA Tour, Charlie would say it was a testament to the players' character and will that they continued to fight for their rights.[41] As for Joe Louis, he got tired of the exclusion of blacks and stopped entering the white tournaments. Despite his efforts, and all of the press attention, Phoenix would remain closed to blacks. Charlie wouldn't play there again until 1959.

Charlie kept going and in 1955 made a splash with the big boys. After finishing 11 strokes off Gene Littler's winning pace at Los Angeles, he had to wait until the St. Paul Open in July to play again on the "white tour," as he called it, where he tied for 22nd. He then went to the Canadian Open and fired a tournament and course record 63 in the opening round. In second place was a promising player who had won the U.S. Amateur the year before. His name was Arnold Palmer. Charlie happened to pass Palmer late that afternoon when he was staring at the leaderboard.

Charlie Sifford was one of several African American golfers struggling to make their mark on the PGA Tour in the 1940s and '50s. The smiles on the faces of Eural Clark (left), Ted Rhodes (center), and Sifford at the 1952 Phoenix Open belie the treatment they received, as in the qualifying round Charlie came to the first green and found human excrement in the cup, a disgusting action from racists protesting their presence. *Courtesy USGA. All Rights Reserved.*

"How on earth did Charlie Sifford shoot a 63?" asked Palmer. "Same way you shot a 64, chief," Sifford shot back, "except I did you one better."[42]

Charlie wasn't used to playing in many four-round tournaments and by his own admission had a lot to learn about maintaining a high level of play over several days. He finished in 19th place but was "nonetheless thrilled." For one day, he had been the undisputed best golfer in the world, beating the likes of Palmer, Billy Casper, and Sam Snead.

The following year, he won the Rhode Island Open, and a few weeks later, in Hartford, he tied for third in a strong field and took home $1,116, his biggest paycheck yet. He felt that if he could just keep persisting, "something would happen. I'd make it happen." In 1957, Charlie won his most significant tournament to date, the Long Beach Open, a 54-hole tournament that was sanctioned by the PGA, with a field composed of many touring pros, including future major winners Billy Casper, Gene Littler, Gay Brewer, Tommy Bolt, and Jay Hebert.

"Man, it's tough to win when you got to win," Sifford would say, "when you need that dough and when you've got every Negro on your back, pulling for you." He won enough money to help buy a home for his wife and son in Los Angeles, but he wasn't allowed to enter the PGA tournament the next week. [43]

The country was changing, but the PGA Tour not so much. The modern civil-rights movement had begun in 1955 with Rosa Parks and the Montgomery Bus Boycott, led by a dynamic 26-year-old minister named Martin Luther King Jr. This followed the Supreme Court decision *Brown v. Board of Education* in 1954, which declared that state laws establishing separate public schools for black and white students were unconstitutional. Among other works, the court cited Gunnar Myrdal's book *An American Dilemma* in its decision. The "Negro problem" remained, however. It was "embarrassing" and made "for moral uneasiness." [44]

There were still few sponsors who welcomed black golfers. One was George S. May, who ran the Tam O'Shanter tournament outside Chicago. In 1942, he opened play to "any American who is willing and able to qualify under the rules of competition which have been set up for all participants." Years later, in face of continued discrimination against blacks, May claimed the PGA and certain white players didn't "want the fellow from the wrong side of the tracks to get into golf. They want to restrict the game and keep it for rich men. . . . They fear a Negro will come along and win one of the tournaments." He wasn't alone in thinking so, even if he voiced a minority opinion. [45]

When Charlie made the cut at the 1959 U.S. Open, sportswriters sat in the clubhouse, wondering what would happen if he finished in the top 16, which earned an invitation to the Masters. Most agreed that if he did, the Masters committee would change the rules. "That's no lie," said one. "They ain't gonna have no Nigras playing at Augusta." [46] In fact, it would be 16 more years before a black man would play in the Masters. Charlie's first concern was just surviving. "I was practically starving and trying so hard to hold onto this dream of making my living at golf," he'd say of those times. "What kept me going? I don't know." His son Charles Jr. would maintain it was his father's "belief in God that kept him going, and my mom who kept him going as well," adding that "those were the two most important things that kept him on the straight and narrow" and gave him the strength to stay on the Tour and pursue his dream. [47]

As the 1961 season dawned, *Sports Illustrated* ran an article highlighting golfers to watch that year. Charlie was featured, but "there's the rub for Sifford. Once the tour leaves Arizona and pushes into the South, he has to leave it, and he can't rejoin the pros until they get back above the color line." [48]

The civil-rights movement was expanding in the South. A year earlier, four students from the North Carolina Agricultural and Technical State University sat down at the "whites only" lunch counter inside the Woolworth's store in Greensboro, North Carolina. Their nonviolent protest set off a wave of like actions across the South. In the spring of 1961, students began Freedom Rides on buses intended to test Supreme Court rulings that banned racial discrimination in interstate travel.

The system was being challenged, and that April, the NAACP believed it was time for a message to be sent to the golf world. To that end, it pushed to have Charlie invited to play in Greensboro. He had started the year well, but when he went south, not one of the six tournament sites accepted his applications to play. Through the efforts of Dr. George Simkins, head of the local chapter of the NAACP, an invitation was finally extended to Sifford. [49]

Charlie knew what he was getting himself into, going into the same hornet's nest that the student sitting at the Woolworth's counters encountered. His invitation made the newspapers, and soon the whole country knew he was heading to Greensboro. His wife, Rose, encouraged him, telling him nothing was going to happen that he couldn't handle and that this was what he had been working toward for years. Charlie would say a prayer to God for strength and protection.

As he drove into North Carolina, however, it was apparent this wouldn't be easy. When he stopped for gas, he couldn't eat in the café; he couldn't use the restrooms in some places. In Greensboro, no hotels were available to him, and Dr. Simkins got him a room with a family. A strong field greeted him, including Sam Snead, Art Wall, Mike Souchak, and Gene Littler. They treated him like any other pro, which he appreciated greatly. Charlie realized a lot was riding on that week. If he could play well and not lose his temper in the event trouble arose, he would open doors not only for himself but also for other black golfers coming up through the ranks.

In the first round, he put up the best score of the day, a 3 under par 68. A great start. That night, he received a phone call. "You'd better not bring your black ass out to no golf course tomorrow if you know what's good for you, nigger." Charlie was stunned but defiant. He told the caller he'd be on the first tee at 10:15 the next morning, no matter what. Before hanging up, the man said, "You'd better watch out, nigger."

Sifford figured it was just talk, but he couldn't shake the fear. He considered withdrawing and going somewhere safe. He called Rose, and after a long discussion, she encouraged him to continue, giving him an added measure of fortitude through her love, as she always had. While warming up on the range the next day, Charlie looked into the faces of the spectators, wondering if the caller from the previous night was among them. He tried to calm himself, knowing he'd be finished if he allowed these sorts of racist attacks affect his game. [50]

After hitting a good opening-tee shot, he walked down the first fairway. A familiar voice came from the gallery, the voice he heard the night before. "Nice shot, Smokey," he yelled. A group of about a dozen young white men were following him, taunting him. "Don't miss it, darkie." "Go back to the cotton fields." [51] And so it went for 14 grueling holes, when the police finally arrived and hauled them away. Sifford wondered why it took so long to get rid of them and called it the longest round of his life. He considered the 72 he shot that day one of the best of his career.

He went out the next day, saddened that nobody said anything about the incident or apologized on behalf of the country club or the tournament. He hung in, played well, and finished fourth, despite the hostile environment. Gary Player, one of the game's all-time great champions, witnessed what Sifford had gone thorough. When Charlie slammed his pencil down in frustration at the end of the second round, Player shook his head and asked him, "Laddie, how can you play like this?" [52]

Charlie had mixed feelings about his experience. On the one hand, going into Greensboro he felt that if he could break into more tournaments he'd be accepted and free to concentrate on his game. That notion was shattered by the racist hecklers he encountered on the course. But on the other hand, he felt he had won a certain victory. Under the pressure of discrimination, and while facing his worst fears, he hadn't cracked or quit. [53]

The next two weeks he was turned away by tournament officials at both Houston and San Antonio. Obviously, the barriers to playing golf in the South weren't going to come down easily. Charlie had found out as the years went that being a pioneer meant you could never quit but had to keep pressing forward. As far as his being called the Jackie Robinson of golf, he told the press: "My job's tougher than Jackie Robinson's was. He had a set salary. I have no sponsor. I have to finance my own way. He had a team backing him. I'm playing alone."[54]

In 1959, Jackie Robinson wrote an article in the *New York Post* devoted to the fact that Charlie hadn't been invited to play in the Bing Crosby or Palm Springs Desert Classic: "Golf is the one major sport in America today in which rank and open racial prejudice is allowed to reign supreme. Though often called the sport of gentlemen, all too often golf courses, clubs and tournaments apply the ungentlemanly and un-American yardstick of race and color in determining who may or may not compete."[55]

As Sifford noted, golf was a game controlled by elite white society, and it wasn't going to change simply for the sake of one black player. Things would only change when someone threatened the PGA where it was most vulnerable—its wallet. The Caucasian clause fell because Charlie happened to send a letter to a smart and tenacious man named Stanley Mosk in 1959. At least that's what Charlie Sifford believed.[56]

Mosk, who was Jewish, knew his own version of discrimination, and when he became attorney general of California in 1958, he used his power to combat discrimination. In six years, he issued almost two thousand written opinions in matters ranging from water rights to voting rights, and in the case of Charlie Sifford, he warned the PGA that his office would block racially restricted tournaments on public golf courses in California.[57]

Mosk presented Sifford as a resident of the state whose civil rights were being violated and asked the PGA to show reasons other than race why Sifford was being denied membership. According to Charlie, the PGA couldn't provide any valid explanation and in December made him an "approved tournament player," the first black man to earn this distinction. This category had originally been set up for members who didn't have five years' experience in a pro shop to gain PGA membership but who were prominent players. Arnold Palmer, Ken Venturi, and foreign players, such as Peter Thomson, Bobby Locke, and Gary Player, fit in this category at various times.[58]

In early 1961, Mosk expanded his pressure on the PGA by telling its leadership that private courses would not be exempt from the reach of the attorney general. The PGA Championship, set to be played in Los Angeles at the Brentwood Country Club the next year, was suddenly in jeopardy. It all came back to article III, section I of the PGA's constitution, which stated: "Professional golfers of the Caucasian Race, over the age of eighteen (18) years, residing in North or South America, who can qualify under the terms and conditions hereinafter specified, shall be eligible for membership." Mosk said that conducting tournaments under such a constitution violated both the public policy and the laws of California. He believed that "society and the law can ultimately defeat overt bigotry every time."[59]

Relenting to Mosk's pressure, the PGA voted on May 17, 1961, to relocate the 1962 tournament to Aronimink in Pennsylvania. The Executive Committee also passed a resolution to eliminate the "Caucasian clause" from its constitution at the November meeting. The issue was not ignored by the press. A week after the decision, *Sports Illustrated* wrote that the PGA was far behind the times if it held that racial segregation still had a place in sports. "Professional basketball, baseball, and football have long permitted Negro athletes to play, and all these sports have thrived in consequence. It's time that the PGA put its musty store in order, too."[60]

In September, Claude Harmon, winner of the 1948 Masters, was reported as saying in the *New York Post*, "I feel that if a Negro is good enough in this game, he's entitled to play. He does in basketball and he competes in the Olympics. Golf can't be different." The article also noted, that, being realistic, "the Negro still is a long way from acceptance in top golf even if the PGA does eradicate the Caucasian clause."[61]

Delegates met two months later and voted on two amendments to the constitution. The first permitted worldwide membership (not just those from North or South America), and the second amendment eliminated the words "of the Caucasian race" as a prerequisite of membership. Both were approved by a vote of 87–0. After 18 years on the books, on November 9, 1961, the PGA officially eliminated the "Caucasian clause." The move, stated PGA president Lou Strong, was "in keeping with the realization of changing world conditions and coinciding with principles of the United States government."[62]

Charlie Sifford would gain full PGA membership in 1964 (after playing the requisite 25 tournaments a year), but the playing field had not been leveled. His best years were behind him. When asked in 2003 when he was playing his best golf, Charlie answered, "I say that 1947 through 1960 I was swinging the clubs pretty good." Those years could not be brought back, but Charlie kept plowing forward, even though the road was still full of obstacles that sapped his physical and spiritual strength and kept him constantly on edge emotionally. [63]

African American writer Richard Wright grew up in the South and told a story of once quitting a job after being intimidated by a boss who thought Wright had failed to call him "Mr." Wright recalled that his sustained expectation of violence had exhausted him. "My preoccupation with curbing my impulses, my speech, my movements, my manner, my expressions had increased my anxiety. While standing before a white man I had to figure out how to perform each act and how to say each word." [64] Might Charlie Sifford have had similar thoughts?

In 1988, Larry Mowry related an incident in *Golf Digest* that sheds light on this aspect of Sifford's experience. It was something Sifford referred to briefly in his autobiography but didn't fully explain. As Mowry told it, in the 1960s (most likely around 1963), he needed a ride to the next tournament in Wilmington, North Carolina. Charlie offered him one but not without issuing a cautionary warning. "Do you know what you're getting into, driving with me?" Mowry said it would be fine. As a young pro still in his 20s, he looked up to Charlie as both a golfer and a person and wanted to talk golf with a proven player. "Color doesn't mean anything to a professional athlete," Mowry said. "Performance is what you admire, and I really admired Charlie's game." [65]

When they stopped for coffee, Charlie would always ask Larry to get it, who thought nothing of it. They had progressed well into Georgia when they stopped for gas at a dimly lit truck stop. Sifford asked Mowry to go get a couple of Cokes while he gassed up the car, but he seemed nervous. As Mowry got the drinks, he noticed two policemen staring at him. "They were dressed like characters in a B movie: open shirts, hats tilted back on their heads and cigars in their mouths. One of them said to me, 'You jes don't care who you drive with, do you, son?'" Somewhat intimidated, Mowry stood there silent before this mean-looking guy with a scar on his face. This drew a four-lettered response, as the police turned and walked toward Charlie and the car.

"Whose car is this, boy?" the man with the scar asked Sifford. "Is it yours?" Charlie, in a high-pitched falsetto voice answered, "Nose-saa.

Ah's drivin' for mistah Larry." This answer seemed to be satisfactory to the officer, and he told them to drive slow and steady out of his county. When Mowry and Sifford crossed the county line, Charlie broke the nervous silence. "If he knew this was my car, we'd both be buried in a cotton field and never be heard from again." This was the same era in which civil-rights workers James Chaney, Andrew Goodman, and Michael Schwerner were killed in June 1964 by the Ku Klux Klan in Philadelphia, Mississippi, and later found buried in an earthen dam.

After driving through the night and reflecting on what had happened, Mowry knew the rules. Restrooms and drinking fountains were off limits to Sifford, unless they said "Coloreds." "Charlie lived in a different country than I did." This conclusion was crystallized after witnessing Charlie adopt a subservient affectation in Negro dialect to extract them from a hostile environment. [66]

A 1963 *Newsweek* poll of Americans' feelings concerning race relations included a quote from a Californian woman, who told the pollster, "We don't hate niggers. We just don't want them near us."[67] Many others shared the same sentiment or worse. Martin Luther King Jr. spoke the same year of his dream that the worth of the individual should be measured by the content of their character rather than the color of their skin, a dream yet to be realized.

In 1965, a year after President Lyndon Johnson signed the Civil Rights Act into law, discrimination hadn't miraculously disappeared. Sifford still couldn't eat in the restaurant at the Pensacola Country Club. Instead, he had to go to the locker room with his breakfast. But other players joined him: Bob Rosburg, Frank Stranahan, and Ken Venturi. Charlie wondered what would have happened if someone had asked Palmer or Nicklaus to take their lunch down to the locker room.[68] Or if Sam Snead showed up and he was the only white player and all the spectators were black— wouldn't that have affected their games?

"I really would like to know how good I could have been with a fair chance," said Sifford in 1992. "I loved the game, and I had a gift, but I had too much pressure. I will never know."[69] Every tournament was a new battle for Charlie, as he had to prove his worth to fans, sponsors, and tournament officials. His anger would rise to the surface, and the stress became unbearable. Fortunately, he was able to find a psychologist in Los Angeles who taught him breathing and mental exercises to help relax him. Charlie kept going. If he could win a big tournament, it would be a vindication of all he had endured.

By the late 1960s, at least he wasn't alone on the tour. Pete Brown and Rafe Botts had come out in 1964, which made Sifford feel like he had managed to open doors for them and other black golfers coming up. But Charlie still wanted to win, and he knew time was running out. In his mid-40s, he realized it was difficult to keep his game together over four rounds of golf, but at least by 1967, he didn't feel as if he were "walking into the enemy camp every single time I showed up somewhere to play golf."[70]

Hartford, Connecticut, had been one of the few sites on the tour that had welcomed black players, and Charlie remembered he "made a lot of friends up there in the '50s."[71] When the 1967 tournament rolled around, he was playing with confidence in a place he always enjoyed, a good combination for any golfer. Its big purse drew a field of big-time names, including Gary Player, Ray Floyd, Lee Trevino, Julius Boros, and Al Geiberger. After two rounds, Charlie was six shots off the lead and going into the final round was still five back.

Truthfully, he had no thoughts of winning, but in that final round something special awaited him. He made the turn only two under par for the day, then birdied the 10th, 13th, and eagled the 14th. He knew from the reactions of the gallery that he was in the hunt. When he sank an eight-foot putt on the 16th for another birdie, he had found himself in the lead. He parred the 17th and hit a good drive on the last. The crowd was yelling encouragement as he bounded down the fairway. "It was like a wave," said Owen Canfield, who covered the tournament for the *Hartford Courant*. "Everybody was like, 'Look at Charlie. Look at Charlie.'"[72]

Sifford pulled his seven-iron approach shot into a bunker. His stomach and throat tightened as he walked into the bunker and surveyed the lie. Nerves jumping inside him, the next few moments would help define his life. As Charlie recalled, "I closed my eyes and prayed to God. 'Please just let me make this shot.'"[73] His prayer was answered, as the ball came out well and rolled gently four feet from the hole. He made the putt for a glorious 64.

Steve Opperman, one shot back, needed a birdie on the last to tie, but failed to secure it. Opperman recalled 30 years later that "inside 80 yards, Charlie was a Houdini. There was nobody better at getting up and down."

Charlie Sifford had won a full-fledged PGA tournament. All those years of fighting for the right to play, of struggling to hang on to his dream, of proving he belonged there, had not been in vain. "I have no bitterness," he told *PGA Magazine* after. "It doesn't do any good to hate anyone. I knew it was tough when I took up the game."[74]

The victory brought tears to Charlie's eyes. "I thanked God for my victory, and for giving me the strength to hang in there all of those years." Ed McManus, the cochairman of the tournament, was struck by the timing of it all. "It was a tough time in America—there was a lot going on," he recalled. "And there was Charlie Sifford, the first black to win a major tournament. That was on everybody's mind." For Charlie, Hartford was the one he remembered most. "I'll never forget how the people were behind me."[75]

Winning on the PGA Tour, the biggest golf stage in the world, Charlie found people treating him differently, like a champion. This in turn boosted his confidence, and he began to play better as a result.[76] He hoped there would be endorsement deals, but none came. Sifford contacted Mark McCormack, who represented Arnold Palmer and Jack Nicklaus, hoping he might be able to look after Charlie's business affairs, but was told that he didn't take on clients who could not bring in at least $200,000 a year in income.

Sifford wondered if some of it had to do with the color of his skin. Since he had been a cigar smoker since the age of 12, Charlie thought some tobacco company might wish to have him as an endorser. Nobody called, and he concluded that his black face wasn't going to sell as many cigars as a white one would.

Charlie kept playing on. Even though the Caucasian clause had been overturned in 1961, the end of discrimination de jure did little to alter the effects of discrimination de facto. Realities, however, can sometimes be more complex than legalities. As Charlie told *Sports Illustrated*, African Americans hadn't been exposed to golf as whites had, and by the late 1960s, they were just coming to the game, even though they might never catch up.

It was even more difficult for black women who sought to play professional golf, who had to fight not only racial discrimination but also gender discrimination. "You know, you can't play the game where they won't let you play," maintained Sifford, "and they didn't let us play nowhere for a long time." It was hard to catch up without money and without good golf courses to play on and without good instruction.[77]

Even though the system was not friendly to them, five other black players joined Charlie in the 1969 Los Angeles Open. As Sifford recalled years later, "Los Angeles was always so good to me." For years, he owned and lived in an apartment complex at Crenshaw and 11th Avenue. "I could play anywhere here. I will never forget that."[78] He almost didn't enter the tournament that year at Rancho Park, after coming down with a bad cold. His lungs were so irritated he was forced to give up his cigars that week, which he didn't like, knowing he felt nervous and uncomfortable without a "stogie" in his mouth.

The first day was "one of those magic rounds where it all comes together and you start thinking about shooting at the pin on every single hole." He was out in 35 and then came home in an incredible 28 on a chilly, breezy day. His 63 led his closest competitor by three shots in a field that included Arnold Palmer, Lee Trevino, and Billy Casper. He held the lead all the way to the final round, when Rose and his two sons joined the thousands of fans who followed him around. Their cheers energized him, and he later claimed he had "never seen or felt anything like it."[79]

Paired with Harold Henning that day, the two traded the lead back and forth on the final nine holes, and Charlie had to sink a three-foot putt for par on the last to force a play-off. The two went to the 15th, a 382-yard par 4, to begin the play-off. After good drives, Henning hit first and put his second to the right of the green.

Charlie was up, grabbed a nine iron from the bag, and put a great swing on the ball, sending it three and a half feet from the hole. The crowd went wild, and he could feel his heart beating against his chest as he walked to the green. Henning chipped up to the hole, leaving Charlie his putt for the win. Summoning all the control he could muster over his nerves, he made a good stroke, and the ball disappeared. A second victory in two years. This time, when they handed him the oversized check for TV, he didn't cry, he laughed. "Rose was at my side and she laughed too. It was one of the best times I've ever had."[80]

"I got one real thought about this," Charlie said to the press. "The Lord gave me some courage to stay in there when it got close. I don't know whether I proved that the black man can play golf, but I proved that Charlie Sifford can."[81] Stanley Mosk, the man who helped overturn the

Caucasian clause, and who was now a California Supreme Court justice, was not forgotten by Charlie's supporters. The next day, a telegram arrived at Mosk's home which read: "Thank you for opening the door for the Charlie Siffords of this world."[82]

At a time when the country was reeling following the assassination of Martin Luther King Jr. a year earlier, with Vietnam War protesters ubiquitous on college campuses, and the Black Panther Party pushing for "black power," there were those who thought Charlie should be more active in promoting the cause of racial justice. But Charlie was a golfer, and his goal was to win tournaments and take care of his family, not be a crusader. As he said after his victory, "I'm here as a golfer, man. I ain't no politician and I don't go along with that militant stuff either."

Maggie Hathaway, a black golfer and activist who wrote a column for the *Los Angeles Sentinel*, writes, "He's never been what you'd call overly involved with the cause. But when he shoots a 63, that's *his* contribution, and no amount of militancy is going to be worth any more than that." Sifford loved the competition, and his goal was not to be the best black golfer on the tour but the best golfer, period.[83]

Sifford was given a parade after his victory. "I would like to say to all the young people in America today, all you have to do is be ready and produce," adding, "It's just so wonderful to think that a black man can take a golf club and become so famous. I just wish I could call back ten years." A fan yelled out, "Next stop, the Masters." Charlie smiled and said, "I hope you're right."[84] He didn't get an invitation after his win in Los Angeles and never did make it to Augusta, convinced discrimination was the reason. "The Masters didn't want blacks in general and didn't want me specifically," Sifford told *Golf Digest* in 2006. "When I got on the PGA Tour, the one thing I was certain of was that I would never get invited to Augusta no matter what I did." He claimed he didn't regret not being invited, since "I don't want to be anywhere I'm not wanted."[85]

It is difficult to determine the true motives of the people who ran the Masters from the time of its founding in 1934 until 1974, when Lee Elder's victory in the Monsanto Open earned him an invitation in 1975 to be the first African American to play. The Masters has always had a certain aura, due to the fact that Bobby Jones gave both the course, Augusta National, and the tournament itself, life. Clifford Roberts, who along with Jones founded the club, served as chairman from 1931 to 1976, and was the man who ran the tournament with an iron fist.

Just before Lee Elder's qualifying victory, Jim Murray wrote in the *Los Angeles Times* that the Masters was "the Queen Mother of golf. Players speak of it in the hushed tones usually reserved for the Vatican. The PGA does not run it. The USGA does not run it. The Masters runs it. It is not a democracy, but a monarchy."[86]

In the 1950s and 1960s, especially, its selection criterion was heavily weighted to include amateurs and foreign players, making for a weak field. As Murray put it, there were so many loopy swings in the field, all "Hogan had to beat was Snead, and all Nicklaus had to beat was Palmer to win it." Perhaps not quite, but by the mid-to-late 1960s, things changed, and tour winners and leading performers were let in as a matter of course.

Murray asserted that there had been blacks in the Masters for years. But they "were carrying somebody else's bag. They had names like 'Chimney' and 'Cemetery' and 'One-Iron.' Also, 'boy.' If they had other names, no one bothered to know them."[87] Augusta National was certainly a part of the culture that for decades made golf virtually inaccessible for black players. Ken Bowden, writer and former editorial director at *Golf Digest*, claimed that Roberts was generous to employees, but "he was sort of oblivious" to racial problems. "He came from a time and a world where black people served white people. I think it was as simple as that."[88]

In that respect, Charlie Sifford was not excluded from the Masters but rather ignored by it. He was a golfer, it would argue, who did not merit an invitation based on its qualification system at the time. From its beginnings, the Masters had various categories for granting automatic invitations, which included major championship winners and top finishers in the Masters, U.S. Open, U.S. Amateur, and PGA. It also included two professionals not otherwise qualified who had the best scoring average on the winter circuit (this increased to four in 1962, to six in 1968, and to eight in 1971).

Past champions had the right to choose a player who otherwise was not invited. They did not select Charlie after his 1967 win at Hartford, although Art Wall (1959 champion) did vote for him in 1969. The system was finally changed in 1972 to allow any tour winner into the field, but this new qualification was never made retroactive for Sifford—it required that the victory had to come in the previous calendar year.

As far back as 1961, in a letter responding to an accusation that black players were banned from the Masters, Bob Jones wrote that the qualifications didn't "include any limitation based on race or color. I can assure you that no such limitation is contemplated for the future." In 1968, he wrote Sifford a letter to personally assure him that if he qualified, he would be invited, adding, "I for one would be particularly happy to see you realize this ambition."[89]

Bob Jones's views on race are not clearly defined. His law partner Arthur Howell, who for 10 years had an adjoining office with Jones, could not recall "any discussion of race with Bob. If somebody asked me where he was on all this, I'll tell you I don't know. I don't know if he ever discussed it with anybody." There is also no record of Jones ever helping black golfers during the push to desegregate public courses in Atlanta in the 1950s. As a boy, he grew up with black nannies looking after him and as a man employed black housekeepers, cooks, gardeners, and chauffeurs in his own household. His whole life, practically speaking, was lived in a segregated world.[90]

In the weeks following Charlie's triumph in Los Angeles, columnists for black newspapers took up his cause. Frank Lett Sr., former president of the United Golfers Association, argued that golf would benefit greatly from Sifford playing in the Masters. Other sports had overcome the barriers of race long ago, and "the popularity that these sports have gained by opening the door is unbelievable."[91] Even with the flood of telegrams to Augusta urging that Sifford be invited, nothing happened. The rules would not be changed on his behalf.

Beyond overt discrimination, personalities may have also had something to do with Sifford not receiving additional consideration. Charlie Sifford was a no-nonsense man, not afraid to speak his mind and stir the pot, and as such, he could rub people the wrong way. Clifford Roberts had risen from his own difficult childhood in the farmland of Iowa to become a Wall Street banker and lived in a world far removed from Sifford's. Like Bob Jones, Roberts never had occasion to deal with black people as social equals and didn't appreciate anyone who told him how to run his tournament.

Pete Brown, who won the 1970 San Diego Open, claimed that Roberts wanted him to play at Augusta before Charlie. "Anybody before Charlie;

he didn't care who it was. He hated Charlie's guts."[92] Perhaps personal animus and class differences played a role, in the same way Sam Snead felt that USGA executive director Joe Dey, a refined Northern gentleman, gave him bad pairings and tee times in the U.S. Open because he didn't like Snead, an unrefined hillbilly from West Virginia. Whatever the truth, to Charlie perception was his reality.[93]

When Lee Elder became the first black man to play in the Masters, Charlie was at the end of his career on the tour. He had given away more than a dozen good years due to the Caucasian clause, and he couldn't get them back. There was no Senior Tour then, only one big tournament for players over 50, the Senior PGA championship, which he won in 1975. Ironically, the first one had been played at Augusta National in 1937. He found a club pro job and tried to be a businessman, but what he wanted to do was play tournament golf.

When the Senior Tour was launched in 1980, he had his chance, and in the inaugural U.S. Senior Open that year, he finished fourth. Life still wasn't perfect, and he continued to encounter problems. There was Utah in 1989 when the man in his pro-am group spoke about his "nigger" cook. There were many times when Charlie would be headed for the locker room only to be told by a security guard who took him for a caddy that it was off limits to him. Endorsement deals that white players might expect weren't abundant, although he was grateful for his business relationship with Toyota.

When Shoal Creek Country Club, site of the 1990 PGA Championship, was thrust into controversy when it was discovered the club practiced open discrimination in its membership practices, golf was clearly still fighting old battles. The club had no black members, and as Hall Thompson, president of the club stated, "That's just not done in Birmingham, Alabama."[94] For Charlie, it was a matter of "What else is new?" The PGA and USGA reacted by making it clear they would not stage future championships at clubs that had discriminatory policies, but the culture was difficult to change.

Charlie Owens recalled playing a senior tournament there in the late 1990s and having someone ask him about his courtesy car. "Boy, who you driving that car for?" the man asked. Owens collected himself and responded, "Well, number one, I'm not a boy. Number two, I am a black player playing in this golf tournament. I've been told to drive this car. So

I went and told the officials. They swept it under the rug. Didn't do no good."[95]

Not much seemed to have changed, as players were still treated with disrespect and confused with being caddies. "That happened to me several times out there," recalled fellow-player Walter Morgan, saying it had happened to him in Boston and Indianapolis, and in Birmingham he was once told, "Caddies park over there."[96]

For players, discrimination was more a problem outside than inside the ropes. Charlie never had problems with his fellow players treating him badly. In fact, in his autobiography, he singles out Bob Rosburg, Ken Venturi, Ed Oliver, and Frank Stranahan (all prominent names in their era) as having gone out of their way to make him feel welcome.

Fellow player Pete Brown said of Rosburg, "He'd fight for us. Anything we'd try to do, he wanted to do it. We always had his vote."[97] (Brown also credited Jackie Burke, Jimmy Demaret, Bob Goalby, and Art Wall as being supportive of him and the other black players on tour). Through it all, Sifford was able to make a living and earned $800,000 in his senior career, to go along with the $324,000 he made on the regular tour.[98]

Charlie was 74 years old when Tiger Woods won his first Masters in 1997, and with all the history surrounding that event, he found himself in the limelight once again. What did he think? Was he a pioneer? Did he talk to Tiger and offer advice? These, and more banal questions, were directed at him.

Steve Opperman, who lost to Charlie at Hartford in 1967, considered the irony. He drove with Sifford once from Tucson to Texas and, after hearing the brutal stories first hand, earned a greater understanding of the man hardened by bitter experiences. Thirty years later, reporters from all over the world were calling Sifford to get his opinion of what someone else was doing. "Charlie never got his full due," Opperman said. "The fact that he's getting it now [in 1997], with all the interest in Tiger Woods. . . . Well, that might just be a little hard for him to take." Sifford didn't disagree. The notoriety might have been nice, but at the end of the day, there was nothing in it for him.[99]

In 2004, when Charlie was elected to the World Golf Hall of Fame, he finally received his due respect from his peers. Gary Player presented him at the induction ceremony that November. Charlie writes in his autobiography that, of all the white players on the tour, Gary Player did the most for blacks. While some thought his actions were in response to his own experiences growing up under an apartheid government in South Africa, Sifford was convinced they were simply an honest expression of "just the kind of man he is." Player maintained that Sifford was essentially "persecuted" as a tour player and deserved the honor "for what he went through."[100]

Sifford gave an emotional speech that night, breaking down when he told the audience that his wife Rose—the "boss"—wasn't there, having passed away in 1998. He spoke of his days growing up as "a little old caddy boy from Charlotte, North Carolina," coming from a very poor family, "out there running up and down the road behind this little white ball," and getting inducted into the hall of fame, taking his place alongside so many of the game's greats. His handkerchief repeatedly wiped tears from his eyes. "How 'bout it?" he said. "It makes me feel like I'm a worthwhile professional golfer. I did my best."

On the 30th anniversary of Sifford's win at Hartford, Lee Elder contended that without Charlie, "there would have been no one to fight the system for the blacks that followed. It took a special person to take the things he took. Myself, I don't think I could have taken it, because I'm a little too thin-skinned." After Sifford won in Los Angeles, Bill Spiller, who fought his own battles with the PGA and was part of a suit following the Richmond Open in 1948, said: "Charlie Sifford never did anything but play golf and play golf and play golf. He was a brave man, old Charlie was. He went through some kind of hell, that man did."[101]

It is a sad reality that, as of 2016, Tiger Woods and Harold Varner III are the only full-time African American players on the PGA Tour. Charlie believed that the collapse of the caddy system blunted the development of black players, as it eliminated a way for poorer kids to get exposure to the game and have an outlet to develop their skills while making a little money. In 2003, he was asked why there weren't more blacks on tour. "A lot of youth today will not put up with the stuff I did back then," he answered. Many are more likely to quit and try something else when the going gets tough. "I had to be strong to deal with the stuff that was placed in front of me."[102]

Sifford told *Golf Digest* in 2006, "I knew what I was getting into when I chose golf." He knew he would never be rich or famous but added, "I was made for a tough life, because I'm a tough man. And in the end I won; I got a lot of black people playing golf. That's good enough. If I had to do it over again, exactly the same way, I would."[103]

Sifford said at the Hall of Fame that he "took the fight up for Teddy Rhodes. He was a wonderful man." Men like Ted Rhodes, Howard Wheeler, and Bill Spiller were not able to succeed in the way Sifford did but were all part of the mosaic that made up the African American golf experience in the 20th century.

Lee Trevino, who had his own hardscrabble upbringing, once said that when one considers what Sifford accomplished and "how he stayed in there, you have to put him in the Jackie Robinson category. Charlie is the one who fought for the Lee Elders, the Tiger Woodses," and others such as Pete Brown, Rafe Botts, George Johnson, Nate Starks, Jim Dent, Calvin Peete, Charlie Owens, Jim Thorpe, Chuck Thorpe, Bobby Stroble, Walter Morgan, Adrian Stills, Harold Varner III—and women such as Althea Gibson and Renee Powell on the LPGA—who followed him. For those who make the comparison to Robinson, it is good to consider the words etched on his graveside memorial: "A life is not important except in the impact it has on other lives."[104]

In November 2014, Charlie Sifford received the Presidential Medal of Freedom. Established in 1963, it is the highest civilian award in the country and recognizes individuals who have made "an especially meritorious contribution to the security or national interests of the United States, world peace, cultural or other significant public or private endeavors." Only two other golfers, Arnold Palmer and Jack Nicklaus, have received it. This added to the honorary doctorate he received from the University of St Andrews in 2006.

Charles Sifford passed away February 3, 2015, after a short hospitalization following a stroke. As his friend Gary Player said when paying tribute to him, Charles was a "fighter and he never, ever gave up." His long life of 92 years was one well lived. As Mr. Sifford explains in his autobiography, he didn't ask for the problems he got—he just wanted to play the game.

He demanded respect and gave it and showed people that "blacks could play at the highest level, too."[105] And when he made it to the World Golf Hall of Fame, he claimed proudly, "That little old golf I played was all right, wasn't it?" It was, but even greater was the strength of his character, which by its dogged persistence broke down the door for others of his race to walk through, bringing change to a system that desperately needed it.

6

KEN VENTURI

"I Still Think It Was a Miracle"

When the good Lord gives you a talent, you shouldn't waste it. [1]
—Ken Venturi

*He was running on fumes. If you had asked him his name, he could not
have told you. It is one of the most heroic things I have ever seen.* [2]
—Ray Floyd, on Venturi's final round of the 1964 U.S. Open

Children, without benefit of the acquired social graces that allow for the
appropriate expression of empathy and compassion when required, can be
extremely cruel. Ken Venturi remembered the gleeful taunts of his little
classmates. "Wh-wh-wha-t's th-th-the ma-ma-atter Ken? Ca-ca-ca-cat
go-go-got yo-yo-your to-to-tongue?" Laughter would follow, and young
Kenny would fly across the room to nail the culprit.

Venturi writes in his book *Comeback* that he wondered "why it was I
didn't become a boxer instead of a golfer." [3] In the United States today,
there are over three million people who stutter, and approximately 5
percent of all children go through a period of stuttering that lasts six
months or more. [4] Ken was such a child.

Many famous people have suffered from this affliction—Lewis Car-
roll, Winston Churchill, Marilyn Monroe, James Earl Jones, B. B. King,
and John Updike, to name a few. King George VI was one of the most
famous, and the 2010 Academy Award–winning movie *The King's
Speech* chronicles his own story, one that certainly left an impression on

Ken Venturi. Watching actor Colin Firth put a pot over his head, Venturi declared, "He did the same things I did!" Ken used to put a big spaghetti pot over his head as he worked to correct his speech because it helped to hear the echo of his own voice. "I got chills watching the movie," he said, recalling his own childhood angst.[5]

Kenneth Paul Venturi was born in San Francisco on May 15, 1931, the only child of Fred and Ethyl Venturi. His father worked for a ship chandler's firm on the busy San Francisco Embarcadero until he was 45, when he quit that job to take over the pro shop at the municipally owned Harding Park golf course. His mother sold real estate and became Ken's biggest cheerleader, boasting of his exploits to her friends and never missing an opportunity to tell him how much she cared about him.

As a kid, Kenny was always busy. He had a newspaper route, cut lawns, washed cars, and did whatever he could to make some extra money. At age nine, two things happened that would change his life. He started to caddy at the San Francisco Golf Club, and his mother changed him from being left-handed to right-handed.[6]

What Ethyl Venturi did was a fairly common practice in the 1940s and still persists today, especially in other countries. As late as 1946, the former chief psychiatrist of the New York City Board of Education warned that unless retrained, left-handed children risked severe developmental and learning disabilities; therefore, children were to "be encouraged in their early years to adopt dextrality . . . in order to become better equipped to live in our right-sided world."[7]

Although the National Stuttering Association now claims that being forced to change dominant hands is not a cause of stuttering, Howard I. Kushner, professor of Behavioral Sciences and Health Education at Emory University, has suggested that recent "imaging studies of stutterers, however, have suggested that stuttering is tied to disturbed signal transmission between the hemispheres" of the brain.[8]

The question of causality between changing handedness and stuttering is difficult to prove because studies since the 1930s have, according to psychologist Lauren J. Harris, "ignored the question of hand training and have focused on the broader question whether speech disorders are more common in left-handers generally." Whatever the reasons, Venturi was convinced that in his case the switch affected his speech, as he "began to stammer very badly."[9]

Sadly, he became the target of school bullies and recalled an incident at recess when a few of them managed to take off his pants and hang them from a flagpole. Yet when school administrators asked him to give up the names of the kids who did it, he refused. "When the other kids discovered that I had not given them away, I gained their respect. From that day forward, they never mimicked me again."[10]

By the time he was 13 years old, a teacher told his mother he would never be able to speak normally. "He's an incurable stammerer," Venturi recalled in 2011. "My mother asked me what I planned to do. I said, 'I'm taking up the loneliest sport I know,' and picked up a set of hickory shafts across the street from a man and went to Harding Park and played my first round of golf."[11]

Although he had been a caddy for four years, this was his first attempt at playing. He wasn't a natural, scoring a 172, but he counted every stroke. The golf course became his safe harbor, a place where he didn't have to talk to people, and he worked at improving his game each time out. He would go to the course by himself and play two balls and invent his own game. With one ball he would have to fade it from left to right, and with the other, he would have to draw the ball from right to left. "If I failed to at least curve the ball in the direction I wanted, that ball lost the hole, and I moved on. By the time I got to the point where the fade and draw won about equally, I was a very good player. To this day, I think it's a wonderful way for a kid to learn how to play golf."[12]

San Francisco turned out to be a great place to learn the game, with plenty of good golf courses to test him. "We had a lot of firemen, policemen and people like that who played golf," Venturi told the *San Francisco Chronicle* in 2012. "They taught you. And the city was really good about it; they let you play Harding and wouldn't charge you."[13] In 1946, when the PGA Tour came to town for the San Francisco Open, he went to watch. Camera in hand, he took a photo of Byron Nelson, the eventual winner, who gently reprimanded him for doing so while he was about to shoot. It didn't matter; Byron Nelson had talked to him.

"I came home to my mother," Ken shared with the Golf Channel's David Feherty in 2012, "and I said I just saw the greatest golfer in the world, and I want to grow up to be just like him." Ken did become an excellent player, yet his father never let it go to his head, telling his son to keep practicing when he won and to work a little harder when he lost.

"No matter how good you get," he'd tell Ken, "there is always someone waiting to knock you off."[14]

Ken also began a concerted effort to overcome his speech impediment, and his parents helped him, waiting for him to sound out words when he stuttered. "Their patience allowed me to recognize the value of self-reliance, of not waiting for somebody else to solve your problems, another early lesson I never forgot."[15] This struggle imbued him with a resilience that would serve him in dealing with future trials.

By the time he was 16, Ken was playing in national junior tournaments and scheduled his high-school classes so that he could finish early enough to get to Harding Park for a full afternoon of practice. He'd arrive at the course by 2:30 and practice until 5:30. He'd return home for dinner at 6:00 and then go to Shaw's Ice Cream Parlor, where he worked until 9:30. Saturday mornings he'd mow lawns to earn another $15 a month, and at the golf course, he washed cars in the parking lot for extra cash.

He was very frugal, he recalled with pride in 1964. "I always seemed to have a lot of jobs." In 1948, the United States Golf Association held its inaugural U.S. Junior Amateur. Top juniors from across the nation gathered at the University of Michigan Golf Course to compete, and Venturi made it all the way to the finals before losing to Dean Lind four and two. Defeat was always hard to take, but Ken's mother had told him never to cry in defeat, words he never forgot. [16]

When he captured the San Francisco City Golf Championship in 1950, a major event for city golfers, he was the youngest player to win it. His ego was growing, but his father put a check on it. Venturi maintained that his father was a man of few words. "My father and I would drive down from San Francisco. I would caddy at Cypress, and he would sell to the fishermen, and then he'd come pick me up, six, seven o'clock at night." Sometimes the ride home would be in silence, due to Ken's stuttering problem. "When my father spoke," Ken recalled, "it was to say something meaningful." When Ken would brag about his accomplishments, his father would stop him. "When you're really good, son," he'd caution, "they'll tell you."[17]

In 1949, Ken entered San Jose State, with the intention of becoming a dentist, but golf directed him in another direction. He earned his way by sweeping out classrooms, waiting tables in a sorority house, and passing out sandwiches in the press box during football games. [18] It was during this time that Venturi met a man who would become quite influential in

Ken Venturi was a teenage golf prodigy, and runner up to Dean Lind (right) in the 1948 U.S. Junior Amateur Championship. As a boy, Venturi's teacher told his mother that he was an incurable stutterer. His mother asked him what he planned to do. "I'm taking up the loneliest sport I know," he told her, and picked up a set of clubs from a man across the street and went to Harding Park in San Francisco to play his first round of golf. *Courtesy USGA. All Rights Reserved.*

his life—Eddie Lowery. Ed, who as a boy had caddied for Francis Ouimet when he defeated Harry Vardon and Ted Ray in the 1913 U.S. Open, became a successful businessman, owning numerous car dealerships. He was also an excellent amateur golfer in his own right and enjoyed high-stakes matches.

Lowery and Venturi began to play regularly, and these matches helped Ken learn how to deal with pressure. Sometimes Lowery would put in $600–$700 of his own money, and Venturi never more than $10–$20, but it was significant to him. "I got used to being where a lot of money was riding, and I didn't get scared off by it," he'd remember and told of their opponents' once shooting a 65 in a match and losing every bet to him and Lowery.[19]

In September 1951, Venturi won the California State Amateur at Pebble Beach, which earned him a very special benefit. He remembered sitting in class one day in early 1952 when someone came to tell him he had a phone call. "So what?" Ken said. "It's Bing Crosby." Not really believing it, he took the call anyway. As he told CBS partner Jim Nantz on air at the 2002 AT&T Classic, "So I went up and I picked up the phone and I said, 'Hello.' 'Hey Ken, it's Bing Crosby.' I said, 'Hey Mr. Crosby, what can I do for you?' He said, 'Well we've lost one of our amateurs, and I hate to call you at this late time, but could you come down, could you fill in, and play in my tournament?' I said, 'I sure will Mr. Crosby.' He said, 'Where are you going to stay?' I said, 'Well I'll find someplace.' He says everything is taken. He says, 'You know where I live on the thirteenth hole?' I said, 'I sure do.' He says, 'You stay with me.'"[20] And so it was that Venturi received his first invitation to play in the Bing Crosby National Pro-Am, which he would go on to win in 1960.

The following year, he would meet another man who would be perhaps the most instrumental influence in his career. After being defeated in the first round of the U.S. Amateur in Seattle, Eddie Lowery introduced Ken to Byron Nelson, the same man he had taken a photo of six years earlier and told his mother he wanted to emulate. Nelson was impressed with Ken's play and asked if he'd like to play a round together. Venturi jumped at the chance, and the two met the next day at San Francisco Golf Club (Nelson flew, Ken drove his 1942 Buick Roadster, fixing a flat tire along the way). Nelson observed him closely as they played their round and offered no advice. After shooting a 66, Venturi thought he'd receive some accolades, but none came. As Nelson remembered it, Ken scored well enough to beat him thanks to great pitching and putting but made a lot of bad swings.

"He was expecting me to brag on him (I knew from my own experience playing with Bobby Cruickshank when I was Kenny's age), but instead I said, 'Kenny, Eddie said he wanted me to work with you and if you're not busy tomorrow, you come out early, because we've got six things we've got to work on right away.'"[21] Venturi worked with Nelson for three days, recalling that Byron told him, "It will take about five or six months before you will be able to fully grasp what I'm trying to get across to you, but I want you to stick with it." Venturi turned out to be an excellent pupil. He claimed Nelson "taught me how to play," changing him from a hands player with a loop at the top of the backswing, to a balanced player with a solid one-piece motion.[22]

It was a meeting that changed Venturi's life. As he described it, "I never realized, honestly, what went into a golf swing until Byron got hold of me. He turned my game inside out." He took copious notes of their sessions and developed a routine for evaluating each round to track his mistakes, both mental and physical. Nelson told reporters years later that Ken "wanted to learn and he listened, never questioning what I told him."[23]

By the time Venturi graduated from college in 1953, his reputation had grown nationally, and he was selected to play on the Walker Cup team, a biennial event begun in 1921 pitting the best amateurs in the United States against those of Great Britain and Ireland. At 6 feet tall and 175 pounds, he had a good build for a golfer, lean and strong, and his future was bright. In 1954, Ken's career took a bit of a detour when he was inducted into the army. But before being stationed in Austria for 16 months, he was able to play in his first Masters, where he tied for 16th.

Before leaving for overseas, Ken married his first wife Conni, a woman with movie-star good looks who was the mother of his two sons, Matthew and Tim. After serving his military duty, he returned home and had to get the rust off his game, having played little golf while in the army. His game came back quickly, which was no surprise to him.

Venturi was confident of his own talents, and people took him as being too cocky at times. He explained part of that perceived cockiness was a byproduct of his stammer. When the press would ask him who would win a tournament he'd say "me" because he didn't have to put together a complex sentence he might stumble over, such as "There are many great players in the field, and a number of them have a chance to win."[24] He also drew confidence from the fact that he was respected by great players such as Byron Nelson and Ben Hogan.

In 1956, two of the best amateurs in the country were Ken Venturi and his good friend Harvie Ward. They were set to play in Bing Crosby's tournament that January, and before the practice rounds began, Eddie Lowery, who they both worked for as car salesmen, made a bet with fellow millionaire George Coleman. Lowery bet that his boys could beat two professionals in a best-ball match, telling Coleman he could bring whomever he wanted to a course of his choosing the next morning and they would play. Coleman came up with an incredible pair, Ben Hogan and Byron Nelson, to face the amateurs.

They would play at Cypress Point, one of the game's most famous courses. The match took place, and when Ben Hogan sank a 10-foot putt on the last hole, his team won the match 1 up. The scores for each: Hogan 63, Nelson 67, Venturi 65, and Ward 67. As Ken Venturi recalled it, the match was tight all the way. At the last hole, Ken hit his second to 12 feet and made the putt, forcing Hogan to make his to avoid a tie. As Hogan prepared to stroke the winning putt, he winked at Ken and told his partner Byron Nelson, "I'm not about to be tied by a couple of amateurs."[25] Hogan made the putt, but the experience proved to Ken that he could compete with the best in the game.

Since Ken had missed the 1955 Masters due to his military service, Ben Hogan persuaded the former champions to offer him a spot in 1956. He came into the Masters a confident man and jumped out to a four-stroke lead going into the final round, poised to become the first amateur to ever win there. In the final round, in which the leader was customarily paired with two-time champion Byron Nelson, the committee felt that it would look bad to pair Ken with his mentor and teacher and asked him to choose someone else to play with. He chose Sam Snead.

"For three dazzling days Venturi was within reach of a prize no amateur in the history of the Masters has ever been able to seize," wrote Herbert Warren Wind in *Sports Illustrated*. "But the Masters is a drama in four acts, not three, and on the fourth day it was exit Ken Venturi and enter Jackie Burke."[26] In blustery conditions, Burke shot a 71 to Venturi's 80 and won by a shot.

Even though Ken hit 15 greens the last day, he three-putted six times. He would remember trying to two-putt every green and "just coast home. The hardest thing in golf is trying to two-putt when you have to, because your brain isn't wired that way. You're accustomed to trying to make putts, and when you change that mind-set, your brain short-circuits, especially under pressure." Venturi finished second, the best performance by an amateur in the history of the Masters, but it was a crushing defeat, in more ways than one.[27]

Ten years later, he said, "There's no way I can put into words the bitterness and humiliation I felt." In the crucible of defeat, he brooded endlessly, having trouble sleeping as he would lie in bed and replay every shot of that final round over and over in his mind.[28] Returning to San

Francisco, he found the press waiting for him. Harry Hayward, a sports-writer for the *San Francisco Examiner*, asked Venturi about playing with Snead, and Venturi gave a number of statements that could well have been left unsaid.

"It wasn't that I didn't say what they wrote," Ken acknowledged. "It's that things were not quoted completely," and his words were put in the worst possible light, like, "Sam Snead gave Venturi the silent treatment" and "Venturi vows revenge, says he'll win the Open" and accusing Mike Souchak of choosing clubs and reading greens for Burke. [29]

The story that was picked up by AP and UPI wires and spread across sports pages throughout the country was that Venturi felt he had been unfairly treated by the tournament committee. Venturi was made to look like an aloof, self-centered crybaby, an impression that persisted in the minds of many people for years. [30] To make matters worse, Eddie Lowery took it upon himself to write a letter of apology, in Venturi's name and without his knowledge, to Bobby Jones and Clifford Roberts, which would strain his relationship with Lowery.

Four decades later, he was still upset about the newspaper story, which he believed intentionally misrepresented his views, and about the letter of apology he feels should never have been written. Of Hayward, Venturi said, "I never talked to him again. I never acknowledged him again." [31] And he never forgave him.

Through this trial, Ken considered quitting and told his father as much. "Well, you can quit if you want to," Fred Venturi told his son, "because it doesn't take any talent. Anybody can quit." Ken would remember this advice during many dark moments in the future, along with his father's admonition that, "When you lose, son, all it means is that you have to practice that much harder." [32]

Ken would defend his personality and attempted to explain himself in a 1964 interview, saying he didn't think he was aloof or intolerant. He admitted to being a loner at heart but that the only way he could be relaxed was to keep his mind completely on the game. "When I talk to people I lose my concentration, and then if I hit a bad shot or a stupid shot I get mad at myself and lose my composure." Other people might be able to be more sociable or talk to the gallery, but that was not in his nature. [33] For him to quietly acknowledge someone in the crowd with a nod was like someone else going over and giving them a slap on the back.

Following the Masters debacle, Venturi got back to the game. He played in the 1956 America's Cup in October, a USGA competition at that time, which featured matches between the United States, Canada, and Mexico. He won his foursomes match (two players on each team play one ball, alternating shots from tee to green) while being quite ill, sneaking off to the rough more than once to throw up, but sealed the match after hitting a nine iron to a couple feet on the last hole. "How I managed to get around that day, I do not know," he said, "but I simply couldn't allow them to substitute for me." His resilience, he believed, was a response to the criticism he endured after the Masters.[34] Later that year, he won the San Francisco City Amateur and the California State Amateur.

After graduating from San Jose State in 1953, he also began working for Eddie Lowery, who owned one of the country's largest Lincoln–Mercury dealerships. As Ken attested, "Lowery was to become in the months and years to follow almost like a second father to me." His own son had been killed in the war, and he would treat Venturi as an adopted one. They became exceptionally close friends, but Lowery never served as his sponsor, as some people inferred over the years. In his book *Getting Up and Down*, written in 2004, he says of Lowery, "I don't know how I would have succeeded without his help."[35]

Venturi turned out to be a good salesman, and in his first three months, he took third place in most cars sold on a staff of 24. "I made good money working for Lowery, about $30,000 in salary and commission. No wonder the thought of turning pro never occurred to me."[36] Like Bobby Jones before him, Venturi had the idea of remaining an amateur for life, especially in an era when the professional game didn't pay that much. As late as 1958, Arnold Palmer was the leading money winner with just over $42,000. Venturi may have faded into obscurity had it not been for a man named Bob Roos.

Roos was a wealthy San Francisco clothing-store executive and a member of Lowery's golfing clique, and Venturi had played with him countless times. But when he beat Venturi in the 1956 U.S. Amateur, it got Ken to thinking. If he could be beaten by Bob Roos, who he gave two strokes a side every time they played together, then he might go the rest of his life and never win the Amateur.

Venturi asked himself, "What the hell am I doing?" When he was selling cars all day, he wasn't practicing golf, and when he was practicing, he wasn't selling cars. Lowery finally forced the issue by offering

Ken his own dealership, but he couldn't take it. He decided to turn pro. "I knew by then how tough being a touring pro was," recalled Venturi in 1964, "that it [could] be Heartbreak Hill. But I was determined to test myself."[37]

Ken turned professional in November 1956. His mentor Byron Nelson thought his chances were good, saying at the time, "He has guts and desire. He grasps whatever I show him so well that I see my old self when I watch him swing. Even on bad days, he has that rare ability to score well."[38] The student had learned well and immediately made an impact, with a sixth-place finish in the U.S. Open and then wins at St. Paul and Milwaukee back-to-back in August. Venturi had turned pro to prove to the world he had the talent and ability to win. "And guts," as he said.[39] He accomplished that goal.

He also showed his mettle by returning to Augusta in 1957, finishing a respectable tie for 13th. With the memory of the news he made in the papers the year before, he was literally booed by the fans. But Venturi remembered Bobby Jones being his "biggest fan," defending Ken against the negative things that had been written about him. Venturi made no excuses because, as his father taught him, "You don't make excuses" and asserted that after people realized what really happened they became his biggest fans. Ken ended up 10th on the money list in 1957 and was named rookie of the year.[40]

The next year was even better, as Venturi captured four titles. Byron Nelson cautioned reporters who were putting his student in the company of the game's best players. "I won't say he will be the next Hogan or Snead. . . . But I will say he has the game and the will to be great." Venturi believed he was not affected by all the accolades, saying later, "I tried not to let what people wrote impress me." Eddie Lowery remembered it differently, telling *Sports Illustrated* in 1964 that Ken's success had gone to his head. "I had people come up to me and say, 'Ed, you're a friend of mine, and I know how you feel about Venturi, but I hope the s.o.b. shoots 100.'"[41]

Ken won twice in both 1959 and 1960, although his loss to Arnold Palmer in the 1960 Masters was almost as painful as his 1956 defeat. Venturi was poised to win the tournament until Palmer made birdie putts of 35 feet on the 71st and 6 feet on the 72nd to win by a stroke. In hindsight, Venturi contended that subconsciously that loss "well may have been the start of my long but certain slide on the toboggan to nowhere." The next year, Arnold Palmer skulled a bunker shot over the green on the last hole, and the resulting double bogey gave the tournament to Gary Player. "After taking it away from me in 1960 with a couple of miracles," Venturi recalled somewhat bitterly in 1966, "Palmer had handed it to Player on a silver platter."[42] He felt the fates were against him, and who could blame him given what would happen next?

In 1961, he was injured in a car accident. Venturi was the passenger, and the impact drove him against the side of the door, injuring his ribs and back. Instead of taking time off, he tried to play through the pain, which was a horrible mistake. "I didn't break anything," he recalled years later, "but I tore muscles in my back and shoulders and my game went down the tubes."[43] Two long years would pass before he would be 100 percent again, and during that time, he lost more than his golf game.

Ken's physical condition deteriorated further in 1962. Early in the year at Palm Springs, during the fourth round of the five-round tournament, he went to pick the ball out of the hole on the 10th green and felt a sharp pain in his chest, like someone had shoved a knife into it. He kept going and finished with a 68, but the next day, he couldn't continue. As he started to take a practice swing on the first tee, pain shot through him in "such waves that the club fell right out of my hands."[44] He returned home and was diagnosed with a back spasm that had pinched nerves leading to the chest and was given injections of Novocain. He then ignored the doctor's advice to rest.

The condition did not improve. Doctors tried cortisone, whirlpool baths, and deep heat treatments, to no avail. Venturi recalled it took several months before he could touch his head with his right hand, and his swing got shorter and flatter. As he described it, "The quicker I could pull the trigger, the quicker the pain would be over." Somehow, he managed to tie for ninth at the Masters but by the end of the year fell to 66th on the money list. With a wife and young sons to support, he was reaching the end of his rope.[45]

The year 1963 didn't seem as if it would be any better, and during this time, his childhood stammer resurfaced. His mother noticed, seeing "his chin twitching frequently, a sure sign of nervous tension in Ken," wrote Alfred Wright in 1964. "He went to doctors and, ultimately, to a hypnotist, but nothing helped." As for his physical ailment, he was ordered to wear a special brace, which he slept in for six weeks and wore daily for a couple of months.[46]

His swing had become a pitiful caricature of the classic one Nelson had helped him mold, although by March the pain in his back had virtually disappeared. As soon as that problem seemed to be lessening, he developed tendonitis in his left wrist. In trying to compensate for his bad swing, he believed he was putting more strain on other parts of his body.[47]

Mentally, Venturi admitted being "in a shambles" at this time and "started to ease both the physical aches and the worries clouding my mind by having a few drinks here and there." They became more and more of a crutch as time went by.[48] By 1963, his game was a total wreck, and he had no idea where the ball was headed. On the 13th hole at St. Petersburg that year, his tee shot ended up two hundred yards out of bounds.

People asked him what happened to his swing, and he shrugged them off, but things were falling in upon him. Palo Alto Hills Country Club fired him because he didn't spend enough time at the club, and by the end of the year, he had won only $3,848. "What Kenny went through in those years," a friend said of him, "was like a millionaire going broke." Yet Venturi kept things to himself and didn't complain to the press or his fellow pros. Dave Marr, winner of the 1965 PGA and longtime television analyst for ABC, said he never forgot how Ken sat with him at dinner one night after missing another cut, "and he never once talked about a shot or mentioned his bad luck. That was real class."[49]

Ken may have been able to put up a good front to the public, but he knew he was in trouble. The drinking got worse. It wasn't that he craved a drink, he said, but that it tasted good and took him away from reality. The more he drank the more belligerent he became, looking for fights and finding them. "I felt that I was the dirt in the bottom of the barrel," he would say of that time, "and I wished that I could disappear completely from the face of the earth."[50]

Ken Venturi, the cocky kid with a golf game that the best players on the tour had come to respect, was too stubborn to ask for help. The same qualities of self-reliance and hard work that had helped overcome his stuttering problem and build a world-class golf game now became a liability for him. His game had deserted him, and he felt powerless to do anything to get it back.[51]

His former boss Eddie Lowery said that during that period Ken thought he knew all the answers. He refused the counsel of friends, and even turned a deaf ear to Byron Nelson when he tried to help. "I remember one time I said to him," Lowery recalled, "'Kenny, have you got a dictionary at your house? Go home and look up the word humble—h-u-m-b-l-e, humble. You have no idea of the meaning of the word.' Oh, he was sore at me. He didn't even speak to me for a while after that."[52]

Venturi did indeed resent Lowery's telling him he needed to learn humility, but in his heart, he knew Lowery was right. The low point came when he went to a local haunt for a drink, and his bartender friend, Dave Marcelli, told him he was wasting his talent and making a total mess of himself and his family. He told Ken that people still believed in him and wanted him to play well.

Marcelli touched a nerve and gave Venturi something to think about on the drive home. "For the entire drive, I kept talking to myself, realizing what a stupid jerk I had become." He resolved to change his course and the following day was back at the club, hitting nothing but nine irons and wedges. His strategy was straightforward: to rebuild his game, "step by step, for as long as it would take."[53]

Lowery's words, and those of his bartender, lit a fire inside him. As Venturi described it, there was something that made him "bristle and fight like a tiger" when he felt people didn't think he could do something. He started fighting back, first by reviewing the pile of notes he had kept from his sessions with Byron Nelson years earlier and then hitting balls until his hands blistered. He kept at it, spending seven or eight hours a day on the practice range.[54]

Ken went to Las Vegas to play in the Sahara tournament to test his game, only to be told by officials at the registration desk that he was not invited. Humiliated, he went back to his hotel room to pack. But he still had friends who had stuck by him, and after Mike Souchak, Gardner Dickinson, and Jay and Lionel Hebert petitioned forcefully on his behalf, he was allowed to play. He made the cut, finished 26th, and felt some measure of success.[55] His game was coming around.

By the end of 1963, Ken began feeling pretty good about the way he was playing and told his wife that they had just enough money to carry him through one more year on the tour. His contract with U.S. Royal, whose ball he played, still had a year to go, and he could borrow the rest if he had to. If he failed, he promised her, he'd find another business. He asked his friend Bill Varni if he might buy into the restaurant he owned in downtown San Francisco. He told Venturi, "You don't want half this restaurant; 1964 is going to be your year."[56] Ken, appreciating the confidence Varni showed him, vowed he wouldn't take another drink until he won again.

Ken began the New Year knowing he was approaching "the end of the line." Almost broke, he had dedicated himself to one more effort to keep playing the game he loved on the biggest stage in the world. He had given up drinking and went to the practice tee to work, in his words, "as I had never worked before."[57]

Things didn't start well when he missed the cut at the Los Angeles Open, and he returned home depressed and bereft of hope. At midnight, he went to his basement workshop to clean his clubs and soon found himself on his knees praying. "Dear God, please don't let me die like this." He begged God to let him play as he had before, and if that happened, he'd accept whatever fate was in store for him after that. "Give me just one more chance to prove that I'm a man."

Venturi experienced an epiphany that night. There was a "new calmness and peace inside" him as he went back upstairs. "It was four o'clock in the morning; I had been down there alone a full four hours."[58] He went back on tour and started making cuts but found himself backing away from important shots, not willing to trust his swing. In March at Pensacola, he tied for ninth and won $1,100, his first four-figure check in two years, but was not invited to the Masters. "That was the killer," he'd remember. "'This is the bottom of the bottom of the barrel,' I thought. Another quarter of an inch lower and I would be out in the dirt."[59]

Then, when he needed it most, the prayer he had made in his basement a couple of months earlier was answered, in the person of Father Francis Kevin Murray. Venturi had met him sometime earlier, but Father Murray had known "with a kind of sixth sense" that Ken wasn't ready to be reached at that point. Still, the 35-year-old parish priest kept in touch and followed Ken at the Lucky International in San Francisco that January. He walked with Ken's wife, Conni, in the gallery and told her he'd like to get to know Ken better. Venturi let his guard down, and Father Murray's comforting personality touched him.

An invitation was offered for the priest to come to the house later, and it was accepted. Father Murray knew of the strain Ken's marriage was under and counseled the couple. He became a frequent visitor, spending a great many hours talking to Venturi, who was impressed by Murray's "wonderful easy way, his own particular brand of psychology" that helped iron out "the wrinkles" in his mind. Ken felt he had been set "back sure-footedly on God's path."[60]

At this most vulnerable time, Ken felt blessed to have found Father Murray. They played a little golf together (Murray was a 10 handicap) and took walks, talking about trust, confidence, dedication, about life. "He showed tremendous faith in me," affirmed Venturi, "which helped me to have more faith in myself." As Byron Nelson had taught Ken golf and worked on his swing, Father Murray worked on his inner self. He encouraged Ken and challenged him to be courageous, telling him if he had "guts" he could always be a winner.[61]

In May, Ken played in the Colonial National Invitation with his friend Ben Hogan, who had taken Ken under his wing in 1958. "Ken, what happened to your hook?" Hogan asked him. For Venturi, the recognition from a man he respected that his swing had improved was vindication of all the work gone into resurrecting his swing. Still, his position remained extremely precarious: years later, Venturi would claim he had about $300 to his name at that point.[62]

Ken set his sights on the Thunderbird Classic in New York, the tour's richest event, that June. A missed cut the week before in Indianapolis meant he needed a sponsor's invitation to get into the field. He made a call to Bill Jennings, the chairman, pleading for an invitation. The previous year, Venturi had withdrawn after a first-round 80, and he knew Jennings didn't owe him anything. Jennings listened patiently and told him he'd get back to him, and after a sleepless night, the call came the next day telling Ken he was in.

In the final round, Venturi found himself with a chance to win. Arriving at the 16th hole, a long par three, he knew that pars all the way in would secure at least third place and a big check. He could play the shot safe and make a sure bogey or go for the pin and maybe make a birdie, but if the shot didn't come off, it would be costly not only to his pocketbook but also his confidence. "I said to myself, 'If you back off now, you'll back off the rest of your life.' So I took the three-iron and hit a great shot to the green and two-putted for my par."[63] A birdie on 17 and par on 18 gave him his tie for third place and a check for $6,250. He called his wife, and they both cried, unable to talk.

The U.S. Open was fast approaching, and two days after the Thunderbird, Ken shot 77 in the morning round of the 36-hole qualifier. Tempted to withdraw, he remembered his father's words that it takes no talent to quit. He went out that afternoon and shot a 70, passing 45 players ahead of him to qualify.[64] He then finished sixth at the Buick and came to the Open with a surprisingly new measure of confidence. That year's venue was Congressional Country Club, in the suburbs of Washington, DC.

The Open had been held once before in the nation's capital, in 1921 at Columbia Country Club in Chevy Chase, Maryland, where winner Jim Barnes was presented the trophy by President Warren Harding. In 1964, the region was experiencing a tremendous heat wave. Temperatures near 100 degrees combined with stifling humidity to create a suffocating atmosphere. It's the kind of heat that starts early—at 7 a.m. you can step outside and find your shirt soaking with perspiration within five minutes.

Not only did the players have to deal with the heat, but also they faced the longest course in the championship's history, at 7,053 yards. That year Ken Venturi's average of 249 yards off the tee ranked him in the top 20 in driving distance. Today, the number is closer to 300 yards, so it is easy to see how long the course was in relation to the equipment and golf balls of that era. With length came tall, heavy rough lining the narrow fairways. Venturi was so overwhelmed by the heat when he arrived— which he likened to being in a furnace—that he and Paul Harney give up their practice round after 13 holes.[65]

The night before the first round, Ken went to church and said a prayer, asking to play well and to handle himself like a man no matter what might befall him.[66] At the end of two rounds, he found himself six shots behind leader Tommy Jacobs, still well within striking distance. Checking his mail that night, he found a six-page letter from Father Murray. Its words offered Ken inspiration.

Most people were in the midst of struggles, Father Murray told him, with their jobs, their families, or their health, to name a few. "For many there is the constant temptation to give up, and to quit trying. Life seems to be too much, and the demands are too great." He told Ken that if he could hang on and win he would be an inspiration "to millions of people that they can be victorious over doubt and temptation to despair."

Father Murray reminded Venturi that he had family and friends who loved him, and they respected him for how he had battled his way back. Ken was "mature and battle-toughened," he said, and urged him to give himself over "entirely to the fulfillment of your one shot at hand. . . . Trust in your swing and in your ability. Trust in your good judgments."[67] Ken took every word of that letter to heart. He was ready. From 1926 to

1964, the final two rounds of the U.S. Open were played on the same day. The finish would be a true test of endurance.

Ben Brundred III of Laurel, Maryland, then 12 years old, followed the play with his father. He thought it was magical seeing Arnold Palmer and Jack Nicklaus. "But the memory that stands out the most," Brundred recalled in 2011, was "how hot it was. There had been thundershowers at various times. . . . After the bad weather cleared, you came back out and play resumed." It was so hot that "steam was rising from the ground. It was an amazing sight."[68]

Venturi's eight-foot putt for birdie on the first hole hovered on the lip of the cup before falling in. It was witnessed by a large gallery that included legendary football coach Vince Lombardi. Venturi later learned that Lombardi told his wife that when he saw Ken's eyes after that putt dropped he knew he was going to win because they showed no fear.[69]

Ken believed "the good Lord was looking after me" after that putt dropped, and he blocked out his discomfort from the broiling temperature that by some accounts reached as high as 108 degrees on the greens that day. He concentrated on doing what was necessary to win and forgot about how badly he felt but admitted he also "forgot to drink water," which would be a horrible mistake.[70]

Venturi found a touch of magic on the front nine, going out in 30. "I hit every fairway, I hit every green, I made every possible putt," he would recall.[71] He continued to play well on the back nine until becoming dizzy on the 17th. With a 13-foot putt for birdie, he hit it a foot by. Approaching his second putt, his body started shaking, and chills rolled down him from head to toe. His vision was blurry. He saw three cups, aimed at the middle one, and missed and then bogeyed the 18th as well but still finished with a 66. As he walked off the 18th green after finishing the round, "I hardly had any idea where or who I was. My body was as limp as a dish towel, my eyes kept wanting to roll up into my skull, I was shaking uncontrollably and I was as deathly white."[72]

What happened next has become an indelible part of golf history. Clearly suffering from heat exhaustion, Venturi was disoriented, dizzy, nauseous, and feeling faint. If not treated, this can lead to heat stroke, in which the body's temperature-control system is compromised and complications involving the central nervous system occur. His face was ashen and eyes glazed over as he walked to his locker.

He couldn't eat and asked for some tea and lemons. Ray Floyd, Ken's playing partner, went looking for Ken's wife. "He's sick," said Floyd. Dr. John Everett, a member of Congress and chair of the Open's medical committee, was called in with another doctor to assess his condition. He had Ken lie down for the 50-minute break between the third and fourth round.[73]

Frank Murphy III, who was 23 years old at the time, was helping his father, chairman of the 1964 Open. "I was there, in the locker room with my dad," he would recall. "All these people were working over him. The big question was whether he should keep playing." "Don't continue," Everett finally said, advising caution. Venturi told the doctor there was no way he was going to quit. Then the doctor added a chilling qualifier: "It could be fatal." To his final days, Ken could not remember the conversation, but Dr. Everett said Venturi looked him right in the eyes and said, "It's better than the way I've been living."[74]

Everett relented but only on the condition that Venturi allow him to walk with him, fearing if Ken's condition worsened he might go into convulsions. "But remember, doc," Venturi told him, "don't touch me unless I give you the okay. Is it a deal?"[75] Everett fed him iced tea and salt tablets (12 during the round, which would be rejected as a treatment today) and dipped a towel in a bucket of ice water for Venturi to drape over his head and neck. "I was going to make it if I had to die in the effort," Venturi maintained. "If I didn't make it I was out of golf. I had failed too often before. That last round became my whole life."[76]

It was to be the round of his life but one which he would hardly remember. He couldn't recall going from the locker room to the first tee for that final round. After cutting the heart out of the fairway with an arrow-straight drive, he slowly walked down the fairway. "Just hit this one shot," he kept telling himself over and over again. When he began to tire, he thought of Father Murray's letter and from some inner reservoir found the strength to keep going.[77] He couldn't worry about what everyone else was doing, that was out of his control. Just one shot and then the next, that was his formula. He went out in par 35. Half way there, and he was still on his feet.

On his walk to the tenth tee, Ken wondered how many people in the crowd of 22,000 were thinking he might fold. He was determined to show them he could finish strong. When Venturi birdied the 13th, he took a five-shot lead with five holes to go. Almost home. On the next hole, he began to feel quite poorly and had to slow down. At the 15th, he said to Joe Dey, the executive secretary of the USGA who was following his pairing, "You can penalize me two strokes if you want to, but I'm slowing down."[78]

After hitting what he called his best shot of the championship at the 16th—a one iron to the par three that missed hitting the pin by inches— Ken two-putted from 12 feet and had the finish within sight. Two pars would force Tommy Jacobs to finish with two improbable birdies to tie. One shot at a time. A par came on 17. A straight but relatively short tee shot found the fairway on 18. After his drive, he asked a friend in the gallery, Bill Hoellie, where he stood. "All you gotta do is stay on your feet," came the answer.[79]

Joe Dey sidled up to Ken and told him to hold his head up, he was a champion now. Steering away from the water hazard to the left, he pushed his four iron into the right greenside bunker. Cheers from the crowd sent chills racing up and down his spine.

Then, as Venturi was walking to the green to complete one of golf's most dramatic finishes, a very odd thing happened. Two overzealous and heat-crazed marshals got into a fist fight near the green. "I saw them rolling in the dust," Ken remembered, and thought, "'Please don't land on my ball.'"[80] The scuffle was broken up, and Ken blasted out of the bunker to within 10 feet of the hole.

He lined up the putt, stroked it firmly, and it fell in the hole. "My God, I've won the Open," Ken said softly, closing his eyes, the putter slipping from his hands and falling to the ground. Ray Floyd, then a 21-year-old just beginning his career, remembered the moment in 1997: "I reached down and picked his ball out of the hole and when I went to give it to him I had tears in my eyes I felt so great for the guy." Venturi said he stayed fairly composed until he saw Floyd sobbing, "and that's when I lost it," as both wept tears of joy and relief.[81]

Floyd called Venturi's 66 that morning the "greatest round I've ever seen. It was so nearly perfect, it made me feel like I was shooting 90. If he had been putting super, he might have shot 59 or 60." Venturi was always grateful to Floyd for the encouragement he provided. "During the round I could hear him say at times, 'Keep going, you've got it, keep going, you're doing fine.'"[82]

Ken always maintained he played the back nine on instinct. "I was in a fog. Actually, it may have been a blessing in disguise. I didn't feel any of the pressure. It was kinda like walking through a dream world and when I woke up, people were telling me I was the Open champ. It was beautiful." His old tutor Byron Nelson said those last two rounds "proved what a great player Kenny really was." His last three rounds of 206 set a 54-hole record, and his closing 136 tied the Open record for the final 36 holes. He had come back from the abyss to win the most prestigious championship in golf, and nobody could ever "take this day of days away from me."[83]

Venturi didn't believe that hard work and renewed dedication were the sole reasons for his inspired play. "Never ever lose faith in God," he would say.[84] In the press conference he spoke of the final putt that was supposed to break to the right. He pushed the putt, but the ball somehow broke left. Years later he'd say it was as though "somebody upstairs turned it and plunked it right in the hole. It was destiny."[85]

Part of that destiny was meeting Father Murray, who encouraged Ken with letters and telegrams, "to let him know I was thinking of him and appreciated our friendship, that I believed he could succeed." Venturi said after the win that he had read Father Murray's letters over and over, that he "used them almost as a Bible." The 1964 U.S. Open was a miracle in the eyes of many people. In 1992, Venturi affirmed, "I still think it was a miracle. It was. If it was written as fiction, you couldn't sell a single book because it's too corny, it could never happen."[86]

Ken won twice more in 1964 and was named PGA Player of the Year. Yet just when he thought he had a rebirth of sorts, another crisis struck him. While at the Piccadilly World Match Play Championship event outside London that October, his hands became cold and had little feeling in them. The condition worsened the following year. A *Sports Illustrated* article in 1965 stated that he suffered from a circulatory disorder "that so drastically reduced the flow of blood into Venturi's hands that the skin began to peel, the fingers felt cold to the touch and they turned white as frozen flounder."[87]

The condition made his fingers numb, and the colder the weather, the worse they got. Venturi said when he tried to play, "it didn't even feel as if I had a golf club in my hands. It might as well have been a broomstick. I never had any idea of what I was doing or where the club head was." At night, when the hands were warm, his fingers would throb. "They felt as if they were about to explode," he said.[88]

Ken Venturi came to the 1964 U.S. Open at Congressional Country Club in Bethesda, Maryland trying to resurrect his career after a three year slump. On the
final day he suffered from heat exhaustion in the 100 degree plus heat, and was
advised by a doctor not to continue, as it could prove fatal. To which Venturi
responded, "It's better than the way I've been living." *Courtesy USGA. All Rights
Reserved.*

Doctor after doctor failed to diagnose the exact problem, as he went
crashing to the bottom once again. Yet this time, he approached his fate
differently. There would be no panic, no withdrawal from the world, no
escape into the bottom of a bottle. Venturi would remember the promise
he made to God "that night when in utter desolation I knelt in my basement workshop all alone."[89] He would cope with what might come, a
stronger man than he had been before.

He tried to play on, taking heavy daily doses of cortisone. He would
soak his hands in near-scalding water to try to warm them up and
restore circulation, with little success. In the winter cold of the Crosby
tournament on the Monterey Peninsula, his hands had no feeling in
them at all, and he had difficulty making a fist or wrapping them
around a club. At one point, they were so painful that he putted wear-

ing a pair of fur-lined leather gloves. "The fingers got so white and awful looking," says Venturi, "that when I showed them to [fellow pro] Bob Goalby one day while we were playing Cypress I scared him half to death."[90]

His hands worsened, shaking as if with palsy, and he began to drop things constantly. The ball would fall out of his hand when he tried to tee it up; his knife or fork would drop onto his plate with an embarrassing clunk. At the Masters, his friend Mike Souchak suggested he go to Mayo Clinic, where he was diagnosed correctly with carpal tunnel syndrome. He suffered withdrawal from the cortisone he had been taking, which led to loud outbursts and tantrums. While driving his car to an exhibition with Souchak, he had a hallucination that almost led to an accident.[91]

Ken needed surgery, but held off until he defended the Open at Bellerive in St. Louis, which he believed was his duty as reigning champion. He missed the cut by 11 shots after shooting rounds of 81 and 79. Bill Campbell, former president of the USGA and captain of the Royal and Ancient Club of St Andrews, who played with Venturi, said, "It was a tremendous demonstration of will power, for he was in pain. He never whimpered or complained at any time." Venturi told the press that he was going to put his clubs away for awhile and wouldn't play again until he was physically able to perform.[92]

Ken submitted to surgery. The doctor spent 16 minutes on his left hand and 18 on the right hand, and a trace of gangrene was found in one finger. Had he waited a little longer, his doctor said after the surgery, Ken might have lost some fingers or perhaps a hand. Ken faced another arduous period of rehabilitation, stretching out scar tissue, and found his left hand worked better than the right. It was a frustrating recovery, and as he said before the operation, "I just wonder how many times I'm going to have to get off the canvas. But whatever happens, I know that God can make everything turn out for the best."[93]

Venturi worked hard to recover but had to overcome a mental block when trying to deliver his full power to a shot. Seeing the scars on his wrist made him fear something tearing as he swung full-out. He was able to get back on the tour in 1966 and in San Francisco found one last bit of inspiration. The Lucky International tournament was played at Harding Park, where Ken played his first round of golf and learned the game. His father, Fred, was now managing the course, and it was a nostalgic home-coming for both.

In the first round, he hit all 18 greens and shot a 68 and then matched the score in the second round. He was in great shape. The third round brought a change in the weather, as it began to rain and turned cold, which was the last thing his hands needed. They started hurting almost immediately, and he thought his chances were gone, but when he reached the sixth hole, play was cancelled for the day, and the round was wiped away. It was an absolute blessing for him. Ken was able to manage a 71 in the third round even though the pain had not subsided and he had trouble feeling the putter in his hands. Trailing leader Frank Beard by three shots, he still had a chance. That's all he ever asked for.

Venturi was paired with Arnold Palmer in the final round. Arnie had his army of fans, but that week, Ken had the advantage. Fired up by the supportive gallery, he made birdies at the sixth and ninth holes to make the turn in 33. He followed with a 30-foot putt on the 14th and then picked up another on the 16th. News came that Beard had bog-eyed three holes, and when Palmer dropped back to even par for the day, Ken took the lead by a single stroke. The butterflies were churning, but he welcomed the feeling. He was on his home course, one he had played hundreds of times, and he knew what he had to do. A par came at 17.

On the final hole, a big drive left him with just a seven iron to the green, which he hit 12 feet from the cup. It was the 18th green in regulation he hit that day. Two putts later, it was all over. His closing 66 gave him a 273 total and victory over Frank Beard. As the winner's check was presented to him, Ken spoke of how nice everyone had been, adding, "What could any man say after all his prayers have been answered?"[94]

It would be the last of his 14 wins on the PGA Tour. He had come back again and would receive the 1966 Ben Hogan Award, given to players who have stayed active in golf despite a physical handicap or serious illness. Ken's hands would never be the same and failed him again, forcing another surgery. He asked his doctor if he would be able to play golf again and was told yes but not at the level he had before. His career was over. Distraught, he discussed the situation with his father, telling him he might never play again. His father said it didn't matter if he ever played again. How could he say that, Ken asked. Because, his father replied, "You were the best I ever saw." With that, Ken felt free to go ahead with the surgery in 1970. His father had said he was the best.[95]

Ken also had a faith in God that sustained him. He was a religious man, he said, but didn't wear it on his sleeve. "You don't have to go to a street corner and let everyone know that you pray," he said. After he won the U.S. Open and his hands failed him, he had been tested again. It was as if God asked him, "Do you still believe?" Ken maintained that he felt like Job in the Bible, "who said to God, 'Do with me what you will but I will not stop believing.'"[96]

When Frank Chirkinian and CBS Sports offered him a job as a commentator in 1968, Ken was apprehensive. A man who stammered in the communications business? How would that work? He knew that he had the composure to speak fluently when he kept his mind on exactly what he was saying, but when his thoughts wandered, he was inclined to stumble over his words.[97] Ken approached his new career with the same professionalism he had his golf career and thrived. "He became an icon by being in our living rooms one weekend after another," noted Michael Bamberger on the occasion of Venturi's retirement, "by being reliable, predictable and comfortable."

Like most announcers, Ken had his own supply of well-worn phrases—for example, "You couldn't walk it out there and place it any better," "He'll take his par and walk to the next tee quietly," "That's class"—and was not light on his feet verbally. On air, Venturi once paid tribute to Jerry Pate, a former U.S. Open champion and CBS announcer, by saying, "He's been a great friend, but he still has that beautiful swing." That didn't mean that most of Venturi's great friends lose their beautiful swings, wrote Bamberger.[98] It was just the way Ken talked, and people accepted him, because he knew his golf from the perspective of a major championship winner. He also knew when to let what was happening on the screen speak for itself and keep his mouth shut. As his boss Frank Chirkinian used to say, "Remember, you're doing television."[99]

With his emotional victory at Congressional in 1964, Venturi had established a bond with viewers, wrote Peter McCleery in a 2002 *Golf Digest* article. His strength as an analyst sprang from the "passion and conviction he brought to the booth. He said things with such authority and in such absolute terms that you believed him, or wanted to." Ken was always ready with his yardage book and his pin sheet, remembered partner Jim Nantz. "You never stopped being a player," Nantz said of him in 2013.[100]

Venturi, as a recovering stammerer, struggled with the flow of spoken paragraphs and realized his thoughts didn't always hold together, but he didn't lament his condition. As he told reporter Jimmy Roberts in a 1996 interview, "I've never beaten it. I am a stammerer."[101] But during his three decades in the broadcast booth, he tried to improve and to be an inspiration to the hundreds of stammerers he counseled.

Ken Venturi retired from CBS in 2002 and still remains the longest-serving lead analyst for any sport in television history, working 35 years. "The greatest gift in life is to be remembered," Venturi told millions of viewers at the end of his final telecast. "Thank you for remembering me. God bless you and God bless America."[102]

After leaving CBS, Ken remained active with a number of causes. For nearly two decades, he was the national spokesman for the Stuttering Foundation of America, pledging to the foundation's founder, Malcolm Fraser, that he would do whatever he could to help people who stammered. "Kenny was emphatic about not getting publicity for it, but his life was dedicated to philanthropy," claimed Jim Nantz. He was involved in many different charities, working on behalf of the blind, battered mothers, and sick children, for black golfers like Charlie Sifford who were the victims of racism, and for struggling players looking for help with their swings.[103]

Nantz said Venturi moved "mountains, and people didn't know that about him." As Ken would describe it, when you give to others you don't have to announce it to the world. "Only two people have to know—you and God."[104] One organization that Venturi worked for was Guiding Eyes for the Blind. For 27 years, he conducted the Guiding Eyes Golf Classic, an outing in New York that raised more than $6 million toward providing guide dogs to blind people.

During the September 11 attacks on the World Trade Center, a blind man named Omar Rivera was on the 71st floor of the north tower. "Omar didn't think he could make it down through the crush of people," recalled Venturi in a 2004 interview, "so he asked another man to save his dog. The man agreed, but the dog shook loose, retrieved Omar, and got them both all the way out." Sometime later, Rivera told his story at a Guiding

Eyes gala at Rockefeller Plaza. Venturi remembered that toward the end of Omar's talk he said, "'This dog came from Ken Venturi.' I cry easily enough as it is, but I cried buckets that day."[105]

Venturi continued to face physical challenges for the rest of his life. Two years after successfully captaining the U.S. President's Cup team to victory over the Internationals 21.5–10.5 in 2000, he underwent treatment for prostate cancer. It was during those treatments that he met his future wife Kathleen (his marriage to his first wife Conni ended in divorce, and his second wife Beau died of brain cancer in 1997).

In 2006, he underwent heart bypass surgery, yet despite all these trials, he never bowed to self-pity. As he once observed, "If you think you've got a bad deal in life, just look around." Ken Venturi gave back to the game as much as he could. He mentored a number of players, including 11-time PGA Tour–winner John Cook. And he did it for free. "How can I charge when [Byron] Nelson only charged me five cents? I asked him how I could repay him and he said, 'Be good to the game and give back.'"[106]

No one soaked up more of Venturi's wisdom than well-known instructor Jim McLean. He met Ken in 1975, an event he called "a life-changing experience. Just from a performance perspective, I had never seen such control of the ball," said McLean. "Even past his prime, he showed me there was a different level of golf that could be played, and how truly great a player he must have been."[107] Venturi's knowledge of the golf swing was passed down from the likes of Francis Ouimet, Gene Sarazen, Byron Nelson, and Sam Snead, to touch the current generation through teachers like Jim McLean and players like John Cook.

People remember Ken Venturi for many things. Most recall his heroic U.S. Open victory. They may not know that Masters founder Bobby Jones told him in 1958 that, had Ken won the 1956 Masters and remained an amateur, he would have asked Ken to be president of the Augusta National Golf Club. "Mr. Jones cherished the fact he was a lifelong amateur," Venturi explained in 2004, "and he really wanted to see an amateur win the tournament and succeed him. That was some high honor. If I'd won in 1956, I for sure never would have turned professional."[108]

Fate would push him in a different direction, however. For all he went through, Ken maintained the only regret he had was wondering what he might have done had he not lost the use of his hands. "For five years there before that happened," he said, "I was favored or co-favored in every tournament I played." But he also was philosophical. "But then again, if I had won the Masters as an amateur, there wouldn't have been an Open, there wouldn't have been all the tournaments that I won, there wouldn't have been CBS, there wouldn't have been a lot of things."[109]

Detractors suggested he was made bitter by some of his experiences, which he rejected. "The way I look at it, I feel the exact opposite," he wrote in 2004. "I don't know of anyone in the history of the game who has been more fortunate." He often said he wondered why he had been so blessed and was thankful for what he had. The values his mother and father instilled in him, as well as people like Byron Nelson, guided his life. When his father died in 1988, Venturi was at his bedside and heard him say, "Son, you have made me very proud." That, Venturi said, "made my whole life."[110]

Ken Venturi was elected to the World Golf Hall of Fame in 2013 but was too ill to attend the induction ceremony, having been hospitalized for two months battling spinal and intestinal infections, along with pneumonia. It was hoped he would be able to make his speech the next year, but it was not to be. Ken passed away May 17, 2013, less than two weeks after his induction, and so ended a life that was connected to a hundred years of golf history.

Francis Ouimet was his stockbroker. He knew Walter Hagen and Tommy Armour. Byron Nelson was his teacher. Ben Hogan mentored him and requested that Ken be a pallbearer at his funeral. Gene Sarazen was his neighbor for many years in Florida, and Ken delivered the eulogy at his funeral. Tiger Woods played for him on a victorious President's Cup team. As Bobby Jones might have said, Ken Venturi had a rich, full life.

In 1992, Ken said, "I've lived in an era when I saw the best that you're ever going to see in golf." It would be hard to argue with that statement. And he also left his own legacy, of heart and determination revealed during his many struggles, which he handled with quiet and resolute strength. Ken was fond of repeating a phrase fellow CBS commentator Jack Whitaker used when describing the many peaks and valleys of his friend's life: "Fate has a way of bending the twig and fashioning a man to his better instincts."[111]

Fate bent Ken Venturi but never broke him and left a man who forever appreciated what the game had given him and moved him to give back more than he took. As he told David Feherty in 2012, "I thank God for all the blessings He's given me, and I wouldn't change a thing." It was a sentiment he'd been expressing for years since winning that historic Open championship, where he said simply, "I think the good Lord is looking after me."[112]

7

BRUCE EDWARDS

"I'm Just Trying to Carry On"

Carrying clubs is one of the most agreeable trades open to the lower orders.[1]
—Sir Walter G. Simpson, *The Art of Golf*, 1892

I knew it the first time I stepped inside the ropes. I just loved the way it felt.[2]
—Bruce Edwards

On a cool summer day in Portland, Oregon, John Solheim of the Ping Company stood near the 18th green at the Jeld-Wen Tradition tournament—bearing gifts. When Tom Watson came off the green after a practice round with his caddy Bruce Edwards, they were surprised to see John waiting for them. After warm greetings and handshakes, John presented them with identical gold-plated putters bearing the inscription: "Tom Watson and Bruce Edwards. Friends, Companions, and Brothers Forever."[3] The kind gesture stirred emotions in them, emotions that would carry them both in the days to come.

Tom went out and won the tournament, fueled by a spectacular second round 62. For a brief moment, he was happy and so was Bruce to be on the bag for another win. It had been a busy and trying spring and summer for both men, as they realized time was running out. Bruce's legs were tan but shockingly thin, and he was forced to ride a cart most of the time between shots. He looked frail and ill and with good reason. In January, he had been diagnosed with amyotrophic lateral sclerosis (ALS), or Lou Gehrig's disease, and was given two to five years to live. "People tell me how courageous I am," Edwards told the Portland *Oregonian* that week. "Hell, that's not courage. I'm just trying to carry on."[4]

He would indeed carry on, just as he had been doing since he began his career on the PGA Tour in 1973. He was proud to be a caddy and even prouder of his friendship with one of the game's greatest players. Bruce was part of a tradition going back hundreds of years. A newspaper article from the late 1800s claimed that a "caddy was part and parcel of the player, as were his clubs."[5] Caddies have carried the clubs of golfers since the game began, and when golf came to the United States, it brought a new industry with it. "Three essential factors are required for good golf in America," wrote John Street in *Golf* magazine in 1897—"The expertness of the players, good clubs and balls, and a good caddie."[6]

Many of the game's greatest players started out as caddies—Old Tom Morris, Harry Vardon, Francis Ouimet, Gene Sarazen, Ben Hogan, Byron Nelson, Charlie Sifford, and Ken Venturi, to name a few. Caddying was the avenue through which many great champions came to the game. It also provided many young men who lacked the talent to become top-notch players a way to make a living.

In the past 40 years, there have been a few well-known caddies—Tip Anderson for Arnold Palmer and Tony Lema, Angelo Argea for Jack Nicklaus, Alfred "Rabbit" Dyer for Gary Player, Herman Mitchell for Lee Trevino, Mike "Fluff" Cowan for Jim Furyk, Steve Williams for Tiger Woods, and Jim "Bones" Mackay for Phil Mickelson. And one who helped usher in a new era of professional caddies in the 1970s and 1980s. He was Bruce Edwards, the man Bones Mackay has called the "Arnold Palmer" of caddies.[7]

Bruce Jay Edwards was born November 16, 1954, the second of four children of Jay and Natalie Edwards. As a kid, he always seemed to be in some kind of trouble at school—his parents believed he suffered from attention deficit disorder (ADD)—but in those days, children who weren't doing well in school were thought to not be trying hard enough. Fortunately, he would find an outlet for some of his energy on the golf course.

Bruce's father, a dentist, was a member of Wethersfield Country Club (site of the Insurance City Open and later the Greater Hartford Open from 1952 to 1983), where Bruce and his brother Brian both would caddy. Part of the attraction was the money. He could carry a double (a bag on each shoulder for two players) for four dollars a bag, plus a dollar tip for each. Some days, when there weren't enough caddies, he'd go 36 holes. "That added up to pretty good money for a thirteen-year-old kid," he'd remember. In addition, he made friends with many of the other caddies and had fun.[8]

Edwards never became a serious player—baseball and soccer were his games—but he was a very good caddy, and the reward for his good work was to get a bag at the Greater Hartford Open. Bruce's first was in 1967—the same year Charlie Sifford won it, making history as the second African American to win on the tour. That year, Bruce caddied for Dick Lotz, who would win three tournaments on the PGA Tour.

When Lotz looked at the skinny youngster the caddymaster brought out to him, he wondered if the boy could heft his bag around for 18 holes. Bruce assured him that he could do the job, and Lotz told him they'd try it in the practice round and see how it went. But a few holes in, Lotz knew he had "someone special." Bruce knew exactly what he was supposed to do to be a good caddy, and it was clear "he loved doing it."

Lotz finished tied for 12th. The $60 check he gave Bruce amounted to 5 percent of his earnings, and it was a fortune to a 12-year-old kid. Even at such a young age, Bruce knew he wanted to caddy on the PGA Tour full-time. He loved being inside the ropes, being part of the action. "I wasn't nervous doing it, I was having fun." He recognized the main requirements of the caddy—to carry the bag, encourage his man, and never show up late.[9]

Bruce entered a profession going back more than three hundred years. In 1893, the forerunner of the *Oxford English Dictionary* defined caddy (or caddie) as: "A lad or man who waits about on the look-out for chance employment as a messenger, errand-boy, errand-porter, chair-man, odd-job man, etc." It also extended to "a golf-player's attendant who carries his clubs (generally a boy or lad)." The earliest documented case of a golfer employing a caddy was in 1628, when James Graham, a student at the University of St Andrews in Scotland, recorded in his expense accounts payments to boys for carrying his clubs. Go to St Andrews today and you will find men who for decades have been helping players around the Old Course.[10]

"In Scotland, the caddy, besides carrying the clubs, is the golfer's most characteristic figure on the greens." So said Charles Blair Macdonald, who went to St Andrews to attend the university there in the 1870s and returned to the United States and built the country's first 18-hole course in Chicago in 1892. "With unsurpassed opportunities of studying human nature," Macdonald continued, "he acquires a keen sense of the strength and weakness of his master, and is prone at all times to express himself freely."[11] This aptly describes the relationship Bruce would have with Tom Watson.

Bruce's parents figured that his caddy work would help keep him out of trouble in his teenage years, and at least they'd always know where he was on summer days. When he graduated from high school, he told his folks he wanted to pursue a career as a caddy on the PGA Tour. "My graduation present was air fare from Hartford to Charlotte," he remembered. His father, Jay, wasn't happy about it, but he knew Bruce was set on doing it, so he let him go. But he didn't want Bruce calling him asking for money if things didn't work out. "If he wanted to do this, okay, but he was going to be on his own."[12] His mother, Natalie, thought Bruce would tire of the lifestyle and be back in a year, but he had different plans.

In the early 1970s, the tour wasn't the huge operation it is today. Big tournament purses amounted to $150,000–$250,000, with first prizes of $30,000–$50,000. Most players didn't have a regular caddy, thus Bruce joined a group of other bag-toters going week-to-week looking for a player needing someone to lug their 40-pound bag four or five miles around the course and offer them some emotional support. He was able to get a couple bags his first two weeks out—future U.S. Open champion David Graham was one of them—and was paid $15 a day plus 3 percent of any winnings.

Edwards was entering a profession that didn't have the best of reputations. Many people thought of caddies as "drunks or people who were down and out or people you couldn't trust," recalled Edwards.[13] The tour caddy, according to one writer at the time, was "that creature society depicts as a drunk, a misfit, and a flophouse bum." Perceptions hadn't changed that much in 100 years.

"Carrying clubs is one of the most agreeable trades open to the lower orders," wrote the author of *The Art of Golf* in 1892. "In it an amount of drunkenness is tolerated which, in any other, would land him in the workhouse. A very low standard of efficiency and very little work will secure a man a decent livelihood." Regulations at St Andrews in 1910 called for caddies to be "tidy in dress, sober when on duty and civil to his man."[14]

Dave Hill, a 13-time winner on the PGA Tour, noted in 1977 that the reputation of caddies, "mixed in the past, [was] getting better," adding that there were probably three dozen caddies then who traveled the tour full-time. Hill contended that a good tour caddy was worth at least a shot a round to him, which could be the difference between winning and losing.[15]

Yet professional caddies at that time were in many cases still treated like second-class citizens. "We had nothing," remembered Jeff Burrell. "In fact, it was so bad that at Tour events they had signs that would say 'Public Welcome, Caddies Not Allowed.'" In fact, Jack Nicklaus's caddie Angelo Argea had been given a 30-day suspension in 1975 for entering the clubhouse at Pinehurst during the World Open.[16]

It wasn't an easy life. Caddies would drive together from tournament to tournament, sharing hotel rooms and eating in cheap diners. Still, Bruce knew it was what he wanted to do. It was the kind of job where you "never have to look at the same four walls" or wear a coat and tie, he'd say years later. "I'm outside, travelling the world. . . . That always appealed to me. I knew as a kid I didn't want to do the normal 9-to-5 routine."[17]

Bruce took his job seriously. There were no yardage books then, so Bruce would walk the course early in the week to write down distances from bunkers and sprinkler heads. He wanted to get it right and filled scorecards with scribbled notes that were sometimes hard to decipher when the time came to give his man a yardage.

In time, Edwards's attention to detail became legendary, to the point where he could pull out a 10-year-old yardage book with notes on how the wind would blow on a particular hole on a particular course when a cold front swept through from the west. He was one of the few caddies who would walk the course before rounds during a tournament, rechecking yardages and counting steps to the flag.[18] But in 1973, Bruce was still learning, and he headed for St. Louis looking for a player in need of a caddy.

On July 17 at the tournament site, the Norwood Hills Country Club, Bruce thought he caught a break. He approached Dale Douglass, who was walking into the clubhouse. Douglass was an established top-60 player, 3-time winner on tour, and member of the 1969 Ryder Cup team. He also had the reputation as a true gentleman and would have been a good fit for Bruce, but he told Bruce he already had a caddy for the week.

At this point, friend and fellow caddy Neil Oxman, who had been watching, stepped in and pointed out another player coming out of the clubhouse. "Hey Bruce, look over there." The young pro with reddish-brown hair and his green McGregor golf bag slung over his shoulder had no caddy in sight. "That's Tom Watson," said Oxman. "He's going to be a real good player someday. Go ask him if he needs a caddy."[19]

Watson would recall that the connection seemed immediate. "I was a long-haired golfer, . . . and he was a long-haired caddie. We fit the bill together right there." Watson had made it to the tour by finishing fifth in the December 1971 Qualifying School. As a rookie in 1972, he finished 78th on the money list, making $30,413 for the year, and almost won a tournament, losing by a shot to Deane Beman at the Quad Cities. The year 1973 had started well, but he was still in need of a steady caddy. "I said I'd like to caddie for him that year," Bruce recalled. "He said he'd see how it went for a week." He gave Bruce the bag, and they headed for the practice range.[20]

Bruce spent four hours with Watson as his new boss hit bucket after bucket of balls. He liked what he saw, especially such dedication in the brutal "million degree" heat, as Bruce called it. During the practice round the next day, Watson was impressed with Bruce's background, and the more they talked, the more he liked him. Tom had a good week, tying for sixth place and earning $6,300. Bruce got $300 and something much more valuable. Tom handed him the keys to his Oldsmobile Cutlass and said he'd see him Tuesday morning at the next stop in Montreal.

Bruce felt as if his life had changed. "That three hundred dollars might just as well have been three thousand or thirty thousand," he'd recall, as rich as he felt.[21] He and another caddy drove 1,200 miles in 36 hours to get to Montreal, where he entered a new world with Tom Watson, who was on tour in order to challenge himself. He had been a good amateur but not a great one, and after his senior year at Stanford, he told his father, Ray, he wanted to give the world of professional golf a try. His father agreed, telling him if he didn't he'd regret it for the rest of his life. Tom was wild off the tee then but a great scrambler, saving countless shots with his putter.

Bruce liked his new boss's style; he played fast and was aggressive, willing to take chances. "The thing I liked about Tom right away was that he was so nice to me. He treated me more like a person than a caddy. He didn't throw clubs or gripe. On the course, what impressed me was that he never gave up." Watson never blamed his caddy, the wind, or a bad lie for a poor shot; he just kept going and didn't sulk. Bruce also thought Tom was a "neat guy" for coming out after a round to act as third-base coach at the caddies' softball games.[22]

At the World Open that fall of 1973, an eight-round tournament, Tom shot a 62 in the fifth round, and they both would point to that round as a key to Watson's future, as he finished the year 35th on the money list. Watson had found a good caddy and also appreciated Edwards for his sense of humor and quick wit. "He knew when to say things that could loosen me up, he knew when to encourage me," and, just as important, "he knew when to yell at me."[23]

As Edwards would say, "You're together six hours a day, six days a week, so it's important that the chemistry works." They were a good match, and Bruce had found a home on the tour. The next year he got a raise—to $25 a day and 4 percent of the winnings. Even though Watson encouraged Bruce to go to college, he resisted. "I knew I was doing exactly what I wanted to do," and there was never a serious thought of doing anything else.[24]

A successful caddy has to not only carry the clubs but also be a good psychologist and friend. "When you are in a tight match and you have no one to turn to, it gets a little lonely out there," said Hall of Famer Johnny Miller. "Not so with a good caddie on your side. He is your closest friend on the golf course."[25]

According to tour caddy Chuck Hart, the emotional strain can become acute at times for a caddy. "They have to know their man and who they're caddying for. They have to recognize when to speak up and when not to speak up, when to be encouraging and when to be pushy. It's a delicate balance." Edwards struck the right balance, saying that "when we're on the last few holes of the tournament, I tell him, 'You're the best—when you're on top of your game, nobody can beat you.' He likes to hear that." He and Watson therefore forged a very strong bond.[26]

After coming close to winning the U.S. Open in 1974, Watson achieved his first victory in the Western Open later that summer and the next year captured the first of five British Opens. Bruce couldn't get a passport in time and was unable to go to Carnoustie that year. In 1977, Watson had his breakout year, winning the Masters and British Open, beating Jack Nicklaus at both.

Bruce, however, was not with him at either. In those days, the Masters did not allow players to use their own caddies. But Bruce did follow Watson at the Masters from the gallery. "When I started to make the run at No. 5 in the final round," Watson recalled, "I hit a 4-iron, and when it was in the air, I heard this, 'Yeaaah!' It was Bruce, because he knew it was a good shot. I ended up making birdie, and I birdied six, seven and eight. He came over that night and we celebrated."[27]

That celebration might not have been possible without the help of Byron Nelson. As he had two decades earlier with Ken Venturi, Nelson saw something special in Watson as a player and a man. While working for ABC Television, Byron met Tom during the telecast at Doral in 1973. "I was very impressed by his demeanor and I liked the quick, aggressive way he played," Nelson said, "so I began to watch him on the tour each week."[28]

When Tom failed to win the U.S. Open at Winged Foot in 1974, Nelson sought him out. "He was in the players' locker room upstairs, sitting with John Mahaffey and having a Coke. 'Tom, I'm sorry you had such a bad day. I've seen quite a few people who've been in the lead but not played good the last round until they had a few tries at it.'" He gave Tom permission to call him if he ever wanted to work with him. After winning Byron's namesake tournament in the spring of 1975, Tom was in the thick of things going into the final round at the British Open that year.[29]

Nelson gave some advice to Tom before the final round, explaining that he had played Carnoustie in the 1937 Open under similar conditions. "Now, even if you make three bogeys in a row, don't think anything about it, because everybody will be making bogeys." No matter what happened, don't quit out there, counseled Nelson. As Watson declared later, Nelson's advice was prophetic—Jack Newton and Bobby Cole each bogeyed three-straight holes near the finish. Tom had his own troubles but didn't quit, and his birdie at the final hole put him in a play-off with Newton, whom he beat the next day for his first major championship.[30]

After a winless 1976, Tom finally took Nelson up on his offer of assistance and called him that October. What followed was a three-day crash course in the golf swing, and for Tom it was the opportunity of a lifetime. "We worked and talked golf all day at Preston Trail. After dinner we sat around each night in Byron's home and talked about everything else but golf." Nelson shortened Tom's swing and showed him how to make a stronger leg drive on the downswing, in an effort to combat Tom's tendency to come over the ball from the top of the backswing. "Byron's instruction really helped my driving," said Tom at the time. "I've never had such confidence on the tee."

They continued to work together three or four times a year, as Tom found a lifelong friend and mentor. It was an easy union, as Byron considered Tom "one of the most intelligent golfers" he ever met.[31] With his newfound swing, Tom began 1977 with a bang, winning the Bing Crosby National Pro-Am and Andy Williams San Diego Open in January and the Masters in April. Bruce savored the victories but decided not to go to Turnberry that year for the British Open.

He would later joke about staying home in 1975 when Watson beat Jack Newton and then going in 1976 only to have Tom miss the cut. He stayed home again in 1977, citing the high cost of traveling overseas in those days, only to miss one of the most historic British Opens ever played. "I'm surprised Tom ever let me caddy for him in any major after that," he'd say with a wry smile. That was the year Watson shot 65-65 on the weekend to beat Jack Nicklaus by a shot. Some older caddies questioned Edwards's credentials in those early years. "They said that if Watson had a better caddy, he'd win more," Bruce recalled.[32]

But Tom never felt that way and continued to find success with Bruce, winning 25 tournaments from 1977 to 1981, although he lost a painful play-off to John Mahaffey in the 1978 PGA. Watson had been four up with nine to play, but the way he handled this spirit-crushing situation impressed Edwards. He was always good at putting a defeat behind him and going on to the next tournament. "I had to learn how to do that," said Edwards. But he still had a front-row seat to one of the best players in the game. "It's been great to watch him get better and better," said Bruce in 1980. "It's really fun to be out here with him when he's making history."[33]

In 1982, Bruce was part of that history when Watson won the U.S. Open at Pebble Beach. Everyone remembers that championship for Watson's dramatic chip-in on the 17th hole, but he came into the championship hitting the ball horribly—"sideways" as he put it. But as he would so many times in his career, he found something on the practice range and after the second round told Bruce the words he wanted to hear. "I've got it," said Tom. "It's like the floodgates opened and the confidence came back, that I could control the ball and play well enough to win the National Open." He hit it well the rest of the way and was also the statistical leader in putting that week—a good combination for anyone.[34]

Watson came to the seventh hole in the final round a shot behind Nicklaus and then missed a two-foot putt for birdie. But he hung on and the putter got hot, making birdies at 11 and 14 and stroking a perfect downhill lag putt to save bogey on 16. He came to the 17th tied with Nicklaus, who had just finished ahead of him. Bruce remembered coming down the stretch and feeling his heart in his throat. "I know how bad Tom wanted this one. And I wanted it just as bad." O. B. Keeler, chronicler of Bobby Jones, once aptly described what Edwards felt. Caddies "fight and bleed and die for their 'man,'" he maintained. "The players get the glory or the sting of defeat. But they don't do all the fighting."[35]

So when Watson pulled his tee shot into the wiry rough left of the 17th green and announced coldly, "That's dead," Edwards wouldn't hear it. "You can still get it up and down." It was that optimism and ability to motivate when the situation called for it that Watson loved about Bruce. "His glass was always half-full," he'd say.[36]

Bruce was fighting for his man and knew there was a chance when he saw the lie, not good but not dead. He told Tom to knock it close. "Close? Hell, I'm going to hole it," responded Watson. With a firm stroke he pitched the ball just to the edge of the green. Perfect touch. The ball tracked right toward the hole, hitting the flagstick and diving in for one of the most improbable birdies at a crucial moment in the U.S. Open ever. Tom ran around the green and pointed at Bruce. "I told you so!" A birdie at the final hole secured his sweetest victory.[37]

When Watson picked the ball from the hole on 18, he gave Bruce a hug and told him, "We did it." For Tom, whose father, Ray, had instilled in him the importance of winning the Open since he was a boy, it was the high point. "Ever since I was ten years old," he reflected, "I had dreamed of winning the title." For Bruce, it would be the first and only major on the regular tour he would partake in as a caddy. Even though he had missed Watson's other majors, this made up for it, because it had been so long in coming and meant so much to both of them. "Pebble Beach, the Open, Nicklaus, the chip-in," Bruce would say. "What more could you ask for?"[38]

That was the acme of Tom's career, and the next years saw it decline to its nadir. The wins started to dry up after 1984, and by the mid-1980s, Tom cut back his schedule as his children were of school age. Watson

Tom Watson won the 1982 U.S. Open at Pebble Beach with Bruce Edwards on his bag. Watson's dramatic pitch-in on the 71st hole to beat Jack Nicklaus is one of the most dramatic shots in golf history. It would be the only major championship Bruce was a part of as a caddy, but as he would say, "What more could you ask for?" *Photograph©Lawrence Levy Photographic Collection. All rights reserved. Image courtesy of the University of St Andrews Library, 2008-1-4118.*

admitted that by 1988 he was like a writer with a permanent case of writer's block—no matter what he tried, nothing worked.

Even though he and Bruce had a great relationship on and off the course, he encouraged Bruce to work for someone else if a good opportunity presented itself. In the summer of 1989, Bruce got an offer from Greg Norman and decided to take it, even though it was a difficult move. Norman was a superstar who did everything in a big way, and his success allowed Bruce to build a dream house in Florida.

Norman had a different personality from Watson and could wear his emotions on his sleeve, getting mad at himself and his caddy. Bruce remembered a defining moment at the British Open in 1990, where Norman was tied with Nick Faldo after 36 holes. After shooting a 76 in the third round and falling well down the leader board, Bruce was mad, not because of the score but rather Norman's attitude.

On the 17th hole, he told Bruce sometimes it was better to be lucky than good. To which Bruce replied, "Greg, I just want to work for someone who plays with guts and heart, no matter the outcome."[39] The breaking point came two years later, as Bruce felt Norman had lost confidence in him. He came to dread going to the golf course—he was working for money and not love for his job.

Conversely, Bruce couldn't remember having a bad day on the golf course with Tom, and he missed that. He broke with Norman in the summer of 1992, and the prodigal son returned home to the welcoming arms of Watson. Years later, Norman would say that he sincerely believed Bruce was meant to return to Tom. Reunited with his old boss and friend, Bruce was happy on the course again and made everyone around him feel good. Jay Haas, winner of nine PGA events, claimed Bruce always "made a day on the golf course more fun" because of his friendly manner and the way he made a point of noticing people and talking about their sports teams and individual interests. [40]

Joe LaCava, longtime caddy for Fred Couples before moving to Tiger Woods in 2011, remembered looking up to Bruce Edwards when he first started out. He appreciated that Bruce and Tom were always doing things for the right reasons. "I respected both of them immensely. Bruce was constantly looking out for caddies and wanting to change things for the better." The late Greg Rita, who caddied for Curtis Strange when he won back-to-back U.S. Opens in 1988 and 1989, said that because of Bruce and caddies like him, the job had been "elevated to a higher level of professionalism."[41]

"Bruce was the most positive person I knew," said Donny Wanstall, a former caddy. "He was always ready to help another guy, give him some advice, or steer him in the right direction."[42] Edwards's popularity with caddies and players alike led to his appointment as an assistant captain to Ben Crenshaw in the 1999 Ryder Cup. His energy and passion were contagious. The late Payne Stewart claimed that if you were on the course with Bruce and didn't get "pumped up, then you can't get pumped up."[43]

Bruce had a gift for motivating all types of people. "He could make me laugh at the worst time and he could kick me in the butt," Watson said. "When a young [caddy] came out on Tour, Bruce wasn't hesitant to show him the ropes or kick him in the butt, too." If they were doing wrong, "he'd tell them to clean up their act."[44]

In 1994, Bruce found even more reason to motivate Watson with his game. It was on the practice tee that spring at Hilton Head that Watson found "the secret" to playing better golf. He was working on trying to get his shoulders more level as they turned around his body—a more rotary motion around the spine—and it "was as if a light switch had finally turned on," he'd say. He took it to the course, and it worked. "The ball started flying for me again like it hadn't flown in years."[45]

With this newfound swing, Tom found a resurgence of sorts late in his career, winning his first tournament in nine years at the 1996 Memorial, the tournament founded by his great rival Jack Nicklaus. Watson's last win on the regular tour came at Colonial two years later, the tournament Ben Hogan won five times. Bruce may not have won as much as he might have with Greg Norman, but he was happy on the golf course. Off the course, things weren't as sanguine. He had married Suzie Oldfield in 1995, but it was a troubled union, and in April 2000, he came back from the Senior PGA to find that she had burned their Ponte Vedra Beach, Florida, home down to the ground.

Suzie was arrested on a charge of arson. The fire destroyed thousands of dollars worth of golf memorabilia, including Ryder Cup mementos and the flag from the 18th green at Pebble in 1982. After she was treated at a mental-health facility and released, Bruce declined to press charges. He didn't want her to go to jail; he just wanted her out of his life and filed for divorce immediately thereafter.[46]

Two years later, Bruce would find his greatest joy amid his most heartbreaking travail. In 1974, Bruce's second year on tour, he had met a girl at the Byron Nelson tournament in Dallas, Texas, named Marsha Cummins, one of several pretty women who served as hostesses for the tournament. He was 19, she was 17. She thought he was cute, but there was something deeper that drew her to him.

The next year, Watson returned and won. Marsha was again there to see the tournament, and when Bruce saw her in the gallery, he asked her out on a date. When Bruce kissed her at the end of the night, "bells went off," according to her, and she was entranced by him. But he moved on to the next tournament, and she was off to college, so their relationship was an intermittent one, as they saw each other off and on until 1984.

In May 2002, Bruce saw Marsha again, this time at the Colonial tournament in Fort Worth, when a mutual friend invited him to a party. She was now Marsha Moore, a mother of four, but in a failed marriage about to end in divorce. "I walked up to the porch and there he was, sitting in a chair, drinking a White Russian," Marsha recalled. Her heart skipped a beat when she saw him. It was as if she was that same 17-year-old girl he had met in 1974.[47]

Through the years, she had kept tabs on Bruce, and when she learned he had married in 1995, she was devastated. She knew it made no sense, a married woman carrying a torch for a man she had hardly seen in years, but she also realized she was not fulfilled in life. She admitted that she was still searching; she didn't know for what, exactly, but searching.

The sparks still flew between the two, and a courtship ensued. Both looked forward to a new, happy chapter in their lives, but dreams of a long life together were quickly shattered. In the spring of 2002, Bruce began noticing that his speech was sometimes slurred, and by the fall, he began having trouble grasping things with his left hand. Marsha had noticed a thickness in his speech that night in May, as if he had been drinking or was very tired. Fellow caddies noticed it, and Greg Rita, whose mother had suffered a stroke a year earlier, saw similarities in Bruce's symptoms.

Watson also noted a worsening of the slurring, among other things. During a tournament in October, he marked a ball on the green and threw it to Bruce, who couldn't close his hand around it. Bruce remembered turning to Tom and saying, "Look at this, I think I have arthritis." Looking back, Watson acknowledged, "I had a black thought right then and there," fearing something was seriously wrong with his friend.[48]

Bruce thought he might have cancer. A lifelong smoker, he realized the dangerous implications it could have on his health. Still, he put off seeing a doctor. By Christmas, he was losing weight and slurring his speech badly. Despite all this, he was in love, and on New Year's Eve 2002, he asked Marsha to marry him. She immediately said yes, and they planned for a summer wedding.

The beauty of the moment was short-lived, as a few days later Bruce woke up during the night with a violent coughing fit. It went on for some time, Marsha recalled, and when it finally ended, a frightened Bruce was left exhausted and out of breath.[49] Watson had seen enough and arranged for Bruce to go to the Mayo Clinic for a thorough physical examination, and he would pay all the medical bills.

Marsha accompanied Bruce to Rochester, Minnesota, and on a cold, dank January 15, a blur of doctors and nurses performed a battery of tests on Bruce. His last appointment was with Dr. Eric Sorenson, a neurological specialist. He had Bruce walk on his heels, tested his reflexes, and measured the strength in his arms and legs.[50] After about 45 minutes, he left the room for a few minutes, and Bruce waited, wondered, hoped, and prayed.

When the doctor returned, he had news for Bruce and delivered it with all the grace and gentleness of a sledgehammer to the head. Bruce had ALS, or Lou Gehrig's disease, Dr. Sorenson told him and gave him one to three years to live. He then coldly advised his patient to go home and get his affairs in order.

Bruce felt sick to his stomach and asked the doctor to bring in Marsha, who was waiting outside. Looking into Bruce's eyes, she knew the news was bad, and when he told her, they were both in shock. She tried to console him, but words couldn't express the hurt in her heart. Back in the hotel that night, while Marsha went out to get sandwiches, Bruce cried for the first time, still unable to believe the horrible news.

French doctor Jean-Martin Charcot first described amyotrophic lateral sclerosis (ALS) in the scientific literature in 1869. A progressive neuro-degenerative disease, it attacks nerve cells and pathways in the brain and spinal cord. When these cells die, voluntary muscle control and movement dies with them. Patients in the later stages of the disease are totally paralyzed, yet in most cases, their minds remain sharp and alert. Every day, an average of 15 people are diagnosed with ALS, and as many as 30,000 Americans may currently be affected by ALS. Annually, 2 deaths per 100,000 people are attributed to it, and there is no cure.

Lou Gehrig, the famous New York Yankee baseball player who appeared in 2,130 consecutive games from 1923 to 1939 before the disease ended his career, brought public awareness to ALS. He was diagnosed in June 1939 with a condition described as "a hardening of the tissues in the spinal column and a wasting of the muscles dependent upon it."[51]

Gehrig would succumb two years later at the age of 37, and since then, his name has been synonymous with it. In the medical world, ALS is classified by the National Institutes of Health as an "orphan disease," that is, one affecting less than 200,000 people. An orphan disease does not get "adopted" by the pharmaceutical industry because there is little financial incentive for the private sector to make and market new medications to treat or prevent it.[52] This has not changed since the days of Lou Gehrig.

The mortality rate is rapid—life expectancy is one to three years after diagnosis for bulbar onset, which Bruce had. This form of ALS starts with the muscles in the face, head, and neck and progresses faster than limb onset, which affects the legs and arms first. Death results from asphyxiation when the paralysis spreads to the diaphragm. Somehow, Bruce retained his sense of humor after receiving such horrible news, telling Watson, "I could have a disease named after Liberace or something. At least Lou Gehrig was a great athlete."[53]

Telling his family he was dying would be the hardest thing he'd ever have to do. "Everything was so bleak," he would say. "I wanted to care, but at that moment it was tough."[54] When he met with his parents and siblings and told them he had ALS, there was an audible gasp. He could never remember seeing his father cry until then. Later in the evening, Jay pulled Marsha aside and told her they would understand if she didn't wish to go through with the wedding. She had let Bruce walk out of her life once, she told Bruce's father, and wasn't going to let it happen again.

Ten days after the diagnosis, Bruce and Marsha flew to Hawaii for the MasterCard Championship. With only 36 men in field and few press covering the event, it was quiet spot for the new golf season to start. It was on Monday that Hilary Watson suggested to Marsha that she and Bruce get married there.

"Being realistic, there was no way to know how much time we were going to have," said Bruce. His family wouldn't be able to come, but he knew they would understand. Hilary did most of the work, and the ceremony took place at sunset on Saturday, after everyone had completed play in the second round. Guests included Jack Nicklaus, Arnold Palmer, Gary Player, and Hale Irwin, among others. Many of Bruce's fellow caddies were there as well. "It was beautiful," said Marsha, like something "straight out of a movie."[55]

After Bruce and Marsha informed friends and family of his condition, the PGA Tour released a story to the press. At least Bruce was not alone in his struggle. Tour player Jeff Julian was also suffering from the same pernicious disease, having been diagnosed in late 2001. Julian was awarded the Ben Hogan Award during the week of the Masters in April 2003, with Marsha and Bruce in attendance. By that time, Julian couldn't talk but would type into a computer as a voice synthesizer spoke the words. Tiger Woods sent a message to both Jeff and Bruce: "The toughness they show really inspires me to do more with my life."[56]

Bruce was quiet that night. As Marsha described it, "He couldn't help but look at Jeff and think, 'This is my future.' It was a very difficult night for all of us." The media attention began in earnest, which was off-putting for Marsha, since nothing could prepare her for being put under the microscope of press attention. Tom missed the cut that week, and Bruce, fearing this may be the last time he would caddy at the Masters, cried, first on Hilary's shoulder and then Marsha's. He just wanted to make one more cut in his favorite tournament and wouldn't give up without a fight.[57]

Edwards told *Golf Digest* that he had always believed "that golf parallels life" and that "what makes you a champion is how you deal with adversity." True champions carry on, and that's what he planned to do. "I'm having a rough nine holes," he said, putting it in golfing terms, "and I hope it's only nine holes, because I'll get through this. That's the way I've always caddied, so why would I not live my life that way as well? I don't want to be the poster boy for this, but if I can make one person see that it's not devastating or it's the battle that's important, not the end result, then maybe I was the right guy to get this."[58]

The late spring and summer began a tour featuring great golf and an outpouring of support and affection for Bruce. His sense of humor still intact, Edwards told reporters, "I talk like the town drunk, but I feel pretty good."[59] When he and Tom arrived in Chicago for the U.S. Open two months later, they were to share one of their most special moments. Watson shot a spectacular 65 in the first round, becoming the oldest player to lead after the first round. Starting the day on the back nine, he began with a bogey and par but then holed a 170-yard six iron for eagle at the 12th. "I started thinking this was going to be one of those days," said Watson.[60]

He turned in two under par and birdied the first hole, then on the seventh made a 35-footer with about 20 feet of break that hung on the lip of the hole. Watson walked slowly to the hole, wondering how the ball couldn't fall, and just as he got to it, it took one last turn and tumbled in. Watson kicked up his left leg in delight, turned to Bruce, smiling and overcome with emotion, and bowed. Another 12-foot putt on the eighth and a good 7-foot putt for par on the last gave Watson his 65.[61]

Bruce, crying by now, gave Watson a hug and whispered in his ear, "Thanks for a great five hours." For Bruce, it was as if they were young again and anything was possible. When he left the course, he said, "I was thinking how lucky I was and not, 'Oh, woe is me.'" Although Tom could not sustain his level of play, finishing in 28th place, the week allowed him a platform to get the word out about Bruce and ALS. "It launched our fight," said Marsha. "It was a big moment." Bruce agreed. "If I use this podium properly, somebody might be saved, even if I'm not."[62]

When Tom was asked what he'd remember most about that round, he said it would be Bruce's tears. "They'll always be with me. They're etched in my heart. I want to find something for him."[63] Watson didn't know why Bruce had to get ALS, but he knew that Marsha coming back into his life had been something of a miracle. Bruce said, "She is my strength. I mean, she has said a lot of things in private to keep me going, not feel sorry for myself, . . . and she has been my pillar, believe me." Marsha had urged Bruce to revisit his Christianity and his faith, which helped him deal with what was happening to him. The experience changed Watson's perspective as well. "There is something beyond what we are, we feel, we smell," he said. "And [Bruce] believed that."[64]

Tom and Bruce were sought out by the media wherever they went and gave countless interviews as the summer progressed. At the U.S. Senior Open two weeks later, Bruce was walking slower due to the heat, the exhaustion apparent on his face. Watson lost by two strokes to Bruce Lietzke, but Edwards was adamant that he and Tom still had a lot of golf left.

Tom continued to play well, finishing 18th at the British Open and then won the Senior British Open. Neil Oxman, the man who told Bruce to seek out Tom in the parking lot in St. Louis all those years ago, caddied for Tom, since the cold weather was not good for Bruce in his condition. "Of course I told both him and Ox before they went over that Tom was a lock to win since I wasn't going," joked Bruce.

Oxman wrote a letter to Bruce, telling him that without exaggerating, during that two-week period, there must have been 50 or 60 times people began a conversation with the same two words, "How's Bruce?" He added, "Tom Watson loves you Bruce. That is for sure. And so do a lot of other people—many of whom have never met you." Oxman thanked Bruce for allowing him to "see a little bit of the world as you've been able

Bruce Edwards and Tom Watson giving each other a hug on the 18th green after Watson shot a 65 to lead the first round of the 2003 U.S. Open. Edwards, suffering from Lou Gehrig's disease, was the focus of much media attention that week and inspired Watson to a stellar round of golf. Afterwards, Bruce told Watson, "Thanks for a great five hours." *Copyright USGA/John Mummert.*

to see it for the past thirty years."[65] He then saved the flag from the 18th green for his friend.

With each passing day, Bruce's condition worsened, but he and Marsha kept fighting, even though she admitted it was "so frustrating to have the medical community look you in the eye and say they don't know." She found a valuable ally in Kim Julian, who shared the treatments her husband Jeff tried and who also knew exactly what Marsha was going through. Tom had called Kim in March, and she was impressed by his knowledge of ALS and desire to do all he could to drive research for a cure. He encouraged Kim to reach out to Marsha, which she did.[66]

"Our husbands were dying of ALS," recalled Kim. "In the months that would follow, we were very lucky to have one another. . . . We were soldiers, fighting side by side, as our husbands became more and more frail." She and Marsha split the possible remedies between them, which helped save valuable time. The idea for fund raising and spreading awareness had begun with Kim and Jeff and picked up steam when Tom agreed to lend his famous name to the effort.[67]

It was decided that the Boston-based ALS Therapy Development Foundation would be the recipient of all funds procured through their campaign, filtered through its 501(c)3 tax-exempt foundation—Driving4Life (the "4" signified Lou Gehrig's number as a Yankee). Its six founders were Jeff and Kim Julian, Bruce and Marsha Edwards, and Tom and Hilary Watson, and it was kicked off at the U.S. Open, with numerous public-service announcements appearing in print and television.[68]

While Driving4Life spread the word across the media world, Bruce was trying many different treatments, including cobra venom in the Bahamas. Kim Julian said that Jeff tried snake venom too, as well as stem-cell infusions. "All we had was hope, and hope is a powerful thing." At the end of August, Tom and Bruce headed west to Portland, Oregon, and the Jeld-Wen Tradition, one of the designated majors of the Champions Tour. Bruce had weakened since the U.S. Open and used a golf cart much of the time to get him around the course. "It allows me to do what I love to do," he said simply. As they had been doing all spring and summer, he and Tom granted interviews to a curious press who wanted to know how they were holding up.[69]

"Golf is not as important as it used to be," said Tom. "It is still important when I'm playing, but there is always the backdrop of Bruce's health and what can we do to help him." He knew Bruce was going through a test, the reasons for which neither could understand. "There is somebody I love who is going through a hard, seemingly dead-end time. But I don't want it to end, and I will do everything in my power to raise funds and the awareness and not leave any detail unturned so I can help Bruce survive this."[70]

Tom was motivated by a promise he had made to Bruce two months earlier—he wanted to win again with Bruce on his bag—and opened with a steady 68. Bruce talked after the round about his friend's dedication to fighting ALS. "He has actually almost become obsessed with it. I wish he would let it go a little, but it shows how concerned he is. I don't want it to get to the point where it is all consuming, because our goal is to accomplish a job, and I would rather he not be occupied with me all the time."

In the second round, Watson shot a 62, tying his career-best, to grab the lead. The gallery was enthusiastic, cheering for both player and caddy at every turn. The good will must have been both appreciated and distracting. Edwards told a reporter for the *Oregonian*, "I'm not dying of ALS, I'm living with ALS. People tell me how courageous I am. Hell, that's not courage. I'm just trying to carry on." It is the people who can't move or talk who should be admired, he said, perhaps foreshadowing his own future. "I hope I have the dignity and class that they have. . . . But when you get to that stage, that's courage."[71]

Tom's 73 on Saturday was the product of a number of missed putts, and he may have been trying too hard. "I wanted very much to win again *with* Bruce," he later acknowledged. "I don't think I was pressing because of it, but I was aware of it and so was he."[72] In the final round, he made a run and was tied for the lead when he stumbled, making a bogey at the easy par-five 16th hole. He was convinced he had lost right there, since the leaders still had it to play, plus another par five on 18. But as always, Bruce was in his ear when he needed it, telling him he could still win the thing.

After a par at the difficult 17th, Watson hit his second shot on 18 into the left greenside bunker. With a good lie, he hit an excellent shot and left the ball four feet from the hole. The putt went down for a 70, and he now had a one-shot lead. Tom and Bruce waited in the scorer's tent and watched on television as Jim Ahern and Tom Kite stroked short birdie putts to force a play-off. When both missed, Tom gave Bruce a hug. "I promised Bruce I was going to win for him before it was over. Today, as he said, it was the first of many. I hope he's right."[73]

Kim Julian had told Tom, Bruce, and Marsha early on to live in denial. Be positive, go forward, and use as much information as they could, and try everything they could to help Bruce, forgetting the diagnosis. This reflected the answer she had given to an ESPN reporter who asked her if she and Jeff were in denial: "Absolutely. In denial is a good place to be."[74] But by the fall of 2003, denial was no longer an option. As Bruce continued to decline, Marsha and Kim consoled one another. Kim called one morning, depressed and worried about her own future. With Jeff's blessing, she traveled to visit Bruce and Marsha.

Kim spent four "uneasy" days with the Edwardses. "A very private person, Bruce spent most of his days in their bedroom with a computer and television," she would recall. "Marsha was frustrated, understandably, because she felt he was giving up." Kim sensed the same tension she had experienced in her own home. In addition to the horrible continued withering of the body, Jeff had also demonstrated mood swings. Brief periods of anger, paranoia, or suspiciousness and increased irritation due to change in routine are also part of the disease. "I talked with Marsha about it," said Kim, "and she was certain she'd seen similar behavior in Bruce. Dementia is indeed part of ALS."[75]

Tom didn't play in September, as was his custom, so Bruce had time to rest. He and Marsha traveled to Boston for a family reunion at his sister Gwyn's house, but the family found it harder and harder to understand his slurred words. He still talked of going to the Masters, his favorite tournament, come springtime, but admitted that his weakened legs would require using a cart.

In October, Bruce was inducted into the Caddie Hall of Fame. The founder of the Professional Caddies Association, Dennis Cone, had known Bruce since 1985 and insisted his induction was due to his professionalism and dedication to the profession, not because of his illness. Bruce was honored by the gesture but insisted his was a low-profile job. "The only thing that's important," he maintained, "is that I do a good job."[76]

At the end of the month, he was on the bag as Tom played in the season-ending tour championship in Sonoma, California. By this time, Bruce's speech had deteriorated to such a degree that Tom couldn't understand him when he asked for yardages to the holes. This was devastating for Bruce, but Tom told him they would get through it, that it would *not* be a problem.

Tom didn't win the tournament, but he did win the Charles Schwab Cup for the best overall performance on the Champions Tour that year and the $1 million tax-deferred annuity that went with it. He donated all of it to Driving4Life, telling the press that in light of how far ALS needed to go in terms of research dollars, it "just seemed to be the right thing to do." Bruce knew he could not ask for a more faithful, caring, and generous friend.[77]

On November 16, 2003, Bruce celebrated his 49th birthday with friends, but by the end of the month, his breathing had worsened, and his tall frame had shrunk to 131 pounds. Tom visited him in early January, and the sight of his friend's deteriorated condition was heart-wrenching. As ALS progresses, it weakens the diaphragm and respiratory muscles, making inhaling, exhaling, and coughing impossible.

When you can't exhale, carbon dioxide builds up in the lungs, and blood oxygen saturation drops, eventually killing you. In March, when the Players Championship came to Florida, players and caddies came to Bruce's home, which was less than a mile from the course, to say hello. He was now so weak that he could barely speak, and his friends knew they might be saying goodbye to him for the last time.[78]

Tom would go to Augusta that April alone. Bruce wanted to attend, but his body could not obey his heart's desire. On the Wednesday night before the first round of the Masters, at the Golf Writers Association of America annual dinner, Watson accepted the Ben Hogan Award on behalf of Edwards, the same award Jeff Julian had won the year before.

Bruce's father, Jay, with resolute strength and considerable grace, spoke eloquently of his son's life, adding that two people had "been saints in all of this—his wife, Marsha, and his boss, Tom Watson." Watson began his speech by looking at Edwards's family and friends and saying, "No long faces," as he spoke affectionately of the man who was more than just a good friend. "You have to understand," Neil Oxman explained, that Tom and Bruce were "not as close as brothers, they're closer than that."[79]

When Hilary dropped off her husband at the Augusta National clubhouse at 6:30 a.m. the next morning, April 8, 2004, she was supposed to return to their rented home. But when a security guard told Tom she was at the door of the Champions Locker Room, Watson knew exactly what that meant. Edwards had gone to sleep about 1:00 a.m. the night before and passed away at 6:26 a.m. that morning.

"Hilary and I just looked at each other," Watson recalled, "and said, that's typical. He wanted to die on the first day of the Masters, his favorite tournament." Added Hilary, "He didn't want to sit in bed watching the Masters. He wanted to be there, sitting right on Tom's shoulder. That's Bruce." Marsha had called Kim Julian after Bruce died. "He looks so at peace, Kimmy." Her voice conveyed equal amounts of relief and angst, as her husband's suffering had ended.[80]

There would be no miracles on the course that sad day, as Watson shot a 76. He met the press after, his eyes red and brimming with tears, but wanting to talk about Edwards. He spoke of the old yardage books Bruce told him to take to Augusta because they had all the lay-ups on the par fives. "He was out there all right. I could just remember him saying, 'All right, you've got 158 to carry over the right front on No. 6 there, go for it.'" Then, in a flash of emotion, he said, "Damn this disease! Damn it! They are going to find a cure. The neurological diseases are really difficult. It's not for naught. Suffice it to say that we don't have a cure yet, but we're going to get there."[81]

Watson then reminded people of how much Bruce loved the Masters. "He always wanted to caddy, obviously, at Augusta. When it came time, we never got all that close to winning. But he sure loved it here." For Edwards, being a caddy was, in Tom's words, "the neatest thing in the world." Ben Crenshaw, remembering his vice-captain of the 1999 Ryder Cup team, would say that Bruce was "a real professional and one of the most positive human beings I have ever been around. I know how much he meant to Tom Watson. It's not fair. They took a really good one there today."[82]

The last time Tom spoke with Bruce face-to-face had been a few weeks earlier. "We talked about death and the fear of death," Watson said. "He said he was not afraid to die." To the three hundred mourners at the Bruce's memorial service the following Monday, Tom told the attendees that Bruce "left us with a lot of smiles. He left us with a lot of heart. He left us in body but he will always be with us in spirit. He was a friend to all of us. Don't feel sorry for him." Bruce's brother Brian spoke of how he loved to laugh and how he found humor in every setting, claiming, "Bruce was Seinfeld before there was Seinfeld."[83]

Jeff Julian had seen Phil Mickelson win that Masters—he was pulling for him—but sadly he knew it wouldn't be long before he would follow Bruce. Jeff wanted to be in Vermont with his family in those last days, and he passed away peacefully on July 15, 2004. Kim Julian and Marsha Edwards were now both widows, but neither Jeff or Bruce and their fight against ALS would be forgotten.

Following Bruce's death, Tom and author John Feinstein (who wrote Edwards's biography, *Caddy for Life*) joined forces to form the Bruce Edwards Foundation for ALS Research (where Feinstein serves as chairman). The foundation and its primary fundraiser, the Bruce Edwards Celebrity Golf Classic, raise funds in support of the search for a cure. The foundation has raised more than $4 million for ongoing research at the Packard Center at John Hopkins University, along with other ALS research facilities.[84]

Bruce Edwards changed Tom Watson. "Maybe he opened up my soul a little bit," Tom acknowledged after Bruce's death. A poem attributed to St. Augustine captured a sentiment Watson liked to share with others. "Don't cry for me, but remember the most important things of my life and what I represented in my life, and make that your memory of me, not my death." Tom was for Bruce the older brother he never had, and felt blessed for it. [85]

Watson summarized their relationship as one of, "friendship, love, respect." As Bruce said, "It's caring." They shared many wonderful moments together, and when asked for his favorite memory, Tom claimed, "I think that hug at the 18th hole at Pebble Beach was probably the most wonderful memory that we both shared together. That was the only major he won on my bag. But, you know, that was the major that I wanted the most and he knew that."[86] Bruce always said, "I was always exactly where I wanted to be when I was out there walking with him," and that never changed, even up to the end. Of his fate, he felt he was trying to "show other people to keep going, never quit."[87]

At that last magical U.S. Open before he died, Bruce summed up his feelings this way: "Everybody has to leave this earth. If I go in a year or less, I've lived a wonderful life. . . . I remember Tom saying, 'The game is a game of moments, and I want my share.' Well, not only did he have his share but I had my share."[88]

NOTES

THE GAME

1. Epigraphs are from Goodreads, www.goodreads.com/quotes.

2. Sidney Matthew, *Bobby: The Life and Times of Bobby Jones* (Ann Arbor, MI: Sports Media Group, 2005), 48.

3. Walter G. Simpson, *The Art of Golf* (Edinburgh, UK: David Douglas, 1892), 5.

4. James Balfour, *Reminiscences of Golf on St Andrews Links* (Edinburgh, UK: David Douglas, 1887), 54.

5. John L. Low, *Concerning Golf* (London: Hodder and Stoughton, 1903), 6–7.

6. Theodore Arnold Haultain, *The Mystery of Golf*, 2nd ed. (New York: Macmillan, 1910), 244.

7. Henry Leach, *The Happy Golfer* (London: Macmillan, 1914), 13.

8. Ibid.

9. Michael Murphy, *Golf in the Kingdom* (New York: Viking Arkana, 1994), 65; David Forgan, "Golfer's Creed," quoted in *The American Golf Teaching Method* (Ft. Pierce, FL: United States Golf Teachers Federation, 1999), 68.

10. Haultain, *The Mystery of Golf*, 24–25.

11. Theodore P. Jorgensen, *The Physics of Golf* (New York: Springer-Verlag, 1994), 9, 19.

12. Alastair Cochran and John Stobbs, *The Search for the Perfect Swing* (New York: Lippincott, 1968), 3, 6.

13. Pembroke Arnold Vaile, *The Soul of Golf* (New York: Macmillan, 1912), 3.

14. Don Wade, *Talking on Tour: The Best Anecdotes from Golf's Master Storyteller* (New York: Contemporary Books, 2001), 153.

15. Haultain, *The Mystery of Golf*, 15.

16. Charles Blair Macdonald, "Golf: The Ethical and Physical Aspects of the Game," *Golf*, January 1898, 21.

17. Romans 12:6; I Corinthians 12:4–6.

18. Horton Smith, "Glory Belongs to Jones Alone," *Golfer's Magazine*, reprinted in *Golf World*, vintage issue 1994, v32.

19. Robert Tyre (Bobby) Jones Jr., *Golf Is My Game* (New York: Doubleday, 1960), 68.

20. Goodreads, accessed March 20, 2014, http://www.goodreads.com/quotes.

21. Forgan, "Golfer's Creed"; Jerome D. Travers and James R. Crowell, *The Fifth Estate: Thirty Years of Golf* (New York: Knopf, 1926), 119.

22. See Dr. Deborah Graham and Jon Stabler, *The Eight Traits of Champion Golfers* (New York: Simon and Schuster, 1999). These traits are: focus, abstract thinking, emotional stability, dominance, tough-mindedness, confidence, self-sufficiency, optimum arousal.

23. Stephen Lowe, *Sir Walter and Mr. Jones: Walter Hagen, Bobby Jones, and the Rise of American Golf* (Chelsea, MI: Sleeping Bear, 2000), 16.

24. Don Weiss, "A Golfing Way Back to Life," *Golf Journal*, February 1965, 27–28.

25. "There Are No Handicaps Here," *Golf Digest*, August 1955, 47; Bill Fields, "Recovery Shots," *Golf World*, August 15, 1997, 10.

26. Steve DiMeglio, "Golf Helps Turn the Tables for a Soldier Wounded in Iraq," *USA Today*, January 25, 2011, accessed January 25, 2015, http://usatoday30.usatoday.com/sports/golf/2011-01-25-pga-hotline-tim-lang-jim-estes_N.htm.

27. "The Armless Golfer and How He Plays," *Golf Monthly*, January 1915, 772–74. The article notes that he had shot 108 at the Buffalo Country Club. Twenty years later, he was shooting in the 90s. See "Gossiping about Golf," *American Golfer*, January 1934, 20. A decade before Thomas McAuliffe, there was the story of Old Tom Morris. His son Tommy, who like his father won four British Opens, died on Christmas Day 1875, three months after his wife and baby died during child birth. Old Tom would see his wife and all five of his children die before him, and he claimed that if not for his God and his golf, he would not have found the strength to go on. See David Joy, *The Scrapbook of Old Tom Morris* (Chelsea, MI: Sleeping Bear, 2001), 223; Charles Blair Macdonald, *Scotland's Gift: Golf* (New York: Charles Scribner's Sons, 1928), 28.

28. Haultain, *The Mystery of Golf*, 47, 50–51, 61.

29. Ibid., 12–13.

30. James Dodson, *Ben Hogan: An American Life* (New York: Doubleday, 2004), 316.

31. "St Andrews Gossip: Funeral of Old Tom Morris," *Golf Illustrated* (UK), June 5, 1908, 211; Haultain, *The Mystery of Golf*, 14.

32. Mark Frost, *The Greatest Game Ever Played: Harry Vardon, Francis Ouimet, and the Birth of Modern Golf* (New York: Hyperion Books, 2002), 77.

I. HARRY VARDON

1. Audrey Howell, *Harry Vardon: The Revealing Story of a Champion Golfer* (Charleston, SC: Tempus, 2001), 14.

2. Jerome D. Travers, "Vardon—Greatest Golfer," *American Magazine*, November 1914, 87.

3. Harry Vardon, *My Golfing Life* (London: Hutchinson, 1933), 108; Harry Vardon, "My Best Round and Some Others," *American Golfer*, June 1920, 22; Frost, *The Greatest Game Ever Played*, 72.

4. "Candid Communings," *Golf Illustrated* (UK), March 27, 1937, 248. As Harry Vardon writes: "How difficult is our task when sometimes we are not feeling as well as we might wish—as must occasionally happen—I will leave the charitable reader to imagine. Has he ever felt like playing his best game when a little below par in either mind or body? This is where the really hard work of the professional's life comes in." *The Complete Golfer* (New York: McClure, Phillips, 1905), 262.

5. Frost, *The Greatest Game Ever Played*, 73. Designed by Old Tom Morris when he moved with his family to the west coast from St Andrews in 1851, Prestwick featured 12 holes until 1883, when it was expanded to 18. The course measured 5,948 yards and played to a par 72 in 1903, sufficiently long in the days when a good drive went 220 yards.

6. Vardon, *The Complete Golfer*, 8.

7. Smaller than the District of Columbia (68 square miles), or Liechtenstein (61 square miles), Jersey had a population of just over 56,000 people when Harry was born. Today, it is around 98,000. "Jersey," *Wikipedia*, accessed May 23, 2013, http://en.wikipedia.org/wiki/Jersey.

8. Harry was one of nine children who lived in a small cottage that stood near the current 12th fairway of the Royal Jersey Golf Club. See Howell, *Harry Vardon*, 15–16; Vardon, *The Complete Golfer*, 3.

9. Vardon, *The Complete Golfer*, 2–4.

10. Howell, *Harry Vardon*, 18; Vardon, *The Complete Golfer*, 4–5.

11. Vardon, *The Complete Golfer*, 5–7.

12. Harry Vardon, *The Gist of Golf* (New York: Doran, 1922), 94.

13. Vardon, *My Golfing Life*, 18, 23.

14. Vardon, *The Gist of Golf*, 93–94; Frost, *The Greatest Game Ever Played*, 14; Howell, *Harry Vardon*, 18.

15. *Wikipedia*, "Child Labour," accessed May 20, 2013, http://en.wikipedia.org/wiki/Child_labour.

16. Howell, *Harry Vardon*, 18; Vardon, *The Gist of Golf*, 94.

17. Vardon, *The Complete Golfer*, 9; Vardon, *My Golfing Life*, 27; Vardon, *The Gist of Golf*, 95–96.

18. Vardon, *My Golfing Life*, 81.

19. Frost, *The Greatest Game Ever Played*, 78.

20. "The Open Championship at Prestwick, Victory of Harry Vardon," *Golf Illustrated* (UK), June 19, 1903, 238.

21. Vardon, *My Golfing Life*, 108–9.

22. Harry Vardon, "My Best Round and Some Others," 22.

23. Howell, *Harry Vardon*, 83.

24. Vardon, *The Gist of Golf*, 96.

25. Ibid.; Vardon, *My Golfing Life*, 28; Howell, *Harry Vardon*, 21.

26. Vardon, *My Golfing Life*, 111. Vardon had suffered from hemorrhages since he was 17, and the doctor he worked for then recommended he get as much fresh air as possible, not overexert himself, and devote himself to golf. In March 1903, Vardon suffered a hemorrhage that was widely reported, and many wondered if he would ever play again. See "Vardon May Not Play Again," *Evening World* (New York), September 14, 1903.

27. Frost, *The Greatest Game Ever Played*, 96; Howell, *Harry Vardon*, 87.

28. Frank Ryan, *The Forgotten Plague: How the Battle against Tuberculosis Was Won—and Lost* (Boston: Little, Brown, 1993), 23–24; "The Forgotten Plague," PBS *American Experience* documentary, aired February 10, 2015, http://www.pbs.org/wgbh/americanexperience/blog/2015/02/10/plague-worldwide-epidemic/; see also David Hamilton's article in the March 2014 issue of *Through the Green* entitled "The Tuberculosis Golfer" for a description of how the disease afflicted a number of players in the 1800s.

29. Ryan, *The Forgotten Plague*, 18–19.

30. Ibid., 28.

31. Howell, *Harry Vardon*, 87; Frost, *The Greatest Game Ever Played*, 97.

32. Vardon, *My Golfing Life*, 112.

33. Ryan, *The Forgotten Plague*, 27.

34. Howell, *Harry Vardon*, 87.

35. Vardon, *The Gist of Golf*, 96–97.

36. Vardon, *My Golfing Life*, 28; Vardon, *The Gist of Golf*, 97.

37. The twin barriers of social rank and finance applied to Harry and his friends, who were gardeners, laborers, and servants and, as such, were precluded

from joining the Royal Jersey Golf Club as members in their own right. See Howell, *Harry Vardon*, 19; Vardon, *My Golfing Life*, 30.

38. Vardon, *The Complete Golfer*, 11.

39. Vardon, *My Golfing Life*, 33.

40. Vardon, *The Gist of Golf*, 111.

41. Ibid., 111–12; Howell, *Harry Vardon*, 174.

42. Charles Price, "He Came to Play," *Golf Magazine*, March 1960, 8.

43. Vardon described the evolution of his grip: "When I first began to play golf I grasped my club in what is generally regarded as the orthodox manner, that is to say, across the palms of both hands separately, with both thumbs right around the shaft." He improved on this and created a new method. "The club being taken in the left hand first, the shaft passes from the knuckle joint of the first finger across the ball of the second. The left thumb lies straight down the shaft. . . . The right hand is brought up so high that the palm of it covers over the left thumb, leaving very little of the latter to be seen. . . . The little finger of the right hand rides on the first finger of the left. The great advantage of this grip is that both hands feel and act like one." See Vardon, *The Complete Golfer*, 59–60; "Vardon Interviewed," *Golf Illustrated* (UK), March 2, 1900, 196; Howell, *Harry Vardon*, 20–21; Vardon, *My Golfing Life*, 37.

44. Vardon, *The Complete Golfer*, 59–60.

45. Vardon, *The Gist of Golf*, 98.

46. Bernard Darwin recalled the first time he saw Vardon play:

> It was the late summer of 1896 and he had won his first championship in the spring. I went over to Ganton, where he was then professional, for a day's golf and there by good luck was the great man driving off. He hit just the sort of drive that he always did—dead straight and rather high, the ball seeming to float with a particularly lazy flight through the air. The shot was obviously a perfect one and yet I was not quite so impressed as I had expected to be. The style was so different from what I had been taught to admire; the club seemed to be taken up in so outrageously upright a manner, with something of a lift. No doubt I was stupid and uneducated. So at least were other people who ought to have known much better than I, and the general impression at first could be summed up in the learned Mr. Edwards's words, "These Vardons are not pretty players." . . . However that may be, all the world soon became converted and by 1898 his swing was recognized not only as one of genius but also as one of surpassing ease and grace.

See Bernard Darwin, "The Old Masters—Harry Vardon," *American Golfer*, October 1929, 13; Herbert Warren Wind, "The Age of Vardon," *Sports Illustrated*,

June 10, 1957, 64; Dick Aultman and Ken Bowden, *The Methods of Golf's Masters: How They Played, and What You Can Learn from Them* (New York: Coward, McCann and Geoghegan, 1975), 13.

47. Aultman and Bowden, 21 (quoting Walter Cavanaugh in the *American Golfer*, 1924); Henry Leach, "The Human Vardon," *American Golfer*, January 1917, 189.

48. Horace G. Hutchinson, "Fifty Years of Golf (Tenth Installment)," *Golf Illustrated and Outdoor America*, February 1915, 24.

49. Price, "He Came to Play," 10; Grantland Rice, "Obtaining 100 Per Cent," *American Golfer*, August 28, 1920, 14.

50. Vardon, *My Golfing Life*, 248–49.

51. Price, "He Came to Play," 8–11.

52. Frost, *The Greatest Game Ever Played*, 97.

53. Howell, *Harry Vardon*, 24, 19. Harry listed his occupation as "gardener."

54. Ibid., 25–27.

55. Ibid., 35, 39.

56. Hutchinson, "Fifty Years of Golf (Tenth Installment)," 22; Howell, *Harry Vardon*, 39, 47.

57. Hutchinson, "Fifty Years of Golf (Tenth Installment)," 23.

58. Vardon, *My Golfing Life*, 58; Vardon, *The Complete Golfer*, 18.

59. Vardon, *My Golfing Life*, 57.

60. Howell, *Harry Vardon*, 88.

61. Travers, "Vardon—Greatest Golfer," 87.

62. Frost, *The Greatest Game Ever Played*, 97–98.

63. Leach, "The Human Vardon," 178; Howell, *Harry Vardon*, 89.

64. Vardon, *My Golfing Life*, 93–94.

65. "Vardon Interviewed" *Golf Illustrated*, 196.

66. Vardon, *My Golfing Life*, 126; *Washington Post*, January 9, 1906.

67. Howell, *Harry Vardon*, 89–90; Frost, *The Greatest Game Ever Played*, 99.

68. *Golf Illustrated* (UK), January 8, 1904, 23.

69. Ross Goodner, *Golf's Greatest: The Legendary World Golf Hall of Famers* (Norwalk, CT: Golf Digest, 1978), 203.

70. Travers, "Vardon—Greatest Golfer," 88.

71. Vardon, *My Golfing Life*, 23.

72. Howell, *Harry Vardon*, 89; Frost, *The Greatest Game Ever Played*, 99–100.

73. Vardon, *My Golfing Life*, 98, 154.

74. Ryan, *The Forgotten Plague*, 23; Frost, *The Greatest Game Ever Played*, 100.

75. Howell, *Harry Vardon*, 89.

76. Frost, *The Greatest Game Ever Played*, 101.

77. Howell, *Harry Vardon*, 91.

78. Ibid., 94; Frost, *The Greatest Game Ever Played*, 71.

79. Daniel Wexler, *The Golfer's Library: A Reader's Guide to Three Centuries of Golf Literature* (Ann Arbor, MI: Sports Media Group, 2004), 8. At least 20 editions were issued at home and a similar amount overseas.

80. Hutchinson, "Fifty Years of Golf (Tenth Installment)," 24.

81. Vardon, *My Golfing Life*, 152.

82. Vardon, *The Gist of Golf*, 151.

83. Howell, *Harry Vardon*, 94.

84. Vardon, *The Gist of Golf*, 151–52.

85. Ibid., 152; Howell, *Harry Vardon*, 94.

86. Vardon, *My Golfing Life*, 153–54.

87. Leach, *The Happy Golfer*, 72.

88. Bill Fields, "Golf's Grey Ghost," *Golf World*, June 9, 2000, 80.

89. Price, "He Came to Play," 8; Wind, "The Age of Vardon," 69.

90. Wind, "The Age of Vardon," 69.

91. Vardon, *My Golfing Life*, 153.

92. "Ouimet is the Winner," 1913 U.S. Open newspaper clippings, United States Golf Association, Arnold Palmer Center for Golf History, Far Hills, NJ (USGA).

93. Leach, "The Human Vardon," 179.

94. Harry Vardon, "How Many Clubs Do I Need?" *American Golfer*, September 5, 1925, 10. He claimed that "no reasonable person would call that a big outfit."

95. Vardon, *The Gist of Golf*, 152.

96. Ibid., 152–53.

97. "Funeral of the Late Harry Vardon," *British Golfer*, May 1937, 161.

98. The Claret Jug is the name of the trophy given to the winner of the British Open.

99. World Golf Hall of Fame biographical information in the USGA Harry Vardon file.

100. Vardon, *My Golfing Life*, 240.

101. O. B. Keeler, "Mr. Keeler Grows Reminiscent," *American Golfer*, February 1934, 39.

102. Keeler, "Mr. Keeler Grows Reminiscent," 39.

103. Grantland Rice, "By the Turn of a Putt," *American Golfer*, August 21, 1920, 19.

104. Keeler, "Mr. Keeler Grows Reminiscent," 39.

105. Rice, "By the Turn of a Putt," 17.

106. Ibid.

107. Keeler, "Mr. Keeler Grows Reminiscent," 39.

108. Howell, *Harry Vardon*, 149–52.

109. "Bobby Jones Conquers the Golf World," *Literary Digest*, July 30, 1927, 56.

110. Vardon, *My Golfing Life*, 263.

111. "Bobby Jones Conquers the Golf World," 56.

112. Howell, *Harry Vardon*, 152.

113. Ibid., 152–53; Fields, "Golf's Grey Ghost," 74.

114. Fields, "Golf's Grey Ghost," 74, 80. Peter Howell passed away in 2012.

115. Ibid., 80.

116. Henry Cotton, *This Game of Golf* (London: Country Life, 1948), 36.

117. Vardon, *My Golfing Life*, 12, 102.

118. Ibid., 272–73.

119. Ibid., 276.

120. "Plain Truths by 'Sam Solomon,'" *American Golfer*, September 1919, 890; 1920 British Open champion George Duncan wanted a five-inch hole, Gene Sarazen an eight-inch hole. Vardon thought this was counterproductive. "Truly the putting has too great an effect on the results of the matches that are played. . . . I would make the hole four inches in diameter instead of four and a quarter. To reduce it by a quarter of an inch would make a big difference."

121. Vardon, *My Golfing Life*, 15.

122. Ibid., 253.

123. Bernard Darwin, "A Tribute to the Late Harry Vardon," *Sports Illustrated and the American Golfer*, April 1937, 32. Jessie Vardon passed away June 3, 1946.

124. Bernard Darwin, "A Tribute to the Late Harry Vardon," 32.

125. Howell, *Harry Vardon*, 177.

126. Ibid., 164.

127. Vardon, *My Golfing Life*, 108–10.

2. BOBBY JONES

1. Jones, *Golf Is My Game*, 68.

2. Tommy Armour, "Penshots of the Masters—No. 6," *American Golfer*, October 1935, 39.

3. Ron Rapoport, *The Immortal Bobby : Bobby Jones and the Golden Age of Golf* (New York: John Wiley, 2005), 274.

4. Ibid., 275.

5. Jones, *Golf Is My Game*, 250.

6. Ibid., 250–51. He played the round in: 4-3-4-4-4-3-4-2-4=32 Out 4-5-4-5-5-5-5-4-3=40 In—for a total of 72. See USGA Bobby Jones Papers, BJJG1/59 (unidentified newspaper clipping).

7. Curt Sampson, *The Slam: Bobby Jones and the Price of Glory* (New York: Rodale, 2005), 13.

8. Richard Miller, *Triumphant Journey: The Saga of Bobby Jones and the Grand Slam of Golf* (Dallas: Taylor, 1993), 29.

9. O. B. Keeler, "How Bobby Jones Started," *American Golfer*, June 5, 1920, 4; William E. Woodward, "What Makes Him Click," *American Magazine*, April 1930, 37.

10. *Hamilton Evening Journal*, July 17, 1926; Keeler, "How Bobby Jones Got Started," 4; O. B. Keeler, *The Bobby Jones Story* (Chicago: Triumph Books, 2003), 3; Robert T. Jones and O. B. Keeler, *Down the Fairway: The Golf Life and Play of Robert T. Jones, Jr.* (New York: Minton, Balch, 1927), 23–24.

11. Mark Frost, *The Grand Slam: Bobby Jones, America, and the Story of Golf* (New York: Hyperion Books, 2004), 19; Keeler, *The Bobby Jones Story*, 3.

12. Woodward, "What Makes Him Click," 38; Jones and Keeler, *Down the Fairway*, 26.

13. Jones and Keeler, *Down the Fairway*, 27.

14. Jones, *Golf Is My Game*, 17.

15. Robert Tyre Jones's Canton cotton mill had earnings of over $1.5 million in 1925. See Miller, *Triumphant Journey*, 25.

16. O. B. Keeler, *The Boy's Life of Bobby Jones* (Chelsea, MI: Sleeping Bear, 2002), 58.

17. Woodward, "What Makes Him Click," 38; Jones beat Howard Thorne 5 and 4 over 36 holes, and his photo appeared in the *American Golfer* magazine; Frost, *The Grand Slam*, 24.

18. Jones and Keeler, *Down the Fairway*, 40–41. Around the age of 11, Little Bob began to append the "Jr." to his name as a tribute to his father (who was actually Robert Purmedus. It was Bobby's paternal grandfather who was Robert Tyre). See Sampson, *The Slam*, 14; Lowe, *Sir Walter and Mr. Jones*, 165.

19. "Golf, Business, and Bobby Jones," *Literary Digest*, April 18, 1925, 64; Grantland Rice, "Never Another Jones," *Saturday Evening Post*, June 8, 1940, 44.

20. Jones and Keeler, *Down the Fairway*, 20.

21. Miller, *Triumphant Journey*, 31; Grantland Rice, "Bobby Jones's Golf Story," *St. Nicholas*, November 1916, 58.

22. Frost, *The Grand Slam*, 75.

23. Rice, "Never Another Jones," 46.

24. Alexa Stirling Fraser, "The Most Unforgettable Character I've Met," *Reader's Digest*, April 1960, 56.

25. Ibid., 56–57.

26. Ibid., 57; Rapoport, *The Immortal Bobby*, 34.

27. Travers and Crowell, *The Fifth Estate*, 125.

28. Jones and Keeler, *Down the Fairway*, 64–65.

29. Rice, "Never Another Jones," 44.

30. Charles R. Yates, interview by Joe Doyle, November 2, 1990, USGA Oral History Collection, 4.

31. Matthew, *Bobby*, 199.

32. Ibid., 21.

33. Clifford Roberts, *The Story of the Augusta National Golf Club* (New York: Doubleday, 1976), 237.

34. Catherine Lewis, *Bobby Jones and the Quest for the Grand Slam* (Chicago: Triumph Books, 2005), 80.

35. Bill Inglish, "The Tournament Record and Other Performances of Robert Tyre Jones, Jr., 1911–1942," appendix 3 in *The Story of the Augusta National Golf Club*, by Clifford Roberts (New York: Doubleday, 1976), 233; Sampson, *The Slam*, 15, 72–73.

36. Jones, *Golf Is My Game*, 92; Miller, *Triumphant Journey*, 87. Jones's outlook on life may also have been affected by how Keeler dealt with his own physical limitation (having a permanently stiff knee), the result of an illness that almost took his life when he was a young man.

37. Keeler, *The Boy's Life of Bobby Jones*, 125.

38. Keeler, *The Bobby Jones Story*, 33; *Washington Post*, August 11, 1920; Vardon, *My Golfing Life*, 240.

39. Matthew, *Bobby*, 186.

40. "I used steel first in 1931 after I retired. It gives an advantage of, perhaps, one or two shots a round. It is lighter, stronger, reacts much faster than hickory, and allows a much greater margin of error. You can hit nearly flat out with safety, whereas it was necessary to 'feel' shots with hickory." See "Master's Voice—On Eve of the Masters—Bobby Jones talking to John Ballantine" *Times of London*, April 7, 1968, from USGA Bobby Jones file.

41. Walter Travis, the great amateur of the early 1900s, gave Jones a lesson in 1922 that had him stand taller and with his feet close together, allowing the wrists to swing freely. He also advised Jones to let his putts "die" at the hole instead of charging them. See Miller, *Triumphant Journey*, 77.

42. Matthew, *Bobby*, 18.

43. Rapoport, *The Immortal Bobby*, 38; Lowe, *Sir Walter and Mr. Jones*, 105.

44. Lewis, *Bobby Jones and the Quest for the Grand Slam*, 95; Rapoport, *The Immortal Bobby*, 41.

45. Miller, *Triumphant Journey*, 94; Lowe, *Sir Walter and Mr. Jones*, 115.

46. Lowe, *Sir Walter and Mr. Jones*, 115; Walker was the grandfather of President George H. W. Bush and founder of the Walker Cup, a biennial competition between amateur teams from the United States and Great Britain and Ireland.

47. Rice, "Never Another Jones," 46; Duncan won the British Open in 1920, Evans the U.S. Open in 1916. See "Golf, Business, and Bobby Jones," 64.

48. Lowe, *Sir Walter and Mr. Jones*, 102; Jones and Keeler, *Down the Fairway*, 65.

49. Al Laney, *Following the Leaders* (n.p.: Ailsa, 1991), 28–29.

50. Ibid., 136; Joseph C. Dey, "Francis Ouimet and His Stories," *Golf Journal*, November 1967, 21; Jones, *Golf Is My Game*, 94.

51. Lewis, *Bobby Jones and the Quest for the Grand Slam*, 80; Sampson, *The Slam*, 76.

52. Jones and Keeler, *Down the Fairway*, 130.

53. Matthew, *Bobby*, 26.

54. Jones and Keeler, *Down the Fairway*, 133.

55. Herbert Warren Wind, *The Story of American Golf: Its Champions and Its Championships* (New York: Knopf, 1975), 135.

56. Jones and Keeler, *Down the Fairway*, 133.

57. O. B. Keeler, "Bobby Jones' Own Story of How He Won," *American Golfer*, August 11, 1923, 144.

58. Keeler, *The Boy's Life of Bobby Jones*, 186.

59. Harry Paxton and Fred Russell, "A Visit with Bobby Jones," *Saturday Evening Post*, n.d., 70; Keeler, *The Boy's Life of Bobby Jones*, 183; Jones and Keeler, *Down the Fairway*, 135; "Jones, An Amateur, Beats Cruickshank, Pro, for Golf Title," *New York Times*, July 16, 1923.

60. Ross Goodner, "Wee Bobby," *Golf Magazine*, August 1974, 55; Rapoport, *The Immortal Bobby*, 72.

61. Lowe, *Sir Walter and Mr. Jones*, 143.

62. Henry Picard, interview by Joe Doyle, November 3, 1990, USGA Oral History Collection, 18–19. Picard remembered saying to Jones, "'I didn't know you were that religious.' He said, 'I am very religious.'" Bob Jones's grandson Bob Jones IV said that "He was not denominational but he had always thought about religious matters. He had been a regular Mass attender every Sunday because my grandmother was devout." See "Robert T. Jones IV, M.Div., Psy.D.," Golf Conversations, accessed March 23, 2014, http://www.golfconversations.com/2011/04/05/robert-t-jones-iv-psy-d-m-div.

63. Lowe, *Sir Walter and Mr. Jones*, 16–17.

64. Woodward, "What Makes Him Click," 170.

65. Rice, "Never Another Jones," 44.

66. Jones and Keeler, *Down the Fairway*, 44; Jones, *Golf Is My Game*, 22.

67. Matthew, *Bobby*, 49.

68. Jones, *Golf Is My Game*, 93.

69. Ibid.

70. Miller, *Triumphant Journey*, 25, 34.

71. Sampson, *The Slam*, 15.

72. Michael Bamberger, " Life with Bub: Robert Tyre Jones IV Is Devoted to the Memory of His Grandfather," *Sports Illustrated*, April 8, 2013, accessed March 29, 2014, http://www.golf.com/tour-and-news/masters-bobby-jones-grandson-remembers-his-grandfather?page=1.

73. Joan Flynn Dreyspool, "Tommy Armour Analyzes the Jones Swing," *Golf Magazine*, September 1960, 23.

74. Sampson, *The Slam*, 15–16.

75. Luke Ross, "I Caddied for Jones When He Threw Clubs," *Golf Digest*, April 1969, 76; Starting in 1928, his first full year with his father's law firm, Jones's routine called for golf each Wednesday with his father and his friends, and he played one or two other times a week. See Sampson, *The Slam*, 15–16.

76. Miller, *Triumphant Journey*, 88–89.

77. Keeler, *The Boy's Life of Bobby Jones*, 134; Jones and Keeler, *Down the Fairway*, 70; Woodward, "What Makes Him Click," 169.

78. Jack Sher, "Bobby Jones, Emperor of Golf," *Sport*, August 1949, 61.

79. Lewis, *Bobby Jones and the Quest for the Grand Slam*, 80; At the end of the fall term in 1927, halfway through a three-year program, Jones took the bar exam, passed, and was admitted to the bar May 8, 1929. Clara Malone Jones was born April 18, 1925, Bob Jones III on November 30, 1926, and Mary Ellen on January 29, 1931.

80. Miller, *Triumphant Journey*, 149–51.

81. Lowe, *Sir Walter and Mr. Jones*, 168.

82. Frost, *The Grand Slam*, 109; During Bobby's early days, the stark example of 1911 and 1912 U.S. Open champion Johnny McDermott's nervous breakdown remained a vivid reminder.

83. Paxton and Russell, "A Visit with Bobby Jones," 68, 70.

84. Sampson, *The Slam*, 93.

85. Paxton and Russell, "A Visit with Bobby Jones," 70; Miller, *Triumphant Journey*, 87; "Evans Sets Record and Wins at Golf," *New York Times*, August 29, 1925, 8; Sher, "Bobby Jones, Emperor of Golf," 63; Jones and Keeler, *Down the Fairway*, 226.

86. Yates, interview by Joe Doyle, 24.

87. Armour, "Penshots of the Masters—No. 6," 39.

88. Matthew, *Bobby*, 64.

89. Ibid.

90. Dreyspool, "Tommy Armour Analyzes the Jones Swing," 23.

91. Chick Evans, "A Great Sportsman," *Golfer*, March 1953, 43; Woodward, "What Makes Him Click," 36.

92. Matthew, *Bobby*, 204; Miller, *Triumphant Journey*, 153.

93. "Bobby Jones' Idealism Keeps Him from Entering Pro Ranks," *Chicago Daily Tribune*, September 11, 1925, 17; Jones and Keeler, *Down the Fairway*, 28.

94. Lowe, *Sir Walter and Mr. Jones*, 195.

95. Miller, *Triumphant Journey*, 133; Frost, *The Grand Slam*, 388; Jones's appearances in the British Open were tied to his Walker Cup appearances, except for 1927, when he defended his championship.

96. Rapoport, *The Immortal Bobby*, 298; Henry Longhurst, "Bobby in Britain," *Golf Magazine*, September 1960, 18; William D. Richardson, "Bobby Jones Is the King of Golf," *New York Times*, July 18, 1926.

97. Steven Reid, *Bobby's Open: Mr. Jones and the Golf Shot That Defined a Legend* (London: Corinthian Books, 2012), 185, 207.

98. Matthew, *Bobby*, 81; Frost, *The Grand Slam*, 273.

99. Jones and Keeler, *Down the Fairway*, 161.

100. Ibid.; Dreyspool, "Tommy Armour Analyzes the Jones Swing," 24.

101. "Golf, Business, and Bobby Jones," 64.

102. Charles Price, "Robert Tyre 'Bobby Jones'—The Headmaster, 1902–1971," *Golf Magazine*, April 1972, 50; Matthew, *Bobby*, 141; Yates, interview by Joe Doyle, 26.

103. Clair Price, "He Denies That His Has Been Ungovernable and Points Out That Moral Discipline Is an Invaluable Asset," *New York Times*, July 31, 1927, xx2.

104. Sampson, *The Slam*, 203; Price, "He Denies That His Has Been Ungovernable," xx2.

105. "Jones to Defend Title," *New York Times*, November 20, 1926.

106. Lowe, *Sir Walter and Mr. Jones*, 205.

107. Keeler, *The Bobby Jones Story*, 175; Keeler, *The Boy's Life of Bobby Jones*, 243.

108. Matthew, *Bobby*, 87.

109. "Cablegrams Flow in on Jones," *New York Times*, July 17, 1927, S9; Price, "He Denies That His Has Been Ungovernable, xx2; Keeler, *The Bobby Jones Story*, 175.

110. "Bobby Jones out of 1928 British Open, but Will Play in U.S. Open and Amateur," *New York Times*, December 18, 1927, S1. Jones said he would not defend his British Open title, citing his law-school schedule. "A lot of people don't take this law school idea seriously," he said. "They ought to try it. It's serious enough for me."

111. Lowe, *Sir Walter and Mr. Jones*, 207–8.

112. Keeler, *The Bobby Jones Story*, 195–96.

113. O. B. Keeler, "Prelude to the 1930 Grand Slam," *Esquire* 23 (June 1945): 44; Sher, "Bobby Jones, Emperor of Golf," 59.

114. Sher, "Bobby Jones, Emperor of Golf," 59.

115. Keeler, *The Boy's Life of Bobby Jones*, 274; Miller, *Triumphant Journey*, 75.

116. Jones, *Golf Is My Game*, 102.

117. Ibid., 130; Frost, *The Grand Slam*, 358.

118. Sampson, *The Slam*, 115; Keeler, *The Boy's Life of Bobby Jones*, 281.

119. Keeler, *The Bobby Jones Story*, 221; Matthew, *Bobby*, 118, 121.

120. Keeler, *The Bobby Jones Story*, 225.

121. Keeler, *The Boy's Life of Bobby Jones*, 28; Rapoport, *The Immortal Bobby*, 209.

122. Miller, *Triumphant Journey*, 120; Rapoport, *The Immortal Bobby*, 224.

123. Letter from Prescott Bush to Everett Seaver, July 22, 1930, from USGA Championship Files, U.S. Open, 1930. "I was standing on the seventeenth tee when Jones hit the ball," writes Bush. "I watched the flight very carefully. . . . His ball was in or lost in a recognized water hazard. . . . There were many eye witnesses on the spot who were absolutely positive that the ball was lodged in that marsh and from the tee it was absolutely clear to me that the ball landed in the marsh. . . . Jimmy Johnston happened to be with me and he later told me that the ball was, in his opinion, at least ten yards inside of the margin of the hazard." Every player was given a local rule sheet defining this parallel water hazard that stated that, if in the hazard, "another ball may be dropped in the fairway as near as possible to the point at which the ball crossed the margin of the hazard, but not nearer the hole." See also Rapoport, *The Immortal Bobby*, 229.

124. Frost, *The Grand Slam*, 410; Rapoport, *The Immortal Bobby*, 210.

125. Robert Sommers, "The 1930 Open Revisited," *Golf Journal*, June 1970, 10.

126. Frost, *The Grand Slam*, 142; "The Coronation of the Emperor Jones," *Literary Digest*, August 2, 1930, 34.

127. Joseph C. Dey Jr., "It Was Always Jones against the Field," *Golf Magazine*, August 1965, 73; Miller, *Triumphant Journey*, 14, 17.

128. Miller, *Triumphant Journey*, 12.

129. Lewis, *Bobby Jones and the Quest for the Grand Slam*, 70.

130. Keeler, *The Bobby Jones Story*, 243; Price, "Robert Tyre 'Bobby Jones,'" 52.

131. Keeler, *The Bobby Jones Story*, 244.

132. In 1931, Jones signed with A. G. Spalding and Brothers to help design a matched set of golf clubs, stamped "Robt. T. Jones, Jr." The line sold an estimated two million sets of 15 different models from 1932 to 1973. See Lewis, *Bobby*

Jones and the Quest for the Grand Slam, 86; Rapoport, *The Immortal Bobby*, 267. In 1937, Jones bought a Coca-Cola bottling plant in Massachusetts and in 1940 another in Vermont. In addition, he and Cliff Roberts had an interest in a South American Coca-Cola venture. See Furman Bisher, "The Southern Gentleman," *Golf Magazine*, September 1960, 37; Miller, *Triumphant Journey*, 236; Lowe, *Sir Walter and Mr. Jones*, 267.

133. Sampson, *The Slam*, 203. The record he left behind was spectacular. Tom McCollister of the *Atlanta Journal-Constitution* looked at the numbers: "From 1923 to 1930, Jones won 13 major national championships in the U.S. and Great Britain, 62 percent of the championships he entered." In his 14-year career, he "played in only 52 tournaments in that span, an average of four a year, and won 23." That's a 44 percent victory rate. See Lewis, *Bobby Jones and the Quest for the Grand Slam*, 70 and Roberts, *The Story of the Augusta National Golf Club*, 238.

134. Alister MacKenzie, "Plans for the Ideal Golf Course," *American Golfer*, March 1932, 20–21.

135. Martin Davis, *The Greatest of Them All: The Legend of Bobby Jones* (Greenwich, CT: American Golfer, 1996), 59; Richard Davis Gordin, "Robert Tyre Jones, Jr.: His Life and Contributions to Golf," (PhD diss., Ohio State University, 1967), 158. Jones served as a captain in the army, inducted June 5, 1942, where he served as intelligence officer and landed on Normandy June 7, 1944. He was discharged August 25, 1944, when his father was ill. See Lewis, *Bobby Jones and the Quest for the Grand Slam*, 86.

136. Rapoport, *The Immortal Bobby*, 297.

137. Miller, *Triumphant Journey*, 225.

138. Lowe, *Sir Walter and Mr. Jones*, 306; See "Full Recovery for Bobby Jones," *New York Times*, November, 11, 1948.

139. Rapoport, *The Immortal Bobby*, 302. Jones's teacher and friend Stewart Maiden died in the same hospital a few days earlier. See "Operated on Neck, Bobby Jones Better," *Clovis News-Journal* (New Mexico), November 6, 1948.

140. Lowe, *Sir Walter and Mr. Jones*, 306–7; "Jones Awaits Operation," *New York Times*, May 17, 1950.

141. Fraser, "The Most Unforgettable Character I've Met," 59.

142. Miller, *Triumphant Journey*, 227; Lowe, *Sir Walter and Mr. Jones*, 308.

143. Fraser, "The Most Unforgettable Character I've Met," 60.

144. Rapoport, *The Immortal Bobby*, 300–302; Miller, *Triumphant Journey*, 226; Gordin, "Robert Tyre Jones, Jr.," 168; "Syringomyelia Fact Sheet," National Institute of Neurological Disorders and Stroke, accessed February 4, 2014, http://www.ninds.nih.gov/disorders/syringomyelia/detail_syringomyelia.htm . The same year Jones was diagnosed, his father died, which was another heavy blow to endure.

145. Rapoport, *The Immortal Bobby*, 303.

146. Ibid., 299, 304; Gordin, "Robert Tyre Jones, Jr.," 169.

147. Rapoport, *The Immortal Bobby*, 305.

148. Miller, *Triumphant Journey*, 234; Rapoport, *The Immortal Bobby*, 318; Davis, *The Greatest of Them All*, 16.

149. Price, "Robert Tyre 'Bobby Jones,'" 52; Charles Price, "The Last Days of Bobby Jones," *Golf Digest*, April 1991, 184; Miller, *Triumphant Journey*, 4, 237.

150. Lowe, *Sir Walter and Mr. Jones*, 331; Miller, *Triumphant Journey*, 238.

151. Frank Christian, *Augusta National and the Masters: A Photographer's Scrapbook* (Chelsea, MI: Sleeping Bear, 2009), 133.

152. "My Shot—Frank Chirkinian," *Golf Digest*, September 2003, 112. Chirkinian recalled at the Masters in 1970 Mary Jones confronting him about removing Jones from the presentation ceremony. Chirkinian maintained he did no such thing. Mary paused a moment, then said, "I knew it. That son of a bitch Roberts, I *knew* he was behind this," 112; Jones's grandson Bob Jones IV recalled, "In the mid-'60s, when my grandfather wanted my father named as club president, Cliff preempted him. He had the board name my grandfather President in Perpetuity. He despised that title. Cliff tried to get my father to resign from the club. He brought him into his office and berated him, in front of another member, and tried to get him to quit. The way Cliff Roberts treated my dad just frosted my grandfather." See Bamberger, "Life with Bub."

153. Mike Towle, *I Remember Bobby Jones* (Nashville, TN: Cumberland House, 2001), 56; Lewis, *Bobby Jones and the Quest for the Grand Slam*, 93.

154. Frost, *The Grand Slam*, 465.

155. Jones, *Golf Is My Game*, 247.

156. Ibid., 95; Miller, *Triumphant Journey*, 246.

157. Herbert Warren Wind, "Will Ye No' Come Back Again?" *Sports Illustrated*, October 27, 1958, 64; Lowe, *Sir Walter and Mr. Jones*, 315. See full text of acceptance remarks in Lewis, *Bobby Jones and the Quest for the Grand Slam*, 112–13.

158. Christian, *Augusta National and the Masters*, 22.

159. Jones, *Golf Is My Game*, 68; Longhurst, "Bobby in Britain," 55.

3. BEN HOGAN

1. John D. Ames, "The New Ben Hogan," *USGA Journal*, July 1950, 9. Ames was president of the USGA from 1958 to 1959 and chairman of the Championship Committee in 1950.

2. Joan Flynn Dreyspool, "Conversation Piece: Subject: Ben Hogan," *Sports Illustrated*, June 20, 1955, 37.

3. Jody Vasquez, *Afternoons with Mr. Hogan: A Boy, a Legend, and the Lessons of a Lifetime* (New York: Gotham Books, 2004), 27.

4. Ibid., 29.

5. Bill Fields, "A Man Apart," *Golf World*, USGA Ben Hogan file.

6. James Dodson, *American Triumvirate: Sam Snead, Byron Nelson, Ben Hogan, and the Modern Age of Golf* (New York: Knopf, 2012), 46–47; Curt Sampson, *Hogan* (Nashville, TN: Rutledge Hill, 1996), 10–12.

7. Sampson, *Hogan*, 11; Martin Davis, *Ben Hogan: The Man behind the Mystique* (Greenwich, CT: American Golfer, 2002), 29.

8. Sampson, *Hogan*, 14–15; Jimmy Demaret, *My Partner, Ben Hogan* (New York: McGraw-Hill, 1954), 46; George Peper, "Ben Hogan," *Golf Magazine*, September 1987, 65; Dreyspool, "Conversation Piece: Subject: Ben Hogan," 37.

9. Demaret, *My Partner*, 47; Bob Brumby, "The Ben Hogan Story," *Sport*, December 1953, 36; Sampson, *Hogan*, 18.

10. Demaret, *My Partner*, 48, 66; Gene Gregston, *Hogan: The Man Who Played for Glory* (Englewood Cliffs, NJ: Prentice-Hall, 1978), 26; Kris Tschetter, *Mr. Hogan: The Man I Knew*, with Steve Eubanks (New York: Gotham Books, 2010), 46; Demaret, *My Partner*, 66.

11. Dreyspool, "Conversation Piece: Subject: Ben Hogan," 38.

12. Arch Murray, "Golf's Biggest Money Winner," *Look*, July 1, 1941, 40, 42.

13. Ibid., 40; Gregston, *Hogan*, 28–30; Sampson, *Hogan*, 135.

14. Dodson, *American Triumvirate*, 78–79.

15. Ibid., 79; Davis, *Ben Hogan*, 29.

16. Gregston, *Hogan*, 29.

17. Dreyspool, "Conversation Piece: Subject: Ben Hogan," 37.

18. Ibid., 38.

19. Sampson, *Hogan*, 39–40; Dodson, *American Triumvirate*, 92.

20. Peper, "Ben Hogan," 66.

21. Vasquez, *Afternoons with Mr. Hogan*, 14.

22. Gregston, *Hogan*, 33; Brumby, "The Ben Hogan Story," 60; Sampson, *Hogan*, 47.

23. Sampson, *Hogan*, 44.

24. Gregston, *Hogan*, 34.

25. Davis, *Ben Hogan*, 31.

26. Ibid., 25.

27. Ibid.

28. Gregston, *Hogan*, 35.

29. Dodson, *American Triumvirate*, 94.

30. Tschetter, *Mr. Hogan*, 71–72.

31. Dodson, *Ben Hogan*, 334.

32. Tschetter, *Mr. Hogan*, 44; Brumby, "The Ben Hogan Story," 57.

33. Dodson, *American Triumvirate*, 102.

34. Ben Hogan, interview by Ken Venturi, transcript, CBS Sports, broadcast on May 14–15 and May 21, 1983, USGA Ben Hogan file; Sampson, *Hogan*, 49; Gregston, *Hogan*, 31.

35. Demaret, *My Partner*, 65.

36. Hogan, interview by Ken Venturi.

37. Brumby, "The Ben Hogan Story," 60.

38. Picard, interview by Joe Doyle, 13.

39. Ibid., 23; Sampson, *Hogan*, 53.

40. Dreyspool, "Conversation Piece: Subject: Ben Hogan," 38; Sampson, *Hogan*, 54.

41. Picard, interview by Joe Doyle, 21–22. Craig Wood would win both the Masters and U.S. Open in 1941; Gregston, *Hogan*, 44–45.

42. Dreyspool, "Conversation Piece: Subject: Ben Hogan," 37.

43. Sampson, *Hogan*, 68.

44. Brumby, "The Ben Hogan Story," 35; Peper, "Ben Hogan," 66.

45. Sampson, *Hogan*, xix.

46. Dodson, *Ben Hogan*, 120.

47. Tschetter, *Mr. Hogan*, 75; In an interview in 1942 Hogan said he had to give his complete attention to every shot played, and after "leaving the first tee, there could be no recess, no loafing spot, on the mental side." See Grantland Rice, "Ice Heart," *Collier's*, May 23, 1942, 35.

48. Demaret, *My Partner*, 152; Jaime Diaz, "What Could Have Been," *Golf Digest*, June 2009, 46.

49. Hogan, interview by Ken Venturi.

50. Ben Hogan, "This Is My Secret," *Life*, August 8, 1955, 61.

51. Peper, "Ben Hogan," 67.

52. Sampson, *Hogan*, 100.

53. Dodson, *American Triumvirate*, 232.

54. Gregston, *Hogan*, 67–68.

55. Hogan, interview by Ken Venturi.

56. Gregston, *Hogan*, 49; Dodson, *Ben Hogan*, 124; Sampson, *Hogan*, 89.

57. Sampson, *Hogan*, xx.

58. Al Barkow, *The Upset: Jack Fleck's Incredible Victory over Ben Hogan at the U.S. Open* (Chicago: Chicago Review, 2012), 195.

59. Murray, "Golf's Biggest Money Winner," 43.

60. Gregston, *Hogan*, 41.

61. Dave Kindred, "Moving Ben's Memorabilia," *Golf Digest*, August 1998, 48.

62. Bruce Selcraig, "Our Friend, Mr. Hogan," *Golf Digest*, October 1997, 135.

63. Davis, *Ben Hogan*, 30.

64. Barkow, *The Upset*, 58.

65. Dodson, *American Triumvirate*, 267.

66. Gregston, *Hogan*, 6; Sampson, *Hogan*, 116.

67. Gregston, *Hogan*, 6; Kindred, "Moving Ben's Memorabilia," 48. Hogan's weight dropped from 142 to 115 pounds after the accident.

68. Gregston, *Hogan*, 8.

69. Bill Rives, "I'll Be Back, Says Ben Hogan," *Sport*, September 1949, 15; Sampson, *Hogan*, 117; Frank Eck, "The Secret of Ben Hogan," *True*, June 1952, 65.

70. Gregston, *Hogan*, 8.

71. Rives, "I'll Be Back, Says Ben Hogan," 98.

72. Gregston, *Hogan*, 9.

73. Ibid., 10; "Hogan to Recover, Surgeon Reports," *New York Times*, March 4, 1949.

74. Gregston, *Hogan*, 10–11; Davis, *Ben Hogan,* 39.

75. Gregston, *Hogan*, 11; Eck, "The Secret of Ben Hogan," 65.

76. Charles Bartlett, "Hospital Interview," *Golf World*, April 6, 1949, 4; Dodson, *Ben Hogan*, 247; Gregston, *Hogan*, 11.

77. Gregston, *Hogan*, 18; "Hogan Back Home Again," *New York Times*, April 2, 1949.

78. Demaret, *My Partner*, 88.

79. Rives, "I'll Be Back, Says Ben Hogan," 98.

80. Bartlett, "Hospital Interview,"4.

81. Rives, "I'll Be Back, Says Ben Hogan," 99; Sampson, *Hogan*, 126.

82. Gregston, *Hogan*, 20; Dodson, *Ben Hogan*, 262.

83. Eck, "The Secret of Ben Hogan," 67.

84. Gregston, *Hogan*, 20–21.

85. Sampson, *Hogan*, 139; Barkow, *The Upset*, 72.

86. Al Laney, *Following the Leaders* (n.p.: Ailsa, 1991), 88.

87. Part of the legend involves his caddy telling him he couldn't quit because the caddy didn't work for quitters. Jim Trinkle, "Ben-Hogan at Merion," *Golf Journal*, June 1971, 21; Sampson, *Hogan*, 142.

88. Trinkle, "Ben Hogan at Merion," 21–22.

89. Tschetter, *Mr. Hogan*, 71.

90. Trinkle, "Ben Hogan at Merion," 22; Dodson, *Ben Hogan*, 297.

91. Nick Seitz, "The Iceman Speaketh," *Golf Digest*, October 1997, 151; John McCafferty, "Hogan Discounts Wrenched Knee," USGA 1950 U.S. Open file.

92. Davis, *Ben Hogan*, 129; Ames, "The New Ben Hogan," 9.

93. Dodson, *American Triumvirate*, 73.

94. Sampson, *Hogan*, 1.

95. Trinkle, "Ben Hogan at Merion," 21.

96. Dodson, *Ben Hogan*, 276.

97. Diaz, "What Could Have Been," 53.

98. Gregston, *Hogan*, 98–99. The average fourth-round score was 75.2, and only one other score under 70 was shot the entire championship. See Sal Johnson, *Official U.S. Open Almanac* (Dallas: Taylor, 1995), 116.

99. Dodson, *American Triumvirate*, 270.

100. Demaret, *My Partner*, 115.

101. Dodson, *Ben Hogan*, 230.

102. Seitz, "The Iceman Speaketh," 150.

103. Fields, "A Man Apart."

104. Sampson, *Hogan*, 181–82.

105. Hogan, interview by Ken Venturi; Ben Hogan, "The Greatest Year of My Life," *Saturday Evening Post*, October 17, 1953, 33; Davis, *Ben Hogan*, 42.

106. Seitz, "The Iceman Speaketh," 150–51; Hogan, "The Greatest Year of My Life," 33.

107. Davis, *Ben Hogan*, 43.

108. Sampson, *Hogan*, 192.

109. Gregston, *Hogan*, 179; Dodson, *Ben Hogan*, 393.

110. Dodson, *Ben Hogan*, 392.

111. Ibid.; Davis, *Ben Hogan*, 45; Gregston, *Hogan*, 158.

112. Hogan, "The Greatest Year of My Life," 33; Gregston, *Hogan*, 153; Davis, *Ben Hogan*, 165.

113. Ben Hogan, "Why I Quit Tournament Golf," *Look Magazine*, November 1, 1955, 94.

114. Barkow, *The Upset*, 58; Hogan, "Why I Quit Tournament Golf," 94.

115. Barkow, *The Upset*, 6.

116. Davis, *Ben Hogan*, 27; Dreyspool, "Conversation Piece: Subject: Ben Hogan," 38.

117. Hogan, "Why I Quit Tournament Golf," 92.

118. Hogan referenced the diminished vision in his eye during a late-1980s photo shoot. Photographer Jim Moriarty thought the shots Hogan was hitting with a four iron were good ones, but Hogan would curse "gawddammit," after hitting them. "When we finished," Moriarty recalled, "he said, 'You know I have only one eye.'" See also Roger Schiffman, "The Last Look He Gave Us," *Golf Digest*, October 1997, 141.

119. Seitz, "The Iceman Speaketh," 156.

120. Fields, "A Man Apart."

121. Dodson, *American Triumvirate*, 332; Gregston, *Hogan*, 67.

122. Dodson, *Ben Hogan*, 453.

123. Hogan, interview by Ken Venturi.

124. Sampson, *Hogan*, 223.

125. Ibid., 218.

126. Lee Trevino, *They Call Me Super Mex*, with Sam Blair (New York: Random House, 1982), 178.

127. Peper, "Ben Hogan," 66.

128. Tschetter, *Mr. Hogan*, 37–38.

129. Mike Towle, *I Remember Ben Hogan* (Nashville, TN: Cumberland House, 2000), 59. Hogan's chauffeur Elizabeth Hudson knew of his pain, saying, "You know, he could have been suffering before, but he never said anything. He never complained. He never said he was in any pain." See Jacqueline Hogan Towery, Robert Lindley Towery, and Peter Barbour, *The Brothers Hogan* (Fort Worth, TX: TCU Press, 2014), 187.

130. Tschetter, *Mr. Hogan*, 61; Gregston, *Hogan*, 133.

131. Hogan, "Why I Quit Tournament Golf," 92.

132. Ibid.

133. Bill Fields, "Ben Hogan," *Golf World*, August 1, 1997, 15.

134. Dodson, *Ben Hogan*, 513.

135. Towle, *I Remember Ben Hogan*, 35.

136. Tschetter, *Mr. Hogan*, 63–64.

137. Selcraig, "Our Friend, Mr. Hogan," 135.

138. Dodson, *Ben Hogan*, 519.

139. Jimmy Demaret, "My Partner, Ben Hogan," *Colliers*, April 2, 1954, 23.

140. Alan Shipnuck, "Right up His Alley," The Vault, *Sports Illustrated*, May 27, 1996, accessed April 7, 2014, http://www.si.com/vault/1996/05/27/213307/right-up-his-alley-ben-hogans-failing-health-cast-a-shadow-over-corey-pavins-conquest-of-colonial .

141. Dodson, *Ben Hogan*, 168; Towle, *I Remember Ben Hogan*, 45.

142. Selcraig, "Our Friend, Mr. Hogan," 134–35.

143. Fields, "A Man Apart."

144. Dodson, *Ben Hogan*, 452.

145. Towle, *I Remember Ben Hogan*, 120.

146. Tschetter, *Mr. Hogan*, 40.

147. Ibid., 56; Diaz, "What Could Have Been," 51.

148. Al Barkow, "Golf Will Still Feel Hogan's Presence," Golf Web.com, USGA Ben Hogan file; Diaz, "What Could Have Been," 52.

149. Diaz, "What Could Have Been," 51.

150. Tschetter, *Mr. Hogan*, 134–52.

151. Nick Seitz, "Hogan Speaks Out," *Golf Digest*, August 1987, 51.

152. Dreyspool, "Conversation Piece: Subject: Ben Hogan," 38.

153. Selcraig, "Our Friend, Mr. Hogan," 133, 137.

154. Tschetter, *Mr. Hogan*, 192–93.

155. Ibid., 193–95; Towle, *I Remember Ben Hogan*, 61; Dodson, *Ben Hogan*, 514–15.

156. Ron Sirak, "Ben Hogan Dead at Age 84," Golf Web.com, USGA Ben Hogan file; Shipnuck, "Right Up His Alley"; Dodson, *Ben Hogan*, 451; Towery, Towery, and Barbour, *The Brothers Hogan*, 182.

157. Dodson, *Ben Hogan*, 517; Towery, Towery, and Barbour, *The Brothers Hogan*, 185.

158. Hogan, "The Greatest Year of My Life," 33.

159. Dodson, *Ben Hogan*, 21.

160. Towery, Towery, and Barbour, *The Brothers Hogan*, 184.

161. Dodson, *Ben Hogan*, 518, 521.

162. Tschetter, *Mr. Hogan*, 194.

163. Ibid., 200.

164. "Hogan Remembered as a Man Who Overcame All Hardships," *New York Times*, July 30, 1997.

165. Dodson, *American Triumvirate*, 125.

166. "Golf Pays Tribute to Ben Hogan," Golf Web.com, USGA Ben Hogan file.

167. Fields, "Ben Hogan," 12; Gregston, *Hogan*, 1.

168. Dennis Walters, *In My Dreams I Walk with You*, with James Achenbach (Chelsea, MI: Sleeping Bear, 2002), 137. Likewise, Hogan had told Kris Tschetter when she was contemplating shoulder surgery: "Don't believe the doctors. They told me I'd never walk again, but I knew they were wrong." See Tschetter, *Mr. Hogan*, 74.

169. Tschetter, *Mr. Hogan*, 74.

4. BABE DIDRIKSON ZAHARIAS

1. Jack Sher, "The Amazing Amazon," *Sport*, June 1948, 33.

2. Thad S. Johnson, *The Incredible Babe: Her Ultimate Story*, with Louis Didrikson (Lake Charles, LA: Andrews Printing and Copy Center, 1996), 74.

3. Babe Didrikson Zaharias, *This Life I've Led* (New York: Barnes, 1955), 6; Susan E. Cayleff, *Babe: The Life and Legend of Babe Didrikson Zaharias* (Urbana: University of Illinois Press, 1995), 226; Don Van Natta Jr., *Wonder Girl: The Magnificent Sporting Life of Babe Didrikson Zaharias* (New York: Little, Brown, 2011), 304.

4. Van Natta, *Wonder Girl*, 304; Cayleff, *Babe*, 226.

5. "The Babe Is Back," *Time*, August 10, 1953 (USGA Babe Didrikson Zaharias file).

6. Byron Nelson, *How I Played the Game* (Lanham, MD: Taylor Trade, 2006), 247.

7. William Oscar Johnson and Nancy P. Williamson, *Whatta-Gal: The Babe Didrikson Story* (Boston: Little, Brown, 1977), 20.

8. Van Natta, *Wonder Girl*, 20.

9. Zaharias, *This Life I've Led*, 34; Johnson and Williamson, *Whatta-Gal*, 53.

10. Johnson, *The Incredible Babe*, 95.

11. Van Natta, *Wonder Girl*, 18; Zaharias, *This Life I've Led*, 7; Sher, "The Amazing Amazon," 84.

12. Zaharias, *This Life I've Led*, 27; Cayleff, *Babe*, 46; Johnson, *The Incredible Babe*, 75.

13. Zaharias, *This Life I've Led*, 15.

14. Van Natta, *Wonder Girl*, 35.

15. Cayleff, *Babe*, 40.

16. Van Natta, *Wonder Girl*, 44; Johnson and Williamson, *Whatta-Gal*, 55. She would arrive to school many times with bruised knuckles and cuts on her face. When asked what happened, she would tell schoolmates and teachers she had to fight some of the African American kids in the neighborhood just to keep them in line. See Johnson and Williamson, *Whatta-Gal*, 52.

17. Betsy Rawls, interview by Alice Kendrick, November 12, 1990, USGA Oral History Collection, 30; Van Natta, *Wonder Girl*, 36.

18. Johnson, *The Incredible Babe*, 163–64; Zaharias, *This Life I've Led*, 30.

19. Van Natta, *Wonder Girl*, 45; Cayleff, *Babe*, 50.

20. Johnson and Williamson, *Whatta-Gal*, 64.

21. Zaharias, *This Life I've Led*, 37; Van Natta, *Wonder Girl*, 51; Jack Newcombe, "The Incomparable Babe Didrikson," *Sport*, December 1959, 70.

22. Cayleff, *Babe*, 53; Van Natta, *Wonder Girl*, 50.

23. Johnson and Williamson, *Whatta-Gal*, 66.

24. Ibid., 75; Van Natta, *Wonder Girl*, 56.

25. Zaharias, *This Life I've Led*, 38; Van Natta, *Wonder Girl*, 76.

26. Johnson and Williamson, *Whatta-Gal*, 76.

27. Ibid.; Zaharias, *This Life I've Led*, 38.

28. Pete Martin, "Babe Didrikson Takes off Her Mask," *Saturday Evening Post*, September 20, 1947, 135; Johnson and Williamson, *Whatta-Gal*, 70.

29. Zaharias, *This Life I've Led*, 50. She competed in the 80-meter dash, long jump, high jump, javelin, shot put, discus, 100-meter dash, baseball throw, winning five events and placing in seven.

30. Paul Gallico, "Farewell to the Babe," *Reader's Digest*, January 1957, 22.

31. Van Natta, *Wonder Girl*, 73.

32. Martin, "Babe Didrikson Takes off Her Mask," 135.

33. Ibid., 134.

34. Jim Moriarty, "One Amazing Babe," *Golf World*, May 2, 2003, 22.

35. Martin, "Babe Didrikson Takes off Her Mask," 135.

36. Moriarty, "One Amazing Babe," 20; Cayleff, *Babe*, 70.

37. William Oscar Johnson and Nancy Williamson, "Babe: Part 1," *Sports Illustrated*, October 6, 1975, 125; Cayleff, *Babe*, 67.

38. Johnson, *The Incredible Babe*, 195.

39. Johnson and Williamson, *Whatta-Gal*, 51.

40. Van Natta, *Wonder Girl*, 95, 110.

41. Van Natta, *Wonder Girl*, 99; Betty Hicks, interview by Joe Doyle, August 5, 1991, USGA Oral History Collection, , 25.

42. Moriarty, "One Amazing Babe," 21.

43. Johnson and Williamson, "Babe: Part 1," 122; Johnson and Williamson, *Whatta-Gal,* 72.

44. Van Natta, *Wonder Girl*, 119; Cayleff, *Babe*, 84.

45. Van Natta, *Wonder Girl*, 126.

46. Zaharias, *This Life I've Led*, 68; Moriarty, "One Amazing Babe," 21. The insurance from Employee Casualty indemnified her when she was involved in a car accident near New Orleans. A car ran a stop sign, Babe broadsided it, and the driver was killed. It was one of the few things in her life she never spoke of afterward. See Van Natta, *Wonder Girl*, 130; Johnson, *The Incredible Babe*, 392.

47. Zaharias, *This Life I've Led*, 77.

48. Dave Anderson, "Remembering the Babe," *Golf Digest*, September 1981, 61.

49. Van Natta, *Wonder Girl*, 152; Cayleff, *Babe*, 120.

50. Martin, "Babe Didrikson Takes off Her Mask," 136; Cayleff, *Babe*, 118; Johnson, *The Incredible Babe*, 322.

51. Van Natta, *Wonder Girl*, 153, 157; Zaharias, *This Life I've Led*, 81.

52. Van Natta, *Wonder Girl*, 140, 144.

53. Ibid., 144; Cayleff, *Babe*, 92; Newcombe, "The Incomparable Babe Didrikson," 73.

54. Johnson and Williamson, *Whatta-Gal*, 74; Van Natta, *Wonder Girl*, 141.

55. Cayleff, *Babe*, 55; Van Natta, *Wonder Girl*, 147; Johnson and Williamson, *Whatta-Gal*, 132.

56. Johnson and Williamson, *Whatta-Gal*, 133.

57. Sher, "The Amazing Amazon," 33.

58. Zaharias, *This Life I've Led*, 85; Johnson and Williamson, *Whatta-Gal*, 77.

59. Zaharias, *This Life I've Led*, 85–86; Cayleff, *Babe*, 114.

60. Martin, "Babe Didrikson Takes off Her Mask," 135–36.

61. Cayleff, *Babe*, 56; Oscar Johnson and Nancy Williamson, "Babe: Part 2," *Sports Illustrated*, October 13, 1975, 50.

62. Zaharias, *This Life I've Led*, 87.

63. Zaharias, *This Life I've Led*, 87–88.

64. Rhonda Glenn, "A Friend Remembers Babe Zaharias," *Golf Journal*, July 1984, 30.

65. Rhonda Glenn, *The Illustrated History of Women's Golf* (Dallas: Taylor Trade, 1991), 136.

66. Johnson and Williamson, *Whatta-Gal*, 142–44; Van Natta, *Wonder Girl*, 166.

67. Cayleff, *Babe*, 157; Glenn, "A Friend Remembers Babe Zaharias," 30.

68. Johnson and Williamson, *Whatta-Gal*, 145.

69. Van Natta, *Wonder Girl*, 173. Later, Sam Snead would contend that Dey deliberately gave him inferior tee times and paired him with people who didn't like him in a deliberate effort to prevent Sam from winning; Johnson and Williamson, *Whatta-Gal*, 145; Johnson, *The Incredible Babe*, 317; Cayleff, *Babe*, 125, 166.

70. Van Natta, *Wonder Girl*, 176–77; Lowe, *Sir Walter and Mr. Jones*, 203. Homer Mitchell, president of the Employers Casualty Insurance Company, claimed the USGA had a "snooty" attitude and that Babe's lack of social standing lead to her suspension. See "Babe Didrikson Golf Ban Laid to 'Snootiness,'" *El Paso Herald-Post*, May 24, 1935.

71. Cayleff, *Babe*, 129.

72. Johnson and Williamson, *Whatta-Gal*, 148; Cayleff, *Babe*, 122.

73. Cayleff, *Babe*, 121; Zaharias, *This Life I've Led*, 101.

74. Johnson and Williamson, *Whatta-Gal*, 148–49; Cayleff, *Babe*, 122.

75. Glenn, *The Illustrated History of Women's Golf*, 142; Cayleff, *Babe*, 123.

76. Van Natta, *Wonder Girl*, 208; Zaharias, *This Life I've Led*, 101.

77. Johnson and Williamson, *Whatta-Gal*, 153; Van Natta, *Wonder Girl*, 186.

78. Cayleff, *Babe*, 87–88.

79. Johnson, *The Incredible Babe*, 95; Cayleff, *Babe*, 90.

80. Cayleff, *Babe*, 136.

81. Ibid., 140.

82. Johnson and Williamson, *Whatta-Gal*, 5; Van Natta, *Wonder Girl*, 370–71 (Babe's record during this time is outlined in the endnotes of Van Natta's book).

83. Cayleff, *Babe*, 173–75.

84. Johnson and Williamson, *Whatta-Gal*, 182; Glenn, *The Illustrated History of Women's Golf*, 141.

85. Martin, "Babe Didrikson Takes off Her Mask," 136.

86. Johnson and Williamson, *Whatta-Gal*, 21.

87. Martin, "Babe Didrikson Takes off Her Mask," 27.

88. Sher, "The Amazing Amazon," 31.

89. Martin, "Babe Didrikson Takes off Her Mask," 136.

90. Johnson, *The Incredible Babe*, 95.

91. Betty Hicks, "Babe Didrikson," *Women Sports*, December 1975, 20.

92. William Oscar Johnson and Nancy P. Williamson, "Babe: Conflict and Glory," *Golf Magazine*, September 1977, 57; Johnson, *The Incredible Babe*, 349; Cayleff, *Babe*, 188.

93. Cayleff, *Babe*, 189.

94. Rawls, interview by Alice Kendrick, 76; Cayleff, *Babe*, 163.

95. Rhonda Glenn, "Professional Pioneer, 1941 Women's Am Champ Hicks Dies," USGA, February 22, 2011, accessed January 22, 2014, http://usga.org/news/2011/February/1941-Women-s-Am-Champ-Hicks-Dies/.

96. Cayleff, *Babe*, 164; Peggy Kirk Bell, interview by Joe Doyle, June 15, 1991, USGA Oral History Collection, 46.

97. Bell, interview by Joe Doyle, 46.

98. Cayleff, *Babe*, 192; Van Natta, *Wonder Girl*, 271.

99. Rhonda Glenn, "The Triumph of Her Life," USGA Babe Zaharias file, 8; Rawls, interview by Alice Kendrick, 76, 27.

100. Rawls, interview by Alice Kendrick, 28.

101. Bell, interview by Joe Doyle, 16; Al Barkow, *Gettin' to the Dance Floor: An Oral History of American Golf* (New York: Atheneum, 1986), 222.

102. Van Natta, *Wonder Girl*, 271; Louise Suggs, interview by Alice Kendrick, January 16, 1992, USGA Oral History Collection, 70; Hicks, "Babe Didrikson," 21.

103. Hicks, "Babe Didrikson," 24; Hicks, interview by Joe Doyle, 54.

104. Rawls, interview by Alice Kendrick, 76; Johnson and Williamson, *Whatta-Gal*, 164; Suggs, interview by Alice Kendrick, 30.

105. Cayleff, *Babe*, 184, 189.

106. Johnson and Williamson, *Whatta-Gal*, 190–91.

107. Suggs, interview by Alice Kendrick, 31.

108. Ibid.

109. Van Natta, *Wonder Girl*, 267.

110. Zaharias, *This Life I've Led*, 90. Both Zaharias and Suggs were recipients of the USGA's Bob Jones Award, given in recognition of distinguished sportsmanship in golf; Johnson and Williamson, *Whatta-Gal*, 189.

111. Van Natta, *Wonder Girl*, 265; Rawls, interview by Alice Kendrick, 28–29.

112. Johnson and Williamson, *Whatta-Gal*, 54; Van Natta, *Wonder Girl*, 269; Johnson, *The Incredible Babe*, 98.

113. Martin, "Babe Didrikson Takes off Her Mask," 27; Cayleff, *Babe*, 199.

114. Cayleff, *Babe*, 216; Johnson and Williamson, *Whatta-Gal*, 152.

115. Van Natta, *Wonder Girl*, 281; Johnson and Williamson, *Whatta-Gal*, 200; Moriarty, "One Amazing Babe," 22.

116. Van Natta, *Wonder Girl*, 219, 283.

117. Johnson, *The Incredible Babe*, 389; Johnson and Williamson, *Whatta-Gal*, 166.

118. Van Natta, *Wonder Girl*, 284; Johnson and Williamson, *Whatta-Gal*, 167; Cayleff, *Babe*, 215.

119. Cayleff, *Babe*, 202; Johnson and Williamson, *Whatta-Gal*, 19.

120. Johnson and Williamson, *Whatta-Gal*, 202; Cayleff, *Babe*, 213–15.

121. Van Natta, *Wonder Girl*, 277, 196.

122. Ibid., 196; Johnson, *The Incredible Babe*, 100; Cayleff, *Babe*, 202.

123. Van Natta, *Wonder Girl*, 255.

124. Cayleff, *Babe*, 205–6; Van Natta, *Wonder Girl*, 287; Zaharias, *This Life I've Led*, 189–90.

125. Hicks, "Babe Didrikson," 24; Van Natta, *Wonder Girl*, 291.

126. Glenn, *The Illustrated History of Women's Golf*, 144.

127. Glenn, "A Friend Remembers Babe Zaharias," 31; Cayleff, *Babe*, 218.

128. Zaharias, *This Life I've Led*, 201.

129. Van Natta, *Wonder Girl*, 297–300.

130. Van Natta, *Wonder Girl*, 300; Cayleff, *Babe*, 219; "3-Hour Operation on Mrs. Zaharias," *New York Times*, April 18, 1953.

131. Cayleff, *Babe*, 200.

132. Ibid., 200, 220; Moriarty, "One Amazing Babe," 22.

133. Van Natta, *Wonder Girl*, 295; Cayleff, *Babe*, 214; Van Natta, *Wonder Girl*, 301.

134. Cayleff, *Babe*, 223; Johnson, *The Incredible Babe*, 74.

135. Zaharias, *This Life I've Led*, 214; Quentin Reynolds, "The Girl Who Lived Again," *Reader's Digest*, October 1954, 54.

136. Zaharias, *This Life I've Led*, 201, 208, 214; Reynolds, "The Girl Who Lived Again," 54.

137. Zaharias, *This Life I've Led*, 5, 209; Cayleff, *Babe*, 230; Van Natta, *Wonder Girl*, 312.

138. Beverly Hanson, "The Babe's Future," *Golf Digest*, May 1954, 10–11.

139. "Babe's Appeal," *USGA Golf Journal and Turf Management*, June 1956, 2; Van Natta, *Wonder Girl*, 235, 329.

140. Van Natta, *Wonder Girl*, 309; Zaharias, *This Life I've Led*, 217.

141. Zaharias, *This Life I've Led*, 217.

142. Glenn, *The Illustrated History of Women's Golf*, 144.

143. William Oscar Johnson and Nancy Williamson, "Babe: Part 3," *Sports Illustrated*, October 20, 1975, 53; Van Natta, *Wonder Girl*, 304.

144. Bill Rives, "The Babe's Toughest Battle," *Sport*, September 1953, 25.

145. Ibid., 60.

146. Ibid., 61.

147. Hanson, "The Babe's Future," 10.

148. "A Good Show," *Golf World*, July 9, 1954, 5; Hicks, interview by Joe Doyle, 28; Moriarty, "One Amazing Babe," 20.

149. Reynolds, "The Girl Who Lived Again," 50.

150. Van Natta, *Wonder Girl*, 312; "Babe's Greatest Victory," *Golf World*, July 9, 1954, 4.

151. Van Natta, *Wonder Girl*, 312; "Babe's Greatest Victory," 4; Newcombe, "The Incomparable Babe Didrikson," 75.

152. "Cancer Fatal to Babe Zaharias," *Corsicana Daily Sun* (Texas), September 27, 1956; Van Natta, *Wonder Girl*, 329.

153. Cayleff, *Babe*, 235–36; Johnson, *The Incredible Babe*, 400.

154. Zaharias, *This Life I've Led*, 231; Cayleff, *Babe*, 233.

155. Johnson and Williamson, "Babe: Part 3," 53; Johnson and Williamson, *Whatta-Gal*, 214.

156. Johnson and Williamson, *Whatta-Gal*, 215; Glenn, "A Friend Remembers Babe Zaharias," 32; Cayleff, *Babe*, 231; Glenn, *The Illustrated History of Women's Golf*, 133.

157. Cayleff, *Babe*, 233.

158. Van Natta, *Wonder Girl*, 326.

159. Johnson and Williamson, *Whatta-Gal*, 20.

160. Johnson, *The Incredible Babe*, 403.

161. Cayleff, *Babe*, 236. Betty Dodd said, "I had such admiration for this fabulous person. I never wanted to be away from her even when she was dying from cancer. I loved her. I would have done anything for her." See Cayleff, *Babe*, 203.

162. Johnson and Williamson, *Whatta-Gal*, 19, 218; Anderson, "Remembering the Babe," 63.

163. Johnson, *The Incredible Babe*, 404.

164. *Golf World*, October 5, 1956, 3; Johnson and Williamson, *Whatta-Gal*, 219.

165. Cayleff, *Babe*, 239.

166. Johnson and Williamson, *Whatta-Gal*, 218; Johnson, *The Incredible Babe*, 407.

167. "Eisenhower Leads Nation in Paying Last Tribute to Babe," *Beaumont Enterprise* (Texas), September 28, 1956; "Cancer Fatal to Babe Zaharias."

168. Fred Corcoran, *Unplayable Lies* (New York: Duell, Sloan and Pearce, 1965), 180.

169. Johnson and Williamson, "Babe: Conflict and Glory," 79.

170. Hicks, "Babe Didrikson," 21.

171. Barkow, *Gettin' to the Dance Floor*, 221.

172. Cayleff, *Babe*, 257; Gallico, "Farewell to the Babe," 22.

173. Gregston, *Hogan*, 132.

174. Moriarty, "One Amazing Babe," 20.

5. CHARLIE SIFFORD

1. Charlie Sifford, *Just Let Me Play: The Story of Charlie Sifford, the First Black PGA Golfer*, with James Gullo (Latham, NY: British American, 1992), 111.

2. Randall Kennedy, *Nigger: The Strange Career of a Troublesome Word* (New York: Pantheon Books, 2002), 161.

3. Sifford, *Just Let Me Play*, 6.

4. Kennedy, *Nigger*, 5.

5. Sifford, *Just Let Me Play*, 5–6.

6. Ibid., 75.

7. Leland Stein III, "Charlie Sifford, A Profile in Courage," AfroGolf.com, USGA Charlie Sifford file, African-American Golf History Archives; Clifton Brown, "On Golf: One Man's History Rings Proudly," *New York Times*, March 1, 1998.

8. Gunnar Myrdal, *An American Dilemma: The Negro Problem and Modern Democracy* (New York: Harper Brothers, 1944), xlvii, xlv.

9. William J. Powell, in response to segregation, was the first African American to design, construct, and own a golf course in the United States, building the Clearview Golf Club in Ohio. See Ellen Susanna Nösner, *Clearview: America's Course* (Haslett, MI: Foxsong), 2000.

10. Pete McDaniel, *Uneven Lies: The Heroic Story of African-Americans in Golf* (Greenwich, CT: American Golfer, 2000), 8.

11. Shippen was born December 5, 1879, and died May 20, 1968; See Daniel Wexler, *The Book of Golfers: A Biographical History of the Royal and Ancient Game* (Ann Arbor, MI: Sports Media Group, 2005), 321.

12. In 1892, after Homer Plessy had taken a seat in the whites-only railway car, he was asked to vacate it and sit instead in the blacks-only car. Plessy refused and was immediately arrested. Justice Henry Brown, writing for the majority, declared, "We consider the underlying fallacy of the plaintiff's argument to consist in the assumption that the enforced separation of the two races stamps the colored race with a badge of inferiority. If this be so, it is not by reason of anything found in the act, but solely because the colored race chooses to put that construction upon it." "Plessy v. Ferguson," Legal Information Insti-

tute, Cornell University Law School, accessed October 23, 2014, http://www. law.cornell.edu/supremecourt/text/163/537#writing-USSC_CR_0163_0537_ZO.

13. "Lynchings: By Year and Race," Famous Trials, UMKC School of Law, accessed June 9, 2013, http://law2.umkc.edu/faculty/projects/ftrials/shipp/lynchingyear.html. The numbers are based on statistics provided by the Archives at Tuskegee Institute. The Dyer Anti-Lynching Bill as it appeared in 1922 states: "To assure to persons within the jurisdiction of every State the equal protection of the laws, and to punish the crime of lynching. . . . Be it enacted by the Senate and House of Representatives of the United States of America in Congress assembled, That the phrase 'mob or riotous assemblage,' when used in this act, shall mean an assemblage composed of three or more persons acting in concert for the purpose of depriving any person of his life without authority of law as a punishment for or to prevent the commission of some actual or supposed public offense."

14. Sifford, *Just Let Me Play*, 10.

15. Ibid., 11.

16. Ibid.; Guy Yocom, "Dr. Charlie Sifford—My Shot," *Golf Digest*, December 2006, 147.

17. Sifford, *Just Let Me Play*, 12.

18. Ibid.; Mary Ann Hudson, "Sifford Blazed a Trail Few Have Followed," *Los Angeles Times*, August 12, 1990, accessed June 11, 2013, http://articles.latimes.com/1990-08-12/sports/sp-1123_1_pga-tour . Sifford was never a great putter and explained it this way: "I was always moving fast to keep from being thrown off the course. I never learned how to take my time on the greens and develop a decent stroke." See Jaime Diaz, "When Racial Barriers Die Hard," *New York Times*, May 24, 1992.

19. John H. Kennedy, *A Course of Their Own: A History of African American Golfers* (Lincoln: University of Nebraska Press, 2005), 188.

20. Sifford, *Just Let Me Play*, 13, 15.

21. Ibid., 18, 20–21.

22. Ibid., 21.

23. Kennedy, *A Course of Their Own*, 43; interview with Charlie Sifford, June 3, 2001, USGA.

24. Yocom, "Dr. Charlie Sifford—My Shot," 150.

25. Sifford, *Just Let Me Play*, 24.

26. Ibid., 29–30.

27. Ibid., 36.

28. McDaniel, *Uneven Lies*, 49, 54.

29. Sifford, *Just Let Me Play*, 40; Yocom, "Dr. Charlie Sifford—My Shot," 145.

30. "Black Golf Recognized for Breaking Barriers," *New York Times*, November 18, 2014. See Sifford, *Just Let Me Play*, 43.

31. McDaniel, *Uneven Lies*, 110; Golf Channel video tribute to Sifford, "Life and Legacy: Sifford Tough during Hard Times," February 4, 2015; Brown, "On Golf: One Man's History Rings Proudly."

32. *Golf World*, January 28, 1948, 3. That summer, Ted Rhodes, who would bring a suit for the actions taken against him, and Solomon Hughes, another top golfer on the United Golfers Association tour, were denied entry in the St. Paul Open in Minneapolis. See also Thomas B. Jones, "Caucasians Only: Solomon Hughes, the PGA, and the 1948 St. Paul Open Golf Tournament," *Minnesota History* 58, no. 8 (Winter 2003–2004).

33. Hannibal Coons, "Please Go Away, Says the PGA," *Sport*, July 1948, 68.

34. Joe Black, the tour's bureau manager in the late 1950s, recalled: "The contract, in those days, gave the sponsors the right to reject players. That was the reason they started calling their tournaments 'invitationals.' I tried to talk sponsors into letting blacks in, and finally we put it in the contract that they had to accept all qualified entrants." See Al Barkow, *The History of the PGA Tour* (New York: Doubleday, 1989), 102; Jones, "Caucasians Only," 389.

35. Kennedy, *A Course of Their Own*, 64; Coons, "Please Go Away, Says the PGA," 69.

36. Sifford, *Just Let Me Play*, 60–62.

37. Kennedy, *A Course of Their Own*, 73.

38. Ibid., 87.

39. Sifford, *Just Let Me Play*, 64; Kennedy, *A Course of Their Own*, 83.

40. Sifford, *Just Let Me Play*, 66.

41. Ibid., 67–68. The *New York Times* ran an editorial January 20, 1952, aimed at the events in San Diego, stating in part that "discrimination in any form is a bad thing in principle and practice. The world of sport is a field in which the stupidity of prejudice has been repeatedly and dramatically shown and it should be a powerful leader in better living and better community understanding."

42. Sifford, *Just Let Me Play*, 73.

43. Ibid., 80–81; "Sifford's First," *Golf World*, November 15, 1957, 4.

44. Myrdal, *An American Dilemma*, xlv.

45. Calvin Sinnette, *Forbidden Fairways: African Americans and the Game of Golf* (Chelsea, MI: Sleeping Bear, 1998), 164; Kennedy, *A Course of Their Own*, 57.

46. Dick Schapp, "Golfer with the Big Handicap," *Sport*, March 1960, 42–43. The article explained that, from Augusta's perspective, "The Club's qualification regulations are the principal means of determining the player invitation list, but such eligibility under these regulations does not oblige the Tournament Committee to issue an invitation, nor does failure to invite imply unfitness of any kind."

47. Sifford, *Just Let Me Play*, 74–75; Interview with Jimmy Roberts at the ceremony inducting Charlie Sifford into the PGA of America Hall of Fame, November 13, 2015.

48. Alfred Wright, "Candidates for a Better Day," The Vault, *Sports Illustrated*, February 13, 1961, accessed April 10, 2014, http://www.si.com/vault/1961/02/13/579547/candidates-for-a-better-day.

49. Sifford, *Just Let Me Play*, 117; Kennedy, *A Course of Their Own*, 130.

50. Sifford, *Just Let Me Play*, 121.

51. Ibid., 122; In 1969, Sifford had to endure more of the same, as four white men were removed from the course after shouting, "Miss it, nigger!" when he was putting. Sifford commented that they must have been drunk, but playing partner Al Geiberger was shaken and said he had "never experienced anything like it." See Lincoln A. Werden, "Racial Taunting Heard on Greens," *New York Times*, April 5, 1969.

52. Kennedy, *A Course of Their Own*, 141.

53. Sifford, *Just Let Me Play*, 128.

54. Kennedy, *A Course of Their Own*, 135, 131.

55. Sifford, *Just Let Me Play*, 95.

56. Email from Al Barkow to Lyle Slovick, October 26, 2015. Al Barkow, upon reviewing this chapter for me, asserted: "I rather believe what Bill Spiller told me, that it was he who wrote the letter to Stanley Mosk. Bill provided some details about it that seemed to me more evidence of that than Charlie offered."

57. Ibid., 90. Biographical information on Mosk is taken from the USGA African-American Golf History Archives, Box 6, "Discrimination and Racism" file.

58. Sifford, *Just Let Me Play*, 98–99; William Johnson, "Call Back the Years," *Sports Illustrated*, March 31, 1969, 64.

59. Sifford, *Just Let Me Play*, 92; McDaniel, *Uneven Lies*, 48; Kennedy, *A Course of Their Own*, 134.

60. Kennedy, *A Course of Their Own*, 135.

61. Gene Roswell, See "PGA Lifting Ban on Negroes," *New York Post*, September 21, 1960.

62. Kennedy, *A Course of Their Own*, 20, 138.

63. Stein III, "Charlie Sifford, A Profile in Courage."

64. Richard Wright, *Black Boy* (New York: Harper Collins, 1998), 195–96.

65. Larry Mowry, "My Rough Ride with Charlie Sifford," *Golf Digest*, March 1988, 41.

66. Ibid., 42.

67. Kennedy, *A Course of Their Own*, 122.

68. Sifford, *Just Let Me Play*, 136; Owen Canfield, "Recalling Charlie Sifford's Courageous and Determined GHO Play," *Hartford Courant*, October 30,

2011, accessed June 11, 2013, http://articles.courant.com/2011-10-30/sports/hc-owen-canfield-column-1030-20111030_1_charlie-sifford-james-gullo-water-spout.

69. Diaz, "When Racial Barriers Die Hard."

70. Sifford, *Just Let Me Play*, 151.

71. Paul Doyle, "Breaking another Barrier: Sifford Takes His Place in History with Hall of Fame Election," *Hartford Courant*, May 9, 2004, accessed June 1, 2013, http://articles.courant.com/2004-05-09/sports/0405090539_1_charlie-sifford-caucasian-only-clause-pga-tour.

72. Greg Garber, "Changing History's Course," *Hartford Courant*, July 20, 1997, accessed June 11, 2013, http://articles.courant.com/1997-07-20/sports/9707170675_1_charlie-sifford-black-pros-hotel-bed.

73. Sifford, *Just Let Me Play*, 151.

74. Garber, "Changing History's Course"; Bob Gorham, "Hartford Meant More Than Money," *PGA Magazine*, October 1967, 46.

75. Sifford, *Just Let Me Play*, 158; Garber, "Changing History's Course."

76. Doyle, "Sifford Takes His Place in History"; Sifford, *Just Let Me Play*, 151.

77. Johnson, "Call Back the Years," 58.

78. Bill Plaschke, "Charlie Sifford Broke Barriers," *Los Angeles Times*, October 24, 2011, accessed June 11, 2013, http://articles.latimes.com/2011/oct/24/sports/la-sp-plaschke-20111025.

79. Sifford, *Just Let Me Play*, 167–68.

80. Ibid., 169–70.

81. Dan Jenkins, "Old Charlie Jolts the New Tour," *Sports Illustrated*, January 20, 1969, 17.

82. Johnson, "Call Back the Years," 58.

83. Ibid., 63.

84. Kennedy, *A Course of Their Own*, 193–94; Johnson, "Call Back the Years," 58.

85. Yocom, "Dr. Charlie Sifford—My Shot," 151.

86. Jim Murray, "Back-of-the-Bus Golf," *Los Angeles Times*, February 10, 1974, C1.

87. Ibid.

88. David Owen, *The Making of the Masters: Clifford Roberts, Augusta National, and Golf's Most Prestigious Tournament* (New York: Simon and Schuster, 1999), 228.

89. Ibid., 245. Jones had claimed: "I am on record, in writing, in the office of Augusta National, that anyone who qualifies for Augusta will play regardless of race, color, or creed. You've just got to meet the qualifications." See Rapoport, *The Immortal Bobby*, 293.

90. Rapoport, *The Immortal Bobby*, 285; "He was not a trailblazer," claims grandson Robert Tyre Jones IV. "The status quo had been good to him. He had no reason to want change." Jones IV noted that, while his grandfather may have had mixed feelings about Martin Luther King Jr. and the civil-rights movement, "I know he appreciated that King preached change through nonviolence." See Michael Bamberger, "Life with Bub: Robert Tyre Jones IV Is Devoted to the Memory of His Grandfather," *Sports Illustrated*, April 08, 2013, accessed March 23, 2014, http://www.golf.com/tour-and-news/masters-bobby-jones-grandson-remembers-his-grandfather?page=1.

91. Kennedy, *A Course of Their Own*, 197.

92. Ibid., 198.

93. Golf historian Al Barkow claimed Joe Dey's "personal dislike of fellow Virginian Snead was perhaps the worst-kept secret in golf." See Dodson, *American Triumvirate*, 310.

94. McDaniel, *Uneven Lies*, 96.

95. Charlie Owens, interview by Rhonda Glenn, 2011, USGA Oral History Collection, 51–52.

96. Walter Morgan, interview by Rhonda Glenn, 2011, USGA Oral History Collection, 35, 31.

97. Pete Brown, interview by Rhonda Glenn, 2011, USGA Oral History Collection, 23–24.

98. Sal Johnson and Dave Seanor, *USA Today Golfers Encyclopedia* (New York: Skyhorse, 2009).

99. Garber, "Changing History's Course."

100. Sifford, *Just Let Me Play*, 185; Steve Elling, "It's about Time: The Long Wait Ends for Charlie Sifford as the Jackie Robinson of Golf Will Join Hall," *Orlando Sentinel*, April 28, 2004, accessed June 11, 2013, http://articles.orlandosentinel.com/2004-04-28/sports/0404280354_1_charlie-sifford-jackie-robinson-hall-of-fame; Sifford said in 1992 that nobody expected him to get far. "It's like Nelson Mandela. They kept him in jail 25 years, but it didn't break his determination. They couldn't break mine." See Diaz, "When Racial Barriers Die Hard." Gary Player introduced Sifford at his induction into the World Golf Hall of Fame in 2004. Player would say later that it had been a great honor for him, a white man who came from a nation that had practiced apartheid for most of his life, to be called on by his good friend to do such a thing. Player had empathy for Sifford and all he went through and recalled fondly that every time Charlie ended a phone call with him, he'd say to Player, "Love you, my man." Golf Channel, *Morning Drive*, interview with Gary Player, February 4, 2015.

101. Garber, "Changing History's Course"; Johnson, "Call Back the Years," 63.

102. Sifford, *Just Let Me Play*, 224; Stein III, "Charlie Sifford, A Profile in Courage"; Golf Channel, "Life and Legacy."

103. Yocom, "Dr. Charlie Sifford—My Shot," 145.

104. Elling, "It's about Time"; Bobby Stroble, interview by Rhonda Glenn, 2011, USGA Oral History Collection, 41–42. Stroble noted that when he came on the tour in 1976 there were about a dozen black players. Bill Wright was the first African-American to capture a USGA event when he won the 1959 U.S. Amateur Public Links championship. The LPGA as of 2016 has had five African-American players: Althea Gibson, Renee Powell, LaRee Pearl Sugg, Shasta Averyhardt, and Sadena Parks.

105. Golf Channel interview with Player, February 4, 2015; Sifford, *Just Let Me Play*, 4; Stein III, "Charlie Sifford, A Profile in Courage."

6. KEN VENTURI

1. Paul Gardner, "Venturi Came to Conquer," *Golf Magazine*, January 1960, 53.

2. Richard Goldstein, "Ken Venturi, U.S. Open Golf Champion and Broadcaster, Dies at 82," *New York Times*, May 17, 2013.

3. Ken Venturi, *Comeback: The Ken Venturi Story*, with Oscar Fraley (New York: Duell, Sloan and Pearce, 1966), 18–19.

4. "FAQ," The Stuttering Foundation, accessed May 25, 2013, www. stutteringhelp.org/faq .

5. Ron Kroichick, "Ken Venturi, Golf Pro Turned Analyst, Dies," SFGate, May 18, 2013, accessed October 27, 2014, http://www.sfgate.com/sports/ kroichick/article/Ken-Venturi-golf-pro-turned-analyst-dies-4527179. php#ixzz2UsBAY3zP .

6. Venturi, *Comeback*, 17; Ken Venturi, *Getting Up and Down: My 60 Years in Golf*, with Michael Arkush (Chicago: Triumph Books, 2004), 19.

7. Howard I. Kushner, "Retraining the King's Left Hand," *Lancet* 377 (June 11, 2011): 1998–99.

8. Howard I. Kushner, "Retraining Left-Handers and the Aetiology of Stuttering: The Rise and Fall of an Intriguing Theory," *Laterality: Asymmetries of Body, Brain and Cognition* 17 (2012): 673–93.

9. Kushner, "Retraining the King's Left Hand," (June 11, 2011): 1998–99. Venturi, *Comeback*, 17–18.

10. Venturi, *Getting Up and Down*, 14.

11. Ibid., 15; "Hall of Famer Ken Venturi, 82, Dies," ESPN, May 20, 2013, accessed June 23, 2013, http://espn.go.com/golf/story/_/id/9287839/ken-venturi-us-open-champion-analyst-dies .

12. Guy Yocom, "My Shot: Ken Venturi," *Golf Digest*, December 2004, 165.

13. Gary Klein, "Ken Venturi Dies at 82, Golfer Had Dramatic Win in 1964 U.S. Open," *Los Angeles Times*, May 17, 2013.

14. Ken Venturi, interview by David Feherty, Golf Channel, April 10, 2012; Venturi, *Comeback*, 21.

15. Venturi, *Comeback*, 19; Venturi, *Getting Up and Down*, 15.

16. Alfred Wright, "Sportsman of the Year: Ken Venturi," *Sports Illustrated*, December 21, 1964, 36; Venturi, *Getting Up and Down*, 28.

17. Venturi, *Getting Up and Down*, 28; Michael Bamberger, "Proud Words," The Vault, *Sports Illustrated*, June 9, 1997, accessed October 27, 2013, http://www.si.com/vault/1997/06/09/228108/proud-words-ken-venturi-the-1964-open-champion-has-faced-lifes-ups-and-downs-by-following-his-fathers-commandments.

18. Wright, "Sportsman of the Year: Ken Venturi," 36.

19. Ibid.

20. Venturi, interview by David Feherty.

21. Nelson, *How I Played the Game*, 178.

22. Venturi, *Comeback*, 29.

23. Furman Bisher, "Venturi Looks like the New Hogan," *Sport*, July 1958, 74; Venturi, *Getting Up and Down*, 41.

24. Ken Venturi, interview by Jimmy Roberts, accessed October 23, 2014, http://www.youtube.com/watch?v=CZPb77ImUB0.

25. Venturi, *Getting Up and Down*, 62.

26. John Strege, "Ken Venturi, 82, Dies 11 Days after Hall of Fame Induction," *Golf Digest*, May 17, 2013, accessed June 3, 2013, http://www.golfdigest.com/golf-tours-news/blogs/local-knowledge/2013/05/ken-venturi-82-dies-11-days-after-hall-of-fame-induction.html#ixzz2qPqr04xI.

27. Yocom, "My Shot: Ken Venturi," 165; Strege, "Ken Venturi."

28. Venturi, *Comeback*, 46.

29. Wright, "Sportsman of the Year: Ken Venturi," 37; Venturi, *Getting Up and Down*, 76.

30. Wright, "Sportsman of the Year: Ken Venturi," 37.

31. Ken Venturi, interview by Robert Blumenthal, May 24 and 31, 2011, accessed May 13, 2013, http://www.golfconversations.com/2011/05/24/ken-venturi-part-1, http://www.golfconversations.com/2011/05/31/ken-venturi-part-2/; Bamberger, "Proud Words."

32. Venturi, *Comeback*, 47.

33. Wright, "Sportsman of the Year: Ken Venturi," 37.

34. Venturi, *Comeback*, 50.

35. Ibid., 23; Venturi, *Getting Up and Down*, 33.

36. Venturi, *Getting Up and Down*, 58–59.

37. Wright, "Sportsman of the Year: Ken Venturi," 37.

38. Al Stump, "Venturi Is out for the Money," *Sport*, June 1957, 83.

39. Venturi, *Comeback*, 48.

40. Venturi, interview by Robert Blumenthal, May 24 and 31, 2011.

41. Bisher, "Venturi Looks like the New Hogan," 75; Wright, "Sportsman of the Year: Ken Venturi," 37.

42. Venturi, *Comeback*, 68–70.

43. "Playing by Heart," *Healthy Living Magazine*, Spring 2015, accessed April 14, 2013, http://www.emc.org/healthyliving.cfm?id=855&action=detail&source=511&issue=579&dataRef=138; Interview with Ken Venturi, June 13, 2011, USGA 2011 U.S. Open file, 3.

44. Venturi, *Comeback*, 72; Wright, "Sportsman of the Year: Ken Venturi," 38.

45. Venturi, *Comeback*, 73; Venturi, *Getting Up and Down*, 2.

46. Wright, "Sportsman of the Year: Ken Venturi," 35; Venturi, *Comeback*, 74.

47. Venturi, *Comeback*, 77.

48. Ibid., 74.

49. Wright, "Sportsman of the Year: Ken Venturi," 35.

50. Venturi, *Comeback*, 78, 84.

51. Ibid., 77.

52. Wright, "Sportsman of the Year: Ken Venturi," 38.

53. Venturi, *Getting Up and Down*, 4–6.

54. Venturi, *Comeback*, 64.

55. Venturi, *Getting Up and Down*, 9.

56. Wright, "Sportsman of the Year: Ken Venturi," 35; Ken Venturi, "Why Me—A Tale of 1964," *Golf Journal*, May/June 1989, 36.

57. Venturi, *Comeback*, 8.

58. Ibid., 90–91.

59. Wright, "Sportsman of the Year: Ken Venturi," 35.

60. Venturi, *Comeback*, 93, 98.

61. Joe Williams, "Venturi Won More Than the Open," *New York World Telegram and Sun*, June 23, 1964; Venturi, *Getting Up and Down*, 136; Venturi, *Comeback*, 101.

62. Venturi, interview by Jimmy Roberts. Venturi played with Hogan first at the 1954 Masters, and the two struck up a friendship that would last the rest of Hogan's life. Sam Snead related asking Hogan for a game once and Hogan telling him, "I'll take Venturi and play anybody in the world." See Towle, *I Remember Ben Hogan*, 79; Wright, "Sportsman of the Year: Ken Venturi," 36.

63. Wright, "Sportsman of the Year: Ken Venturi," 36.

64. Ibid., 38; Venturi, "Why Me," 37; "From my father—Giving up is the easiest thing to do—anyone can do it. Takes no talent." Letter from Ken Venturi to Lyle Slovick, January 18, 2013.

65. Venturi, *Comeback*, 105.

66. Ibid., 107.

67. Ibid., 109–12.

68. Kathy Chenault, "The Longest Day," *Bethesda*, May–June 2011.

69. Venturi, *Getting Up and Down*, 150; Venturi, "Why Me," 33; USGA 1964 U.S. Open file.

70. Chenault, "The Longest Day." "We know today that taking salt tablets on a hot day can further dehydrate you. In the end, I beat a tough golf course and a great field, but I also overcame my own mistakes." See Yocom, "My Shot: Ken Venturi," 166. Venturi lost eight pounds that day, beginning the day weighing himself at 172 pounds and ending at 164. See interview with Ken Venturi, June 13, 2011, USGA 2011 U.S. Open file, 3.

71. Alfred Wright "'Poor Ken' Rich Again," *Sports Illustrated*, June 29, 1964, 17.

72. USGA 1964 U.S. file, "Background File," 2; Venturi, *Comeback*, 116.

73. Wright, "'Poor Ken' Rich Again," 17–18.

74. Ibid.; Ray Didinger, "1964: Venturi's Wonderful Year" *Philadelphia Daily News*, June 12, 1981; Kenneth P. Venturi, interview by Joe Doyle, USGA Oral History Collection March 9, 1992, 54.

75. Didinger, "1964: Venturi's Wonderful Year"; Venturi, *Comeback*, 117.

76. Wright, "Sportsman of the Year: Ken Venturi," 39.

77. Irwin Smallwood, "The Last Marathon," *Golf Journal*, June 1997, 13; Venturi, *Comeback*, 118–19.

78. Venturi, *Comeback*, 120, 129; USGA 1964 U.S. Open file, "Background File," 2.

79. Wright, "Sportsman of the Year: Ken Venturi," 39.

80. Venturi, "Why Me," 38.

81. Smallwood, "The Last Marathon," 15; Venturi, *Getting Up and Down*, 156; Joe Dey said the Venturi story demonstrated how "a deeply human experience transcended a great golfing drama." See *Golf Digest*, August 1976, 16.

82. Smallwood, "The Last Marathon," 15; Venturi, interview by Joe Doyle, 70.

83. Didinger, "1964: Venturi's Wonderful Year"; Nelson, *How I Played the Game*, 196; Smallwood, "The Last Marathon," 15; Venturi, *Comeback*, 122; Venturi was so spent at the end of the round that he couldn't remember what he had shot for each hole and was afraid he might be disqualified for signing an incorrect scorecard. "I kept going over it, and couldn't sign it. I had one thing in mind, a girl that I knew from Hawaii, Jackie Pung." Pung had been disqualified

from the 1957 U.S. Women's Open for signing an incorrect scorecard. When Joe Dey of the USGA assured Ken the scores were correct, Venturi finally signed his card. See interview with Ken Venturi, June 13, 2011, USGA 2011 U.S. Open file, 5.

84. Letter from Ken Venturi to the Lyle Slovick, January 18, 2013.

85. Venturi, *Getting Up and Down*, 167; Venturi, *Comeback*, 129; Kay Hawes, "Comeback Ken Venturi," *Golf Course Management*, December 1997, 36. (Venturi was the 1998 Old Tom Morris Award winner); Venturi, "Why Me," 38; Dick Taylor, "Faith, Wife, Salt Tablets Revive Venturi," *Golf World*, June 26, 1964, 4.

86. Wright, "Sportsman of the Year: Ken Venturi," 38; Venturi, interview by Joe Doyle, 63. The *Washington Post* reported the next day that Venturi was among 398 people, including volunteers and spectators, who received first aid for heat-related problems at the Open that week. The USGA changed the format of the Open the next year, playing four rounds over four days. See Chenault, "The Longest Day." Venturi would say years later: "I don't know if I could have played the next day. I might have been in a hospital." He would tell USGA executive director Joe Dey, "Don't ever use me as an excuse because 36 holes was a blessing [to me]. You're doing it because of television and because of the money." See Smallwood, "The Last Marathon," 14.

87. Gwilym S. Brown, "Warm Hopes for a Man with a Cold Touch," The Vault, *Sports Illustrated*, March 15, 1965, accessed May 12, 2013, http://www.si.com/vault/1965/03/15/607526/warm-hopes-for-a-man-with-a-cold-touch.

88. Brown, "Warm Hopes for a Man with a Cold Touch."

89. Venturi, *Comeback*, 145.

90. Ibid., 148; Brown, "Warm Hopes for a Man with a Cold Touch."

91. Venturi, *Comeback*, 150, 157. Carpal tunnel is the strangulation of the nerves, tendons, ligaments, and veins in the hands by a band of tendons that encircle the wrists.

92. Lincoln A. Werden, "Venturi, Palmer Are Eliminated," *New York Times*, June 19, 1965; Venturi, *Comeback*, 159.

93. Venturi, *Comeback*, 164; "Ken Venturi and the Open," *Golf Journal*, June 1965, 2.

94. Venturi, *Comeback*, 170–71, 180, 182–83.

95. Venturi, *Getting Up and Down*, 192; Interview with Ken Venturi, June 13, 2011, USGA 2011 U.S. Open file, 4.

96. Hawes, "Comeback Ken Venturi," 40; Venturi, interview by Joe Doyle, 61.

97. Venturi, *Comeback*, 19.

98. Michael Bamberger, "So Long, Kenny," The Vault, *Sports Illustrated*, June 10, 2002, accessed May 23, 2013, http://www.si.com/vault/2002/06/10/

324905/so-long-kenny-after-35-years-of-calling-the-shots-on-cbs-telecasts-ken-venturi-will-take-his-career-and-walk-away-quietly.

99. Venturi, interview by Robert Blumenthal, part 1.

100. Goldstein, "Ken Venturi"; Jim Nantz, "A Letter to My Mentor," Golf, May 4, 2013, accessed June 13, 2013, http://www.golf.com/tour-and-news/jim-nantz-pays-tribute-ken-venturi-world-golf-hall-fame.

101. Venturi, interview by Jimmy Roberts.

102. Bamberger, "So Long, Kenny."

103. "Ken Venturi: A Champion to Those Who Stutter," The Stuttering Foundation, accessed May 23, 2014, http://www.stutteringhelp.org/content/ken-venturi-champion-those-who-stutter; Strege, "Ken Venturi"; Nantz, "A Letter to My Mentor."

104. Strege, "Ken Venturi"; Hawes, "Comeback Ken Venturi,"40.

105. Yocom, "My Shot: Ken Venturi," 165.

106. Hawes, "Comeback Ken Venturi," 40–42.

107. Jaime Diaz, "The Golf Genius of Ken Venturi," *Golf Digest*, May 13, 2013.

108. Yocom, "My Shot: Ken Venturi," 165.

109. Venturi, interview by Robert Blumenthal, part 1.

110. Venturi, *Getting Up and Down*, 258; Michael Bamberger, "Proud Words."

111. Venturi, interview by Joe Doyle, 13; Venturi, *Getting Up and Down*, 258.

112. Venturi, interview by David Feherty (41:28); After winning the U.S. Open, Venturi said: "If I had it to do all over again, I wouldn't change a thing. I've found out a lot about myself, about my friends, and about life. Nobody knows all the answers and nobody should, but I think the good Lord is looking after me." See USGA 1964 U.S. Open file.

7. BRUCE EDWARDS

1. Simpson, *The Art of Golf*, 30.

2. John Feinstein, *Caddy for Life: The Bruce Edwards Story* (New York: Back Bay Books, 2004), 23.

3. Feinstein, *Caddy for Life*, 269. I witnessed this episode and took photos, which I sent to Tom Watson, receiving a gracious reply in return.

4. Jason Quick, "Life's Lie Tougher Than Golf for Watson's Caddie," *Oregonian*, August 29, 2003, C9.

5. Joy, *The Scrapbook of Old Tom Morris*, 157.

6. John Phillips Street, "The Training of Caddies," *Golf*, November 1897, 32.

7. David Shefter, "Bruce Edwards Succumbs to ALS," USGA, April 8, 2004, accessed May 31, 2013, http://www.usga.org/news/2004/April/Bruce-Edwards-Succumbs-to-ALS; Dave Anderson, "Sports of the Times: For Watson's Caddie, It's More Than a Game," *New York Times*, April 8, 2004.

8. Feinstein, *Caddy for Life*, 17–18, 22.

9. Feinstein, *Caddy for Life*, 23–24.

10. Neil Millar, "Golf Caddies in the 17th to 19th Centuries," *Through the Green*, March 2013, 36.

11. Charles Blair Macdonald, "Golf: The Ethical and Physical Aspects of the Game," *Golf*, January 1898, 21.

12. Dave Anderson, "Carrying the Load for Watson," *San Bernadino County Sun*, January 28, 1980, 20; Feinstein, *Caddy for Life*, 27.

13. Feinstein, *Caddy for Life*, 33.

14. Dick Mackey, "I Caddied on the Tour and Lived to Tell about It," *Golf Digest*, November 1973, 107; Simpson, *The Art of Golf*, 30; Richard Mackenzie, *A Wee Nip at the 19th Hole: A History of the St Andrews Caddie* (New York: Bantam Books, 1998), 10.

15. Dave Hill and Nick Seitz, *Teed Off* (Englewood Cliffs, NJ: Prentice-Hall, 1977), 49–50.

16. Greg "Piddler" Martin, *Caddie Confidential: Inside Stories from the Caddies of the PGA Tour* (Chicago: Triumph Books, 2009), 57; Dwayne Netland, "Who's That Tagging Along with Angelo?" *Golf Digest*, April 1978, 158.

17. Maggie FitzRoy, "Caddie Adds Hope to Game Bag," *Florida Times-Union*, October 11, 2003, accessed June 30, 2014, http://jacksonville.com/tu-online/stories/101103/nep_13747208.shtml.

18. Garry Smits, "Golf World Mourns Loss," *Florida Times-Union*, April 13, 2004, accessed May 31, 2013, http://jacksonville.com/tu-online/stories/041304/spg_15330087.shtml; FitzRoy, "Caddie Adds Hope to Game Bag."

19. Feinstein, *Caddy for Life*, 41; Anderson, "Carrying the Load for Watson."

20. Tim Rosaforte, "A Sad Start," *Golf World*, April 16, 2004, 70; FitzRoy, "Caddie Adds Hope to Game Bag"; Feinstein, *Caddy for Life*, 43.

21. Feinstein, *Caddy for Life*, 45.

22. Anderson, "Carrying the Load for Watson."

23. Feinstein, *Caddy for Life*, 57.

24. FitzRoy "Caddie Adds Hope to Game Bag"; Feinstein, *Caddy for Life*, 63.

25. "Do You Listen to Your Caddie?" *USGA Golf Journal*, February 1965, 6.

26. Martin, *Caddie Confidential*, 14; Anderson, "Carrying the Load for Watson."

27. Ivan Maisel, "Edwards Made Watson a Better Man," ESPN.com, April 8, 2004, accessed April 16, 2014, http://sports.espn.go.com/golf/masters04/columns/story?columnist=maisel_ivan&id=1778608 .

28. Nelson, *How I Played the Game*, 209.

29. Ibid., 209–10. In 1974, the Western Open didn't allow tour caddies but required players to use caddies provided by the club. The Byron Nelson in 1975 would be the first tournament Watson won with Edwards on the bag.

30. Dwayne Netland, "The Story behind Tom Watson's Sudden Surge," *Golf Digest*, April 1977, 142; Tom Watson, "How I Won the Battle with Myself," *Golf Magazine*, November 1975, 32.

31. Netland, "The Story behind Tom Watson's Sudden Surge,"142.

32. Feinstein, *Caddy for Life*, 86; Anderson, "Carrying the Load for Watson."

33. Feinstein, *Caddy for Life*, 96; Anderson, "Carrying the Load for Watson."

34. Tom Watson, interview in USGA Tom Watson file, 5; GOLFstats, http://www.golfstats.com/.

35. Feinstein, *Caddy for Life*, 103; Keeler, *The Bobby Jones Story*, 139.

36. Tom Watson, interview in USGA Tom Watson file, 6; Tom Watson, interview by Charlie Rose, PBS, May 5, 2010.

37. Tom Watson, "Read My Mind as I Play the Open," with Nick Seitz, *Golf Digest*, February 1983, 50; Tom Watson, interview in USGA Tom Watson file, 7.

38. Adam Schupak, "Watson Is Miraculous in 1982," article in USGA Tom Watson file; Feinstein, *Caddy for Life*, 109.

39. Feinstein, *Caddy for Life*, 140.

40. Ibid., 144, 119.

41. Martin, *Caddie Confidential*, 122; Smits, "Golf World Mourns Loss."

42. Smits, "Golf World Mourns Loss."

43. Feinstein, *Caddy for Life*, 120.

44. Jeff Rude, "2004 Masters: The Masters Say Goodbye to Caddie Bruce Edwards," *Golfweek*, March 28, 2011, accessed April 13, 2014, http://golfweek.com/news/2004/apr/17/masters-say-goodbye-caddie-bruce-edwards/?print.

45. Feinstein, *Caddy for Life*, 141; Tom Watson, *The Timeless Swing*, with Nick Seitz (New York: Atria Books, 2011), 115–16.

46. Dana Treen, "Caddy's Wife Arrested on Arson Charge," *Florida Times-Union*, April 25, 2000, accessed June 23, 2013, http://jacksonville.com/tu-online/stories/042500/met_2893670.html; Feinstein, *Caddy for Life*, 164.

47. Feinstein, *Caddy for Life*, 176–77.

48. FitzRoy, "Caddie Adds Hope to Game Bag"; Feinstein, *Caddy for Life*, 183.

49. Feinstein, *Caddy for Life*, 185.

50. Ibid., 188.

51. Dr. Morris Fishbein, editor of the *Journal of the American Medical Association*, quoted in the *Emporia Gazette*, June 21, 1939, 6.

52. "Amyotrophic Lateral Sclerosis," Bruce Edwards Foundation for ALS Research, accessed June 7, 2014, http://www.bruceedwardsfoundation.org/about_ALS_lou_gehrig's_disease.htm.

53. FitzRoy, "Caddie Adds Hope to Game Bag"; Feinstein, *Caddy for Life*, 192.

54. Feinstein, *Caddy for Life*, 196.

55. Ibid., 205–6.

56. Doug Ferguson, "Julian Keeps a Weird Week in Perspective," *Salina Journal*, April 17, 2003, 20.

57. Feinstein, *Caddy for Life*, 217–18.

58. David Kindred, "He Will Carry On," *Golf Digest*, May 2003, 111.

59. Tim Dahlberg, "Watson's Caddie Shares in Golfer's Early Success," *Salina Journal*, June 13, 2003, 20; Dave Anderson, "Sports of the Times: Watson and Caddie Add a Memory," *New York Times*, June 13, 2004.

60. Feinstein, *Caddy for Life*, 236.

61. Ibid., 239.

62. Feinstein, *Caddy for Life*, 240–42; FitzRoy, "Caddie Adds Hope to Game Bag"; Scott Micheaux, "Edwards, Watson Spread Word about ALS," *Morris News Service*, June 16, 2003, accessed May 31, 2013, http://jacksonville.com/tu-online/stories/061603/spg_watson.shtml.

63. Micheaux, "Edwards, Watson Spread Word about ALS."

64. Interview with Bruce Edwards, June 15, 2003, USGA 2003 U.S. Open file, 2; Rosaforte, "A Sad Start," 70.

65. Feinstein, *Caddy for Life*, 262–63.

66. FitzRoy, "Caddie Adds Hope to Game Bag."

67. Kim Julian, *Golf Widow: A Memoir* (printed by author, 2011), 155–56.

68. Julian, *Golf Widow*, 157; Dave Anderson, "Sports of The Times: He's Carrying Sport's Most Human Story," *New York Times*, July 3, 2003.

69. Julian, *Golf Widow*, 150; FitzRoy, "Caddie Adds Hope to Game Bag."

70. Quick, "Life's Lie Tougher Than Golf for Watson's Caddie," C1, C9.

71. Ibid., C9.

72. Feinstein, *Caddy for Life*, 268.

73. Feinstein, *Caddy for Life*, 271; John Strege, "Oregon Tale," *Golf World*, September 5, 2003, 15.

74. Kindred, "He Will Carry On," 111; Julian, *Golf Widow*, 132.

75. Julian, *Golf Widow*, 203, 201.

76. Feinstein, *Caddy for Life*, 272; FitzRoy, "Caddie Adds Hope to Game Bag."

77. Feinstein, *Caddy for Life*, 278; Smits, "Golf World Mourns Loss."

78. Feinstein, *Caddy for Life*, 294; Julian, *Golf Widow*, 178.

79. Anderson, "Sports of the Times: For Watson's Caddie, It's More Than a Game"; Maisel, "Edwards Made Watson a Better Man"; Feinstein, *Caddy for Life*, 90.

80. Gary Van Sickle, "Clouds over Augusta," Sports Illustrated.com, April 8, 2004, accessed April 14, 2014, http://sportsillustrated.cnn.com/2004/golf/specials/masters/2004/04/08/vansickle.column; Maisel, "Edwards Made Watson a Better Man"; Paul Newberry, "Caddie's Spirit Stays with Watson," *Indiana Gazette* (PA), April 9, 2004, 17; Julian, *Golf Widow*, 214.

81. Dave Anderson, "Watson Recalls Caddie's Last Reminder," *New York Times*, April 9, 2004.

82. Maisel, "Edwards Made Watson a Better Man"; Newberry, "Caddie's Spirit Stays with Watson."

83. Van Sickle, "Clouds over Augusta"; Maisel, "Edwards Made Watson a Better Man"; Smits, "Golf World Mourns Loss."

84. Bruce Edwards Foundation for ALS Research, accessed June 14, 2014, http://www.bruceedwardsfoundation.org.

85. Maisel, "Edwards Made Watson a Better Man"; Glenn Sheeley, "Watson, Ailing Caddy Turn Back Clock," *Indiana Gazette* (PA), June 13, 2003, 13.

86. Kindred, "He Will Carry On," 11; Shefter, "Bruce Edwards Succumbs to ALS."

87. Feinstein, *Caddy for Life*, 91; Dahlberg, "Watson's Caddie Shares in Golfer's Early Success," 20.

88. Tim Rosaforte, "Brothers in Arms," *Golf World*, June 20, 2003, 42; Anderson, "Sports of the Times: For Watson's Caddie, It's More Than a Game."

APPENDIX: PLAYERS' RECORDS

HARRY VARDON

Professional Majors: 7

> Open Championship: 1896, 1898, 1899, 1903, 1911, 1914
> U.S. Open: 1900

Additional Wins: 53

> 1893: Ilkley Professional Tournament
> 1894: Didsbury Professional Tournament, Ilkley Professional
> Tournament
> 1896: Yorkshire Professional Tournament, Yorkshire Union of
> Golf Clubs Tournament
> 1897: Southport Professional Tournament, Wallasey Professional
> Tournament
> 1898: Barton-on-Sea Opening Festivities Tournament, Carnoustie
> Professional Tournament, Royal County Down Professional
> Tournament, Elie Professional Tournament, Royal Lytham and
> St Annes Professional Tournament, Manchester Professional
> Tournament, Musselburgh Open Championship, Norbury Pro-
> fessional Tournament, North Surrey Club House Opening Tour-
> nament, Prestwick Professional Tournament, Windermere Invi-
> tational Professional and Amateur Tournament
> 1899: Buxton Professional Tournament, Cruden Bay Professional
> Tournament, Ganton Invitational Foursome Match (with John

Ball), Mid-Surrey Open Professional Tournament, Newcastle County Down Tournament, Porthcawl Professional Tournament, Portmarnock Irish Professional Tournament

1901: Mid-Surrey Professional Championship, Penarth Professional Tournament

1902: Edzell Professional Tournament, Lord Dudley's Tournament, Northern Section PGA Tournament

1903: Eastbourne Professional Tournament, Enfield Professional Tournament, Richmond Golf Club Tournament, South Gailes Professional Tournament, Western Gailes Professional Tournament

1904: Irvine Professional Tournament

1905: Montrose Professional Tournament

1906: Musselburgh Open Tournament

1907: Blackpool Professional Tournament

1908: Costebelle Invitational Professional Tournament, Harrowgate Golf Week Tournament, Nice Invitational Professional Tournament

1909: St Andrews Professional Tournament

1911: German Open

1912: Cooden Beach Professional Tournament, Hanger Hill Invitation Tournament, Monte Carlo Professional Tournament, "News of the World" Professional Match Play Championship, Sandy Lodge Stroke Competition, Sphere and Tatler Foursomes Tournament (with T. Williamson)

1913: Deal Professional Foursome Tournament (with T. Williamson), Sphere and Tatler Tournament

1914: Cruden Bay Tournament

BOBBY JONES

Professional Majors: 7

U.S. Open: 1923, 1926, 1929, 1930
Open Championship: 1926, 1927, 1930

Additional Wins: 25

1908: East Lake Children's Tournament

1911: Junior Championship Cup of the Atlanta Athletic Club

1915: Invitation Tournament at Roebuck Springs: Birmingham, Davis and Freeman Cup at East Lake, East Lake Club Championship, Druid Hills Club Championship

1916: Georgia Amateur, Birmingham Country Club Invitation, Cherokee Club Invitation, East Lake Invitation Tournament

1917: Southern Amateur

1919: Yates-Gode Tournament

1920: Davis-Freeman Tournament, Southern Amateur, Morris County Invitational

1922: Southern Amateur

1924: U.S. Amateur

1925: U.S. Amateur

1927: Southern Open, U.S. Amateur

1928: Warren K. Wood Memorial, U.S. Amateur

1930: Southeastern Open, British Amateur Championship, U.S. Amateur

BEN HOGAN

Professional Majors: 9

Masters Tournament: 1951, 1953
U.S. Open: 1948, 1950, 1951, 1953
Open Championship: 1953
PGA Championship: 1946, 1948

PGA Tour Wins: 55

1938: Hershey Four-Ball

1940: North and South Open, Greater Greensboro Open, Asheville "Land of the Sky" Open, Goodall Palm Beach Round Robin

1941: Asheville Open, Chicago Open, Hershey Open, Miami Biltmore International Four-Ball, Inverness Four-Ball

1942: Los Angeles Open, San Francisco Open, North and South Open Championship, Asheville "Land of the Sky" Open, Hale America: Illinois, Rochester Open

1945: Nashville Invitational, Portland Open Invitational, Richmond Invitational, Montgomery Invitational, Orlando Open

1946: Phoenix Open, San Antonio Texas Open, St. Petersburg Open, Colonial National Invitation, Western Open, Winnipeg Open, Golden State Open, Dallas Invitational, North and South Open, Goodall Round Robin, Miami International Four-Ball, Inverness Four-Ball

1947: Los Angeles Open, Phoenix Open, Colonial National Invitation, Chicago Victory Open, World Championship of Golf, Miami International Four-Ball, Inverness Round Robin Four-Ball

1948: Los Angeles Open, Motor City Open, Reading Open, Western Open, Denver Open, Reno Open, Glendale Open, Inverness Round Robin Four-Ball

1949: Bing Crosby Pro-Am, Long Beach Open

1951: World Championship of Golf

1952: Colonial National Invitation

1953: Pan American Open, Colonial National Invitation

1959: Colonial National Invitation

BABE DIDRIKSON ZAHARIAS

Amateur Majors: 1

U.S. Women's Amateur: 1946

Professional Majors: 10

Western Open: 1940, 1944, 1945, 1950
Titleholders Championship: 1947, 1950, 1952
U.S. Women's Open: 1948, 1950, 1954

LPGA Tour Wins: 31

1947: Tampa Open

1948: All American Open, World Championship

1949: World Championship, Eastern Open

1950: Pebble Beach Weathervane, Cleveland Weathervane, All-American Open, World Championship, 144 Hole Weathervane

1951: Ponte Vedra Beach Women's Open, Tampa Women's Open, Lakewood Weathervane, Richmond Women's Open, Valley

Open, Meridian Hills Weathervane, All-American Open, World Championship, Texas Women's Open
1952: Miami Weathervane, Bakersfield Open (tied with Marlene Hagge, Betty Jameson, and Betsy Rawls), Fresno Open, Women's Texas Open
1953: Sarasota Open, Babe Zaharias Open
1954: Serbin Open, Sarasota Open, Damon Runyon Cancer Fund Tournament, All-American Open
1955: Tampa Open, Peach Blossom Classic

CHARLIE SIFFORD

Professional Majors: 1

PGA Seniors' Championship: 1975

PGA Tour Wins: 2

1967: Greater Hartford Open
1969: Los Angeles Open

Champions Tour Wins: 1

1980: Suntree Classic

Additional Wins: 17

1952: UGA National Negro Open
1953: UGA National Negro Open
1954: UGA National Negro Open
1955: UGA National Negro Open
1956: UGA National Negro Open, Rhode Island Open
1957: Long Beach Open
1960: UGA National Negro Open, Almaden Open
1963: Puerto Rico Open
1971: Sea Pines
1988: Liberty Mutual Legends of Golf–Legendary Division
1989: Liberty Mutual Legends of Golf–Legendary Division
1991: Liberty Mutual Legends of Golf–Legendary Division
1998: Liberty Mutual Legends of Golf–Demaret Division
1999: Liberty Mutual Legends of Golf–Demaret Division

2000: Liberty Mutual Legends of Golf–Demaret Division

KEN VENTURI

Professional Majors: 1

U.S. Open: 1964

PGA Tour Wins: 13

1957: St. Paul Open Invitational, Miller High Life Open
1958: Thunderbird Invitational, Phoenix Open Invitational, Baton Rouge Open Invitational, Gleneagles–Chicago Open Invitational
1959: Los Angeles Open, Gleneagles–Chicago Open Invitational
1960: Bing Crosby National Pro-Am, Milwaukee Open Invitational
1964: Insurance City Open Invitational, American Golf Classic
1966: Lucky International Open

Amateur Wins: 2

1951: California State Amateur Championship
1956: California State Amateur Championship

Additional Wins: 1

1959: Almaden Open

BIBLIOGRAPHY

BOOKS

Aultman, Dick, and Ken Bowden. *The Methods of Golf's Masters: How They Played, and What You Can Learn from Them*. New York: Coward, McCann and Geoghegan, 1975.

Balfour, James. *Reminiscences of Golf on St Andrews Links*. Edinburgh, UK: David Douglas, 1887.

Barkow, Al. *Gettin' to the Dance Floor: An Oral History of American Golf*. New York: Atheneum, 1986.

———. *Golf's Golden Grind: The History of the Tour*. New York: Harcourt, Brace, Jovanovich, 1974.

———. *The History of the PGA Tour*. New York: Doubleday, 1989.

———. *The Upset: Jack Fleck's Incredible Victory over Ben Hogan at the U.S. Open*. Chicago: Chicago Review, 2012.

Barrett, David. *Making the Masters: Bobby Jones and the Birth of America's Greatest Tournament*. New York: Skyhorse, 2012.

———. *Miracle at Merion: The Inspiring Story of Ben Hogan's Amazing Comeback and Victory at the 1950 U.S. Open*. New York: Skyhorse, 2010.

Browning, Robert. *A History of Golf: The Royal and Ancient Game*. London: Dent, 1955.

Carrick, Michael. *Caddie Sense*. New York: St. Martin's, 2000.

Cayleff, Susan E. *Babe: The Life and Legend of Babe Didrikson Zaharias*. Urbana: University of Illinois Press, 1995.

Christian, Frank. *Augusta National and the Masters: A Photographer's Scrapbook*. Chelsea, MI: Sleeping Bear, 2009.

Clark, Robert. *Golf: A Royal and Ancient Game*. London: Macmillan, 1893.

Cook, Kevin. *Tommy's Honor: The Story of Old Tom Morris and Young Tom Morris, Golf's Founding Father and Son*. New York: Gotham Books, 2007.

Corcoran, Fred. *Unplayable Lies*. With Bud Harvey. New York: Duell, Sloan, and Pearce, 1965.

Davis, Martin. *Ben Hogan: The Man behind the Mystique*. Greenwich, CT: American Golfer, 2002.

———. *The Greatest of Them All: The Legend of Bobby Jones*. Greenwich, CT: American Golfer, 1996.

Dawkins, Marvin P., and Graham C. Kinloch. *African American Golfers during the Jim Crow Era*. Westport, CT: Greenwood, 2000.

Demaret, Jimmy. *My Partner, Ben Hogan*. New York: McGraw-Hill, 1954.

Dodson, James. *American Triumvirate: Sam Snead, Byron Nelson, Ben Hogan, and the Modern Age of Golf*. New York: Knopf, 2012.

———. *Ben Hogan: An American Life*. New York: Doubleday, 2004.

Feinstein, John. *Caddy for Life: The Bruce Edwards Story*. New York: Back Bay Books, 2004.

Fields, Bill. *Arnie, Seve, and a Fleck of Golf History: Heroes, Underdogs, Courses, and Championships* . Lincoln: University of Nebraska Press, 2014.

Frost, Mark. *The Grand Slam: Bobby Jones, America, and the Story of Golf*. New York: Hyperion Books, 2004.

———. *The Greatest Game Ever Played: Harry Vardon, Francis Ouimet, and the Birth of Modern Golf*. New York: Hyperion Books, 2002.

———. *The Match: The Day the Game of Golf Changed Forever*. New York: MJF Books, 2007.

Glenn, Rhonda. *The Illustrated History of Women's Golf*. Dallas: Taylor Trade, 1991.

Goodner, Ross. *Golf's Greatest: The Legendary World Golf Hall of Famers*. Norwalk, CT: Golf Digest, 1978.

Graham, Deborah, and Jon Stabler. *The Eight Traits of Champion Golfers*. New York: Simon and Schuster, 1999.

Gregston, Gene. *Hogan: The Man Who Played for Glory*. Englewood Cliffs, NJ: Prentice-Hall, 1978.

Haultain, Theodore Arnold. *The Mystery of Golf*. 2nd ed. New York: Macmillan, 1910.

Howell, Audrey. *Harry Vardon: The Revealing Story of a Champion Golfer*. Charleston, SC: Tempus, 2001.

Hutchinson, Horace. *The Book of Golf and Golfers*. London: Longmans Green, 1900.

Johnson, Thad S. *The Incredible Babe: Her Ultimate Story*. With Louis Didrikson. Lake Charles, LA: Andrews Printing and Copy Center, 1996.

Johnson, William Oscar, and Nancy P. Williamson. *Whatta-Gal: The Babe Didrikson Story*. Boston: Little, Brown, 1977.

Jones, Robert Tyre (Bobby), Jr. *Golf Is My Game*. New York: Doubleday, 1960.

Jones, Robert T., Jr., and O. B. Keeler. *Down the Fairway: The Golf Life and Play of Robert T. Jones, Jr.* New York: Minton, Balch, 1927.

Joy, David. *The Scrapbook of Old Tom Morris*. Chelsea, MI: Sleeping Bear, 2001.

Julian, Kim. *Golf Widow: A Memoir*. Printed by author, 2011.

Keeler, O. B. *The Autobiography of an Average Golfer*. New York: Greenberg, 1925.

———. *The Bobby Jones Story*. Chicago: Triumph Books, 2003.

———. *The Boy's Life of Bobby Jones*. Chelsea, MI: Sleeping Bear, 2002.

Kennedy, John H. *A Course of Their Own: A History of African American Golfers*. Lincoln, Nebraska: University of Nebraska Press, 2005.

Kennedy, Randall. *Nigger: The Strange Career of a Troublesome Word*. New York: Pantheon Books, 2002.

Kerr, John. *The Golf-Book of East Lothian*. Edinburgh, UK: Constable, 1896.

Kirkaldy, Andra. *Fifty Years of Golf: My Memories*. London: Unwin, 1921.

Labbance, Bob. *The Vardon Invasion: Harry's Triumphant 1900 American Tour*. Ann Arbor, MI: Sports Media Group, 2008.

Leach, Henry. *The Happy Golfer*. London: Macmillan, 1914.

Lewis, Catherine M. *Bobby Jones and the Quest for the Grand Slam*. Chicago: Triumph Books, 2005.

———. *Considerable Passions: Golf, the Masters, and the Legacy of Bobby Jones*. Chicago: Triumph Books, 2000.

Low, John. L. *Concerning Golf*. London: Hodder and Stoughton, 1903.

Lowe, Stephen. *Sir Walter and Mr. Jones: Walter Hagen, Bobby Jones, and the Rise of American Golf*. Chelsea, MI: Sleeping Bear, 2000.

Macdonald, Charles Blair. *Scotland's Gift: Golf*. New York: Charles Scribner's Sons, 1928.

Mackenzie, Richard. *A Wee Nip at the 19th Hole: A History of the St Andrews Caddie*. New York: Bantam Books, 1998.

Malcolm, David, and Peter E. Crabtree. *Tom Morris of St Andrews: The Colossus of Golf*. Edinburgh, UK: Birlinn, 2010.

Martin, Greg "Piddler." *Caddie Confidential: Inside Stories from Caddies of the PGA Tour.* Chicago: Triumph Books, 2009.

Martin, H. B. *Fifty Years of American Golf.* New York: Dodd, Mead, 1936.

Matthew, Sidney L. *Bobby: The Life and Times of Bobby Jones.* Ann Arbor, MI: Sports Media Group, 2005.

———. *Bobby Jones: Extra.* Tallahassee, FL: I. Q. Press, 2004.

McDaniel, Pete. *Uneven Lies: The Heroic Story of African-Americans in Golf.* Greenwich, CT: American Golfer, 2000.

Miller, Richard. *Triumphant Journey: The Saga of Bobby Jones and the Grand Slam of Golf.* Dallas: Taylor, 1993.

Murphy, Michael. *Golf in the Kingdom.* New York: Viking Arkana, 1994.

Myrdal, Gunnar. *An American Dilemma: The Negro Problem and Modern Democracy.* New York: Harper Brothers, 1944.

Nelson, Byron. *How I Played the Game.* Lanham, MD: Taylor Trade, 2006.

Nösner, Ellen Susanna. *Clearview: America's Course.* Haslett, MI: Foxsong, 2000.

Owen, David. *The Making of the Masters: Clifford Roberts, Augusta National, and Golf's Most Prestigious Tournament.* New York: Simon and Schuster, 1999.

Price, Charles. *A Golf Story: Bobby Jones, Augusta National, and the Masters Tournament.* Chicago: Triumph Books, 2001.

Rapoport, Ron. *The Immortal Bobby: Bobby Jones and the Golden Age of Golf.* New York: John Wiley, 2005.

Reid, Steven. *Bobby's Open: Mr. Jones and the Golf Shot That Defined a Legend.* London: Corinthian Books, 2012.

Ryan, Frank. *The Forgotten Plague: How the Battle against Tuberculosis Was Won—and Lost.* Boston: Little, Brown, 1993.

Sampson, Curt. *Hogan.* Nashville, Tennessee: Rutledge Hill, 1996.

———. *The Masters: Golf, Money, and Power in Augusta, Georgia.* New York: Villard Books, 1998.

———. *The Slam: Bobby Jones and the Price of Glory.* New York: Rodale, 2005.

Sarazen, Gene. *Thirty Years of Championship Golf: The Life and Times of Gene Sarazen.* London: Black, 1990.

Sifford, Charlie. *Just Let Me Play: The Story of Charlie Sifford, the First Black PGA Golfer.* With James Gullo. Latham, NY: British American, 1992.

Simpson, Walter G. *The Art of Golf.* Edinburgh, UK: David Douglas, 1892.

Sinnette, Calvin H. *Forbidden Fairways: African Americans and the Game of Golf.* Chelsea, MI: Sleeping Bear, 1998.

Stirk, David. *"Carry Your Bag, Sir?" The Story of Golf's Caddies.* London: Witherby, 1989.

Taylor, Dawson. *The Masters: Golf's Most Prestigious Tradition.* Chicago: Contemporary Books, 1986.

Towle, Mike. *I Remember Ben Hogan.* Nashville, TN: Cumberland House, 2000.

———. *I Remember Bobby Jones.* Nashville, TN: Cumberland House, 2001.

Travers, Jerome, and James R. Crowell. *The Fifth Estate: Thirty Years of Golf.* New York: Knopf, 1926.

Tschetter, Kris. *Mr. Hogan: The Man I Knew.* With Steve Eubanks. New York: Gotham Books, 2010.

Vaile, Pembroke Arnold. *The Soul of Golf.* London: Macmillan, 1912.

Van Natta, Don, Jr. *Wonder Girl: The Magnificent Sporting Life of Babe Didrikson Zaharias.* New York: Little, Brown, 2011.

Vardon, Harry. *The Complete Golfer.* New York: McClure, Phillips, 1905.

———. *The Gist of Golf.* New York: Doran, 1922.

———. *My Golfing Life.* London: Hutchinson, 1933.

Vasquez, Jody. *Afternoons with Mr. Hogan: A Boy, a Legend, and the Lessons of a Lifetime.* New York: Gotham Books, 2004.

Venturi, Ken. *Comeback: The Ken Venturi Story.* With Oscar Fraley. New York: Duell, Sloan, and Pearce, 1966.

————. *Getting Up and Down: My 60 Years in Golf*. With Michael Arkush. Chicago: Triumph Books, 2004.

Wexler, Daniel. *The Book of Golfers: A Biographical History of the Royal and Ancient Game*. Ann Arbor, MI: Sports Media Group, 2005.

Williams, Bill. *Harry Vardon: A Career Record of a Champion Golfer*. Bloomington, IN: Xlibris Press, 2015.

Wind, Herbert Warren. *The Story of American Golf: Its Champions and Its Championships*. New York: Knopf, 1975.

Zaharias, Babe Didrikson. *This Life I've Led*. New York: Barnes, 1955.

ORAL HISTORY TRANSCRIPTS

USGA Oral History Collection

Bell, Peggy Kirk

Brown, Pete

Dent, Jim

Hicks, Betty

Morgan, Walter

Venturi, Kenneth P.

Picard, Henry

Rawls, Betsy

Stroble, Bobby

Suggs, Louise

Owens, Charlie

Yates, Charles R.

Magazines

American Golfer

Golf Digest

Golf Illustrated (UK)

Golf Illustrated (US)

Golf Journal

Golf Magazine

Golf Monthly

Golf World

Literary Digest

Reader's Digest

Sport Magazine

Sports Illustrated

Saturday Evening Post

Through the Green (UK)

Newspapers

Chicago Daily Tribune

Hartford Courant

Oregonian

Orlando Sentinel

Los Angeles Times

New York Post

New York Times

USA Today

Washington Post

WEBSITES

Harry Vardon (Tuberculosis)

World Health Organization (WHO), http://www.who.int/tb/en.

Bobby Jones (Syringomyelia)

Chiari and Syringomyelia Foundation, http://www.csfinfo.org.
National Institute of Neurological Disorders and Stroke, http://www.
ninds.nih.gov/disorders/syringomyelia/detail_syringomyelia.htm.

Ben Hogan (Suicide Survivor, Alzheimer's Disease)

American Foundation for Suicide Prevention, http://www.afsp.org.
Alzheimer's Association: http://www.alz.org.

Babe Didrikson Zaharias (Cancer)

American Cancer Society, http://www.cancer.org.

Charlie Sifford (Racism)

National Association for the Advancement of Colored People
(NAACP), http://www.naacp.org.

Ken Venturi (Stuttering, Carpal Tunnel Syndrome)

The Stuttering Foundation of America, http://www.stutteringhelp.org.
National Institute of Neurological Disorders and Stroke, http://www.
ninds.nih.gov/disorders/carpal_tunnel/detail_carpal_tunnel.htm.

Bruce Edwards (Amyotrophic Lateral Sclerosis)

ALS Association, http://www.alsa.org.

Bruce Edwards Foundation, http://www.bruceedwardsfoundation.org.

INDEX

ABOUT THE AUTHOR

Lyle Slovick is a historian and golf enthusiast, having played and studied the game for over 40 years. Born in Portland, Oregon, January 10, 1960, he became enamored with both sports and history at an early age and was introduced to golf at age 13. In junior high school, he saw a photo of Old Tom Morris from the 1890s in a book one day. That moment gave him pause to consider the game's rich past and thus began his interest in collecting books that chronicle the fascinating stories of this five-hundred-year-old game. Since the age of 15, he has added over 170 books to his personal collection.

After earning a BA degree in history and political science from Pacific Lutheran University in Tacoma, Washington, Lyle worked various jobs before returning to graduate school to pursue his love of history. While working on a master's degree in American history at George Washington University in Washington, DC, he gained new insights into the political and social history of this county during internships at the Smithsonian Institution and the U.S. Senate.

After earning his MA degree in 1993, Lyle spent 13 years working at George Washington University (GWU) among the rare books and manuscripts in the Special Collections Department of the Gelman Library. The last eight of those years he served as assistant university archivist, where he oversaw more than one thousand collections documenting the administrative and social history of GWU. He assisted an eclectic mix of researchers from around the world, including entities such as the BBC,

History Channel, NPR, Discovery Channel, ESPN, and ABC News *Nightline*.

Among the many collections he processed and organized were the papers of Dr. Janet G. Travell, personal physician to Presidents Kennedy and Johnson, and the papers of Drs. Walter Freeman and James Watts, pioneers in the surgical procedure known as lobotomy (featured in a 2008 documentary for PBS's *American Experience* series).

Lyle served as coeditor of the *GW Historical Encyclopedia*, an online publication, contributing over 330 articles to the database. Lyle enjoys telling stories that shed new light and offer new perspective on often well-trod subjects—what he describes as "augmented interpretation." His published articles include: "George Y. Coffin: A Schoolboy's Life in 19th-Century Washington," *Washington History* (Fall/Winter 2006–2007); "The St. Andrews Rabbit Wars of 1801–1821," *Through the Green* (journal of the British Golf Collectors Society, September 2012); "In Memory of Francis Ouimet's 'Shots Heard Round the World,'" *Through the Green* (June 2013), and "Trials and Triumphs of Harry Vardon and Bobby Jones," *Through the Green* (September 2015).

This book is an expression of Lyle's passion for the game of golf, which has taken him to various major championships over the years (including four British Opens, one U.S. Open, two Senior U.S. Opens, as well as numerous PGA and LPGA tournaments). His research interests have taken him to the British Golf Museum in St Andrews, Scotland (as well as the University of St Andrews), the World Golf Hall of Fame in St. Augustine, Florida, and the USGA Museum and Library in Far Hills, New Jersey.

Lyle enjoys traveling, reading (especially biographies), and shares his particular impressions of the game on his blog From Featheries to ProV1s. He resides in Bedminster, New Jersey, where he currently works as a consultant for the United States Golf Association and spends parts of the year in Córdoba, Argentina, where his girlfriend, Isis, lives.